Dear Da,

No more bird feeders for squirrels to gnaw!

We think this is safe from them!

Merry Christmas. Happy bird watching & bird feeding!

Love,
The O'Ds

The Birds Around Us

Editor
Alice E. Mace

Associate Editor
Suzanne Sherman

Designer and Text Illustrator
Ron Hildebrand

Layout Editor
Linda Bouchard

Created and designed by the editorial staff
of ORTHO BOOKS

Featured Artist
John Dawson

Acknowledgments

Consulting Editorial Services
W. Foulsham and Co. Ltd.

Contributing Editor
Jim Beley

Writers
Kenneth P. Able
Robert F. Cardillo
Peter G. Connors
Susan Roney Drennan
Kimball L. Garrett
George Harrison
Kit Harrison
Bette J. Schardien Jackson
Jerome A. Jackson
J. P. Myers
Roger Tory Peterson
William E. Poole

Contributing Writers
Jeff Kopachena
Michael McKinley

Text Consultants
John Farrand, Jr.
John LaShelle
Roger Pasquier

Contributing Associate Editor
Don Mosley

Design Consultant
Christine Brundage

Photo Editors
Pamela K. Peirce
Raymond F. Quinton

Copy Editors
Melinda Levine
Toni Murray
Rebecca Pepper

Proofreaders
Barbara Ferenstein
Judy Weiss

Indexer
Elinor Lindheimer

Production Artists
Deborah Cowder
Lezlly Freier
Anne Pederson

Special Thanks to
Dolores Campbell
Frank Hildebrand
Ronda Hildebrand
James Murray

Printed and Bound by
Amilcare Pizzi, S.p.A.

Front-Cover Painting
by John Dawson

Two Northern Cardinals—a brilliant red male and a multicolored female—descend from a winter lilac bush to feast on sunflower seeds.

Chapter-Opener Paintings
by John Dawson

Page 8: Great Horned Owls
Page 18: Tufted Puffins
Page 42: Ruffed Grouse
Page 82: Peregrine Falcon
Page 114: Broad-tailed Hummingbirds
Page 136: Greater White-fronted, Snow, and Canada Geese
Page 162: Northern Cardinals
Page 234: American Robin
Page 268: (Top) Steller's Jay, Yellow-rumped Warbler, Downy Woodpecker; *(Center)* Ring-billed Gull; *(Bottom)* House Finch, Wood Duck, Red-shouldered Hawk

Title-Page and Back-Cover Photograph
by Thomas D. Mangelsen

Sandhill Cranes such as these flying at sunset migrate hundreds of miles between their breeding and winter ranges.

Publisher
Robert L. Iacopi

Editorial Supervisor
Robert J. Dolezal

Production Director
Ernie S. Tasaki

Managing Editors
Anne Coolman
Mike Smith
Sally Smith

System Manager
Leonard D. Grotta

National Sales Manager
Charles H. Aydelotte

Marketing Specialist
Susan B. Boyle

Operations Assistant
Georgiann Wright

Senior Technical Analyst
J. A. Crozier, Jr.

Printed in Italy

To bird enthusiasts across North America—
from the child who wants to know how
birds fly to the ornithologist who
unravels such mysteries.

Writers

Kenneth P. Able

Dr. Able is a professor of biology at the State University of New York at Albany. He has authored or co-authored numerous papers, reviews, and articles on migration and orientation. His research interests include animal migration and orientation—especially of birds—and behavioral ecology; his teaching interests include animal behavior, ecology, ornithology, evolution, biogeography, and vertebrate zoology. Dr. Able has been a guest lecturer at a number of universities throughout the United States, and he is a member of several professional societies, including the American Ornithologists' Union, the American Association for the Advancement of Science, and the American Society of Zoologists.

Susan Roney Drennan

Dr. Drennan is editor of *American Birds*, the ornithological field journal of the National Audubon Society. In 1985 the prestigious Arthur A. Allen medal, given by the Cornell University Laboratory of Ornithology, was awarded to her for "outstanding contributions to the written interpretation of ornithological endeavors." Dr. Drennan is the author of *Where to Find Birds in New York State* (Syracuse University Press, 1981) as well as numerous popular and scientific articles. She is past president of the Linnaean Society of New York. Her active pursuit of birds has taken her throughout North and South America, Iceland, Europe, and Antarctica.

Robert F. Cardillo

Mr. Cardillo is the technical director of Visual Resources for Ornithology (VIREO) and manages an international collection of over 60,000 bird photographs. As a biologist, his field studies have led him to the discovery of a large Permian fossil quarry in the Southwest and to the first photographic documentation of an African Heron on Nantucket Island. Mr. Cardillo's current photographic interests focus on the rain-forest birds of South America. He has taught and written about nature photography for years and has won several awards for his photography. His photographic work is published frequently in natural-history publications.

Kimball L. Garrett

Mr. Garrett is ornithology collections manager in the Section of Birds and Mammals at the Natural History Museum of Los Angeles County. He is co-author of *Birds of Southern California, Status and Distribution* (Los Angeles Audubon Society, 1981) and has published numerous articles on problems of bird identification. Mr. Garrett's research expeditions and tour leading have taken him around the world. Mr. Garrett lives in Southern California, where he frequently teaches ornithology courses for the University of Los Angeles Extension Program, the Los Angeles Audubon Society, and the National Park Service.

Peter G. Connors

Dr. Connors is a research ecologist at the Bodega Marine Laboratory of the University of California. He has published numerous articles in scientific journals and books, reporting his research in such diverse fields as molecular biophysics, pollution ecology, and ornithology. Over the past decade, his avian research, which includes studies of behavior, ecology, taxonomy and evolution—principally of migratory shorebirds—has been based on extensive field work, mainly in western North America. For several years Dr. Connors migrated following the same route and schedule as his favorite birds, spending summers in the Alaskan Arctic and winters in Northern California, where he now resides.

George H. Harrison

Dr. Harrison is a writer, photographer, and consultant in the field of natural history and the outdoors. He was managing editor of *National/International Wildlife* magazines for nine years and is now their first field editor. He is also field editor for *Ranger Rick* nature magazine for children and nature editor of *Sports Afield*. Dr. Harrison has authored or co-authored a number of books, including *Roger Tory Peterson's Dozen Birding Hot Spots* (Simon & Schuster, 1976), *The Backyard Bird Watcher* (Simon & Schuster, 1979), *America's Favorite Backyard Birds* (Simon & Schuster, 1983), and *America's Favorite Backyard Wildlife* (Simon & Schuster, 1985).

Kit Harrison

Dr. Harrison is a writer and photographer in the field of natural history and nature adventure/travel. She is the conservation editor of *Sports Afield* magazine and the nature editor of *Exclusively Yours* magazine. She is a former member of the staff of *National/International Wildlife* magazines, where she currently works on special projects. Dr. Harrison co-authored *America's Favorite Backyard Birds* (Simon & Schuster, 1983), *America's Favorite Backyard Wildlife* (Simon & Schuster, 1985), the *Treasury of American Wildlife*, 4 vol. (Encyclopaedia Britannica, 1979), and a section in the *New International Wildlife Encyclopedia* (Raintree Publishers, 1979).

J. P. Myers

Dr. Myers is associate curator of ornithology and director of Visual Resources for Ornithology (VIREO) at the Academy of Natural Sciences, in Philadelphia. This Baltimore native has chased, studied, and photographed birds throughout the Western Hemisphere in his research on the migration and behavior of shorebirds. Dr. Myers received a BA from Reed College and a PhD in Zoology from the University of California, Berkeley. His writings and photographs appear in scientific literature and in natural-history magazines.

Bette J. Schardien Jackson

Dr. Jackson is a research associate at Mississippi State University. She is former associate editor of the *Journal of Field Ornithology* and is currently president of the Mississippi Ornithological Society. Dr. Jackson has published numerous popular articles about birds and is author of more than 30 scientific publications. She and her husband, Dr. Jerome A. Jackson, have travelled throughout North America and to South and Central America and the Bahamas.

Roger Tory Peterson

Dr. Peterson is an internationally known ornithologist, writer, artist, and lecturer. Since the publication of his first book, *Field Guide to the Birds* (Houghton Mifflin, 1934), Dr. Peterson's writings and art have appeared in numerous bird and flower guides, and other nature books. In addition to the many honors and awards he has received for contributions to science, education, and conservation, Dr. Peterson was nominated for the Nobel Peace Prize in 1983. The Jamestown, New York, native is a member of many scientific and professional societies and holds honorary doctorate degrees from a number of colleges and universities. He has traveled worldwide, and his checklist of bird species seen and identified might set a new record.

Jerome A. Jackson

Dr. Jackson is professor of biological sciences at Mississippi State University. He is past president of the Wilson Ornithological Society, former team leader of the Red-cockaded Woodpecker Endangered Species Recovery Team, and former editor of *The Wilson Bulletin, Inland Bird Banding, North American Bird Bander*, and the *Journal of Field Ornithology*. Dr. Jackson is currently editor of *Bird Conservation*, regional editor of *American Birds*, and is a director of the U.S. Section of the International Council for Bird Preservation. He has published more than 130 scientific articles in numerous popular publications on birds.

William E. Poole

Mr. Poole grew up in Massachusetts, where he attracted finches, grosbeaks, siskins, nuthatches, and chickadees to a spacious, rural backyard. He now lives in San Francisco, where he feeds juncos, warblers, doves, and hummingbirds on a narrow city balcony. Mr. Poole is a registered nurse with a background in pediatrics. He is a frequent contributor to *Image*, the Sunday magazine of the *San Francisco Examiner*, writing on health and natural history.

Contents

The Joy of Birds

by Roger Tory Peterson

*B*irds—*the most beautiful, the most dynamic, the most observable of all wild things—have been the focus of my life since I was a boy of eleven. For well over 60 years they have occupied my daily thoughts, filled my dreams, and dominated my reading. What, you may wonder, happened when I was eleven that changed me from a rebellious youngster to an obsessed bird-watcher?*

When I was in the seventh grade in Jamestown in western New York, my teacher started a Junior Audubon Club. The club piqued my interest in birds, but one incident hooked me on birds for life. I can even remember the date—April 8, 1920, about 9:00 in the morning. It was a Saturday, one of the first warm days of spring. A friend and I crossed the railroad tracks and climbed Swede Hill to explore new terrain south of town. As we entered a woodlot on the crest of the hill, I spotted a bundle of brown feathers clinging to the trunk of an oak. It was a flicker, probably in migration. The bird was sleeping with its face buried in the fluffed feathers of its

Moments after its first flight from the nest, a young Great Horned Owl rests on a tree limb. Its parent watches from a higher perch among the leaves of a California Sycamore.

Tom A. Schneider/DRK Photo

For many people, watching birds instills a closeness to nature and a reverence for life around them. The sight of a family of Rose-breasted Grosbeaks excites a sense of freedom, an escape from the rigors of day-to-day activities.

scapulars, but I thought it was dead. Gingerly I touched it on the back. Instantly this inert thing jerked its head around, looked at me with startled eyes, then exploded in a flash of golden wings and fled into the woods. It was like a resurrection—what had appeared to be dead was very much alive. Ever since, birds have seemed to me the most vivid expression of life. As a teenager regimentation and restriction rubbed me the wrong way. Many times I wished that I could fly like the birds and be free. The mere glimpse of a bird would change my listlessness to fierce intensity. My interest was neither thoughtful nor academic—it was so spontaneous that I could not control it, much to my parents' puzzlement. Today there are youngsters all over the country whose eyes light up for the same reason. Indeed, youngsters of any age—from eight to eighty—find release on the wings of birds. Birds are an affirmation of life.

Guided by Nature

As we learn more about birds, we find they are not quite the gloriously unrestrained beings we had imagined them to be. They are bound by all sorts of natural laws. They go north and south almost by the calendar. They seem to follow certain flyways and routes between their summer and winter homes. A robin that lives in Connecticut this year is not likely to go to Michigan next year. Some behaviorists—Tinbergen, Lorenz, and others—caution us against saying that birds *think*. They tell us that birds are creatures of action and reaction. A night-heron newly arrived in the rookery performs a step-by-step ritual of song and dance. Leave out any one of the steps, and the sequence is disrupted—the reproductive cycle does not carry through to fruition.

We learn, too, that most birds have territories. The males hold down a plot of ground as their own—it may be an acre, or it may be 5 acres. They are property owners just as we are. Song, instead of being only a joyous outburst, is a functional expression—a proclamation of ownership, an invitation to a female, a threat to another male.

Most thought-provoking of all is to discover the balance of nature: the balance between a bird and its environment, the interrelation between the hawk that eats the bird, the bird that eats the insect, and the insect that eats the leaves—perhaps the very leaves that grow on the tree in which the hawk nests. We learn that each ecosystem has a carrying capacity, and that predation harvests only a surplus that otherwise would be leveled off in some different way; hence, putting up fences and shooting all the hawks and cats will not raise the number of Red-eyed Vireos to any significant degree. Birds, then, are almost as earthbound as we are. They have freedom and mobility only within prescribed natural limits.

I have often likened birds to litmus paper. Their high rate of metabolism and fast pace cause them to react sensitively to anything in their habitat that is out of kilter. Thus, they are much more than cardinals, jays, or chickadees to brighten the suburban garden, ducks or quail to fill the hunter's bag, or rare shorebirds to be ticked off on the birder's list—they are indicators of the environment that send out signals that we must heed to ensure our own survival, as well as theirs.

Bird-Watchers

Bird-watching, one of the fastest growing national hobbies, takes many forms. It can be a science, an art, a recreation, a sport, an environmental ethic, or a religious experience. After all, birds are the only creatures that share with the angels the attribute of feathered wings.

A bird-watcher by any other name—ornithologist, bird lover, bird bander, bird fancier, bird spotter, birder—is still someone who watches birds. I favor *bird-watcher* for general use because the term is inclusive. It describes almost everyone who looks at birds or studies them—from the watchers at the window who simply feed birds to the elite level of the fellows of the American Ornithologists' Union (AOU), and Nobel laureates such as Konrad Lorenz and Nikko Tinbergen, who have won distinction for their work on bird behavior. As for myself I am primarily a bird artist and bird photographer, a visual person with a consuming passion for birds. To paraphrase the late E. B. White, I watch them and they undoubtedly watch me.

Around 1920, when I was cutting my teeth, so to speak, on Junior Audubon leaflets, people who watched birds fell into two categories: ornithologists, who usually shot birds, and bird lovers, who did not. In

Wayne Lankinen/DRK Photo

A Northern Bobwhite keeps a watchful eye for danger. Predators are only one of several factors that serve to regulate bird populations. For example, in northern areas the Bobwhite population is limited by harsh winter weather. In other areas population may be limited by the availability of food, water, or cover.

The Great Egret is a visible facet of a delicate web of life. The continued health and survival of birds like these are the signs of a healthy environment, a safe place for humans as well as for birds.

Thomas D. Mangelsen

Don & Pat Valenti/DRK Photo

Wardene Weisser/Berg & Associates

Right: *Bird-watchers enjoy the life and color that birds like this male Northern Cardinal bring to their backyards. Serious birders may wander far afield in search of more elusive subjects.*

Far right: *An ornithologist is one who studies specific aspects of bird biology. By examining the nesting behavior of this Scott's Oriole, for example, an ornithologist may gain insight not only into bird behavior but into the nature and evolution of life on earth.*

Color Key to North American Birds, published in 1903, Frank Chapman addressed this dichotomy: "From the scientific point of view there is but one satisfactory way to identify a bird. A specimen of it should be in hand." Then, aware of an increasing dilemma, he wrote, "[but] we cannot place a gun in the hands of these thousands of bird-lovers we are yearly developing." He used the term bird lover freely in his writing. If we insist on speaking of dog lovers and horse lovers, bird lover would be a logical usage. Dogs and horses are pets, however, almost like members of the family; wild birds are not. Loving involves reciprocation, and birds do not reciprocate in an affectionate way. They could not care less about us, even though we feed them and call them our feathered friends.

When I am asked by the media how many birders exist I must ask "Do you mean birders or bird-watchers? It depends on your definition." The term *bird-watcher* includes anyone who feeds birds. In my neighborhood, everyone up and down our road puts out sunflower seeds and other goodies for chickadees, nuthatches, cardinals, and finches. If I go for a midwinter holiday with my wife, Ginny, I rest assured that if the birds eat all the birdseed, our chickadees will not perish; they will simply go to the neighbors' yards. Then there are those several million people who watch birds through a gunsight rather than binoculars; their focus, however, is generally limited to ducks, quail, pheasants, and a few other species.

If we include these and other peripheral categories, we could contend that there are between 20 and 40 million bird-watchers in the United States. The United States Bureau of Outdoor Recreation came up with a figure of 11 million. Robert Arbib, former editor of *American Birds*, arrived at a far more conservative estimate of the number of true *birders*. A birder, according to Arbib, is one who occasionally goes out looking for birds beyond the confines of the backyard. Most birders own binoculars, field guides, and scopes. Although millions of people own field guides and other bird books, Arbib puts the maximum number of bonafide birders countrywide at 150,000. Only a fraction of these would be called hard-core, but the number is growing and will continue to increase as advanced or specialized bird guides become available.

Ornithologists, on the other hand, possess a high level of expertise of a scientific nature. It is presumptuous to call yourself an ornithologist

Frans Lanting

simply because you identify birds or make bird lists. Most ornithologists are professionals with college degrees—either a doctorate or at least a master's. A very few nonprofessionals who devote their time year after year to some specialized problem of avian research might be included in this category. We could make the generalization that the average person who watches birds is interested in what the bird *is;* an ornithologist is more interested in what it *does.*

Most fellows and many of the elective members of the AOU look with disdain on the field-identification buffs. They contend that anyone who watches birds seriously should work on a problem of some kind. This rather lordly attitude was why the American Birding Association (ABA) was formed—as an antidote of sorts, to promote birding as a competitive game or sport. The ABA aspired to form an elite of its own that would set itself apart from the hundreds of thousands, indeed millions, who call themselves bird-watchers.

The Art of Bird-Watching

Field birding has gone through a remarkable metamorphosis in recent years. A greater sophistication has developed among binocular addicts, and a polarization has taken place as a result.

At one extreme is the holistic approach; at the other is the micro-method. Using the holistic approach, the experienced raptor-watcher perched on a boulder on Hawk Mountain or the seabird buff sailing off the coast no longer relies only on the obvious field marks described in field guides. Instead, while the bird is still half a mile away, the holistic birder uses shape, manner, flight, wing beat, and a number of other subtle visual clues to come up with an identification. Birders who use the micro-method bring field birding almost full cycle; their spotting scopes provide the type of bird-in-hand detail that used to be restricted to the specimen tray. With high-powered spotting scopes, birders can even see the parasites on a Peregrine Falcon. Micro-method birders might refer to worn tertials and other characteristics of minute detail.

Birds are a perfect vehicle for understanding the natural world, and there are many ways to watch them.

Using the micro-method, a birder may observe subtle differences in plumage pattern to determine the age and gender of birds like this Sharp-shinned Hawk.

Douglas R. Herr

Identifying and Listing

Some birders ignore butterflies, flowers, and other components of eco-systems to concentrate on listing. Listing is a perfectly valid sport or recreation; but most birders—the ones who have really done their home-work—are usually good all-around naturalists and conservationists. They move on from identification and listing to the level where they inquire into the whys and wherefores. Curiosity keeps their interest meaningful and alive and contributes to the body of ornithological knowledge as well as to knowledge of the environment.

My first years as a birder were full of the joy of discovery. Then bird-watching became a competitive game. I wanted to see how many birds I could identify in a day, to discover rare birds, to record a bird a day or two earlier in the spring or a day or two later in the fall than anyone else. This was my listing stage. But as I tore about the countryside ticking off the birds on my checklist, I gradually became interested in their way of life. At home I pored over ornithological journals such as *The Auk, The Wilson Bulletin*, and *The Condor*. This has been the pattern that many dedicated bird-watchers have followed, but to a few aficionados, the continued pursuit of rarities and the fine points of field identification may almost become a way of life.

Birders enjoy making lists, and there are all kinds of lists: backyard lists, January 1 lists, Big Day lists, Christmas-count lists, birds-on-movie-soundtracks lists. The variations are endless.

Some 70 years ago, when the field-glass fraternity was expanding and it was no longer necessary to check every observation over the sights of a shotgun, a fellow with good legs, good ears, and sharp eyes found he could list 100 species of birds in a day. I know of three such lists that were compiled prior to 1916—two in New York State and one in Ohio. As early as 1930 Charles Urner and his party ran up a total of 162 species in a day in New Jersey. Since then such high totals have become commonplace.

Life-lists. Dear to the hearts of most birders is the life-list, the list of birds sighted anywhere in the world during a lifetime. My own life-list contains under 4,000 species. For some time Stuart Keith held the record for the longest life-list—his list tabulated more than 5,500 birds—but according to the *Guinness Book of World Records* (1985), Norman Chester-field of Ontario is ahead with 5,556 entries. However, rumors maintain that Stuart Stokes of Australia claims more than 6,000.

North American lists. The ABA's North American checklist en-compasses more than 840 species, including well over 100 accidentals (strays). I still do not have Bachman's Warbler on my own list, and I am still just one bird short of qualifying for the ABA's *700 Club*, birders who have seen 700 species north of Mexico. If I include the ABA accidentals that I have seen outside the prescribed area—in the West Indies, Mexico, Japan, on the high seas—my count comes closer to 800.

By zigzagging from one outpost of the continent to another in 1983, Benton Basham of Tennessee was the first birder to pass the 700 mark in one year—he counted 711 to be exact. His efforts boosted the count on his life-list for North America over 750; Basham's North American list is undisputedly the longest.

Less traveled birders may derive the same sense of excitement and accomplishment by completing the ABA state or county lists.

Photography lists. Another kind of list records the number of birds a photographer has photographed. The late Allan Cruickshank's goal was to photograph every bird in North America. It has also been Don Bleitz's dream and that of several other bird photographers I know.

Although normally found only in southeastern North America, Anhingas often wander far to the north and west after the breeding season. Vagrants such as these are hot items on a birder's local list and add a touch of competitive excitement to compiling lists.

Rod Planck/Tom Stack & Associates

A. Cruickshank/VIREO

Photographs are vivid trophies for those who prefer to hunt birds with a lens. In this shot, a young American White Pelican feeds from its parent's pouch.

The hard-core birder who makes a game or a sport of listing may graduate to a 400-mm lens when the binocular affords diminishing returns, and new species become increasingly hard to find. The hard-core birder may photograph rarities through the lens (the modern substitute for the collector's gun) or build up a collection of species photographs that is much like a life-list.

Photographing Birds

Bird photographers have made a significant contribution to our awareness of other two-legged creatures. Bird photography can be an art, a science, a sport, a teaching device, or simply a recreation. To me it is therapy—quite unlike my painting where I seem to sweat blood.

Unlike the millions of people that still shoot birds for sport, photographers enjoy the thrills of the chase by bagging their quarry with a long lens. This takes as much skill as handling firearms, and photography has fewer limitations. The photographer encounters no closed seasons, no protected species, and no bag limits. The same bird can be "shot" repeatedly yet live to give pleasure to others besides the photographer. The picture is the trophy, as tangible as a stuffed bird on the mantelpiece.

Bird photography is a highly popular practice in which much money is invested each year. In a 1980 study by Dr. Stephen Kellert and Miriam Westervelt of the Yale School of Forestry, the *Survey of Wildlife Associated Recreation,* funded by the U.S. Fish and Wildlife Service, it was estimated that nature and wildlife photographers spend at least one billion dollars each year for camera equipment and another three-quarters of a billion for film and processing. Add to this 140 million dollars for binoculars and spotting scopes and the expenditures of wildlife photographers total nearly two billion dollars per year!

Listening to Birds

When John James Audubon created his famous portraits of birds in the first half of the nineteenth century, he had no photographs to jog his memory, and the sophisticated binoculars that now give a bird-watcher the visual acuity of a hawk were not available. If we are to judge from Audubon's writings, his vision was sharp indeed, but his hearing was not. He could not hear the high sibilant songs of birds such as the Prairie

J.P. Myers/VIREO

By recording bird songs on tape, it is possible to save the sound of summer for a quiet winter evening. Recordings of bird songs are important aids for identifying many species that are often heard but rarely seen.

Warbler, and a number of others—probably because he had been banging away so incessantly with his fowling piece that he had lost sensitivity to the higher register.

Some birders rely 90 percent on their ears. I do. Today, a half century after the Cornell University Laboratory of Ornithology initiated the recording of bird songs in 1932, such tape recordings have become commonplace. The deluge of records and cassettes are useful tools in the field birder's stock of handy, accurate identification aids. Formerly we had to learn some of the bird songs anew each spring the hard way. Now, with bird songs on a record or cassette, we can sit in the armchair and listen—when the migrating warblers and thrushes come through, we are ready for them.

My friend, the late William Gunn of Canada, the premier bird song recordist, said: "Birds have made what would otherwise have been a humdrum life a great experience." The story goes that Gunn's father, to correct his young son's mumbling, bought him a tape recorder so that he could hear himself and learn to project his voice properly. Already fascinated by birds young Bill trundled the bulky tape recorder outdoors and started recording bird songs.

Dr. Gunn was a modest genius whose library of bird sounds was and is still widely used by birders and the media. Thousands of birders throughout the United States and Canada have honed their field identification skills by listening to Gunn's records and cassettes, a number of which are keyed into my own eastern and western field guides (see page 233).

Feeding Birds

Another indication of the level of interest in bird-watching today is the financial investment people are making in feeding birds. The 1980 *Survey of Wildlife Associated Recreation* also reveals that Americans spend more than half a billion dollars each year on bird feeding. This estimate may be conservative; the total could be closer to one billion dollars.

Such widespread feeding has had positive effects for North American birds. Feeding has enhanced the winter survival of a number of species. Fifty years ago cardinals and titmice were not found east of the Hudson; they now sweep through most of New England and are also pushing northward to the Great Lakes region. The Evening Grosbeak—a species that even the great Audubon had never seen—has moved east and south and now even breeds in New England. If anyone questions the value of feeding, they need only to look at the credit side of the ledger.

Bird-Watching Events

I had not heard of a bird-watching tournament before I met the birders of the big cities along the East Coast in the late 1920s. New Yorkers and Bostonians called their tournament the Big Day, Philadelphians called it the Century Run, New Jerseyites looked forward to the Lethal Tour, and Washingtonians to the Grim Grind. One academic with a hint of condescension dubbed it ornithogolfing, and modern devotees bear the name binocular junkies.

No matter the name, most bird-watching tournaments are in mid-May, when spring migration is at flood tide. Some imaginative entrepreneur saw the fund-raising possibilities and funneled all that birding expertise and effort into a bird-watching event, the first Birdathon. As far as I know, the first one was in Ontario in 1977 to raise funds for the Long Point Observatory of Lake Erie. The lucrative idea was soon copied by the Manomet Observatory in Massachusetts, the Point Reyes Observatory in California, the Gull Island Project of the Linnaea Society of New York,

Frans Lanting

and—on a national level—by the National Audubon Society. A "world series" of birding—the Biggest Day—on which a number of teams compete
against each other is now staged each year in New Jersey. Another recent
feature in the bird-watcher's world is the North American Rare Bird Alert,
a continent-wide telephone hookup that gives information about the
sighting of rare birds.

Driven by mild spring tailwinds that
foreshadow the warm days of sum-
mer, Snow Geese rise northward into
a twilight sky, embarking on a voy-
age to distant and mysterious nesting
grounds.

A Guide to The Birds Around Us

Prepared by an outstanding team, this book is neither a field guide nor a
manual—it is a colorful, informative introduction to the world of birds
and the many faces of ornithology.

Kimball L. Garrett explains how birds are classified and describes avian
diversity from the past to the present. An in-depth look at bird behavior
by Peter G. Connors and J. P. Myers follows. Jerome A. Jackson and
Bette J. Schardien Jackson discuss the habitats, the ecosystems, and the
conservation efforts that affect and are affected by birds. From there we
look at birds in flight, from the fine points of flight itself by Susan Roney
Drennan to the mysteries of migration and navigation by Kenneth P.
Able. Then we move into home territory with William E. Poole's chapter
on attracting birds to a backyard. Those interested in learning how to
photograph birds should read the in-depth chapter by J. P. Myers and
Robert Cardillo. The final chapter, by Kit and George Harrison, is a gallery filled with range maps, descriptions, and stunning photographs of
125 species of birds from across the continent.

If you are not already a confirmed bird-watcher you will undoubtedly
be seduced.

Changes Through Time

By Kimball L. Garrett

*B*irds are among the most easily seen, widely distributed, and well-studied of our wild creatures. Ornithologists currently recognize some 9,000 species worldwide; about 850 occur in North America. It is perhaps in part their diversity that has captured the curiosity of bird enthusiasts.

We find avian diversity in size, colors, songs, habits, and movements. In size, for example, birds range from humming-birds, some of which weigh less than 3 grams and are only slightly over 2 inches in length, to ostriches, which weigh about 300 pounds and are more than 8 feet tall. Through the ages birds have provided food and companionship. In recent years, birds have been useful as a yardstick for measuring the quality of the environment.

Ornithologists trace the ancestry of birds back some 140 million years to the first known bird and beyond, to the reptilian progenitors of birds. Throughout recorded history, birds have shared our world, filling our lives with delight and inspiration.

Among the oddest-looking birds, Tufted Puffins reside along the Pacific Coast. They feed mainly on fish, but also use their strong bills to crush the shells of mollusks and sea urchins.

O.S. Pettingill, Jr./VIREO

Waxwings are so named because of small waxy red tips on the secondary wing feathers, as seen on this Cedar Waxwing. Silky plumages, sleek crests, and yellow tail bands distinguish waxwings from all other types of birds.

Classifying Birds

In order to obtain information about birds, scientists have grouped them into an orderly sequence of categories that are based on apparent kinship. Most ornithologists agree that all but one or two percent of living birds have been classified; species that are "new" to science are still being discovered, but at a low rate—only two or three species per year. These new additions are usually discovered in isolated areas that had previously received little study.

Early efforts at classifying the bewildering assemblage of birds emphasized general appearance. Birds that shared certain physical features were grouped together under one name to yield groupings such as thrushes, larks, finches, ducks, falcons, and pigeons. During the mid-eighteenth century, the Swedish botanist, Linnaeus, applied a system of binomial nomenclature to the groupings. His system incorporated scientific names such as *Sylvia* (for warblers), *Muscicapa* (for flycatchers), *Turdus* (for thrush-like birds), *Falco* (for diurnal birds of prey), and *Tringa* (for sandpipers). We now know that these early groupings included many unrelated species, which is not surprising since no understanding of evolution existed at that time.

In the latter decades of the nineteenth century and into the present, classification has undergone much refinement that more accurately reflects evolutionary branchings. Morphological characteristics (characteristics that relate to body form and structure) such as skull structure, arrangement of the bones of the palate, shape of the hind limb girdle, and the shape of the middle ear bone establish relationships among bird groups. The presence, absence, and arrangement of muscles and tendons also provide clues to bird relationships, and so do the number and arrangement of toes. Even the scales covering the bare part of the leg, the structure of the intestine, and the shape, structure, and color of eggshells yield useful information. Plumage patterns, feather colors, feather arrangement, and the number of flight feathers in the tail and wing provide additional external clues. In some cases, behavioral characteristics such as vocalizations, preening mechanics, nest building, and sociability are also useful in determining relationships.

Jack Wilburn

Kerry A. Grim

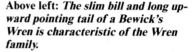

Robert J. Shallenberger

Arnold Small

Above left: *The slim bill and long upward pointing tail of a Bewick's Wren is characteristic of the Wren family.*

Above center: *The Tufted Titmouse exhibits the short bill and compact body that places it among the family that includes all titmice and chickadees.*

Above: *This Red-billed Leiothrix is a type of babbler that shares some body features with thrushes.*

Left: *The Wrentit, as its name implies, resembles superficially both the wren and the titmouse in appearance. For many years it was placed in its own unique family. However, recent studies using behavioral, morphological, and biochemical techniques have shown that Wrentits are related more closely to Asian babblers, which are members of a large grouping that includes thrushes.*

In the last few decades, biochemical techniques—such as studies of DNA—have become increasingly prevalent in determining avian taxonomy. Because such analyses focus on the genetic material or proteins that are the immediate products of genes, scientists believe that biochemical techniques express evolutionary relationships with great validity. Ornithologists are pleased to discover that biochemical studies often corroborate the taxonomies constructed through the analysis of anatomical characteristics.

The Levels of Classification

In all biological classification, taxonomic categories—created specifically to determine relationships between one form of life and another—build on one another. The largest, or highest, taxonomic category, is the kingdom. This broad category encompasses every lower, or more specific, taxonomic category: phylum, subphylum, class, order, family, genus, species, and subspecies.

Kingdom, phylum, and subphylum. Kingdoms are divided into phyla—groupings of organisms that are similar in general form and structure. In the animal kingdom birds are placed in the Phylum Chordata and are known as chordates. Biologists unite the familiar vertebrate groups and some more primitive marine groups in a single phylum because their similar physical characteristics suggest evolution from a common ancestor. The vertebrates are in a subgroup called the Subphylum Vertebrata, which distinguishes them from more primitive chordates. Within the Subphylum Vertebrata, birds constitute the Class Aves.

Class. Most avian characteristics are insufficient to define the Class Aves because they are shared by other living creatures. The characteristic that is unique to birds and clearly distinguishes the avian class is the birds' body covering, the feathers.

From the bones to the digestive system, the features that characterize birds evolved as adaptations for flight: a light, fused skeleton; a muscular stomach near the bird's center of gravity instead of teeth and heavy jaws; air spaces and sacs in the body cavity and major bones; a constant high body temperature and a high metabolism to supply the power for flight; an efficient, specialized respiratory system; and acute vision and advanced development of the vision and balance centers of the brain. (For more on physiological adaptations for flight, see page 117.)

Orders. An order is a group of families and the major subdivision of the Class Aves. Most ornithologists recognize 28 orders of modern living birds (additional orders are known only from fossils). The names of orders always end in *iformes.*

Orders are diverse in size. Some, such as the order of ostriches, Struthioniformes, contain only a single family; others, such as the order of perching birds, Passeriformes, contain as many as 73 families.

Many orders contain birds that are clearly alike. For example, marine birds of the order Procellariiformes share a distinctive feature: a set of external tubular nostrils; little debate surrounds the classification of these birds. Flamingos, on the other hand, do not seem to have any single uniting characteristic that sets them apart from other orders. Taxonomists usually classify flamingos within the order of stork-like birds, Ciconiiformes, but many believe that flamingos are closer to the waterfowl of the order Anseriformes, and others conclude that they are offshoots of certain shorebirds within the order Charadriiformes. As a compromise many recent checklists place flamingos in their own order, Phoenicopteriformes, and list them between the orders Ciconiiformes and Anseriformes. (For more relationships of orders, see page 27.)

Families. Families are groupings of genera with shared anatomical and behavioral characteristics. Family names always end in *idae.*

Sandy L. Schuler

A Lesser Yellowlegs spreads its wings in takeoff. Feathers are believed to have evolved from the scales of reptilian ancestors and are characteristic of birds, distinguishing them from all other types of animals.

Although the Greater Flamingo is similar in general appearance to storks and herons, its webbed feet are characteristic of waterfowl. Because of this mixture of traits, it is not clear to which order flamingos should be assigned. They are often placed in their own separate order.

Sharon Chester

About 170 families are currently recognized worldwide. However, taxonomists by no means agree on the prerequisites for family status, and the many revampings of songbird families are evidence of the disagreement. Many families are divided into subfamilies, groupings of yet more closely related genera. Unfortunately, this category cannot be further defined because it has no strict biological basis.

Genera. Genera are groups of species that share certain adaptive characteristics—characteristics that are quite distinguishable from those of other groups. Like the definition of subfamilies, the definition of genus is only a working definition; biological criteria cannot be applied at this time. Genus is, therefore, a grouping that is solely for the purpose of classification.

Many distinctive species have no known close relatives and are placed in their own, single-species genera.

Species. Species, as a category, is the foundation on which the higher taxonomic classifications are built. Biologists usually define species with regard to the degree of reproductive isolation (the failure to interbreed). Members of a species do not normally interbreed with members of a different species.

Some species are uniform; they vary little in appearance throughout their geographical range. Uniform species are often wide-ranging, and extensive interbreeding occurs among populations. Frequently, however, species show some degree of geographical variation. Taxonomists recognize this variation by naming subspecies, or races.

In North America many familiar species classifications encompass numerous *subspecies*. All subspecies interbreed where their ranges overlap, or taxonomists believe the populations would interbreed if the subspecies were in contact. Where subspecies interbreed frequently, distinguishing traits are often weak; where subspecies are separated geographically, the differences tend to be greater.

Below left: *In the western subspecies of Rufous-sided Towhees, the back is spotted with white. Although generally different in appearance, in areas where the subspecies overlap in distribution, the different forms interbreed freely. This results in a variety of intermediate plumages as well as the categorization of the subspecies as a single species.*

Below right: *Rufous-sided Towhees of the Northeast bear a close resemblance to those found in the Southeast but have red eyes.*

Bottom: *In southeastern North America, Rufous-sided Towhees have white eyes.*

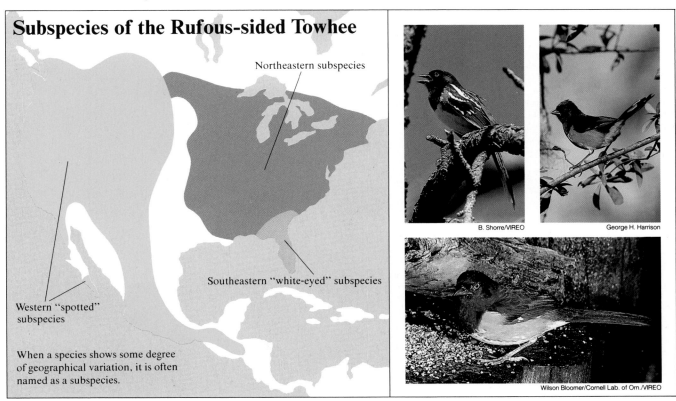

Subspecies of the Rufous-sided Towhee

Northeastern subspecies

Western "spotted" subspecies

Southeastern "white-eyed" subspecies

When a species shows some degree of geographical variation, it is often named as a subspecies.

B. Shorre/VIREO

George H. Harrison

Wilson Bloomer/Cornell Lab. of Orn./VIREO

Because of the relative conspicuousness of birds and the cues they use to recognize each other, birds are probably better known at the species level than any other group of organisms. Still, it is often difficult to distinguish populations as species or subspecies. These difficulties usually result from inadequate information on the degree of interbreeding and the fact that great variation can occur within species throughout their ranges.

Superspecies include two or more closely related species that evolved from a common ancestor but now inhabit separate ranges. Members of a superspecies are not expected to interbreed to a significant degree if their ranges overlap. For example, taxonomists believe that the Indigo Bunting of the eastern and central United States and the Lazuli Bunting of the western United States diverged from a common ancestor during the Pleistocene era. They are morphologically similar, and they interbreed to only a limited degree where their ranges meet.

In North America the classification superspecies frequently refers to characteristic variation between eastern and western species pairs or trios, such as the Rose-breasted and Black-headed Grosbeaks and the Ruby-throated and Black-chinned Hummingbirds. Some superspecies components are separated by extremely large geographical gaps, such as the Pygmy Nuthatch of the western pine forests and the Brown-headed Nuthatch of the southeastern pine bottomlands.

It may seem contradictory to use the criterion of reproductive isolation to define a species and yet label two forms as distinct species when a certain degree of hybridization between the two takes place. For example, in eastern North America the Blue-winged and Golden-winged Warblers regularly interbreed but at a level low enough that most modern taxonomists consider them distinct species. In the West, Townsend's and Hermit Warblers interbreed with regularity, yet they are not considered a single species. These cases represent what are known as secondary contacts: species that have evolved in geographical isolation from each other have since expanded their ranges and come into partial contact.

Evaluating whether groups of secondary contacts represent distinct species is often difficult. Studies ideally conducted throughout the zone of

Below: *Indigo Buntings like this one inhabit brushy areas of eastern North America, but are expanding their range to the West and Southwest.*

Below right: *Closely related to the Indigo Bunting, the morphologically similar Lazuli Bunting is found in western North America. Together the two species form a superspecies and only occasionally hybridize where their ranges now overlap.*

Douglas R. Herr

H. Cruickshank/VIREO

contact should seek to establish the percentage of mixed versus pure pairings, taking into account the viability of hybrid offspring, the differences in habitat preferences, the changes in the size of the contact zone, and the extent of interbreeding over time. Even over the relatively short period of three decades, studies show that the geographical zone of overlap between Baltimore and Bullock's orioles and the degree of hybridization within that zone changed. Such changes are also evident among the forms of the Yellow-bellied Sapsucker in western North America. Taxonomists are far from being in complete agreement about how many species the orioles and the sapsuckers comprise.

What's in a Name?

Like all living organisms each bird species has a unique Latin name. This two-part name specifies the genus, which is always capitalized, and the species, which is never capitalized. Scientific names convey some information about relationships. For instance, although chickadees and titmice are distinctive groups, the names *Parus bicolor* (Tufted Titmouse) and *Parus atricapillus* (Black-capped Chickadee) denote the close relationship between the two.

Birds' English names may vary from region to region; their assignment is not formal, and the rules that govern Latin names do not apply. For example, the bird we recognize in North America as the Common Murre is known as the Guillemot in Britain. To add to the confusion, the name *guillemot* refers to a related but different bird in North America. Throughout the world, however, our Common Murre is known by its scientific name, *Uria aalge.*

Three-part names describe subspecies, and the forms of the names are similarly invariable. Thus, the eastern North American subspecies of the Long-eared Owl (*Asio otus*) is called *Asio otus wilsonianus;* the western North American subspecies, which differs slightly from the eastern subspecies, is called *Asio otus tuftsi;* and the Eurasian subspecies, which differs from both North American subspecies, goes by the name *Asio otus otus.* Subspecies are often informally given English names for convenience. Thus, *Asio otus tuftsi* has been called the "Western" Long-eared Owl. English names are, however, best reserved for distinctive subspecies, such as the Myrtle warbler and the Audubon's warbler, which are subspecies of the widespread Yellow-rumped Warbler.

Recently, a trend has emerged toward the use of modifiers to clarify names. These modifiers usually reflect distinctive physical traits of the bird. The bird we have long known simply as the catbird, for example, is now more properly called the Gray Catbird to avoid confusion with a black species of catbird from southeastern Mexico.

Stability of nomenclature is highly desirable, and the rules for establishing and changing scientific names are rigorous. The rules are designed to avoid the inevitable confusion that would result from endless synonyms. In North America a committee of the American Ornithologists' Union (AOU) decides on the English and the scientific names for North American birds. The AOU also publishes the standard nomenclatural reference for North and Central America, the *Check-List of North American Birds* (Sixth Edition, 1983).

When name changes do occur, they are most frequently the result of the grouping or splitting of species or genera. For example, when the genus *Pyrrhuloxia* was merged into the genus *Cardinalis* to reflect the similarities between the two genera, the species *Pyrrhuloxia sinuata* became *Cardinalis sinuatus.* (The ending on the species name was also changed to agree in gender with the generic noun.)

In North America these birds are known as Common Murres; in Britain they would be called Guillemots. In addition to these widely used names, local regions may have their own colloquial names. To avoid confusion, scientists use an internationally accepted Latin name.

Stephen J. Krasemann/DRK Photo

Archaeopteryx

Ichthyornis

Birds of the Past

Fossils—the impressions or mineralized remains of ancient organisms—provide the most concrete evidence of birds' evolutionary past. The relatively lightweight, toothless skeletons of birds are far from ideal material for fossilization; nevertheless, an extensive fossil record of birds exists, and it has yielded fascinating insights into the history of birds. The fossil record has also shown us the past geographical distributions of birds.

In the evolutionary saga of the Class Aves, no series of fossils has had as great an impact on human understanding of avian origins as Archaeopteryx (Latin for ancient wing). First discovered in 1861 in Europe in the Solnhofen limestone quarries of what is now Bavaria, Archaeopteryx (dubbed *Archaeopteryx lithographica*) is thought to have lived some 140 million years ago in the Jurassic period of the Mesozoic era.

In addition to being the first known bird, Archaeopteryx is significant as a representation of intermediacy between the reptilian and avian grades of evolution. Its feathers are indistinguishable from those of modern birds, and the asymmetry of the wing feathers suggests that Archaeopteryx was capable of at least limited flight. Some aspects of the pectoral girdle of Archaeopteryx are also avian, particularly the fusion of the clavicle bones into a wishbone. The sharp teeth set into sockets of the jaw and the bony tail vertebrae are decidedly reptilian as are the claws on the tips of the hand digits.

The first known birds after Archaeopteryx existed from 135 to 65 million years ago in the Cretaceous period. Most of these birds appear not to be the ancestors of any living orders of birds. The earliest Cretaceous bird known, Ambiortus, lived some 15 to 20 million years after Archaeopteryx. It is not known whether Ambiortus had teeth, but it did have a keeled sternum and was capable of flight. The Ambiortus fossil was discovered only recently in central Mongolia.

Fossils of two orders of Cretaceous marine birds were discovered in west-central North America in the late 1800s. The fossils show that birds of both orders had toothed jaws. (No modern bird has true teeth.)

Time Scale of Bird Evolution

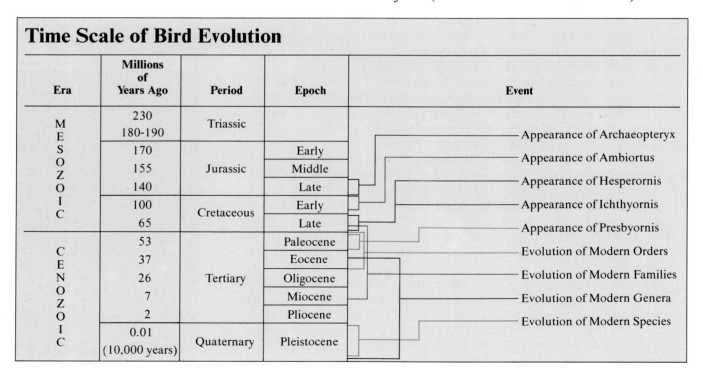

Era	Millions of Years Ago	Period	Epoch	Event
M E S O Z O I C	230 / 180-190	Triassic		Appearance of Archaeopteryx
	170	Jurassic	Early	Appearance of Ambiortus
	155		Middle	Appearance of Hesperornis
	140		Late	
	100	Cretaceous	Early	Appearance of Ichthyornis
	65		Late	Appearance of Presbyornis
C E N O Z O I C	53	Tertiary	Paleocene	Evolution of Modern Orders
	37		Eocene	
	26		Oligocene	Evolution of Modern Families
	7		Miocene	Evolution of Modern Genera
	2		Pliocene	Evolution of Modern Species
	0.01 (10,000 years)	Quaternary	Pleistocene	

Hesperornis and its relatives are grouped into the extinct order Hesperornithiformes, and were flightless, fish-eating birds. The order Ichthyornithiformes was represented by a toothed flying bird called Ichthyornis. This bird was similar in appearance to a tern, and like other modern flying birds it had a keeled breastbone for the attachment of the flight muscles.

Modern bird families branched out on a large scale during the Tertiary period, which began some 65 million years ago. Presbyornis, one of the well-preserved fossils from that period, has contributed mightily toward our understanding of bird relationships. Though generally classified with the order Charadriiformes, which includes modern shorebirds, Presbyornis had a distinctly duck-like skull and tongue apparatus, which suggests that the order Anseriformes (ducks, swans, and geese) may have arisen from a primitive charadriiform stock.

By the end of the Tertiary period most—if not all—of the bird families that we know today had appeared along with many modern genera. But modern bird life was shaped by the ice ages of the Quaternary period, from two million to ten thousand years ago. The repeated occurrence of the evolution of species in separate geographical distributions through the ice ages resulted in the diversity of bird species we see today.

Hesperornis

Presbyornis

Modern Birds

Though some orders bear no clear relationship to others, ornithologists postulate close relationships between enough of them to have established the groupings of birds that follow. These particular classifications are primarily based on the *Reference List of the Birds of the World* by John J. Morony, Jr., Walter J. Bock, and John Farrand, Jr. (American Museum of Natural History, 1975). Some changes, especially regarding the grouping and splitting of certain families, have been made to bring the list into closer agreement with the AOU *Check-List of North American Birds* (Sixth Edition, 1983). For an overview of modern birds, see pages 28 and 29.

Ratites

Taxonomists group several orders of large flightless birds under the term *ratite*. The word refers to the flat, raft-like shape of the sternum, which lacks the keel shape typical of the breastbone of flying birds. Ratites include several orders: ostriches of Africa that also used to inhabit western Asia (Struthioniformes); rheas of South America (Rheiformes); emus of Australia and cassowaries of Australia and New Guinea (both Casuariiformes); New Zealand kiwis (Apterygiformes); and families such as the moas and elephant birds, which are now extinct. Ornithologists generally agree that ratites evolved from flying ancestors, but they are uncertain if the different orders are closely related to each other. All ratites have powerful legs, and the open-country ostriches, rheas, and emus are excellent runners. Most species of ratites feed on a variety of plant material, although the kiwis of the forest floor use their long bills to capture earthworms and insects.

Tinamous

Tinamous are a uniform group of some 45 species, which represent their own order, Tinamiformes. Tinamous inhabit one region, the American tropics. They are ground-dwelling, quail-like weak fliers that traditional taxonomy relates to one or more of the ratite orders. Most species are difficult to observe in their dense forest-floor habitats, but they are often detected by their haunting, whistled calls. The glossy appearance of their colorful eggs is also remarkable.

Ratites are large ground-dwellers that have lost many of the adaptations that other birds require for flight. This Greater Rhea is typical of most ratites; it has large, strong legs for running across the open plains of South America.

Kenneth W. Fink/Berg & Associates

An Overview of Modern Birds

The 22 groups listed here represent all the species of living birds. The list is arranged to reflect, in theory, an evolutionary progression of older "primitive" groups to more recent "advanced" groups. Orders may contain only a single family or as many as 73 families; families are composed of anywhere from 1 to 1,350 species. For more information on each group, see pages 27 to 41.

Ratites

Order: Ostriches (Struthioniformes)
  Families: 1
  • Ostriches (Struthionidae)
    1 species

Order: Rheas (Rheiformes)
  Families: 1
  • Rheas (Rheidae)
    2 species

Order: Cassowaries and Emus (Casuariiformes)
  Families: 2
  • Cassowaries (Casuariidae)
    3 species
  • Emus (Dromaiidae)
    1 species

Order: Kiwis (Apterygiformes)
  Families: 1
  • Kiwis (Apterygidae)
    3 species

Tinamous

Order: Tinamous (Tinamiformes)
  Families: 1
  • Tinamous (Tinamidae)
    47 species

Grebes

Order: Grebes (Podicipediformes)
  Families: 1
  • Grebes (Podicipedidae)
    20 species

Loons

Order: Loons (Gaviiformes)
  Families: 1
  • Loons (Gaviidae)
    5 species

Penguins

Order: Penguins (Sphenisciformes)
  Families: 1
  • Penguins (Spheniscidae)
    18 species

Tube-Nosed Marine Birds

Order: Tube-noses (Procellariiformes)
  Families: 4
  • Albatrosses (Diomedeidae)
    13 species
  • Diving-Petrels (Pelecanoididae)
    4 species
  • Shearwaters and Petrels (Procellariidae)
    66 species
  • Storm-Petrels (Hydrobatidae)
    21 species

Pelicans and Their Relatives

Order: Pelicans and their relatives (Pelecaniformes)
  Families: 6
  • Anhingas (Anhingidae)
    4 species
  • Boobies and Gannets (Sulidae)
    9 species
  • Cormorants (Phalacrocoracidae)
    33 species
  • Frigatebirds (Fregatidae)
    5 species
  • Pelicans (Pelecanidae)
    8 species
  • Tropicbirds (Phaethontidae)
    3 species

Long-Legged Wading Birds

Order: Storks and their relatives (Ciconiiformes)
  Families: 5
  • Hamerkop (Scopidae)
    1 species
  • Herons (Ardeidae)
    64 species
  • Shoebill (Balaenicipitidae)
    1 species
  • Storks (Ciconiidae)
    17 species
  • Ibises and Spoonbills (Threskiornithidae)
    33 species

Order: Flamingos (Phoenicopteriformes)
  Families: 1
  • Flamingos (Phoenicopteridae)
    6 species

Waterfowl

Order: Waterfowl (Anseriformes)
  Families: 2
  • Ducks, Geese, and Swans (Anatidae)
    147 species
  • Screamers (Anhimidae)
    3 species

Birds of Prey

Order: Birds of Prey (Falconiformes)
  Families: 4
  • Falcons (Falconidae)
    60 species
  • Hawks, Eagles, Kites, and Osprey (Accipitridae)
    218 species
  • New World* Vultures (Cathartidae)
    7 species
  • Secretary-Bird (Sagittariidae)
    1 species

Game Birds

Order: Game Birds (Galliformes)
  Families: 3
  • Curassows and Guans (Cracidae)
    44 species
  • Grouse, Quail, and Pheasants (Phasianidae)
    212 species
  • Megapodes (Megapodidae)
    12 species

Cranes, Rails, and Their Relatives

Order: Cranes, Rails, and their relatives (Gruiformes)
  Families: 12, such as . . .
  • Bustards (Otididae)
    24 species
  • Button-Quails (Turnicidae)
    14 species
  • Cranes (Gruidae)
    15 species
  • Kagu (Rhynochetidae)
    1 species
  • Limpkin (Aramidae)
    1 species
  • Mesites (Mesitornithidae)
    3 species
  • Rails and Coots (Rallidae)
    141 species
  • Seriemas (Cariamidae)
    2 species
  • Sunbittern (Eurypygidae)
    1 species
  • Sungrebes (Heliornithidae)
    3 species
  • Trumpeters (Psophiidae)
    3 species

Shorebirds, Gulls, Auks, and Their Relatives

Order: Shorebirds, Gulls, Auks, and their relatives (Charadriiformes)
Families: 13
- Auks, Murres, and Puffins (Alcidae)
  23 species
- Avocets and Stilts (Recurvirostridae)
  13 species
- Coursers (Glareolidae)
  16 species
- Crab-Plover (Dromadidae)
  1 species
- Ibisbill (Ibidorhynchidae)
  1 species
- Jacanas (Jacanidae)
  8 species
- Oystercatchers (Haematopodidae)
  7 species
- Painted-Snipes (Rostratulidae)
  2 species
- Plovers (Charadriidae)
  64 species
- Sandpipers (Scolopacidae)
  86 species
- Sheathbills (Chionididae)
  2 species
- Skuas, Gulls, Terns, and Skimmers (Laridae)
  98 species
- Thick-knees (Burhinidae)
  9 species

Pigeons and Doves

Order: Pigeons and Doves (Columbiformes)
Families: 2
- Pigeons and Doves (Columbidae)
  304 species
- Sandgrouse (Pteroclididae)
  16 species

Parrots

Order: Parrots (Psittaciformes)
Families: 3
- Cockatoos (Cacatuidae)
  18 species
- Lories (Loriidae)
  55 species
- Parrots (Psittacidae)
  269 species

Cuckoos and Their Relatives

Order: Cuckoos and their relatives (Cuculiformes)
Families: 3
- Cuckoos (Cuculidae)
  130 species
- Hoatzin (Opisthocomidae)
  1 species
- Touracos (Musophagidae)
  19 species

Owls

Order: Owls (Strigiformes)
Families: 2
- Barn-Owls (Tytonidae)
  12 species
- Typical Owls (Strigidae)
  133 species

Nightjars and Their Relatives

Order: Nightjars and their relatives (Caprimulgiformes)
Families: 5
- Frogmouths (Podargidae)
  13 species
- Nightjars (Caprimulgidae)
  77 species
- Oilbirds (Steatornithidae)
  1 species
- Owlet-Nightjars (Aegothelidae)
  8 species
- Potoos (Nyctibiidae)
  5 species

Swifts and Hummingbirds

Order: Swifts and Hummingbirds (Apodiformes)
Families: 3
- Hummingbirds (Trochilidae)
  320 species
- Swifts (Apodidae)
  82 species
- Crested-Swifts (Hemiprocnidae)
  4 species

Colies

Order: Colies (Coliiformes)
Families: 1
- Colies (Coliidae)
  6 species

Kingfisher and Woodpecker Assemblage

Order: Kingfishers and their relatives (Coraciiformes)
Families: 10
- Bee-eaters (Meropidae)
  24 species
- Cuckoo-Rollers (Leptosomatidae)
  1 species
- Ground-Rollers (Brachypteraciidae)
  5 species
- Hoopoes (Upupidae)
  1 species
- Hornbills (Bucerotidae)
  45 species
- Kingfishers (Alcedinidae)
  92 species
- Motmots (Momotidae)
  9 species
- Rollers (Coraciidae)
  11 species
- Todies (Todidae)
  5 species
- Wood-Hoopoes (Phoeniculidae)
  8 species

Order: Trogons (Trogoniformes)
Families: 1
- Trogons (Trogonidae)
  37 species

Order: Woodpeckers and their relatives (Piciformes)
Families: 6
- Barbets (Capitonidae)
  81 species
- Honeyguides (Indicatoridae)
  14 species
- Jacamars (Galbulidae)
  17 species
- Puffbirds (Bucconidae)
  34 species
- Toucans (Ramphastidae)
  33 species
- Woodpeckers (Picidae)
  200 species

Perching Birds

Order: Perching Birds (Passeriformes)
Families: 73, such as . . .
- Buntings, Grosbeaks, Tanagers, Wood-Warblers, and their relatives (Emberizidae)
  795 species
- Crows and Jays (Corvidae)
  105 species
- Finches (Fringillidae)
  122 species
- Thrushes and their relatives (Muscicapidae)
  1350 species

Phil & Loretta Hermann/Tom Stack & Associates

This Western Grebe is typical of all grebes, with lobed toes and legs placed well back on the body. Weak flyers, grebes are seldom seen in flight.

Grebes

The order Podicipediformes contains only the grebe family, some 20 species of diving birds. Grebes are characterized by lobes (rather than webs) on their toes, and their legs are so far to the rear of the body that locomotion on land is awkward. Grebes breed on freshwater lakes and ponds, but some species spend nonbreeding periods along seacoasts. Grebes do not appear to be closely related to any other living order of birds. Although taxonomists have placed grebes next to the order of loons, ornithologists now speculate that grebes' relationships may lie elsewhere—perhaps with the order of cranes, rails, and their relatives (Gruiformes).

Loons

The five living loon species of the order Gaviiformes constitute the genus *Gavia*. Loons inhabit only the Northern Hemisphere, where they breed on inland lakes and ponds and winter along seacoasts. These fish-eating divers have webbed toes and bear a superficial resemblance to grebes. Like grebes, the loon's muscular legs are set far back on the body, an adaptation for foot-propelled diving. Loons may represent an early offshoot of the lineage that gave rise to the order of shorebirds, gulls, and auks (Charadriiformes).

Paddlelike wings propel this King Penguin through the water when it pursues its prey. These and other penguins rely on thick layers of insulation to protect them from the cold waters they inhabit.

Sharon Chester

Penguins

Supremely adapted diving birds of the cold oceans of the Southern Hemisphere, penguins form the only family within the order Sphenisciformes. Represented by some 18 living species, penguins pursue fish, squid, and crustacea under water. The modified wings that they use as flippers are useless for flight. Dense, short feathers and a heavy layer of fat insulate penguins from the extremely cold waters they inhabit. The relationship of penguins to other groups of birds is not yet well understood.

Tube-Nosed Marine Birds

The order Procellariiformes, the "tube-noses," contains four major families. Procellariiformes are highly specialized for life in a marine environment. The tubes marking the external nostrils are part of a salt-excreting apparatus and characterize all birds of this order. Groups within the order include albatrosses, petrels, shearwaters, storm-petrels, and diving-petrels. They are most diverse in the oceans of the Southern Hemisphere. Only a few species—Manx Shearwaters, Northern Fulmars, and Fork-tailed and Leach's Storm-Petrels, for example—breed at northern temperate latitudes. Many southern species undertake long migrations to the northern oceans, however. These travelers include two species that are quite abundant in North American waters during the nonbreeding season: the Sooty Shearwater and Wilson's Storm-Petrel. The family of albatrosses, Diomedeidae, are large narrow-winged birds that are highly specialized for gliding flight. The family of gull-sized petrels, shearwaters, and fulmars—Procellariidae—are also narrow-winged and exhibit a strong flapping and gliding flight. The family of more buoyant storm-petrels, Hydrobatidae, contains the smallest of the tube-noses—some species are hardly larger than a swallow. The family of diving-petrels, Pelecanoididae, have an auk-like appearance and reduced wings that the birds use for underwater propulsion. Albatrosses and storm-petrels feed at the surface of the water as do many gull-sized petrels, shearwaters, and fulmars. Diving-petrels and some shearwaters pursue prey under water.

Pelicans and Their Relatives

The order Pelecaniformes includes pelicans, cormorants, and several tropical waterbird families. Members of this order are unique in having all four toes joined by webbing, although this webbing is nearly lacking in the frigatebirds, which are primarily aerial.

Feeding adaptations within this order are diverse. Pelicans use their long pouched bills to scoop fish and other prey from shallow lakes or marshes, and the Brown Pelican, a marine bird of the American coasts, plunges into the water to capture prey. This plunge-diving is further developed in the family of boobies and gannets, marine birds that may plunge from great heights to capture fish and squid.

Cormorants are birds of both fresh and saltwater. They pursue fish under water, propelled by strong fully webbed feet. The cormorant family is easily the largest in the order. Closely related to cormorants are anhingas, sometimes called darters, snake-birds, or water-turkeys. These freshwater birds resemble slender cormorants, but the hooked cormorant beak is replaced by a dagger-like beak—an effective weapon for spearing fish.

Douglas T. Cheeseman, Jr.

The Royal Albatross is a typical tube-nosed marine bird. The tubes around its nostrils help excrete excess salt, which would otherwise build up in the bird's body. This adaptation allows these birds to wander across the ocean without requiring fresh water.

Cormorants, like this Double-crested Cormorant, are one of several families classified under the order Pelecaniformes. Though the members of this order vary dramatically in appearance, all possess webbing between the four toes.

David S. Soliday

The three species of tropicbirds in this order inhabit warm tropical oceans. Somewhat tern-like in appearance, they share the terns' habit of plunging into the water for prey. Adults are noteworthy for their long tail streamers, which may extend some 20 inches.

The final family of the order Pelecaniformes contains five species of frigatebirds. These large distinctive birds soar over tropical oceans and coasts, obtaining food from the surface of the water with their long, hooked bills or pirating fish or squid from other seabirds with a remarkable display of aerobatic skills.

Long-Legged Wading Birds

Several bird families have been traditionally considered to form the diverse order Ciconiiformes: herons, storks, ibises, and flamingos. All are long-legged birds that live in or near shallow water. The Flamingo family is uniquely adapted for filtering algae, diatoms, and invertebrates from the sediments of shallow lakes by using their peculiar down-bent bills and fleshy tongues. It is possible that the flamingos' relationships lie with either the shorebirds or ducks and geese. Today, taxonomists often place them in their own order, Phoenicopteriformes.

Over sixty species strong, herons form the largest family of the order Ciconiiformes. North American herons range in size from the Least Bittern, which is less than a foot tall, to the 4-foot-tall Great Blue Heron. All are slender long-necked birds that capture prey with their dagger-like bills. Unlike other long-legged wading birds, herons fly with the neck folded into an "S" shape.

The 17 species of storks range from large to exceptionally large birds and all have heavy bills. Storks are capable of soaring flight, and they feed on a variety of animal matter. Some species are frequent carrion scavengers. In feeding on carrion and in many other anatomical and behavioral characteristics, these storks resemble condors and other New World vultures. It is possible that storks are the New World vultures' closest living relatives.

In addition to two single-species African families, the final family within the order Ciconiiformes contains ibises and spoonbills. Ibises are characterized by long, down-curved bills and spoonbills have flattened bills with an expanded spoonlike tip. Most birds of this order live in tropical and subtropical climates, though many herons and some storks and ibises live in more temperate zones.

This Green-backed Heron is representative of long-legged wading birds, which also include storks, ibises, and flamingos. All of these birds frequent the shallow waters of lakeshores, rivers, and marshes.

Kent & Donna Dannen

John Gerlach/DRK Photo

Waterfowl, such as this Canvasback, compose the relatively uniform order, Anseriformes. Most species are aquatic and show a variety of behavioral and morphological adaptations for exploiting different types of aquatic prey.

Waterfowl

Ducks, swans, and geese make up the rather uniform order Anseriformes. These birds have webbed feet and a bill that is usually broad, flat, and somewhat rounded at the tip. Distributed worldwide, these waterfowl usually feed on aquatic plants and animals. Some species dive deep for fish or mollusks, others feed at or near the surface, some filter through shallow bottom sediments, and others even graze on land. Most species of waterfowl are migratory. Offshoots of the order are three species of South American screamers, which are more terrestrial and have chicken-like bills. The fossil of the bird Presbyornis shows a long-legged shorebird-like form with a duck-like bill. This fossil, which is some 50 million years old, may suggest an evolutionary relationship between Anseriformes and shorebirds.

Birds of Prey

Hawks, eagles, and falcons of the order Falconiformes are widespread and diverse. All birds of prey are characterized by strongly hooked, sharp beaks, and most have sharp, curved talons. Within bird-of-prey species, the sexes frequently differ noticeably in size, and it is generally the female that is larger and heavier.

Different groups within this order show a variety of hunting techniques. Some—such as vultures, and some caracaras and kites—are primarily scavengers. Strong flyers, birds of prey generally pursue and often capture prey on the wing. Many species cover great distances while soaring in search of prey. Some species are adapted for capturing fish at or near the surface of the water. Other species specialize in capturing rodents, birds, reptiles, and insects. Unusual among birds of prey is the long-legged secretary-bird of the African plains, which feeds largely on reptiles.

The two major groups of carrion feeders, the Old World vultures and the New World vultures and condors, are superficially similar. They are large to massive birds with unfeathered heads and excellent powers of soaring flight. Old World vultures are in the same family as hawks and eagles, but New World vultures may actually be more closely related to storks than to the birds of prey. Similarly, many ornithologists believe that the relationship between the family Accipitridae (hawks, eagles, harriers, Old World vultures, and kites) and the family Falconidae (falcons and caracaras) is rather distant.

A hooked beak and sharp talons characterize this Red-shouldered Hawk as a member of the birds of prey. Birds of prey, often called raptors, are usually superb flyers. Some are strong soarers; others are capable of flying through dense forests without disturbing a branch.

Sandy L. Schuler

Don & Pat Valenti

Ben Goldstein/Valenti Photo

Above: *The Wild Turkey, shown here during a courtship display, exhibits features common to all game birds: Heavy bodies with stout legs and often elaborate courtship rituals.*

Above right: *These American Coots are members of the order Gruiformes, which includes cranes, rails, limpkins, and a number of other groups. These birds are generally weak flyers, although the cranes provide an exception to this rule.*

Game Birds

Chicken-like fowl constitute the order Galliformes. Order members include quail, grouse, pheasants, peafowl, guineafowl, and turkeys. These strong-legged, ground-inhabiting birds feed on seeds, berries, and other vegetable matter. Their wings are short and rounded, and flight is explosive but not prolonged. The young hatch fully covered in down, and they are able to run and feed. Also included in this order are the family of chachalacas, guans, and curassows of the New World tropics. These species are unusual game birds in that they are primarily tree-dwellers. Of interest to those studying breeding biology are megapodes, the mound builders or brush turkeys of Australia. These long-tailed hen-like birds bury their eggs in decaying vegetation, in warm sand, or in volcanic soil. The parent birds are then free of the task of providing the temperature regulation necessary for incubation. The common game birds of North America are quail, grouse, ptarmigan, the Wild Turkey, and—as far north as southern Texas—the Plain Chachalaca. Other species, including pheasants and partridges, have been introduced into North America for sport hunting.

Cranes, Rails, and Their Relatives

Cranes, rails, and about ten other families form the order Gruiformes. The most widespread family, Rallidae, consists of rails and coots. Rails are secretive birds of dense low vegetation, such as marshes. They occur through much of the world, and have even colonized many oceanic islands. Rails are short-winged, and their flight appears labored, although many species are highly migratory. Some forms from oceanic islands are flightless and have been tragically susceptible to extinction. Rails have long toes which enable them to walk on floating vegetation. Coots are heavy duck-like birds that paddle through the water with lobed toes.

Cranes form a family of 15 species and are found through most of the temperate and tropical areas of the world. They are large long-necked, long-legged wading or land birds, that are superficially heron-like (although cranes fly with their necks outstretched). Cranes are noted for their resonant calls and elaborate courtship dances. Many species of cranes are threatened with extinction.

The remaining families that taxonomists traditionally place within the order Gruiformes consist of aquatic, grassland, and forest species. Most are small families of uncertain relationships including such groups as limpkins, sungrebes, sunbitterns, and bustards. Some of these groups may actually be related to the order Charadriiformes.

Shorebirds, Gulls, and Auks

Few bird orders contain more species than the diverse order Charadriiformes. This order includes such groups as plovers, sandpipers, gulls, terns, and auks—some of our most familiar coastal and waterside birds.

The family Alcidae (auks, murres, puffins, and their relatives) consists of highly specialized diving birds. They are compact in shape, with relatively small, thin wings. The wings propel them in flight with rapid, whirring wingbeats and also propel them through the water in their pursuit of fish, squid, and crustaceans. Birds of this family, often called alcids, live only in northern oceans. Penguins and diving-petrels, unrelated to the Alcidae, fill a similar ecological role in the southern oceans.

Gulls and terns are united in the family Laridae. Gulls are opportunistic and abundant coastal birds, scarce only in tropical regions. Gregarious by nature, they feed by scavenging and by exploiting abundant prey such as fish, insects, and—on occasion—bird eggs and nestlings. Terns resemble slender gulls. Most species capture prey such as small fish by plunge-diving or by picking prey from the surface of the water while the terns are in flight. Terns are widespread even on tropical coasts and seas.

Related to the gulls and terns is a small group of predatory birds known as jaegers and skuas. Breeding at high latitudes in both the Northern and Southern Hemispheres, these birds habitually pirate prey captured by gulls or terns. They are also scavengers and voracious predators within colonies of birds such as penguins. Arctic-breeding jaegers feed mostly on rodents during the nesting season. Related to terns and somewhat similar in appearance are three species of skimmers. These species possess a remarkable knife-like bill which the birds skim over the surface of the water to capture prey.

Richard Carver

The diverse order Charadriiformes consists of shorebirds, gulls, auks, and related species. The American Avocet pictured here is typical of most shorebirds. Other members of the order range from sleek, agile terns to the heavy-bodied murres and the flightless, extinct Great Auk.

Of the various families of wading birds within the order Charadriiformes, the most familiar are the Sandpiper family (Scolopacidae) and the Plover family (Charadriidae). The 85 or so species of sandpipers are distributed worldwide, although the greatest diversity of breeding species inhabits the higher northern latitudes. Many species undertake long annual migrations. The legs of sandpipers may be short to quite long, and the wide variety of bill shapes and lengths reflects a corresponding diversity in feeding habits. A subfamily within Scolopacidae includes the three species of phalaropes, which have evolved lobed toes and are excellent, buoyant swimmers. The Plover family, with over 60 species, consists of compact, short-billed sandpiper-like birds that inhabit shorelines, grasslands, and other open areas. The distribution of plovers is nearly worldwide. Other families of shorebirds include stilts and avocets, oystercatchers, jacanas, and thick-knees.

Fossil evidence and living bird families suggest a relationship between the orders Charadriiformes, Anseriformes (waterfowl), and Gruiformes (cranes, rails, and their relatives).

Pigeons and Doves

The long list of land-bird groups is headed by the order Columbiformes, which is dominated by the largely uniform family of pigeons and doves. These are tree- or ground-inhabiting birds that feed primarily on seeds and fruit. Nearly 300 species strong, members of the pigeon and dove family are found worldwide except in the highest latitudes. Pigeons and doves feed their young with a milky substance produced by the adult birds—a trait that is unique to the family. Ornithologists believe that pigeons are related to the extinct dodos and solitaires of the islands of the Indian Ocean. The order Columbiformes also includes the sandgrouse family. The open-country birds of Africa and southern Eurasia share some of the characteristics of pigeons and some of the characteristics of the Charadriiformes. As a result taxonomists sometimes assign these birds to the order Columbiformes and sometimes to Charadriiformes.

W. Peckover/VIREO

This Brown-backed Emerald Dove is typical of most pigeons and doves. These birds are characterized by plump bodies and the habit of bobbing their heads as they walk. Many have become well adapted to feeding on the ground.

Parrots

Parrots belong to the order Psittaciformes. Members of this order are easily recognized by their strong, uniquely hooked bills and their toe arrangement (two toes face forward and two face to the rear). Most species are brightly colored—frequently with bright greens. Parrots range from the size of a sparrow to about 3 feet in length. Parrots are found throughout the tropical and south temperate regions of the world, and are most diverse in South America and Australia. Nearly all species dwell in trees, and they feed on fruits, nuts, and other vegetable matter. The relationships of this order to other bird groups is not yet well understood.

Cuckoos and Their Relatives

The order Cuculiformes contains three rather divergent families which are sometimes placed in their own orders: the family of cuckoos, roadrunners, anis, and their relatives (Cuculidae); the family of touracos (Musophagidae); and the family of the South American hoatzin (Opisthocomidae). Because of the gross similarities between Archaeopteryx and some cuckoos, touracos, and hoatzin, some taxonomists consider Cuculiformes among the most primitive of living avian orders.

Birds of the cuckoo family have yoke-toed feet—two toes face forward and two face to the rear. Female cuckoos often deposit their eggs in the nests of other birds, a trait called brood parasitism.

Although the cuckoo family is distributed worldwide, the touraco family lives only in Africa. The Touraco family contains some 20 species of large, long-tailed, tree-dwelling birds. These birds are brightly colored, and are among the few birds whose feathers possess true green pigment.

The hoatzin lives in woodlands along Amazonian river banks. It is a long-tailed, chicken-like bird that exists on a diet of leaves and fruit. Some taxonomists believe that the hoatzin belongs in the order Galliformes, but the evolutionary relationships of the hoatzin, like those of the other birds of the order Cuculiformes, are unknown.

Ben Goldstein/Valenti Photo

The massive hooked bill, the arrangement of toes, and brilliantly colored plumage identify this Blue-and-yellow Macaw as a type of parrot. Most species are noisy and highly gregarious.

Kenneth W. Fink/Berg & Associates

The Coral-billed Cuckoo in this picture is one of a variety of species that make up the order Cuculiformes. North American members include roadrunners, anis, and some nonparasitic cuckoos.

Maslowski Photo

The Eastern Screech-Owl is typical of the order Strigiformes. Mainly nocturnal and highly adapted predators, owls possess keen eyesight and acute hearing.

This Common Nighthawk is a member of the order Caprimulgiformes, which consists of nightjars and their relatives. These birds are keenly adapted to nocturnal activities. Many have extremely wide mouths and well-developed bristles around their bills to aid in the capture of aerial insects.

Jack Wilburn

Owls

The two recognized families that comprise the order Strigiformes contain typical owls and barn-owls. For the most part both types are primarily nocturnal predators. They share many features with the birds of prey of the order Falconiformes: strong talons, a sharply hooked beak, and the tendency for females to be larger than males. Taxonomists think these similarities are convergences—similar characteristics that have evolved independently in unrelated groups—rather than indicators of close relationship.

Owls are found nearly worldwide. Most owl species are cryptically colored in browns and grays. Owls range in size from the sparrow-sized Elf Owl to the powerful species—Snowy Owls, Great Gray Owls, and Great Horned Owls—which may be over 2 feet in length. Adaptations for nocturnal hunting include acute hearing (some species can locate prey in total darkness) and excellent night vision. The eyes are located relatively far forward on the face, an arrangement that yields good binocular vision (for more on binocular vision, see pages 44 and 45).

Nightjars and Their Relatives

The birds of the order Caprimulgiformes are brown, buff, gray, black, or any combination of those colors. They have soft plumage and feed primarily at night or at dawn and dusk. Most species obtain their food on the wing. The smaller families include frogmouths, potoos, owlet-nightjars, and oilbirds. The major family within the order, Caprimulgidae, has some 70 species in all, including nighthawks, nightjars, and Whip-poor-wills. These birds live in most temperate and tropical areas of the world. The cryptic plumage patterns and nocturnal habits of the members of this order are reminiscent of those of owls, though there appears to be no close relationship between these two groups.

Oilbirds are unique within the order in that they feed on fruits, especially palm fruits. These birds roost in caves and navigate the darkness by using a form of sonar.

Swifts and Hummingbirds

Taxonomists often categorize these two groups of small, strong-flying birds—swifts and hummingbirds—in the order Apodiformes, though a close relationship between the two has been disputed. The family of swifts includes some 70 species, whose members live nearly worldwide. A small group of Southeast Asian birds, the crested-swifts, are placed in their own family. Swifts' superficial resemblance to swallows is a result of evolutionary convergence. Swifts are highly aerial birds that hunt insects while flying. Their wings are long and slender, and their flight is rapid and agile. Many species of swifts attach their nests to a vertical surface with a sticky salivary secretion. In certain parts of the world—especially in the Far East—nests entirely of saliva are the key ingredient in bird's nest soup, which many consider a delicacy.

The short legs and wing shape of hummingbirds and swifts are quite similar; both species have long flight feathers with extremely short wing bones. The more than three hundred species of hummingbirds, all in the Western Hemisphere, show a dazzling array of iridescent plumage. The thin bills may be straight or strongly curved and short to extremely long and are adaptations for feeding at different types of flowers.

Some species of hummingbirds feed mainly on small invertebrates, such as insects and spiders, but the majority feed on nectar. Hummingbirds are active and territorial birds that often defend nectar sources aggressively. Some temperate-zone and high-altitude species enter a torpid state of inactivity and lowered body temperature on cooler nights to conserve energy.

Colies

The order Coliiformes contains only six species of African colies (or mousebirds). These slender, long-tailed birds climb about vegetation in a mouse-like fashion, and they feed on fruits and other vegetable matter. The unique order has no known close relatives.

Kingfisher and Woodpecker Assemblages

Taxonomists believe that the relationship between these two large assemblages of land birds—the order Coraciiformes (kingfishers, rollers, hornbills, and their relatives) and the order Piciformes (woodpeckers, barbets, toucans, and their relatives)—is close. Assignment of certain families to one order or the other is, in fact, a controversial matter.

The birds of the order Coraciiformes, as the order is currently defined, are not numerous in North America. Of the over 85 species of kingfishers found worldwide, only three enter the United States, and only one—the Belted Kingfisher—is common. Kingfishers are strong-billed, short-legged birds with a variety of foraging styles. A large number of species dive from the air for fish and other aquatic animals, but many others feed away from water on insects and vertebrates. Todies and motmots are the other New World representatives of the Coraciiformes. These birds sit quietly in trees and occasionally dart out after prey. At present the tiny todies live only in the West Indies; the larger motmots occur in Central America and northern South America. Additional Old World families of this large order include bee-eaters, ground-rollers, hoopoes, wood-hoopoes, and hornbills.

Coraciiform birds show some degree of fusion at the toes, but they do not have the yoke-toed foot that characterizes the Piciformes. Certain families within the order Piciformes appear to fill a similar ecological role as those of some families of the order Coraciiformes. Jacamars and puffbirds of the New World tropics resemble todies, bee-eaters, and

Steve Maslowski/Photo Researchers, Inc.

A special salivary secretion adheres the nest of this Chimney Swift to the vertical face of a chimney. Characterized by long wings and short, weak legs, hummingbirds and swifts are placed together in the order Apodiformes.

M.P. Kahl/VIREO

The Lilac-breasted Roller in this photograph shares the same order as do the kingfishers, but prefers to forage in more terrestrial environments.

motmots in many ways. Feeding on fruits, insects, and vertebrates with their lightweight but gigantic bills, toucans are reminiscent of the hornbills of the Old World tropics. A small family of African and tropical Asian birds known as honeyguides are notable for their brood parasitism and the fact that some species eat beeswax. The family of barbets, of which there are over 70 species, is a group of strong-billed arboreal birds that are occasionally terrestrial. Barbets live in tropical regions, and their ability to excavate nest cavities with their beaks suggests a close relationship to woodpeckers.

More than 200 species of woodpeckers comprise the family Picidae of the order Piciformes. Woodpeckers inhabit wooded regions throughout the world, with the exception of Madagascar and the Australia and New Guinea region. Special adaptations of the bill, skull, neck, claws, and tail contribute to the woodpeckers' skill at obtaining food by climbing on vertical surfaces and chiseling into wood.

It appears that trogons, which taxonomists often place alone in the order Trogoniformes, are closely related to Coraciiformes. The Trogon family contains about three dozen tropical species that are brilliantly garbed in greens, reds, and other colors. They are arboreal birds which often capture their food—fruits, insects, and small animals—in hovering flight. The most spectacular of the trogons are quetzals of Central America and northern South America, some of which show a dazzling train of feathers formed by the upper tail coverts.

Perching Birds

The order Passeriformes contains perching birds, which are often called passerines. This large and diverse order of over 70 families accounts for well over half of the bird species of the world; it contains many rapidly evolving groups with large numbers of related species. Because the evolution of passerines has been rapid and relatively recent and because of their relatively small stature, the fossil record has shed little light on our understanding of passerine relationships.

Passerines fill a diversity of ecological roles. There are aerial insect eaters such as swallows; bark gleaners such as woodcreepers and nuthatches; heavy-billed seed eaters such as finches, sparrows, and grosbeaks; and

Isidor Jeklin

Leonard Lee Rue III

Above left: *Suboscines are the smaller division of perching birds. This suboscine, a Great Crested Flycatcher, is a noisy cavity-nesting bird that swoops from one perch to another, capturing dozens of different insects in midair.*

Above: *This Dark-eyed Junco is an oscine passerine, one of many familiar songbirds that inhabit temperate North America. Ornithologists consider oscines to be the most recently evolved group of birds.*

hook-billed predators such as shrikes. In addition there are nectar specialists, flycatchers, foliage gleaners, and even aquatic forms (the dippers). Despite this remarkable ecological diversity, passerines share a number of anatomical characteristics. The most notable characteristic is the perching foot—three toes point forward and one, known as the hallux, points backward at the same level.

Major divisions in this order are oscines and suboscines. The suboscine group includes families of tyrant flycatchers, antbirds, ovenbirds, woodcreepers, and other smaller families—diverse components of the avifauna of the New World tropics.

Oscines, or songbirds, represent the vast majority of familiar temperate-zone land birds. Experts are continually studying the relationships of the families within this group with increasingly sophisticated techniques. The oscines are exceedingly diverse, but several major lineages have been identified. One giant assemblage, which is especially diverse in the Old World, is comprised of thrushes and their relatives, which most taxonomists place in the family Muscicapidae. Another large lineage which is most diverse in the New World consists of such groups as wood warblers, tanagers, cardinals, grosbeaks, buntings, and New World blackbirds and orioles. These birds have only nine primary feathers on each wing instead of ten and are members of the Emberizidae family.

Bird Evolution Today

The study of avian evolution continues to generate excitement. Progress stems from the discovery and description of new fossils and the development of increasingly sophisticated techniques that analyze small evolutionary steps over a relatively short time. The long-accepted composition of many orders is likely to undergo extensive reevaluation and reshuffling as avian fossils receive further study and as modern biochemical techniques enhance our understanding of the relationships of living birds. Among the many topics currently under investigation are the independent evolution of flightlessness from flying ancestors, the reconstruction of past distributions of extinct and living groups, and the continuing investigation of gaps in the fossil record.

Behavior for Survival

by Peter G. Connors
and J.P. Myers

*I*t is 3 a.m. on a spring morning. Why is a mockingbird pouring forth its song from atop the highest backyard tree, raising the neighborhood from slumber?

A male mockingbird singing at that hour is almost surely without a mate. His predawn effort is one of the many behaviors this species uses to bring to life the next generation.

Besides the beauty of birds, it is their behavior that makes them fascinating to watch and to study. Bird behavior involves many different abilities and takes many different forms. Birds have a style of singing that identifies them to one another and to us. Each species has a repertoire of movements that it uses to indicate its territory or availability for mating. Every movement and sound a bird makes—however subtle—communicates a message to other birds.

Like other animals, birds have two basic tests that indicate successful behavior: They must survive and they must reproduce. Birds have developed a rich diversity of behaviors that help them pass these tests.

The male Ruffed Grouse pauses before beginning its drumming ritual. The whirring sound it makes by "clapping" its wings announces territory, attracts females, and repels other males.

Ben Goldstein/Valenti Photo   Ben Goldstein/Valenti Photo

Right: *With its feathers erected and bill poised, this Great Blue Heron presents a formidable adversary for nest predators. Behaviors such as this increase the reproductive potential of individual birds and, as a result, are favored by natural selection.*

Far right: *Behavior and body form evolve hand in hand. For example, the bill of this Roseate Spoonbill allows the bird to feed efficiently on minute planktonic organisms and is associated with specialized feeding behaviors.*

The Basics of Behavior

Just as the shape of a bird's bill, the length of its wing, and the size of its tail have evolved, so has bird behavior evolved for survival. Some behaviors are more appropriate than others in a given ecological setting.

To illustrate this point, consider an example from our own lives. Swimming is much better than running for crossing a lake. Running may be efficient in other environments, say on a grassy plain, but if you must cross the lake, you are far more likely to succeed if you can swim. Scientists would call swimming "fitter" than running, at least in lake environments.

Natural selection, in effect, makes comparisons between behaviors. Birds with fitter behaviors leave more offspring; their offspring in turn leave more offspring. Over time, birds with the same sorts of behaviors become increasingly common within the population.

To face the challenges of survival and reproduction, birds have evolved a number of behaviors. These behaviors, different for each species, can be categorized in a three-level hierarchy—individual characteristics, one-on-one interactions, and societal interactions—in which one level of behaviors forms the basis for the next.

Individual Characteristics

The first level of this hierarchy of behaviors is composed of the two most basic survival tools: senses and movement. A bird's sensory abilities and characteristic movements enable it to do everything from finding its food or prey to detecting and hiding from a predator to finding a warm perch in the sun.

Vision. Based on the size of their eyes alone, you might guess that birds see extremely well. Their eyes are much larger in proportion to the sizes of their heads than our eyes are. In fact, some owls and eagles have eyes that are the same size as human eyes, though their heads are much smaller than ours.

Birds' sense of sight is of much higher resolution than ours. Hawks, for example, see two to three times more detail than people do. But most birds do not have the depth perception that we do because of the placement of their eyes. Depth is perceived when each eye provides a slightly different view of the same scene, when there is an overlap in the field of vision. This is known as binocular vision. Birds such as owls, which have both eyes facing forward, have binocular vision similar to our own, but most nonpredatory birds have eyes whose fields of view do not overlap enough to provide this ability. Instead, their laterally placed eyes give them a wider total view, the better to detect an approaching predator. Scientists believe that to compensate for their lack of binocular vision, some birds bob their heads, thereby viewing the same subject rapidly from different angles. Dippers bob nonstop along mountain streams. Many shorebirds bob rapidly when a predator appears nearby.

Some birds have developed extremely unusual vision to detect predators. Woodcocks have enormous eyes that sit so far back in their heads that their fields of view actually overlap to the rear, so that they can see directly behind them. A woodcock probing with its bill in the soil will never be easy to surprise from behind. A bittern's eyes look horizontally at an approaching predator even when its bill points skyward.

Birds' vision is also different from ours in how they see color. Birds are sensitive to the same wavelengths of light as we are, but scientists have recently learned that they can also see ultraviolet light. Because of this, their perception of flowers and other natural objects that have ultraviolet patterns is quite different from ours.

Fields of Vision

Susan Roney Drennan

The eyes of this American Woodcock are placed far back on its head, resulting in a field of vision that completely encircles the bird. Although its depth perception is minimal, the woodcock can detect the presence of a predator in any direction.

D. & M. Zimmerman/VIREO

The eyes of this Eastern Screech-Owl are placed well forward on its head, creating maximum overlap of the fields of view from both eyes. Binocular vision of this sort enables the owl to perceive depth, an important feature when trying to locate its prey.

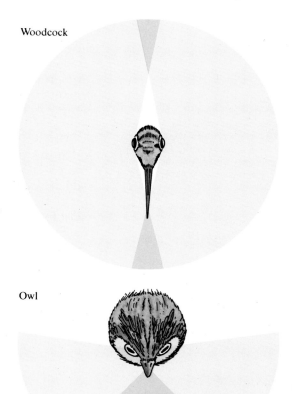

Woodcock

Owl

Frans Lanting

This Northern Harrier is capable of cueing in on the sounds of birds and small rodents as a means of locating these prey species.

These Turkey Vultures can detect the presence of carcasses by their odors. On warm days these odors may be carried by rising air currents, and this may be one reason why soaring vultures often gather over carcasses.

Don & Pat Valenti

Hearing. Similar to their acute vision, birds' sense of hearing is also more refined than ours. Barn-owls, for example, can track their prey by sound, without any visual cues. Researchers discovered this by putting an owl and a mouse in a darkened cage. Even without light, the owl pounced unerringly on its prey.

The Northern Harrier also uses sound to locate its prey—small birds and meadow mice—as it flies in the daytime over meadows and brush. If you are out in a field and a Northern Harrier flies by, try squeaking a bit. It may fly around you, searching for the source of the sound. This also works with Short-eared Owls.

Almost all birds rely on hearing for communication with mates, rivals, offspring, or flock members, and many use it to locate prey or predators, but two unusual tropical birds take hearing one step farther. Gray Swiftlets of Southeast Asia and oilbirds of South America use their hearing much like bats and porpoises. Emitting sharp, short clicks as they fly about in the dark, they listen for the echoes of their sounds bouncing off cave walls. Using these echoes, the birds avoid crashing into obstacles.

Sense of smell. The sense of smell in most birds is not highly developed. Just as a bird's eyes are large in relation to ours, the part of its brain that processes odors is relatively small. There are, however, some exceptions. Turkey Vultures locate their food—decaying meat—through smell. Not long ago, engineers trying to stop leaks in a pipeline took advantage of the Turkey Vulture's ability. They filled the pipeline with fumes that smelled like rotting meat and then watched along a 42-mile pipeline to see where the vultures gathered. It worked!

The Turkey Vulture is not the only bird with a good sense of smell. This sense is also well developed in many seabirds, such as albatrosses and shearwaters. These birds follow odor trails in the wind and gather around the source of the smell. Scientists made this discovery when they put out special rafts equipped with an odor source and then watched as the birds began tracing the smells upwind. Bird-watchers take advantage of this behavior by *chumming,* just as fishermen sometimes do. To see as many seabirds as possible on a boat trip off the coast, bird-watchers throw strong-smelling fish pieces overboard. This can attract hundreds of birds that might otherwise have remained far from the boat.

Luring Seabirds

Seabirds use their highly developed sense of smell to track odors on the winds.

Many birds also use their sense of smell for navigating back to their home lofts. (For more on this type of navigating, see page 160.)

Movement. Most birds run and fly, some dive, and they all stretch, poke, scratch, and probe. Directed by their senses, movements allow birds to search for food, preen their feathers, flee predators, fly south from cold weather, and display to a mate.

Bird muscles are quite similar to ours in their basic physiology, but think of what bird muscles achieve. The pectoral muscle on a Ruby-throated Hummingbird weighs less than one tenth of an ounce, yet it powers the bird in its flight from Vermont down to the Yucatán Peninsula or farther each year! (See page 121 for more on muscle-powered flight.)

Not all birds use their muscles for flying. Many seabirds, such as puffins, use their wings to swim underwater in addition to flying in the air. Their Southern Hemisphere counterparts, penguins, use their wings to swim and do not fly at all. Birds with a diminished capacity for flight, such as quail and pheasants, fly only in short, fast bursts and cannot manage the great distances undertaken by many other birds. Roadrunners rely more on their strong leg muscles than their wings to take them where they want to go.

One-on-One Interactions

The second level of the hierarchy of bird behavior is the way individual birds interact with one another for such purposes as communication, aggression, and territorial defense. Without this level, there would be no mates, flocks, territories, or any way for a baby bird to convey its hunger.

Most communication among birds occurs along two channels: sound and sight. Each species has its own system of communication, combinations of movement and sound that act as signals to another bird. For instance, many birds use song and visual displays to establish a territory and to attract a mate.

The nature of a bird's message changes from situation to situation. Sometimes the message simply identifies the species of the singer to others of its kind; sometimes it signals desire for a mate. At other times it communicates possession of a territory and warns competing males to keep their distance.

Thomas D. Mangelsen

Thomas D. Mangelsen

Above: *This Downy Woodpecker communicates its presence by drumming on a telephone pole. Although many birds have only a limited number of acoustic signals, a single call may have a variety of functions, depending on the situation.*

Above right: *By spreading its red epaulettes, this Red-winged Blackbird conveys a visual message to a particular receiver. Visual communication often involves subtle changes in posture. For the Red-winged Blackbird, the intensity of the message is controlled by the extent to which the epaulettes are exposed.*

Male Downy Woodpeckers, for example, make their presence known in winter and spring by drumming on a resonant surface and by voicing their strident calls. They peck loudly and continuously on a favorite dead tree in their territory. This behavior informs other males that the site is claimed and also advertises the male's presence to prospective mates. Several males may drum simultaneously from adjacent territories, setting up a clamor throughout the wood.

Downy Woodpeckers also use visual displays to send territorial signals, especially at close range. Both males and females wave their bills from left to right at competing members of their own sex. They are also known to raise the feathers at the top and back of their heads, at which time the male's red patch is prominent.

The absence of movement can be as important a communication as movement itself. In one territorial display, known to ornithologists as the "still pose," Downy Woodpeckers stop all movement and remain completely still for up to 20 minutes.

Societal Interactions

The third level of the hierarchy involves the combination of signaling patterns into a social organization. Societies among birds, though simpler than those of humans, can be surprisingly complex. Like humans, birds live in societies that are governed by rules. Though no written laws govern the behavior of birds within their societies, natural selection makes it difficult for individuals to be too far out of line with the rest of their species. An individual who violates the norm too flagrantly simply will not be able to secure a nesting site or attract a mate and therefore will not leave descendants. But some variation does occur because there is always a way to do something a little bit better. Improvements lead to more descendants and an advantage in the evolutionary struggle.

Two key attributes make up a bird society: the way its members occupy a habitat, and the mating pattern its males and females follow during the mating season. Birds occupy habitats in various ways. Most birds in the backyards of North America defend their own territories, birds as different as Red-tailed Hawks, Downy Woodpeckers, and Carolina Wrens. Other birds, such as Brown-headed Cowbirds, American Goldfinches, and to some extent American Robins, are nonterritorial and share their nesting

Stefan Harnes

Wardene Weisser/Berg & Associates

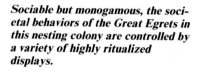

Sociable but monogamous, the societal behaviors of the Great Egrets in this nesting colony are controlled by a variety of highly ritualized displays.

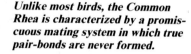

Unlike most birds, the Common Rhea is characterized by a promiscuous mating system in which true pair-bonds are never formed.

and feeding areas with other members of the same species. Yet other birds, such as Great Blue Herons, House Sparrows, and Common Terns, nest and feed only in colonies. (For more information on types of spacing patterns, see page 61.)

Societies among birds are much more varied than those among different nationalities of people. In some species family groups are strong; in others they are almost nonexistent. In most species birds mate as monogamous pairs and share in the task of raising their young. Many geese, for example, mate for life, returning to the same nesting areas each summer. Some birds, like the rhea, a 5-foot-tall bird of southern South America, are promiscuous. Male rheas incubate clutches of 20 to 40 eggs, laid by a number of different females. A gaggle of females moves from the nest of one male to the nest of another, each female laying one egg in a particular male's nest. A male rhea thus fathers the young of many females, and a female mates with several males. The male takes on all responsibilities of raising the young. (For more on mating patterns, see page 70.)

Survival

During most of the year, a bird's chief task is survival. For the Tufted Tit-mouse, typical of many songbirds, the season for display, courtship, and nesting in most areas of the United States lasts only from March through June. The rest of the year is spent in small flocks, flying from tree to bush in search of insects and seeds.

In northern regions, the nesting season is even shorter. Arctic-breeding songbirds, such as Lapland Longspurs, reach their breeding grounds in northern Alaska in late May, and by early July all chicks have hatched. For Lapland Longspurs, the annual cycle involves many months of wait-ing for the next breeding season.

Between breeding seasons, the greatest challenges that birds face in or-der to survive include finding food and water and avoiding predators.

Feeding

As could be expected, birds vary widely in the diversity of their diets. Blue Jays, for example, eat myriad kinds of seeds, grains, nuts, berries, and fruit, favoring acorns, corn, and sunflower seeds. They also eat a wide variety of insects, including caterpillars, grasshoppers, beetles, and snails, and they even capture mice, small birds, frogs, salamanders, and occa-sionally eggs stolen from other birds' nests. This broad diet classifies the Blue Jay as a "diet generalist." "Diet specialists," on the other hand, con-sume a much shorter list of food items. The Belted Kingfisher, for exam-ple, depends almost entirely on one kind of food—small fish it captures by plunging into shallow water. To ensure a year-round supply of fish, it must migrate southward in winter to find water that remains unfrozen. The Blue Jay is not as limited in its food sources and therefore can remain as a permanent resident over many parts of its winter range.

The diets of some birds, mainly tropical species, are even more special-ized than that of the kingfisher. Hawaii's bright red Iiwi, a nectar-feeding honeycreeper, feeds mainly on flowers of a single species of tree, the ohia, a dominant tree in Hawaii's native forests.

Like most temperate birds, this Tufted Titmouse spends only a small portion of each year engaged in breeding activities. During the rest of the year, bird behavior is aimed solely at the survival of the individual.

J.R. Woodward/VIREO

Robert J. Western

Maslowski Photo

H. Cruickshank/VIREO

Above left: *This Iiwi is extremely specialized in its diet, feeding mainly on flowers of the ohia tree. Like many highly specialized feeders, the body and, particularly, the bill of this bird have become modified to accommodate its foraging behavior.*

Above: *The Belted Kingfisher is also a diet specialist, feeding only on small fish. Since they are unable to change their diet, these birds must migrate to warmer climates when the lakes, ponds, and streams that they frequent freeze over.*

Left: *The Blue Jay is a diet generalist and is capable of changing its diet with seasonal changes in the availability of particular food items.*

Foraging behaviors. All birds must employ foraging behaviors that let them do the best job possible of surviving. This basic principle has selected for a bewildering variety of foraging techniques over the entire bird world, with generalists often displaying a large number of behaviors and specialists using very few. Generalists may not be particularly efficient at any single task but, being jacks-of-all-trades, they can switch from one food to another as conditions change.

Bill shapes and sizes—and to some extent, feet, legs, and wings—vary among species according to the foods the birds eat or the feeding methods they use. Imagine a cardinal, with its blunt bill, trying to probe deeply for earthworms in a forest floor; or a woodcock, with its long, slender bill, struggling to open a sunflower seed; or a Mallard attempting to glean insects from the furrowed bark of a maple tree. It is a picture of frustrated and hungry birds. But it is a false picture, since the evolution of bird bills has proceeded in step with the evolution of bird foraging behaviors and diets. (For more on bill shapes, see page 96.)

There is, however, a difference between the evolution of bill shapes and that of foraging behavior: Behavior can be much more variable than bill shape. A bird trying to adapt to different foods in different seasons or in different localities has no choice but to use the bill it was given. But it can

Wardene Weisser/Berg & Associates

R. Van Nostrand/Berg & Associates

Leonard Lee Rue III

Douglas R. Herr

Top: *Though particularly adapted to probing for invertebrates with its long bill, the Whimbrel is equally adept at picking insects off vegetation.*

Top right: *The heavy, blunt bill of this Northern Cardinal is ideally suited for a diet of seeds.*

Bottom: *The habit of foraging down the trunks of trees enables this White-breasted Nuthatch to find insects missed by woodpeckers and creepers that forage upward.*

Bottom right: *This American Dipper can exploit aquatic invertebrates by foraging beneath the surface of swift-flowing streams.*

acquire many different foraging behaviors, each suited to a particular food source or habitat. Whimbrels and Hudsonian Godwits, for example, can use their bills to peck at insects on arctic tundra plants during the summer, as well as probe for small invertebrates in the mud of a coastal estuary during the winter. These pecking and probing behaviors have evolved for these situations, and each bird must learn how to probe deeply for different prey and how to follow tide lines in order to obtain the most food.

To a great extent, the kinds of food available determine the feeding behaviors of birds. A particular kind of food may exist in many different situations requiring different feeding techniques. For example, many birds feed on insects, but their methods vary depending on whether the insects are found on tree bark, in leaf litter, on surface vegetation, in rotting wood, in the soil, underwater, or flying through the air.

Feeding on insects. Insect-eating species have developed specialized behaviors for finding insects in places such as leaf litter (towhees scratch with their feet), in soil (snipes probe with long bills), or in the air (swallows, swifts, and nighthawks perform high-speed aerial acrobatics). Of the species that spend time on tree trunks, nuthatches alone have developed a facility for walking down the trunk, with their heads toward the ground, while searching for insects in bark crevices. This may help them locate insects that would be missed by birds such as Brown Creepers that walk up tree trunks, with their heads tilted toward the sky. In fact, most of the special adaptations and feeding techniques we observe in birds have evolved to give a species access to foods that are overlooked by other, differently adapted species.

The Dipper is a remarkable songbird with special adaptations to reach insects that are unavailable to other birds. This inhabitant of areas near streams in western North America actually dives and swims beneath the surface of fast-flowing streams, clinging to rocks with its feet to capture insect larvae from the stream bottom.

Sapsuckers employ a fascinating variation of the tree-drilling techniques used by their woodpecker relatives. These birds drill a series of small, shallow holes, typically in rings around a tree trunk, to tap the sap that flows through the inner layers of bark. Each small hole is shaped to collect a tiny pool of sap. The bird then repeatedly flies to each hole in succession to imbibe. Insects are attracted to the sap holes, providing both meat and drink at a single sitting.

Feeding on plants. For birds that eat plant foods, adaptations are necessary more for handling than for capturing food, since seeds, grasses, and berries are seldom elusive. Wide differences exist among birds in their methods and abilities for dealing with such plant materials: Blue Jays hammer holes in acorns with their bills; White-winged Crossbills pluck seeds from between the scales of spruce cones; Cedar Waxwings, traveling in flocks, easily gorge themselves on soft berries in treetops; Canada Geese graze on succulent grasses and nibble at ripe grains; Northern Pintails dabble with their bills in shallow water to extract soft tubers and shoots of aquatic plants. Observing how different species handle different foods can be a rewarding pastime for the interested bird-watcher. Start by watching the birds at your feeder. Notice how they choose the foods that are best for their bill sizes.

O.S. Pettingill, Jr./VIREO

By drilling parallel holes into the sapwood of living trees, this Yellow-bellied Sapsucker can feed on the energy-rich sap that oozes out. In addition, sapsuckers benefit by foraging on the multitudes of insects that are attracted to the sap.

These Brants, like most other forms of geese, depend on grains, grasses, and aquatic vegetation to form the bulk of their diets. As with most plant-eating birds, geese are highly sociable and usually feed in flocks.

Herbert Clarke

Douglas R. Herr

Above: ***This Black-shouldered Kite has brought a meadow mouse up to its lofty perch to be eaten. Kites generally hunt for insects and small rodents; other hawks prefer primarily rodents, and the large Golden Eagle specializes on jack rabbits.***

Above right: *A Merlin swoops over a flock of shorebirds. Like other falcons, these swift and agile flyers are adept at pursuing other birds in the air.*

Frans Lanting

Feeding on animals. Compared with watching the peaceful scene of birds foraging for seeds at a feeder, watching birds of prey capture other birds is a thrill-a-minute experience. A Merlin hunting Sanderlings on a California beach flies low behind a dune to approach its intended prey unseen. Suddenly this small, swift falcon streaks over the dune heading for the Sanderlings in the surf zone. The Sanderlings instantly take flight, joining in a small flock, to try to evade the death that is hurtling their way. The chase may continue over a large area of the beach and may include several dashes by the Merlin into the flock, while pursuer and pursued display the best flying of which they are capable. For the potential victim, the stakes are high indeed.

Predatory birds hunt in several styles, taking advantage of keen eyesight, hearing, and a swift, surprise attack. Many hawks and owls, such as the Red-tailed Hawk and the Great Horned Owl, hunt from a perch; some birds, like the American Kestrel and the Black-shouldered Kite, hover over open country; others, like the Northern Harrier and the Short-eared Owl, fly low over likely prey habitats.

Feeding on fish. Fish are another food source for which birds have evolved many different foraging styles. Herons and egrets wade quietly, waiting to strike at a fish in shallow water. Kingfishers, pelicans, terns, and boobies all dive from above the water, using their bills to capture fish they have already sighted. Ospreys also hover above the water, folding their wings to dive, seemingly headfirst, after sighting their prey. But high-speed photography shows that just before impact the Osprey reverses its body position and stretches its legs downward with talons open. Like all other hawks and eagles, the Osprey uses its talons, not its bill, to capture prey. Upon emerging from the water with a fish, an Osprey grasps the fish in its two talons, one behind the other, so that the fish faces in the same direction as the flying Osprey. It also usually shakes violently to rid its plumage of water. Both these behaviors prepare it for more efficient flight to a feeding site on a cliff, nest, or telephone pole.

The Brown Pelican dives from the air, pursuing small fish that live just beneath the surface of the water. A split second after the pelican hits the water in its dive, its bill pouch balloons out to an enormous size, acting like a net to help capture the fish. The pelican's bill then drains of water almost as quickly as it was filled, and the bird is left with a delicious and satisfying meal.

R.J. Shallenberger/VIREO

Cattle Egrets, such as this one, stalk fish by slowly wading through shallow water. Other herons may use different techniques to catch fish; the Green-backed Heron will sit still and wait for fish to swim by, and the Reddish Egret spreads its wings to create shade, thus attracting fish toward it.

By swimming in tight circles, this Red Phalarope creates eddies that draw its minute invertebrate prey within reach of its bill.

Steve Maslowski

Feeding on invertebrates. Some birds' adaptations allow them to feed on invertebrates such as snails, clams, worms, shrimp, and other inhabitants of estuaries and mud flats. Shorebirds, seabirds, ducks, and even some land birds concentrate on prey such as these. Black Oystercatchers jab with their sharp bills into the mussels that live along the rocky coast. With a single probe they can sever the muscle that closes the mussel's shell.

Avocets sweep the water with their delicate, upturned bills. The bill's unusual twist allows the bird to skim a horizontal layer of water or the top surface of mud, where the food it seeks is most abundant.

Gulls sometimes pick up clams, fly over a hard surface such as a nearby parking lot or a house roof, and drop them to smash the clam shells, revealing the good food inside. This technique is sometimes misdirected; gulls have occasionally stolen large numbers of golf balls from coastal driving ranges, or dropped stones through glass skylights in a coastal city.

Phalaropes feed on much smaller prey—tiny insects and other invertebrates in the ocean or in shallow pools. By spinning around rapidly in the water, phalaropes bring their prey to the water's surface. The spinning creates small currents that move the prey up to where the bird can reach it by jabbing its bill in the water.

Frans Lanting

Above: *This Peregrine Falcon feeding on a freshly killed duck is the culmination of a complex series of steps involving interactions between predator, prey, and the environment.*

Above right: *These Gray Gulls, foraging along the Chilean coast, place their nests in harsh desert regions far inland where they are safe from predators. Remote, predator-free nesting sites are common among a wide variety of birds.*

J.P. Myers/VIREO

Predation

In the world of birds, surviving means more than just finding food and shelter. For birds of prey, it means hunting other animals, sometimes extremely elusive ones; for other birds it means taking many precautions.

Predation involves a sequence of steps. Consider the hunting sequence of a Peregrine Falcon. The bird must first choose a place to hunt, locating regions and habitats where the food is abundant. The next step is the search itself. For a Peregrine Falcon, this often entails soaring high above the earth, circling over places where ducks or other prey feed, until a likely victim appears.

Once the falcon locates its prey, a chase begins. Peregrine Falcons stoop from on high, diving at enormous speeds and taking their victims by surprise. The chase may take several minutes of drama as the prey wheels and turns, frantically trying to avoid the fatal clasp of the talons. Falcons pursuing shorebirds on a mud flat stoop repeatedly after sandpipers and turnstones, forcing one bird to leave the flock and then hounding it with powerful, deep wing strokes that leave little hope of escape. The bigger victims may struggle, but most of the prey of Peregrine Falcons are too small to put up much of a fight.

To reduce its chance of becoming a predator's dinner, every bird utilizes some type of antipredator behavior. But the evolution of both hunting behavior and antipredator behavior has proceeded in a long series of steps, each a response to the other. Each time a species of prey develops a new trait that enables it to more successfully avoid predation, the process of evolution may lead to a solution to the new trait, making the prey vulnerable once again. Sharp-shinned Hawks have made sparrows cautious; sparrows have made Sharp-shinned Hawks swift.

Living in safe habitats. The simplest and surest way for a bird to avoid being eaten is to live in an area where there are few predators. For example, a duck might reduce its risk of becoming falcon food by living in the desert. The Gray Gull of Chile nests only in the extraordinarily harsh Atacama Desert, well away from the coastal waters in which it feeds. The adults make long daily flights to bring food to the chicks and to share in the duties of keeping chicks warm at night and shaded during the day. The single advantage of this nesting site is safety from predators, none of which are willing to live in such an inhospitable location. Most birds, however, cannot abandon the habitats in which their foods are found.

Jack Wilburn

J.R. Woodward/VIREO

P.J. Connors/VIREO

P.J. Connors/VIREO

   Staying out of reach. Besides choosing an out-of-the-way habitat, another way for birds to avoid predators is to remain in such dense cover
that predators cannot enter even if they hunt in the area. Here the game
becomes complex, because there are many kinds of predators with many
different hunting techniques. The Sora (a type of rail) chooses the dense
cover of cattails, rushes, and other marsh plants to hide from hawks and
owls, but this does not buy it safety from such marshland predators as raccoons, minks, or snapping turtles. Snowy Plovers nestle into depressions
on a sandy beach and can evade a falcon simply by not flying when the
falcon attacks. But sometimes the attacker is a Northern Harrier instead of
a falcon. The plover's tactic suddenly becomes a liability, because Northern Harriers readily pick prey from the ground. Ground-nesting species
such as Eastern Meadowlarks and Rufous-sided Towhees are generally
immune to aerial predators, but they are vulnerable to attacks by snakes
and weasels.
   Camouflage. Natural selection has resulted in such masters of camouflage as the Whip-poor-will, which seems to disappear when sitting on
dead leaves or a log on the forest floor. The American Bittern has vertical
breast stripes and a skyward-pointing bill that blend with the lines of
rushes and cattails around it. The female Willow Ptarmigan is almost invisible on its nest on the tundra; the Snowy Plover is colored in hues of
gray and tan that blend with the surrounding beaches or sand dunes. Most

Top left: *Only rarely does the Sora
emerge from dense marsh vegetation
like this one has. By staying under
thick cover, Soras can avoid being
detected by flying predators.*

Top right: *By placing its nest on the
ground, this Rufous-sided Towhee
can eliminate aerial predation but is
left vulnerable to ground predators.*

Bottom left: *The camouflaged plumage of this Willow Ptarmigan makes
the bird invisible to most predators.
Such birds often remain on their
nests even when predators are
close by.*

Bottom right: *When a predator approaches the nest too closely, the
Willow Ptarmigan bursts off the
nest in a flurry of feathers and begins a distraction display. This has
the effect of startling the predator
and diverting its attention away from
the nest.*

birds that rely on camouflage are adept at "sitting close," remaining very still on a nest or at rest until just before a predator comes dangerously close, and then often flushing noisily.

Distraction displays. Birds carry out some of their most elaborate behaviors in protecting their nests from predators. Many species of shorebirds combine the subtle camouflage patterns of their plumage and their eggs with distraction displays aimed at drawing a predator away from the nest or chicks.

The broken-wing display of the Killdeer is a good example of a distraction display that can be observed in areas across North America. When approached by a predator—including people—the incubating bird steals away from the nest or flies near the predator and then begins calling plaintively, "*kill-dee, kill-dee*," while squatting and beating one wing against the ground. The bird broadly fans its bright rust-colored tail to lure the predator away from the nest. Any predator looking for an easy catch will surely try for this poor "cripple," which flees just before the predator gets close. The bird then proceeds to move farther from the nest, where it repeats its histrionics.

Finding the nest of a Killdeer presents formidable challenges for predators and bird-watchers alike. Its four spotted eggs blend so well with the gravel area on which they sit that they are difficult to find without behavioral clues from the adult bird. The best strategy is to withdraw and watch for the bird to return to the nest, but even this is not without frustration. The adult may indulge in "false brooding," sitting on nothing in particular in order to further confuse observers. Many sandpipers on the arctic tundra present similar difficulties to the predator or ornithologist trying to locate nests, often using a rodent-run display, running from the nest while crouching and squeaking like a mouse or lemming.

Fleeing. A simple and direct means of avoiding predators is to flee, which is the reason many small birds have such quick reflexes. The sudden burst of a Cooper's Hawk across a clearing or over a backyard feeder area will produce a frantic flash of movement as small birds scatter to the shelter of surrounding bushes. If the predator is a mammal, this fleeing response is even more effective since the small birds are safe as soon as they

The distraction display of this Killdeer is both convincing and effective. Such birds often allow predators to approach remarkably close before fluttering out of reach.

Don & Pat Valenti

Thomas D. Mangelsen

One of the best means of avoiding a predator is to flee. Although this young Tundra Swan is fleeing from the photographer, the same response can be expected in the presence of any terrestrial predator.

fly clear of the predator's grasp. It is only when the birds have nests or chicks nearby that this escape becomes complicated. A few large birds or birds with formidable weapons, such as hawks or owls, may stand up to potential predators, but for most birds, fighting back is not an option. Smaller birds must reach safe refuge if pursued, or must remain at least out of reach of a less mobile predator, which may keep adults away from their eggs or young for long periods. One example of this behavior was observed in Massachusetts at the site of a nesting colony of terns. A Great Horned Owl, which began hunting adult terns every night, forced the terns to abandon their nests at night and to incubate only during the day. Although the hatching was considerably delayed, it was still successful.

Aggressive defense. Many small birds furiously harass predators, carefully remaining just beyond the enemy's grasp. This harassment appears to make the larger bird (or other predator) uncomfortable enough to leave the immediate vicinity.

Since diving at a predator does entail some risk, many small birds join in what is known as mobbing. Mobbing birds surround a predator, calling incessantly from nearby branches, the ground, or the air. Even if a predator is not driven away, mobbing is probably beneficial because it is safer to at least know the location of a predator.

Chickadees are enthusiastic mobbers, giving their buzzy calls as they flit from one perch to another around a predator. Their behavior usually attracts nearby birds of other species to join in the commotion. For an owl trying to sleep quietly at midday, all the attention and noise may be disturbing enough to cause it to find another spot for its perch. Birdwatchers can take advantage of the mobbing behavior of many songbirds, giving a repeated lispy call *(pish-pish-pish)*, which draws birds in for a close look at the trespassing predator.

Survival training. How does a young bird learn what its predators are, what to ignore, what to mob, what to flee? Through a series of clever experiments using mirrors, scientists discovered that young birds learn these things by observing older birds. When older birds in a cage were shown a stuffed owl, they started mobbing it. Younger birds watching from an adjacent cage could not see the owl; what they saw instead was a reflection in a set of mirrors that made it look as if the older birds were mobbing a milk can. Later, a milk can put in the cage with the younger birds was mobbed with all the enthusiasm that normally greets an owl. After the first experiment, mirrors were no longer necessary to fool the young birds. Other young birds learned to mob the milk can by simply watching the birds that had been fooled with mirrors.

Although it is unlikely to harm the Merlin, the constant harassment by this Black-billed Magpie will be aggravating enough to drive the predator away, eliminating it as a potential risk.

Douglas R. Herr

Hawk Alerts

If you listen closely when a hawk is first detected by a flock of feeding birds, you will hear a sudden change in the tone of the birds' chatter. Small birds have special tones that they use when sounding an alert. Normally, it is easy to tell where a small bird is simply by listening. Their chips and chirps have sharp beginnings and endings. These are tonal qualities that make it easy to locate the source of the sound. But when a hawk approaches a flock, a small bird's tone changes to reduce the sharp beginnings and endings of the chirps. These changes in tonal qualities make it more difficult to tell where the sounds are coming from. The birds become ventriloquists so as not to give away their location to the threatening predator. When you hear the change, it may mean a hawk is about to visit your feeder.

By whirling in a tight mass, these Western Sandpipers make it difficult for an aerial predator to strike into the flock without risking serious injury. Through group vigilance, predators can be detected before they are close enough to be dangerous.

Flocking for protection. The birds flocking at your feeder scatter almost instantly when a Sharp-shinned Hawk flies over. Though only one might actually have seen the hawk, all react. This scene illustrates how valuable feeding in a flock can be in avoiding a predator. In a flock, there are many eyes, which means each bird can spend more time feeding and less time looking over its shoulder.

Being in a flock helps avoid predation in other ways too. For a bird in a big flock that is attacked by a hawk, probability alone makes it less likely that a particular individual will be the victim taken. This is small solace to the captured bird, but a benefit to all the others. Another benefit is the factor of danger and confusion a mass of flying birds presents to a predator. Imagine the challenge of picking a single sandpiper out of a flock of a hundred or a thousand birds, all wheeling rapidly in tight formation. The effect must be confusing and bewildering, and the predatory bird is likely to be frustrated unless it can isolate a single individual.

Within the flock, some places are safer than others. Birds that can remain at the center of the flock are less likely to be picked off by a predator than are those flying at the edges. The importance of being at the center of the flock makes flock behavior all the more coordinated. Any available space within the flock gets filled by birds at the edge, and birds are unlikely to stray beyond the edges of the flock.

Sandpipers whirling in tight formation over a bay provide a spectacular ballet for anyone who watches. They achieve their coordination quite simply. Each bird pays attention to the few birds beside it, just like dancers in a chorus line. When the bird in front turns, the rest turn. Thus, even though it looks as if the whole flock turns in unison, each time the flock changes direction it does so in a progressive wave—first one bird, then another, and then another. But the members of the flock react to each other so rapidly that it looks as if the turn takes place all at once.

J.P. Myers/VIREO

Frans Lanting

Establishing and Defending Territories

Whirling flocks of thousands of blackbirds descend at dusk upon a nighttime roost near Indianapolis. They have been foraging all day on the grain of local farms and have now come to roost in a shelter belt of trees. They land, then take off in a nervous leap, the whole roost exploding into excited calls and a rush of rapid wingbeats. The whir of the wings alone would drown out all other noises. Add to that their calls and whistles, and the total force of sound seems too great for any one collection of birds. But when you consider the numbers—in a winter roost of blackbirds more than a million birds may gather—you can understand how it is possible for them to make so much noise.

Walking along the seashore beach of Assateague Island, Maryland, in September, you find a solitary Sanderling feeding in the surf. It runs to the base of a receding wave, sticks its bill into the sand, then scurries away just in time to avoid the next crashing wave. Fifty yards up the beach you spy another. It repeats the behavior, looking not too different from a windup toy. Beyond it there is another, and another beyond that one. Each bird is "alone" and each is separated from its neighbor by about the same distance. As you continue up the beach, each bird moves along in front of you, but only just so far. Before it reaches the next bird, it stops, hesitates, and then flies in a wide circuit out over the waves, returning to the point you just passed. It is as if you never went by. The next bird goes a bit too far; it transgresses the boundary of its neighbor's feeding territory, and there is suddenly a fight.

These two examples illustrate extremes in the spacing behavior of common birds. Blackbirds flock, Sanderlings defend territories. The bird world is full of both behaviors: A band of raucous crows flys silhouetted against a cold winter sky above a cornfield in eastern Pennsylvania; Redtailed Hawks battle over a territorial boundary in Ohio; hundreds of Barn Swallows perch upon a wire, each delicately positioned just far enough away from its neighbor to be out of reach; a Gray Catbird in the midst of a New York forest stakes out a private breeding territory with its constant, melodious song.

Accompanied by noisy chatter, these blackbirds prepare to settle into a night roost. Participants in such roosts often forage in flocks. This type of flocking behavior is usually associated with birds that exploit rich, undefendable patches of food, which may change in location from one day to the next.

The relatively even distribution of food items near the water line enables this Sanderling to defend an area large enough to meet its daily requirements. In most species territorial behavior varies seasonally.

Leonard Lee Rue III

Jack Wilburn

Since the female Brown-headed Cowbird lays her eggs in the nests of other birds, the male has little need to defend a territory. The lack of territoriality in this species seems to result in a promiscuous mating system.

Spacing behaviors govern the distances between individual birds. All birds indulge in some form of spacing behavior. While some birds flock and others defend territories, many birds switch between different styles in different circumstances. A male Red-winged Blackbird does not tolerate another male on its nesting territory during the breeding season. But Sanderlings may suddenly abandon their territories and form a flock if a Peregrine Falcon flies overhead searching for prey. Often in the very same site you can observe individuals of the same species behaving in different ways, some being territorial, others not. These individual variations are especially prevalent on territories away from the breeding ground, as in Sanderlings on winter beaches.

The Brown-headed Cowbird is an interesting example of a bird that is not territorial. Cowbirds lay their eggs in other birds' nests. A female cowbird scouts the egg-laying activities of birds over several acres of habitat and adds one or two eggs to the nests of other species while the owners are absent. Male cowbirds display to the female throughout its scouting area. The males follow the female wherever it goes, showing no evidence of territoriality among themselves.

Seasonal changes in territoriality. During the breeding season most birds defend their territories with song and visual display. Watch your feeder as spring approaches. Gradually the social pattern of the birds using it will change. Birds that had been feeding in flocks, such as chickadees and White-throated Sparrows, begin appearing more and more as pairs or solitary birds. They may burst unexpectedly into song or fly off pell-mell, hurriedly dashing after some real or imagined violation of their territorial sovereignty.

Just the opposite occurs in late summer. Species that had shown no signs of sociability begin to gather into flocks. In part this is due to newly flying young that move around in small groups. These groups coalesce, adults join them, and they grow into large flocks. By early fall, flocks of blackbirds, grackles, starlings, robins, or swallows may number in the hundreds or thousands. The chickadees once again begin to move in small foraging groups. White-throated Sparrows stop their singing and join small flocks.

Flocking in the winter has the advantage of making birds less vulnerable to predators and can also make finding food a little easier; when one flock member finds a good feeding site, the others join.

Black-capped, Carolina, and Chestnut-backed Chickadees are good examples of birds with seasonal changes in spacing behavior that you can easily witness in your own backyard. During the breeding season these three species are highly territorial. Pity the individual bird who wanders into a neighbor's area—the greeting will be all the belligerence a tiny bird can muster. In the fall, however, the local birds that were so intolerant of one another in spring now seek out company. The birds join in a foraging flock that includes adults as well as the young that hatched during the summer. Other species also may join in, such as Plain Titmice on the West Coast or Tufted Titmice in the East. Bushtits, Ruby-crowned Kinglets, and even Downy Woodpeckers may drift along as well, forming mixed-species flocks that forage together.

Come spring, the old intolerance reappears. The first sign usually comes in late winter, when males begin singing near their old territories on sunny days. Pairs begin dropping out of the flock. Instead of ten chickadees coming to your feeder, only two appear. The flock soon dissolves, and individual pairs stake out their old territories.

Year-round territoriality. Some species, particularly shorebirds and some birds of prey, commonly defend territories both summer and winter. This pattern is unusual in songbirds. The Northern Mockingbird is one of the few species common on the East Coast that defends a territory the year around. During the breeding season its territory centers around the nest and is no different from that of any other territorial breeder. In fall, however, the pair separates and each begins to defend its own feeding territory.

J.R. Woodward/VIREO

Northern Mockingbirds, such as this one, represent one species that is territorial at all times of the year. As with other territorial birds, mockingbird territories seem to correspond to the use of defendable resources. It has been suggested that territorial behavior may help to regulate population densities.

Frans Lanting

Don & Pat Valenti

Right: *These Cliff Swallows, like their close relatives the Bank Swallow, often form large colonies of several thousand birds. For its territory, each bird defends the area immediately around the entrance of the nest.*

Far right: *These Wood Storks are colonial wading birds, placing their nests high in trees and out of the reach of predators.*

The Atlantic Puffins in this picture are colonial seabirds that nest on isolated islands. The location of a colony may be limited by the availability of suitable sites. However, many researchers feel that by nesting together, colonial species can take advantage of a variety of benefits associated with group foraging.

Ben Goldstein/Valenti Photo

Colonial nesting. In many species, including herons, swallows, and most seabirds, individual birds come together each year to build their nests near the nests of many others of their species. The resulting aggregations are called nesting colonies. Colonial nesting involves a number of factors. Seabirds, for example, often forage widely over the ocean surface, where the only available nesting land may be an island of limited area. The birds may also prefer an island over mainland nesting sites because it is safer, being inaccessible to most land predators. Also, by watching their neighbors returning to the colony with food for their chicks, colony-nesting gulls, or puffins may learn from one another where they can forage most successfully. Bank and Cliff Swallows, for example, build their nests in sites protected from ground predators such as foxes, skunks, and weasels.

Because residents in a colony usually share their feeding sites, colonial nesters are not, strictly speaking, territorial birds. They do, however, defend their nests. Each pair has its own nest within the colony, which it ardently defends against the adjacent birds, and with good reason: Colony members are known to sometimes steal nesting material from one another. They have also been known to sneak eggs into other birds' nests and to seduce other birds' mates. On the positive side, a few colony nesters have also been known, on rare occasions, to feed a neighbor's chicks.

Courtship and Mating

A bird without a mate is a bird without offspring. Since natural selection has placed the burden on each bird to leave descendants, birds have evolved into creatures that use a variety of methods to meet the challenge of producing the next generation.

Courtship and mating rituals are among the most varied and fascinating of all bird behaviors. The sequence and variety of courting behaviors vary widely among species, but they typically begin with territorial defense and song followed by mate-attraction displays, courtship feeding, and selection of a nest site.

Display

The mating displays of North American songbirds are essential steps in pair formation and can be extremely interesting to watch. A male songbird, such as the Northern Mockingbird, Northern Cardinal, or Black-headed Grosbeak, establishes its nesting territory by singing repeatedly from different perches, announcing its presence to competitors and potential female mates alike, and by vigorously chasing away intruders. In some species the male initially treats the female as an intruder to be chased away. Eventually, the male establishes a peaceful coexistence with neighboring males of its own species.

In many species females arrive on breeding grounds after males each spring, and to some extent have the privilege of choice among prospective mates. The female may base its choice on the song or appearance of the male, on the size or quality of the territory the male defends, or on aspects of compatibility not apparent to us. Whatever method the female uses, the goal is the same: to find a mate likely to provide the offspring with the best chance of survival and continued reproduction. The potential pair may then engage in a series of displays by one or both birds over the next several hours, days, or weeks, to initiate and strengthen a bond between them. The early displays may be subtle, or they may be quite apparent. Rufous-sided Towhees of both sexes briefly spread their wings or tails, revealing white spots; a Scarlet Tanager male may droop its wings to expose its red back while a female perches in a tree above. A male Northern Oriole performs an exaggerated bow in front of its mate, while Herring Gulls toss and turn their heads and provide choking or pecking displays.

Alexander Lowry

The ritualized display of this Ruddy Duck is an important step in the formation of pair-bonds. In waterfowl such as these, displays are believed to have evolved as extreme exaggerations of day-to-day behaviors such as preening and bathing.

Mating displays can also be quite spectacular, as in the sky dance of the Northern Harrier. Over fields or marshes across North America in April you may see this usually low-flying hawk climbing skyward on powerful wing strokes, and then plunging toward the ground while uttering a faint chipping call. The dive is usually repeated in a continuous series by the male, who traces a deep U-shaped pattern or cartwheels in the sky.

Western Grebes perform an equally entertaining dance, "running" in pairs over the surface of their nesting lake. Many cranes perform mating dances together, jumping, turning, and bowing in a display that is at once graceful and ungainly. The secretive American Woodcock of the eastern forests seeks out a forest clearing as dusk settles in the springtime and begins a remarkable performance. This squat, long-billed bird begins by making a "peenting" sound, similar to the sound a clown makes by squeezing his bulbous nose. After a series of these laughable notes, the woodcock flies in a loose spiral above the clearing until it is out of sight in the sky. Its final move is a tumbling, seemingly suicidal fall to earth, ending in sudden control back on the ground of the clearing, where the ritual is begun again.

Courtship nests. Some species use other methods to attract mates or develop pair-bonds. The male Marsh Wren builds several almost spherical courting nests that are lashed into stands of sedges or cattails. Each nest is sturdily woven of grasses and contains a small side entrance. While the male sings and displays, the female enters its territory and inspects the nests. If the female accepts the male, it adds a lining to one of the courting nests to prepare it for a clutch of eggs. The female may judge a male's potential as a mate by the number and quality of his nests.

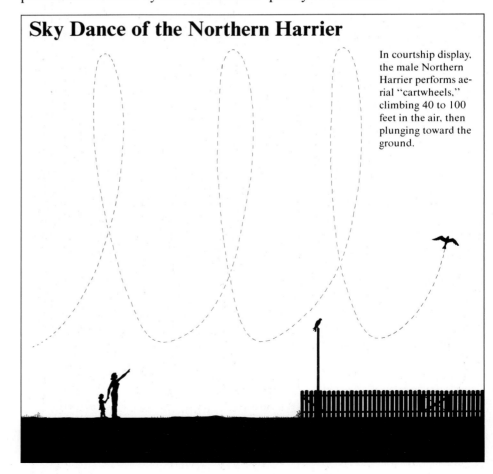

Sky Dance of the Northern Harrier

In courtship display, the male Northern Harrier performs aerial "cartwheels," climbing 40 to 100 feet in the air, then plunging toward the ground.

Donald Waite/Cornell Lab. of Orn./VIREO

Larry West/Valenti Photo

A Marsh Wren delivers a dragonfly nymph to its hungry nestlings. Male Marsh Wrens build several courtship nests within their territory, and females use the number and quality of these nests to assess the suitability of the males.

Courtship feeding, as exhibited by these Northern Cardinals, may be another way in which females assess the suitability of their mates. It is possible that courtship feeding also helps to build the female's energy reserves for the production of eggs.

Feeding. Courtship feeding is a common behavior that cements the pair-bond between mated birds. The male offers a tidbit of food to the female, sometimes at the nest site if it has already been chosen. The male Northern Cardinal offers seeds to its mate at a feeder, placing the seed in the female's bill. Many male gulls bring food to the nest site in an island colony, regurgitating a half-digested mixture of fish and squid at the feet of the females, who eagerly accept the gift.

Courtship feeding is most pronounced, and often most exciting to watch, in birds of prey. The male American Kestrel brings food to a perch on the territory, usually near the nest site. It announces the offering with a call and a fluttering flight. The female follows the male, and they perch side by side, bowing their heads several times before the female takes the mouse or large insect from the talons of its mate.

The male Snowy Owl of arctic tundra regions catches a lemming (a large, brown rodent) in its talons and carries the food in its bill to a mound within sight of the female. Then, standing on the mound and facing the female, with wings displayed behind like a cape, the male offers the dark gift of food, which is dramatically outlined against the background of its snow-white plumage.

Thomas D. Mangelsen

A male Marsh Wren, such as this one, may sing during the night as well as during the day. Singing may function to attract mates, to define territorial boundaries, and to keep other males away.

In the case of the Northern Harrier, the food transfer takes place in midair. The male calls the female to fly out to meet it and then passes the prey—a mouse, snake, or small bird—from its talons to those of its mate. Sometimes the female flies below the male, turning over to grasp the prey dropped from above.

Singing. Although territorial display and singing are restricted to the male in many species, there are some species in which both sexes sing. Male and female Northern Cardinals both sing beautifully, and perform counter-singing during courtship and early pair formation. Perching in different areas of the territory, the two birds alternate their singing, with one echoing the phrases of the other.

The male Anna's Hummingbird is rarely quiet during the breeding season. It perches on a bush or an exposed branch and squeaks incessantly. The bird uses this vocal expression both to attract a female and to alert other males to its presence. As it sings, the male hummingbird darts about in the sunshine, flicking its head back and forth to broadcast the deep red glint on its iridescent throat.

Communal display grounds. Display is highly elaborate in species with less traditional social systems, such as the lekking species (see "Lek mating" on page 72), which use communal display grounds. Male display territories in these species are small sites on the display grounds. Since these territories do not provide shelter for the nest or food for the young, the female's choice of a mate depends on the physical characteristics of the male. As a result, the sexes in most lekking species have evolved great differences in size, plumage, and other adornment.

Natural selection has long favored males of lekking species with larger, brighter, or more ostentatious decorations. The orange neck pouches of the Greater Prairie-Chicken or the purple neck pouches of the Sage Grouse are examples of male adornments in lekking species. In both species the males inflate their pouches to enhance their remarkable displays.

The male Greater Prairie-Chicken displays with its head bent forward, its ear tufts raised, its throat pouch expanded, its wings held close and aquiver, and its tail broadly fanned. In this posture the bird steps and turns around the display ground, all the while producing a resonant, booming sound. Females that visit the lek choose among males on the basis of this display and on the males' relative location in the lek. The birds mate quickly, before a rival male can disrupt them, and then the female leaves to nest elsewhere. In this brief encounter no real pair-bond is formed, and the male has no participation in raising the young.

Many other males of the Grouse, Quail, and Pheasant family have developed elaborate plumage to dazzle the females in display, as in the famous tail spread of the peacock. The many species of birds of paradise of Papua New Guinea, however, rank as the world's most extreme examples of specialized and gaudy male plumage. Some of these tropical birds have special display feathers growing from the head, back, or tail that are much longer than the rest of the bird. These feathers vary from broad plumes to narrow "wires," and have a breathtaking variety of colors. As part of the display, the feathers are erected, fanned, vibrated, or swung. The Blue Bird of Paradise even displays its splendid body and tail feathers while hanging upside down from a tree branch.

Male Buff-breasted Sandpipers display in small, clustered territories, usually along a tundra ridge or on a hillside. From these sites the flashes of their white underwings can be seen for miles, especially as the summer midnight sun approaches the horizon during the late-night hours. The females respond to this distant advertisement, visit the lek, mate, and leave again to build their nests.

Sandy Schuler

Left: *The Sharp-tailed Grouse shown here is an example of a lekking species with an elaborate courtship display. Females judge the suitability of the male by the intensity of the display and the position of the male within the lek, central birds usually being dominant.*

Below: *The Peacock is an example of a species in which selection by females for males with elaborate displays has resulted in the evolution of extremely showy plumages in males.*

Robert & Linda Mitchell

Pair-Bonds

During the breeding season a pair-bond is formed as a result of mating rituals. In most species, the pair-bond lasts only as long as both parents cooperate to feed and care for their young. Pair-bonds vary widely in character and duration, however. At one extreme are species such as the Sage Grouse, Buff-breasted Sandpiper, and Anna's Hummingbird that barely pair at all; the male and female associate for little more than the mating act itself. At the other extreme are species such as the Canada Goose that commonly mate for life, remaining together during summer, migration, and winter. Most birds fall somewhere between these two extremes, annually forming a pair-bond with the same mate on the same territory but separating sometime after the breeding season to migrate and winter apart from each other. In these species, the attachment may be more to the same territory than to a particular partner.

Trumpeter Swans, such as this family, represent a highly monogamous species. Pairs often remain together for as long as both members are capable of successful breeding.

Mating Systems

The mating system is the underlying social organization of a bird society. Mating systems range from the pair-bonds formed by swans, which last many years, to fleeting associations of male and female hummingbirds around a feeding site. The range of mating systems in birds can be divided into a few principal types.

Monogamy. More than 90 percent of the world's bird species are monogamous. In monogamous species, the male and female remain together for the purpose of raising a brood of young. The male and female pair early in the breeding season and share parental duties. The responsibility for territorial defense usually falls upon the male, which is one reason why males sing so much in spring; it is their principal contribution to the nesting effort.

The female's main task is to produce the eggs. The female invests enormous energy in this task, supplying each egg with nutrients that will sustain the chick before hatching. Although the male cannot produce eggs itself, it often provides the female with food to make the job a little easier. In many species the male also assists by preparing the nest, incubating the eggs, and, after the eggs hatch, by bringing food to the young.

In many species "couples" last for more than one year, though they may not be lifelong pair-bonds. Even swans, renowned for their long-term pairing, go through a "divorce" on occasion. Studies show that roughly 5 percent of breeding pairs of Mute Swans separate each year. In many species pairs are more likely to remain together the next year if they have been successful in raising young during the current year.

Polygamy. Polygamy occurs in two forms in bird societies: *polygyny* (a male with several female mates) and *polyandry* (a female with several male mates). Polygyny is much more common than polyandry. Among backyard birds, three masters of polygyny are Red-winged Blackbirds, House Wrens, and Eastern Meadowlarks. Males of each of these species may have several female mates during the same breeding season.

A. Cruickshank/VIREO

The male Red-winged Blackbird achieves its polygyny by impressing first one female, then another. At any one moment it may have several females nesting on its territory, all in different stages of breeding. One may be just beginning, the second well into incubation of eggs, and the third busy feeding the young. This scheduling of the females allows the male to devote different levels of effort to the various females on his territory, thereby not spreading himself too thinly.

Why should a female Red-winged Blackbird select a male that already has a mate? The answer is still unknown. With a bachelor, a female is more likely to receive undivided attention during the hard weeks when food has to be brought to the chicks every few minutes. By choosing a male who already has at least one female on his territory, a female is certain to receive only partial help. The female is not unaware of the situation; it interacts with the other females on a male's territory. The most plausible explanation is that a female's priority is a male with the best territory. The males without mates may have chosen such bad sites that a female would be worse off with them than it would be sharing a mate with another female.

Polyandry is rare among birds, especially in North America. Of all the species regularly found in the lower 48 states, only the Spotted Sandpiper and Wilson's Phalarope are polyandrous. Several more can be found in Alaska, including the Red Phalarope, a species that carries polyandry to its extreme. The female Red Phalarope is bigger and more colorful than the male and plays no role in incubating or caring for the young. The female spends a week or so with one male, courting it and laying eggs in its nest. Once the nest is full, the female begins searching for another mate. Long before the eggs have been hatched by any of the dedicated males, the female Red Phalarope has headed south in migration.

Promiscuity. A few species of North American birds are best called promiscuous. This term describes a rather chaotic social structure in which a female may mate with many males or a male with many females. Promiscuous mating may appear to be a combination of polygyny and

Frans Lanting

Western Meadowlarks, such as this one, may be polygynous, males often mating with two or three females. Polygynous mating systems may result from females selecting high-quality territories despite the presence of other females.

This Red Phalarope is an example of a polyandrous species. As with many polyandrous birds, female Red Phalaropes are more brightly colored than the males.

Herbert Clarke

polyandry, but polygynous and polyandrous birds make some commitment, however brief, to their mates. The polygynous Red-winged Blackbird, for example, actually helps care for its young; the polyandrous Spotted Sandpiper defends a territory upon which the males nest. Promiscuous birds form no lasting associations whatsoever.

All of North America's hummingbirds are promiscuous breeders. The males defend large territories around important sources of food and then display to females coming to feed. Females may fly well beyond the territories of local males to find males with whom to mate. The male will almost certainly never see its offspring or the nest, and most likely will not see the female for more than one brief visit. But what energy he displays to each and every female who comes to call!

Lek mating. Lekking is a curious variation on promiscuous mating. This word, of Swedish derivation, describes a pattern of mating behavior seen in only a small number of birds around the world. In North America its chief practitioners are Greater and Lesser Prairie-Chickens, Sage and Sharp-tailed Grouse, and Buff-breasted Sandpipers.

During the mating season, the males of lekking species gather into small clusters of territories, called leks, or arenas. Each male defends a territory within the lek, although the area may be only a few yards across. Thirty or more males can gather at a large lek. They display with frantic intensity, sometimes oblivious to most everything around them (though their intensity increases when females are present).

Females visit the lek and wander among the displaying males as if comparing their virtues. Eventually a female accepts the advances of a particular male and mates with it. Usually only a few males out of all those present on the lek ever successfully mate. The female then lays its eggs in a nest that may be distant from the lek and that will never be visited by the chosen male.

Lekking species, like the Sage Grouse shown here, reserve mating activities to traditional lekking grounds. In these birds, incubation and parental care is left to the females.

Leonard Lee Rue III

J.P. Myers/VIREO

R. Villani/VIREO

Extremes within a family. In most cases, closely related species have similar mating systems. This is probably due to their similar habitat and feeding behaviors. Ornithologists now believe that the ecological setting of a species helps determine what mating system it uses.

The Sandpiper family, however, stands out among North American birds for its diversity of mating systems. This family runs the gamut of approaches to mating, from highly monogamous Dunlins to promiscuous Pectoral and Buff-breasted Sandpipers. In winter, all members of the Sandpiper family are remarkably similar in their behavior; most move about in great flocks and migrate enormous distances. On the breeding ground, however, their societies are organized in different ways.

Dunlins breed across the Arctic and are common in western and northern Alaska. The Dunlin is an excellent example of a monogamous species. The male arrives from its winter site in early June and immediately starts defending a territory. Within a week, the female, who might be his mate from the previous year, has joined him. Together they build a nest and incubate eggs. The male usually incubates at night, and the female generally takes the day shift. When the eggs have hatched, the parents once again divide their duties, and the family remains together for several weeks while the young learn to fly. Semipalmated, Stilt, and Western Sandpipers are also monogamous.

At the other extreme are promiscuous Pectoral and Buff-breasted Sandpipers. The Pectoral Sandpiper mates on huge territories spread broadly over the tundra's wet surface. A male Pectoral Sandpiper displays at virtually anything entering its territory that remotely resembles a female. Moreover, the Pectoral male is a bully who never ceases in its amorous advances to females, regardless of whether they are receptive or not. Sometimes as many as ten males pursue a female in flight, chasing it for half an hour or more. By the time the eggs hatch, all the local males have left the Arctic, headed south in migration to wintering grounds in Argentina. Who could imagine their antics in the Arctic when seeing them in quiet flocks in a Minnesota marsh as they pause along the way in the wetlands of the lower 48 states?

Above left: *This Dunlin forms a monogamous pair-bond with its mate. Throughout the breeding season, care for the eggs and young is divided equally between the two birds.*

Above: *This Pectoral Sandpiper forms loose promiscuous pair-bonds. Care of the eggs and young is left strictly to the females, the males migrating south before the eggs hatch.*

Wardene Weisser/Berg & Associates

This male Acorn Woodpecker likely belongs to a group of related individuals which cooperate in feeding the young, storing acorns, and chasing predators. Communal breeding helps the adults raise their young and gives the juveniles valuable experience when it comes to raising their own young.

Female Pectoral Sandpipers are no more virtuous. They may dally with the male on whose territory they nest or may visit any of the male's neighbors. Within one clutch, a female Pectoral Sandpiper may have eggs sired by several different males.

Communal breeding. Picture this scene at a large valley oak in the coastal woodlands of California near Monterey: A female Acorn Woodpecker comes out of a nest hole in a dead snag, a large, whitish oval egg in its bill. Calling, the bird flies to a nearby tree and places the egg in one of thousands of small holes patterned along the trunk of the tree. Another woodpecker flies in to join her, and then three more arrive, all calling loudly. One bird breaks open the egg and the group consumes its contents. The female then returns to its nest hole. Within a few hours the female has laid an egg of its own in the nest.

This scene regularly occurs each year in the social life of the Acorn Woodpecker, one of the few communal-breeding birds of North America. The small holes in the tree trunk are holes the woodpeckers made to store acorns for the winter. The egg the female was carrying was laid by one of the group-mates, who does the same to the female's newly laid egg. They trade back and forth like this for several rounds, until at last they stop eating the eggs and start incubating them. The egg-eating is probably prompted by competition among the females, but the control of this behavior remains a puzzle to ornithologists.

Acorn Woodpeckers cooperate to raise their young. They live in groups of varying size, from 3 to 15 birds. Within the group, only one or two males and one or two females breed; the rest remain to help raise young, store food, and protect the group from predators and acorn thieves. One major task they share is digging the thousands of holes in the storage tree. It takes several generations to dig enough holes for the group to store acorns for the winter. The storage tree is thus a family heirloom, passed from generation to generation. As one tree grows old and begins to totter, the group begins working on another one, thereby ensuring the survival of future generations.

For most species, fledging is usually the last interaction between parent and offspring. But with Acorn Woodpeckers, son and daughter stay for at least one year and sometimes even remain on their parents' territory for life. Usually the daughters leave after a year or two, and the sons stay a little longer. Throughout their stay the offspring assist in communal duties— feeding young, storing acorns, chasing squirrels from the storage tree. They do not breed during this time. If a daughter Acorn Woodpecker remains with its family group, it does not become a breeding member of the group until its father dies. Likewise, unless it has moved to another group, a son does not mate until its mother dies.

This cooperative living is not motivated by sheer altruism. The birds need a storage tree to survive the winter. The only way they can obtain access to one is by being in a group, and the only group that will accept them without a fight is their own family. After a year or two they can fight their way into another group.

How common is cooperative breeding in the United States? There is no other species quite like the Acorn Woodpecker. A few, such as the Florida Scrub Jay, the Gray-breasted Jay, and the Red-cockaded Woodpecker, share similar patterns: Family groups remain together for up to several years to share parenting. Quite a few species show some aspects of cooperation in that young from a previous clutch will help at the nest.

Nesting

Nest building is a demanding activity for birds, as well it should be. Nests provide birds with support and insulation, concealment from predators, and shelter from rain. What could be more important?

Building a nest takes time, time that might otherwise be spent feeding or hiding from predators. Early during its nesting season, the Great Tit devotes up to three hours each day to its nest-building efforts. The male Marsh Wren spends hour after hour building a courtship nest, and as soon as one is finished, he begins to build another. Some species, however, build no nest at all, and instead lay their eggs directly on rock ledges.

The nesting habits of each species have evolved over the ages and are matched to climate and habitat, size, amount of threat by predators, clutch size, longevity, physiology, and chick development patterns. Nests can be on bare ground, in trees, in marshes, or on cliffs, and may hold from only a single egg to more than a dozen.

Nest Locations

If asked to picture a typical bird nest, most people think of a bowl-shaped nest woven of twigs and grasses and situated in a tree, a shrub, or in dense grass. This is the kind of nest used by almost all the common songbirds of our fields, forests, and gardens. But birds nest in places ranging from treetops to holes in the ground.

Nesting in dense cover, especially off the ground, provides safety from predators. For the same reason, many species nest in cavities in trees, or in birdhouses. Woodpeckers excavate their own holes in trees; bluebirds, House Wrens, starlings, Tree Swallows, and screech-owls use abandoned woodpecker holes or other existing tree cavities. The hornbill of Africa takes the protection aspect a step further: The male seals the cavity opening with mud after the female is on the nest. The male passes food to its mate, and later to the chicks, through a small opening in the wall.

Birds and Their Mating Systems

Monogamous Birds
Bittern, American
Blue Warbler, Black-throated
Cardinal, Northern
Chickadee, Carolina
Crow, American
Eagle, Bald
Falcon, Peregrine
Flicker, Northern
Golden-Plover, Lesser
Grebe, Pied-billed
Gull, Herring
Hawk, Red-tailed
Heron, Great Blue
Jay, Blue
Junco, Dark-eyed
Kestrel, American
Killdeer
Loon, Common
Nuthatch, White-breasted
Redstart, American
Sparrow, Fox
Sparrow, White-throated
Swan, Mute
Swift, Chimney
Tanager, Scarlet
Thrush, Wood
Titmouse, Tufted
Towhee, Brown
Woodpecker, Downy

Polygynous Birds
Blackbird, Red-winged
Bobolink
Bunting, Indigo
Dickcissel
Grackle, Great-tailed
Harrier, Northern
Meadowlark, Eastern
Ptarmigan, Willow
Sandpiper, White-rumped
Sparrow, Savannah
Warbler, Yellow
Wren, House
Wren, Marsh
Wren, Winter
Yellowthroat, Common

Polyandrous Birds
Phalarope, Red
Phalarope, Wilson's
Sanderling
Sandpiper, Spotted

Promiscuous Birds
Grouse, Sage
Hummingbird, Anna's
Hummingbird, Ruby-throated
Prairie-Chicken, Greater
Sandpiper, Pectoral
Woodcock, American

Richard Carver

Michael Hopiak/Cornell Lab. of Orn./VIREO

Ben Goldstein/Valenti Photo

Above: *These Burrowing Owls find the abandoned burrows of prairie-dogs and other mammals as safe retreats for their own nests.*

Above center: *Northern Orioles, such as this one, make their nests inaccessible by suspending them from the tips of tree branches.*

Above right: *The nest of this Bald Eagle is typical—an enormous mass of sticks balanced at the top of a dead snag. The nests are added to each year, and old nests can grow to spectacular sizes, sometimes becoming so heavy that they fall under their own weight.*

A wide variety of nests are made in holes in the ground. The Belted Kingfisher excavates a tunnel and nest chamber in the face of a bank, usually near a stream. Burrowing Owls often nest in dens abandoned by prairie dogs or other mammals. Many seabirds such as puffins, auklets, and storm-petrels escape the dangers of predatory gulls, which nest on the same islands, by laying and incubating their eggs in dirt burrows or crevices in piles of rocks. For these species the choice of an island colony nest site provides them with protection from mammalian predators.

No birds nest underwater, but Western and Pied-billed Grebes have developed a way of using the waters of the lakes and marshes where they breed to protect their nests from predators. These birds construct floating nests of mats of dead reeds and other vegetation, and lay their eggs on these platforms just above the water line.

Some birds, including the Northern Oriole, make their nests even more inaccessible to reptiles and mammals by suspending them from the tips of tree branches. The typical teardrop shape of this covered nest makes it one of the easiest bird nests to identify in North America.

Ospreys and Bald Eagles are tree nesters, but their large size prevents them from choosing sites hidden among the branches. Typical nest trees have broken tops that support the huge mass of sticks. The nest sites are often used year after year, with some remodeling done each spring. An eagle nest, which can be several feet thick, can become too heavy for an old, dead tree to support. Such a tree eventually falls under the weight of the nest, and the birds must begin building a new one in a new site.

Many seabirds and some songbirds and birds of prey nest on cliffs, another location that is safe from predators. The nest site, or *aerie*, of the Peregrine Falcon often has an overhanging roof above the nest ledge, affording protection from rain. Before Peregrine Falcon populations declined sharply in eastern North America allegedly because of DDT in the food chain, a few birds had become famous for nesting on a new type of "cliff": the skyscrapers of New York, Philadelphia, and Montreal. One Peregrine that nested on ledges of two tall buildings in New York City during the 1950s could be seen diving to capture pigeons over the canyons of Manhattan.

Another way of keeping the nest safe from predators, of course, is energetic defense, provided the bird is strong or noisy enough. Most tern nests are easy to reach in the open habitats near mainland beaches, but the raucous cries and frantic diving of the parent birds deter most egg-seeking predators. Large owls bring formidable weapons to the task of nest defense. Snowy Owls, for example, place their eggs in a depression on a tundra mound, where the female incubates them, exposed to the view of any predator. When a fox or a human comes too close, however, the male dives or flies directly at the intruder, bill clacking fiercely and talons held ready. A Great Horned Owl has been known to slice the back of a man with its sharp talons when he tried to climb its nest tree, and another attacking owl once succeeded in knocking a man out of a tree.

Some species, especially shorebirds such as the Killdeer, Lesser Golden-Plover, and Ruddy Turnstone, have an open nesting habitat that is accessible to predators. These species rely on camouflage and distraction displays to protect their nests.

Building the Nest

Birds use as many materials to construct their nests as they find available in their environments. Twigs and grasses are common, with mud for cement. Some swallow nests are composed primarily of dried mud. The linings of bird nests are usually much softer and more elegant than the outer shell. Materials such as fine grasses, horsehair, thistledown, sheep's wool, spiderwebs, plant down, and feathers may grace the interiors. Tree Swallows are especially fond of feathers; nesting swallows will collect white chicken feathers offered near a nesting box (see page 207).

Many ducks and geese line their ground nests with a warm, insulating layer of down plucked from the female's breast, and pull this layer over the eggs when they leave to feed or flee from a predator.

Many shorebirds form a rather sparsely lined depression in the ground. Some sandpipers line the depressions with grasses, golden-plovers use bits of lichen, and Killdeer use small pebbles, hardly a warm and comforting receptacle for their precious eggs. But the Common Murre, an abundant seabird that nests on rock cliffs, does even less than this, laying its single egg on the bare rock of the cliff ledge. The pointed shape of the egg causes it to roll in a small circle, helping to keep it from falling off the ledge.

Most birds carry nest material to the nest site exactly as they carry food: Birds of prey carry it in their claws, and other species carry it in their bills. The African Rosy-faced Parakeet cuts strips of bark and inserts them among specialized feathers on its back, an unusual but effective way of carrying material to its nest site. Many North American birds can be seen collecting grasses or fibers or carrying twigs in the spring, a sure sign of nesting activity and one of the easiest ways to locate a nest.

Frans Lanting

Many waterfowl nests, like this Mallard nest, are lined with soft down feathers that the female plucks from her breast.

This Red-winged Blackbird nest is typical of the nests of most songbirds. Most songbird nests are carefully woven of grasses and twigs and sometimes held together with mud. The inner linings are usually composed of fine, soft materials.

F.E. Hester/VIREO

The Brood

Though the number of eggs in a clutch varies widely among species, each species seems to follow one of two laying patterns. *Determinate layers* almost always lay the same number of eggs per clutch. For some birds with long life spans the full clutch is only a single egg. Most shorebirds never lay more than four eggs, and seldom lay three. Many songbirds are also determinate layers, usually with clutches of three to six eggs.

Other species are *indeterminate layers*, capable of laying more eggs if any are lost, until a full set (a number typical of each species) is in the nest. Experiments show that when eggs are removed from the nest before the full clutch is present, the bird will keep replacing them. A Northern Flicker once laid 71 eggs in 73 days when this trick was repeatedly played on it. This behavior has been selectively encouraged in domestic chickens for several centuries.

Another clutch size pattern is exhibited by species such as Snowy and Short-eared Owls. These birds nest only when densities of their prey, mainly mice and lemmings, are high enough to feed their young, and they lay larger clutches—up to 10 or 12 eggs—when prey densities are very high. In this way they invest in large clutches only when there is enough food for a large number of hungry chicks.

Incubation. Once laid, the eggs must be incubated, and a warm temperature must be maintained to promote embryo development. This places a burden on the parent or parents, who must devote hours, even days and weeks, to sitting still. Incubation has some risks, too, since the adult is not out feeding during this time, and predators are a hazard.

Among songbirds most incubation is done by the female, but the males of some species share these duties. Among shorebirds and seabirds, males commonly take turns with females, each parent sitting for about 12 hours at a time in shorebirds and up to several days at a stretch in seabirds. The female is responsible for all the incubation among hawks and owls, with the male standing guard and bringing food. The female does all the work in lekking species, and the male knows nothing of the nest site. Females must leave the eggs unattended while they feed away from the nests.

In a few species, the male does all the incubation. Among the species of phalarope, for example, the female abandons all nesting duties shortly after laying the fourth egg, leaving the male alone on the nesting grounds.

Below: The eggs of many birds, particularly arctic species, can be extremely hardy. Golden-plover eggs, for example, can be exposed during periods of freezing temperatures and still hatch into healthy young such as this one.

Below right: Many seabirds, like this Wandering Albatross, may incubate for several days before exchanging duties with their mates.

J.V. Remsen, Jr./VIREO

Sharon Chester

Karl Maslowski

The young of this Rose-breasted Grosbeak are typical of most song-birds, being helpless, blind, and virtually naked at hatching. At this stage the young are totally dependent on their parents for food and protection, and to regulate their body temperature.

The short periods when a foraging bird must leave the nest uncovered do not seem to harm the developing eggs. In some instances, especially early in incubation, even lengthy pauses are not harmful. After an unseasonal June snowstorm on the arctic coast of Alaska, biologists noticed a Lesser Golden-Plover walking repeatedly in a small area on top of the snow. After digging down to uncover a clutch of four eggs, they moved away from the spot and watched the bird settle down to incubate. Two and a half weeks later the eggs hatched, producing healthy golden-plover chicks, bundles of yellow, spotted down that are among the cutest chicks.

Incubation lasts from one-and-a-half weeks to one month in most species, but may be longer, especially in large birds. In extremely cold Antarctic weather, the male Emperor Penguin incubates a single egg for nine weeks, keeping it warm enough to develop and hatch. The bird does not feed during this time, living only on stored body fat. Wandering Albatross incubation lasts even longer, but at least it is shared by both parents.

Caring for the chicks. Do birds make good parents? Male Emperor Penguins, after incubating an egg for nine weeks and then feeding and huddling over their chick for weeks after hatching, certainly deserve credit for effort. But what of the male hummingbird, which never goes near the nest or chicks?

Parental care systems vary widely among bird species, and are an important component of the different social systems. Along with other behavior patterns, parental care systems have evolved to meet the challenge of survival of the species. In general, every adult bird contributes just enough to the child-care effort to give its offspring a reasonable chance to survive and reproduce without greatly decreasing its own opportunity to survive and reproduce in the next season. In some species, one parent contributes nothing to the child-care effort in return for a chance to mate with more than one partner, thereby increasing its number of potential offspring. In other species, including most of the songbirds, both parents share many of the duties of feeding, brooding, and protecting the young birds until they fledge.

Frans Lanting

This young Killdeer is typical of most precocial birds. Thickly covered with camouflaging down and capable of moving about shortly after hatching, such birds are almost independent of their parents.

Patterns of development. To a great extent, the kind of care required is determined by the development pattern of the chicks. Ornithologists separate these development patterns into two kinds: *altricial* and *precocial.*

The chicks of altricial species—which include songbirds, woodpeckers, hummingbirds, hawks, and owls—are naked and blind when they hatch, and are too weak to do anything but open their mouths to be fed by the parents. Altricial chicks usually remain in the nest for two or more weeks, until they have developed enough plumage, strength, and coordination to fly short distances. After fledging they may remain dependent upon the parents several weeks longer for protection and feeding. You may see full-sized young birds at this time begging and harassing their parents for food.

In contrast, the chicks of precocial species, such as ducks, geese, grouse, pheasants, shorebirds, and grebes, are appealing and capable birds at birth. At hatching they are covered with a thick layer of down, have well-developed legs and bills, and their eyes are open. Sandpiper and plover chicks may leave the nest within hours of hatching, and before they are one day old can run, hide, and peck at insects on low vegetation. The parent or parents do not need to carry food to these chicks, which is the most time-consuming job of the parents of altricial chicks. Precocial parents need only lead the chicks to appropriate feeding habitats, keep them warm during their first days by occasional brooding, and protect them from predators.

This last job is especially critical. Since the chicks are moving around in open habitat, they are easily noticeable; since they are unable to fly, they are easy prey. Among shorebirds the solution is a combination of remarkable chick camouflage and energetic adult distraction displays. Baby shorebirds have special down feathers that create a finely spotted effect to break the outline of the chick, and their response to an alarm call from a parent is to crouch, motionless, amid the vegetation. The parent then employs the rodent run, broken wing, or other distraction display, as described on page 58. The distraction displays are often so artful and insistent that the predator is drawn far away from the chick area. Afterwards, the parent circles back, gives an all-clear whistle, and gathers the brood together again. Many precocial waterfowl chicks are even better equipped to avoid predators, since they can swim almost from birth.

Precocial development does, however, impose some limitations. It is well suited mainly to species that nest on the ground and that feed on foods that can be taken by chicks on the ground or on water. For many songbird species that forage on insects in treetops, or for hawks and owls, which kill relatively large prey, precocial chicks would still be unable to feed themselves. Furthermore, precocial chicks must accomplish much more development than altricial chicks while still in the egg, which means that females must lay large eggs and spend more time incubating them in a vulnerable, ground nest site. Altricial birds shift more of their parental care effort into the post-hatching stage.

A few other differences in parental care systems arise from these differences in chick development patterns. Whereas altricial species must be stay-at-home parents, always returning with food to the same spot, precocial species are quite free to travel.

Precocial chicks' ability to care for themselves lessens the burden on parents, permitting single parenting to be more successful and more prevalent among these species. In many shorebirds one adult leaves the nesting grounds before the chicks fledge; in some the second adult may even depart when chicks are barely able to fly. In species such as Pectoral, Baird's, or White-rumped Sandpipers, the parents depart from arctic nesting areas in July and August, headed for wintering areas in southern South America. Their barely grown chicks are left to fend for themselves while they continue to feed for a few more weeks to build up their stores of fat. Before the early arctic winter appears, these four- to six-week-old birds begin the same several-thousand-mile flight themselves, with no adults to guide them. It sounds impossible, but it works every year.

Behavior and Survival

A suite of well-adapted behaviors is essential to the successful reproduction and survival of birds of every species. The evolutionary process has guided the development of appropriate behavior patterns to enable birds to find food, escape predators, obtain mates, build nests, and produce offspring. How these behaviors are matched to a bird's environment plays a major part in determining how successful the species will be. In our role as observers of nature, the behavior of birds provides us with a fascinating array of sights to ponder as we try to understand the birds around us.

H. Cruickshank/VIREO

That the young are precocial, enables this Common Goldeneye to leave the nest site with her brood and eliminates the need for the male to remain with the young.

Avian Ecology

*by Jerome A. Jackson and
Bette J. Schardien Jackson*

*W*ho has not joined the poets in admiring how birds
"loose the bonds of earth"? Their ability to climb to
great heights and cross vast expanses of rugged terrain allows
some birds to reach the highest mountain peaks and know the
limits of land on the most remote islands. Insulating feathers
and an ability to maintain a constant high body temperature
under extremes of heat and cold allow birds to cross scorching
deserts and icy polar regions. Only the ocean depths below
the reach of light remain off limits for birds. To discuss bird
"homes," then, is to discuss the entire surface of the earth.

The word "ecology" brings to mind conservation and recycling programs, but the true meaning of the term is much
broader. "Ecology" derives from "oikos," the Greek word for
home, and it refers to the interrelationships of organisms and
their environments. Where do Least Bitterns lay their eggs
and raise their young? Where do they feed, court, and carry
on their other daily activities? Avian ecology addresses the
questions of how birds use their homes in the ways they do.

**Although now an endangered species, the Peregrine Falcon has
traditionally been one of the most widely distributed birds. With
its long, graceful wings, it soars on wind currents, scouting prey.**

Jack Wilburn

H. Cruickshank/VIREO

Above: *Two Great Blue Herons exchange duties at a tree-top nest. These colonial nesting birds prefer the seclusion of remote islands or inaccessible swamps as nesting sites. By placing their nest high, herons avoid ground-dwelling predators and enjoy an unobstructed view of their feeding habitat.*

Above right: *The shy and secretive Least Bittern is a solitary nester and depends on dense marsh vegetation to conceal its nest. More often heard than seen, these birds seldom stray from the cover that provides them with food and nesting materials.*

The Basics of Avian Home Life

The concept underlying the study of bird homes is that, like people, birds do more than live in their homes—they interact with them. The home provides the resources of everyday survival; the use of the resources influences the home. People decorate their houses, mow their lawns, plant trees, and pollute the environment with accumulations of waste. Similarly, birds adorn their nests with found items, disperse seed from the fruit they eat, and also pollute, such as when the excrement of nesting herons or roosting blackbirds kills the vegetation below them.

Rocks and soil form the foundation of the avian environment, and North America provides an array of home sites—from rugged coasts to gently rising plains; from steep mountains to stark, dry deserts.

Ranges and Barriers

With varied landscapes come varied resources. Different bird species need different resources; therefore, they are limited to certain areas. The broad area that a species occupies is called its range. Knowledge of the range of a species will disclose whether you will see a particular species in your backyard at some time during the year. It would be fruitless, for example, for a bird-watcher in Pennsylvania to sit by the window in the hope of spotting a Steller's Jay. Although the Steller's Jay and its eastern cousin, the Blue Jay, are somewhat similar in appearance and behavior, the Steller's Jay rarely ventures east of the Rocky Mountains, and the Blue Jay rarely roams west of them.

The mountains may be a barrier to the Blue Jay and the plains a barrier to the Steller's Jay. Other variables in the environment may serve as barriers to limit a species' range. Many land birds, for instance, will not cross a large body of water; conversely, many aquatic birds avoid large land areas. A forest can effectively block the spread of a grassland bird like the Horned Lark, and grasslands are an effective barrier to many forest birds.

The ranges of species fluctuate in response to changes in the limiting effects of barriers. Large areas of the eastern deciduous forest that were cleared for crops and livestock have created habitat for the Eastern Meadowlark, Brown-headed Cowbird, and Horned Lark; these species have been able to expand their ranges eastward. In similar fashion the

Above left: *The Steller's Jay is the western counterpart of the Blue Jay. It inhabits coniferous and pine-oak woodlands of the Rocky Mountains and Pacific Coast and only rarely wanders east onto the Great Plains.*

Above: *The Blue Jay is a familiar resident of gardens, parks, and deciduous woodlands in eastern North America. The practice of planting windbreaks in the central prairies has allowed this species to spread westward to the eastern Rockies. In some areas, the ranges of Blue and Steller's Jays now over-lap and the two species have been known to interbreed.*

Left: *Mountain ranges like this one effectively block the dispersal of many bird species, preventing them from colonizing new habitats on the other side.*

planting of trees near farms in the Great Plains has allowed westward expansion of birds of the eastern deciduous forest, such as the Red-bellied Woodpecker and the Northern Oriole. Several of our common backyard species have expanded their ranges as a result of the food provided for them in winter. The ranges of the Northern Mockingbird, Northern Cardinal, and Tufted Titmouse have expanded northward, and the range of the Evening Grosbeak has expanded southward.

Ranges also change with each passing season. For example, many birds migrate to more favorable climates for the winter. The portion of a migratory bird's range in which it nests and raises its young (generally in the spring and summer) is called its breeding range; the area in which it spends the winter is called its winter range. Bird-watchers refer to a bird as a transient if they see it in an area through which it normally passes on migration. If a bird wanders outside of its normal range, it is called a vagrant. Nonmigratory birds are called permanent residents.

Every region of the United States has its own set of permanent residents, migrants that only spend the summer, migrants that only spend the winter, and birds that are transients. The color-coded range maps in many field guides and in "The Gallery of Birds" beginning on page 269 tell which birds we can expect in our backyards and at what time of year we can expect them. We usually see the greatest variety of bird life in any area in spring and fall when migration is under way.

Ecosystems

The basic relationship of a bird to its home begins with the *ecosystem* in which it lives. An ecosystem is an area that has a common structural framework. Ecosystems encompass soil and water as well as plants and animals. Most ecosystems are characterized by and named after the most conspicuous plants in the ecosystem. These plants usually provide the framework for the homes of birds.

North America contains a variety of ecosystems. Each has unique characteristics and an avifauna that is more or less unique to it. Each also shares some plants and animals—including birds—with other ecosystems.

Some bird species are restricted to a single ecosystem because they specialize in using the resources of that ecosystem. For example, the Greater Prairie-Chicken is restricted to the prairie ecosystem of Texas; only an environment that contains a specific type of native grass provides suitable feeding and nesting areas. The Red-cockaded Woodpecker is restricted to the mature pine forest ecosystems of the southeastern United States; it too is specialized to the point that it will only feed and nest there. In contrast, some species, such as the Brown-headed Cowbird and Blue Jay, inhabit a number of ecosystems. These birds are generalists; although they can live in a variety of habitats, they are really "masters" of none. They could not compete well with the specialists for resources, but as generalists, they can turn to other foods and nest sites.

A categorization of some of the major North American ecosystems and some of the birds that characterize them follows.

Blue Jays, such as this trio of fledglings, are typical of the eastern deciduous forest. These members of the Crow and Jay family are extremely adaptable and have been expanding their range beyond the limits of this ecosystem.

Leonard Lee Rue III

Eastern deciduous forest. Most of the eastern United States and southern Canada were once covered by deciduous forest dominated by oak, hickory, maple, beech, and elm. European settlers opened the forest and replaced it with cities, towns, and agricultural land. Remnants of the eastern deciduous forest are still extensive enough, however, to support a diverse avifauna. Characteristic birds of this ecosystem include the Wild Turkey, the Red-bellied Woodpecker, the Black-capped Chickadee, the Blue Jay, and the Red-eyed Vireo.

Northern coniferous forest. Stretching in a belt from the Atlantic to the Pacific across central Canada and reaching into some of the northeastern United States is the northern coniferous forest, a vast ecosystem that is much the same today as it has been for hundreds of years. Spruce, fir, and tamarack trees dominate the landscape and provide homes for Spruce Grouse, Three-toed Woodpeckers, Great Gray Owls, Gray Jays, Boreal Chickadees, Ruby-crowned Kinglets, Black-throated Green Warblers, and many other warbler species.

Grant Heilman/Grant Heilman Photography

Grant Heilman/Grant Heilman Photography

Left: *This climax deciduous forest is dominated by birch, beech, and maple. Such forests are characterized by tall trees with broad spreading crowns, an open understory, and a forest floor of rich herbaceous growth.*

Below left: *The northern coniferous forest forms an almost impenetrable belt of evergreen trees across the northern portion of the continent. Dense stands of fir, tamarack, and spruce are interrupted by acidic bogs and in northern regions give way to tundra.*

Below: *Known in some areas as the Canada Jay or the Whiskey Jack, the Gray Jay has a reputation with picnickers as the "camp robber" of the northern forests.*

Leonard Lee Rue III

Jack Wilburn

Steve Maslowski

Stephen J. Krasemann/DRK Photo

Stephen J. Krasemann/DRK Photo

Top left: *A male Summer Tanager claims his territory from a song perch. These birds are typical inhabitants of the southeastern coniferous forests.*

Top right: *The southeastern coniferous forest is characterized by open stands of mature pines. In such areas, undergrowth is minimized by frequent fires.*

Bottom left: *The Ruddy Turnstone is one of many species that breeds on the tundra during the brief arctic summer.*

Bottom right: *Due to harsh winters and a layer of permafrost just below the surface of the soil, tundra is usually treeless. A few sheltered areas, such as this low arctic valley, support thin stands of stunted spruce.*

Southeastern coniferous forest. South of the eastern deciduous forest is the southeastern coniferous forest, an ecosystem characterized by open stands of shortleaf, loblolly, longleaf, and slash pines. Characteristic birds of this ecosystem include Red-cockaded Woodpeckers, Brown-headed Nuthatches, Carolina Chickadees, Summer Tanagers, Pine Warblers, and Bachman's Sparrows.

Tundra. To the north of the northern coniferous forest and extending from the Atlantic to the Pacific and north to the Arctic Ocean is a soggy, open environment called the tundra. The trees of the tundra—birches, willows, and evergreens—are so dwarfed that the ecosystem has the appearance of a wet, treeless meadow. Even in summer the tundra is usually soggy; not far beneath the surface is a permanently frozen layer that prevents surface water from seeping into the ground. The moisture and long days in summer contribute to lush summer vegetation that supports a rich variety of nesting birds. Most North American geese and many of our shorebirds are tundra species: the Canada Goose, the Snow Goose, the Tundra Swan, the Lesser Golden-Plover, and the Ruddy Turnstone. The Snowy Owl, the Lapland Longspur, and the Snow Bunting further characterize the tundra. Although the tundra is a good nesting area, the bitter winter environment requires that most species migrate to more hospitable regions. Only a few, such as various species of ptarmigan, are year-round residents.

Grant Heilman/Grant Heilman Photography

Grant Heilman/Grant Heilman Photography

Gary R. Zahm/DRK Photo

Stephen J. Krasemann/DRK Photo

Grasslands. From the edge of the eastern deciduous forest to the slopes of the Rockies, grasslands (also called prairies) dominate the landscape through the center of our continent from coastal Texas to the central provinces of Canada. Inadequate rain prevents the expansion of the eastern deciduous forest, but grasses thrive. Big and little bluestems and blue grama grasses dominate the vegetation. The grasslands are sometimes divided into several ecosystems on the basis of grass species. (The prairie ecosystem has been gradually disappearing because of needed agriculture, as explained on page 110.) Characteristic birds of the grassland ecosystem include Prairie Falcons, Greater Prairie-Chickens, Upland Sandpipers, Short-eared Owls, Lark Buntings, and Grasshopper Sparrows.

Deserts. Most of the deserts of North America are in the western and southwestern part of the continent where a combination of latitude and high mountains reduces the precipitation; few plants can survive. By definition, a desert is less than half-covered by vegetation. Many species of cacti are common in the southwestern deserts; sagebrush dominates the deserts of the northern high plains. Differences in temperature, altitude, and vegetation define several different desert ecosystems. The majestic saguaro, several species of cholla, and the ubiquitous prickly pear are among the better-known desert cacti of the southwest. Creosote, Joshua trees, yuccas, and mesquite define other desert environments. These desert ecosystems are home to a diversity of birds—all specialized to

Top left: *At one time most of central North America was a vast treeless plain. The tall-grass prairie shown here forms the eastern portion of the grassland ecosystem. In the higher, more arid regions to the west, there is a transition from a mixed- to a short-grass prairie.*

Top right: *The Greater Prairie Chicken symbolizes untouched grasslands. Unable to cope with modern agriculture, these bird populations have become dangerously low.*

Bottom left: *Ocotillo and prickly pear typify the deserts of the southwest. More northernly deserts are dominated by sages.*

Bottom right: *The Greater Roadrunner is a familiar inhabitant of North American deserts, placing its nest in the protective confines of a cactus clump.*

George J. Sanker/DRK Photo

Joseph R. Pearce/DRK Photo

Robert J. Western

Robert J. Western

Top left: *Throughout the year, Canada Geese, such as this one with its goslings, are typically found near aquatic ecosystems. Water provides food as well as protection from predators.*

Top right: *Lakeside marshes such as this are important for a wide variety of birds, but represent only one kind of aquatic environment. Rivers, streams, bogs, estuaries, bays, and the open ocean all support unique avian faunas.*

Bottom left: *The Amakihi, here on a Trematolobelia, is a representative species of a subtropical ecosystem.*

Bottom right: *A Hawaiian Acacia with climbing Pandanus exemplifies the subtropical ecosystem. Subtropical ecosystems are complex communities of plants and animals that are extremely sensitive.*

survive the extreme aridity. Characteristic species of the southwestern deserts include the Scaled Quail, the Elf Owl, the Gila Woodpecker, the Verdin, the Cactus Wren, the Greater Roadrunner, and the Phainopepla. The high sagebrush deserts include the Sage Grouse, the Sage Thrasher, the Sage Sparrow, and the Black-throated Sparrow.

Aquatic ecosystems. The aquatic ecosystems in North America vary from saltwater to freshwater, from shallow fast-flowing streams to deep slow-moving rivers, from small prairie "potholes" to the Great Lakes, from cold sphagnum bogs in the north to the Everglades in the south. The aquatic ecosystems support a diverse and specialized avifauna. For example, consider the prairie potholes, small lakes and ponds in the northern Great Plains created by huge melting chunks of glacial ice lodged in the ground. These wetlands are the main nesting area for many of our Mallard, Northern Pintail, and other duck populations. Gulls and terns nest in large colonies around the Great Lakes and along all the coasts. Herons and egrets abound in marshes and swamps throughout the continent, although no swamp seems so rich in bird life as the Everglades.

Subtropical ecosystems. Parts of southern California, southern Florida, and the Hawaiian Islands have subtropical ecosystems. Of the three areas, Hawaii has a unique avifauna because of its isolation from the mainland.

Deserts separate Southern California from the tropics; the Caribbean separates southern Florida. As a result, the native birds in these two regions are the same as those in adjacent temperate areas. The subtropical areas are, however, home to some tropical birds, including several species of parrots, New World tanagers, and Old World bulbuls. Introduced to the country by humans, the birds have been successful because of favorable climate and because of tropical plants which were also introduced.

Many of the exotic species are such recent immigrants that their potential impact on the native avifauna has not yet been assessed. In Hawaii, however, it is suspected that diseases brought in with certain exotic species have been detrimental to native birds (see page 111).

Habitats

A habitat is an environment—a portion of an ecosystem—that fulfills a bird's needs for food, water, shelter, and nesting. If a species habitually chooses a particular habitat—and many do—it is known as a habitat specialist. Even widespread species may be extremely narrow in their choice of habitat. For example, the Killdeer is common through most of North America, but within the varied ecosystems of the species' range it specializes in one habitat: open areas with patches of bare ground. The Killdeer particularly favors habitats close to bodies of water. The widespread Blue Jay, in contrast, always requires groves of trees.

Plants are often the most important element in any habitat. Fruit, berries, nuts, sap, and nectar completely satisfy the dietary needs of some birds. Because plants provide nourishment for insects, they are also essential to insect-eating birds. Additionally, plants provide various nest sites and shelter from weather and enemies. In arid environments, plants are an important source of moisture.

Some species are intimately associated with a particular plant. The Kirtland's Warbler, for example, nests only in young jack pine trees that spring up after a fire. When the trees grow large enough to shade the scrubby growth beneath, the warblers will no longer use them. This specific habitat requirement is one reason why the Kirtland's Warbler is now an endangered species—probably fewer than a thousand remain. They live on Michigan's lower peninsula where the U.S. Forest Service periodically burns jack-pine forest to provide the young trees that the birds need.

Larry West/Valenti Photo

The Kirtland's Warbler nests in the secondary growth of jack pines that springs up after a fire. When the pines mature the warblers must move to new, more recently burned areas. Many birds specialize in these and other kinds of temporary habitats and form what are called successional communities.

D. Cavagnaro/DRK Photo

Although wide ranging, the Killdeer only nests where there are patches of bare ground. In urban areas these birds have adapted by nesting in vacant lots, on flat rooftops, and along graveled parking lots.

An understanding of the habitat requirements of particular species can help you provide an appealing environment in your own backyard. (For information on bird-attracting plants, see the chart on page 167.) Such an understanding is also helpful if you are interested in locating particular species. Veteran bird-watchers know that one of the best places to look for a diversity of birds is at the boundary between two different kinds of habitat. Edges often provide an opportunity to see the birds that specialize in each bordering habitat. Some species—such as some of the hawks—prefer edge environments because the edges provide a greater diversity of prey.

"The Gallery of Birds" beginning on page 269 includes information on the habitats of many species. Used in conjunction with the range maps, this information will help you determine which birds are near you.

Niches

A niche is the role of a particular species—what it does—within its habitat. No two species perform precisely the same role in a particular habitat, at least not for long. If they do, competition for food and a place to live results, and one species eventually excludes the other. The competing species may also "compromise" by developing different niches. A great deal of ecological study is directed toward defining the niches of a species. Without that knowledge we cannot examine how human activities affect a given species or manage the conservation of species.

Competition is a powerful force that molds species' niches and sex- and age-specific niches within a species. For example, if males and females had to compete for limited food, pair-bonds might be weakened and nesting success diminished. Where resources are limited, the sexes of some species use the resources differently. For example, if you watch a Downy Woodpecker from a distance for 15 to 20 minutes, you can almost certainly guess the sex of the individual by its behavior. Males characteristically forage on small trees or on small branches of large trees; females typically forage on the trunks and larger limbs of large trees. The niches overlap, but the slight distinction limits competition between the sexes.

The three habitats represented in this picture—stream, pasture, and wooded slope—attract a greater diversity of birds than any single habitat. Boundaries between habitats also provide a greater variety of food and shelter. Some birds are found only in these areas.

Grant Heilman/Grant Heilman Photography

Ben Goldstein/Valenti Photo

H. Cruickshank/VIREO

Stephen J. Krasemann/DRK Photo

Creatures of Habitat

Ask any bird-watcher where to find a Cactus Wren or a Pileated Wood-pecker, and chances are that a veteran will be able to describe the kind of place the bird inhabits. An experienced birder can stop along a highway in the Southwest at a thicket of cholla cactus and say, "There ought to be a Cactus Wren here" or walk into a mature forest in the eastern United States and say, "This is right for Pileateds."

A species' habitat is predictable because it has traditionally provided food, nest sites, defendable territories, and conditions conducive to attracting mates. Through our efforts to find birds, we learn about their habitats; we learn that both quality and quantity are important. Pileated Woodpeckers, for example, may require 200 acres of mature forest.

Finding a bird that is rare within its normal range, or one with a special-ized niche, is not a matter of luck. First, by studying a particular species in depth, we find that its roosting sites, nesting sites, feeding sites, and song perches are quite predictable. Sometimes this predictability holds for only one region or one season; sometimes it holds anywhere or anytime. Later, as we become more familiar with a species, we can find it just by knowing the right combination of habitat characteristics—by having a mental im-age of the species' habitat and looking for a place that matches that image. Field guides often describe general habitats, but with experience the birder learns the particular combination of features within a habitat that attracts a particular species.

In central Wyoming, for example, Western Meadowlarks often place their nests in the midst of a dense patch of prickly-pear cactus where the pads are spread close to the ground. Once you have found one nest, the mental image of that nest helps you find a dozen more in a short time. But that image would be of little help in searching for Western Meadowlark nests in a Nebraska prairie, where there are no cacti, but where the species is just as common. There each nest is a little tent of grass, often with an opening to the south.

Above left: *A Cactus Wren builds its nest deep among the protective spines of a cholla cactus. These birds only nest where there are suitably dense thickets of cactus.*

Above center: *When the Pileated Woodpecker is not hammering at a post or tree, it may be found in a dense, mature coniferous or mixed woodland, where fallen logs provide abundant carpenter ants as food.*

Above: *In the eastern and central prairies the domed nests of the Western Meadowlark are built of grasses. Farther west the nests are more likely to be found in a clump of cactus. For many birds the choice of food or nest sites depends on re-sources most readily available, which vary from one place to another.*

O.S. Pettingill/VIREO

Irene Vandermolen/Leonard Rue Enterprises

Above: *The Upland Sandpiper likes to survey its domain from the top of a fence post. Look for these birds in upland meadows and pastures.*

Above right: *This Carolina Wren has chosen a potted begonia as a place to build its nest. Close proximity to humans and unlikely nest sites identify this bird over much of its range.*

Similarly, if you see a long-legged bird perched atop a fence post in the middle of a Kansas prairie, you can be fairly certain it is an Upland Sandpiper. If you see a group of white birds walking beside cows in an Alabama pasture, they are probably Cattle Egrets. Other birds have long legs and others are white, but they do not perch on fence posts or walk beside cows. The characteristics of the habitat coupled with behavior provide immediate cues for identification.

Say you live in the southeastern United States. You find a nest in an old shoe in your garage or in the fern in the hanging basket on your porch. You have probably found the work of a pair of Carolina Wrens. Other birds may nest close to humans, but in the Southeast such nest sites combined with proximity to humans is most characteristic of Carolina Wrens.

Some species have specific habitat needs related to their selection of a nest site, other species have needs related to their food supply, and for other species habitat specificity relates to nest site and food resources.

Nest-Site Specialists

Among the birds with narrow nest-site requirements are those that nest in cavities. Some birds, like woodpeckers, are called primary cavity nesters because they excavate their own cavities. Secondary cavity nesters are totally dependent on finding a ready-made home—often the work of one of the primary cavity nesters. Bluebirds, some swallows, wrens, flycatchers, kestrels, screech-owls, and vultures are secondary cavity nesters. Chickadees, titmice, and nuthatches often use ready-made cavities, but they can excavate their own if necessary.

Of these cavity-nesting birds, some can make their homes in a wide variety of nest sites, including the birdhouses that people build for them. Others, such as the Bank Swallow, are limited by the availability of suitable sites. A colony of these swallows may excavate a hundred or more cavities into steep earth banks along streams or at gravel pits. Suitable sites are few, and sites that are not flooded are fewer. The lack of suitable banks may explain why the Bank Swallow's nesting range barely reaches the southeastern states. A close relative, the Cliff Swallow, builds its cavity out of mud. The availability of mud of the right consistency and of nest supports limits the range of the Cliff Swallow. Today, it is common

Herbert Clarke

C.H. Greenewalt/VIREO

H. Cruickshank/VIREO

Far left: *This female American Kestral peers from a nest cavity that was originally excavated by a flicker. Old cavities are often scarce, which in some areas may limit the populations of these and other secondary cavity nesters.*

Left: *The Eastern Bluebird is a secondary cavity nester. These birds take readily to nest boxes that are placed in a preferred location such as an open field adjacent to a hedgerow or woodlot.*

The need for suitable banks in which to excavate nest burrows may, in part, limit the geographical range of these Bank Swallows. Such banks must be free from flooding, soft enough to excavate, and hard enough to prevent collapsing.

to see many Cliff Swallows nesting under the eaves of buildings and under concrete bridges as well as in traditional cliff sites.

The deserts of the Southwest provide another example of nest-site specialization. The cavities that many species of woodpeckers excavate deteriorate rapidly as fungi invade the moist environments. As a result these primary cavity nesters must create new nests each year, and nest sites for secondary cavity nesters are in short supply. The Gila Woodpecker, on the other hand, displays a useful specialty. It excavates cavities in giant saguaro cacti. The sap of the saguaro forms a hard glaze on the inside of the cavity, so a bird can use the same hole for several years. A Gila Woodpecker does not have to excavate a nest as frequently as other species in the same area, and abandoned Gila Woodpecker nests provide habitable sites for secondary nesters. The Gila Woodpecker is, therefore, an essential component in the habitat of some southwestern deserts.

The Red-cockaded Woodpecker, another nest-site specialist, is adapted for life in a mature pine forest. This bird usually selects a living pine over 75 years old as a nest site. These older trees are often infected with a fungus that softens the heartwood, making their nest excavation easier.

Other species are also limited by specific nest-site requirements. For example, Common Loons in Minnesota and other northern states seem best suited to lakes with tiny islands. A loon's legs are at the very back of the body. They are well adapted for swimming underwater, but they are not of much use for walking on land. A loon must nest on the ground where it can easily slip in and out of the water. Unless on an island, its nests are quite vulnerable to predators.

Food Specialists

Food specialization commonly limits habitat. For example, though the Snail Kite lives throughout Central and South America, its range in North America is limited to southern Florida by its extreme preference for the apple snail. In North America the Snail Kite can live only in the Florida marshes where the apple snail is found.

Most food specialists have physical adaptations, such as specially modified bills, that maximize efficiency of prey capture. It is no accident that

Right: The Snail Kite lives only in areas where the apple snail is found. The long hook on its beak helps to extract the snail from its broken shell.

Below: The specialized bill of the Red Crossbill is an efficient tool for extracting the seeds from pine and spruce cones. Because of their feeding requirements these birds must constantly wander in search of areas where trees are heavily laden with cones.

Below right: The bill of the American Oystercatcher is flattened from side to side, enabling the bird to pry open the shells of clams and mussels.

Wayne Lankinen/DRK Photo

H. Cruickshank/VIREO

H. Cruickshank/VIREO

an oyster shucker's knife resembles the flat, blunt, knife-like bill of the oystercatcher. The habitat of the American Oystercatcher is defined by its mollusk prey.

The Red Crossbill goes through life with its upper beak twisted in one direction and its lower beak twisted in the other. With such a bizarre tool it can deftly extract pine seeds from an open cone. Other birds have to wait until the seeds fall. Since it has such a narrow food preference, and since the abundance of pine cones varies with the weather, crossbills cannot remain in one area as most birds do. They must wander, searching for areas where the pines have had a good year. Movements that take crossbills out of their usual range are called irruptions. When the pine cone crop fails in the far north, for example, crossbills may irrupt into southern states to feed and nest, then move to another area when the food again becomes limited.

Habitat Generalists

Species that occur in a wide variety of habitats and that make do with whatever the habitat provides are called generalists. Their adaptability in choice of nest sites and food enables the generalists to be successful under diverse conditions. Food generalists can often remain in a cold climate, whereas insect specialists such as warblers must migrate to warmer climates. One of the reasons that the list of generalists contains so many familiar species is that they not only adapt to humans, they actually benefit from our presence. Generalists are, in fact, often most abundant near human habitation.

Perhaps the best-known generalist is the House Sparrow. Like most of us, its ancestors were immigrants; the House Sparrow was originally a European bird that was brought here to control garden insects. Many wagon trains in the last century took along a few caged House Sparrows to release at their destination. Although not prone to much wandering, this species has spread over most of North America.

As with most generalists, House Sparrows are nearly omnivorous and are not too particular about their nest sites, although they are generally cavity nesters. Extremely prolific birds, House Sparrows nest in outdoor lighting fixtures, in birdhouses, and in the nooks and crannies of buildings, as well as in trees. They are as adaptable in finding food as they are in finding nest sites. This adaptability makes them sturdy survivors. They have been known to feed at night under electric lights, to glean insects

Warren Jacobi/Berg & Associates

A House Sparrow demonstrates its adaptability by obtaining water from a drinking fountain. Opportunistic behavior such as this is characteristic of generalist species.

H. Cruickshank/VIREO

The Common Grackle is an example of a native generalist. In many places, grackles are more common in urban habitats than they are in their more natural rural habitats.

from car radiator grills, and to survive severe winters in Manitoba by taking advantage of the warmth of buildings, and of waste grain and other foods resulting from human activities.

It is hard to imagine a native North American species with as broad a niche as the House Sparrow, but the niche of the American Robin may exceed it in some ways. The House Sparrow, though more adaptable in terms of food and nest site, is never far from human habitation; the robin is at home in urban areas and wilderness forest. Other notable North American generalists include the Northern Mockingbird, the Common Grackle, crows, and jays.

Climate

The habitat of a species and what the species does within that habitat, are, to a large extent, orchestrated by climate. Climate is the great equalizer among species—all have to cope with it or die.

Photoperiod

Although we cannot predict all aspects of climate—the precise temperature or the direction and force of the wind on a certain day, for example—seasons and the progression of night to day are predictable. We know that it is cold in certain seasons and warm during others. We know that June 21 is the longest day of the year, and that December 21 is the shortest day of the year. We also know that in the Arctic there are 24 hours of darkness for a time in winter and 24 hours of daylight for a time in summer. This information is predictable because of the regularity of the earth's rotation around the sun and the earth's spinning on its axis.

In temperate latitudes perhaps the single greatest influence on the activities of birds is photoperiod, the number of hours of daylight in a day. The length of daylight seems to be the primary cue for birds to initiate different phases of activity. For example, long before the winds of winter put a chill in the air, birds begin to accumulate body fat in preparation for the cold weather.

In temperate zones, the changes in photoperiod provide birds, flowers, and humans with a natural calendar. The changing photoperiod is particularly important to migrating birds; it stimulates the return migration, the

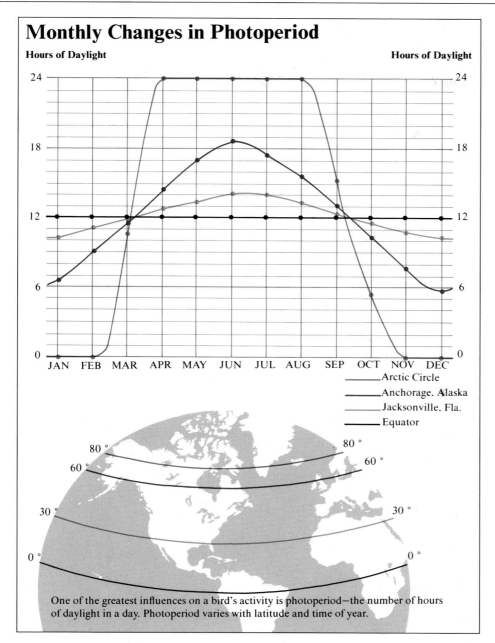

Monthly Changes in Photoperiod

Hours of Daylight

Hours of Daylight

_____ Arctic Circle
_____ Anchorage, Alaska
_____ Jacksonville, Fla.
_____ Equator

One of the greatest influences on a bird's activity is photoperiod—the number of hours of daylight in a day. Photoperiod varies with latitude and time of year.

development of reproductive organs, and the initiation of courtship, nest-building, and egg-laying. In tropical environments the photoperiod is relatively constant—12 hours of daylight and 12 hours of darkness. In the tropics nature provides other cues, such as the beginning of the rainy season.

Changes in photoperiod do more than provide natural cues. The longer days of summer allow adult birds to feed their young for a longer period each day. A shorter period of night means a shorter period of fasting for young birds. Therefore, birds at northern latitudes can often raise more young than birds of the same species farther south. In the same manner, however, birds at northern latitudes may not be able to spend the winter where they breed, even if they can tolerate the cold. They cannot eat enough during the hours of daylight to sustain the high rate of metabolism they need to survive the long, cold night. Other factors influence birds' activities, but most relate in one way or another to photoperiod.

Temperature

Although temperature is related to photoperiod, temperature as a single factor does affect bird behavior. A freeze kills much of the vegetation and the insects that many northern birds need. The loss of a reliable food source without a change in photoperiod could cause some birds to migrate. (For more on migration, see the chapter beginning on page 137.)

Maintenance of a constant high body temperature becomes increasingly difficult in cold environments, especially for smaller birds. Thus, many of the small northern birds that overwinter in cold environments must take advantage of tree cavities or other shelter, or they must roost in groups to minimize heat loss. For example, 20 or more Brown Creepers might roost in a tight mass beneath a piece of loose tree bark. On a cold Tennessee night, several bluebirds might crowd into the same birdhouse or roosting box for warmth. (For information on helping birds keep warm during periods of cold weather, see page 219.)

Physical adaptations. Many species have adapted physically to regional variations in climate. One type of adaptation is summarized by Bergmann's Rule, which states that within a species, individuals that live in colder climates have larger bodies than do those in warmer climates. A bird with a larger body has less surface area relative to the volume of its body. This means that it has relatively less area through which it can lose heat; it is more efficient at retaining heat. Think back to a time when you were cold and did not have a jacket. You probably pulled your arms in close to your body or even huddled down—you decreased the surface area from which you could lose heat.

The Mallard is one species of waterfowl that spends the winter as far north as open water will permit. Waterproof feathers, a layer of fat, and specially adapted blood circulation through the feet help to minimize heat loss.

Don & Pat Valenti

Another rule, Allen's Rule, also explains patterns of variation. This rule suggests that birds in colder environments have relatively smaller appendages than those in warm environments. The result is an increased ability to retain heat. In warm environments, smaller body size and relatively longer appendages enable a bird to keep cool by ridding itself of excess body heat.

The Hairy Woodpecker provides an example of both these rules. Found from near the tree line in Alaska and Canada to western Panama in Central America, this single species encompasses birds in Alaska that weigh more than 120 grams to birds in the tropics that weigh less than 40 grams. Other body proportions vary similarly. Because colder climates are associated with montane areas as well as northern latitudes, we also find larger Hairy Woodpeckers—or the larger birds of most species—farther south in the mountains. The ocean also affects climate; coastal areas do not get as cold as adjacent inland areas, and we find smaller birds of most species extending farther north along the Pacific coast. Within a species, the changes are so gradual that each population is capable of interbreeding with the next.

Birds show other morphological, physiological, and behavioral adaptations to the rigors of climate. For example, have you ever wondered how a duck can tolerate icy water on a cold winter day? First realize that no matter how cold the air temperature is, the temperature of unfrozen water cannot be below 32° F (0° C). The water may actually be the warmest place in the area. In addition the duck has physical adaptations that protect it from any chilling effect of the water. A thick layer of down covered by waterproof feathers traps air in and keeps water out. A thick layer of fat just under the skin provides additional insulation. But what about those bare legs sticking down into the cold water? They also provide an example of adaptation to climatic extremes. The arteries carrying warm blood from the body lie right next to the veins carrying cold blood from the feet. The warm blood going to the feet warms the cold blood so effectively that the blood going back to the body is nearly the same temperature as the blood that is leaving. In addition the vessels are constricted; they allow just enough warm blood to flow to the feet to keep them from freezing. During summer heat the blood vessels dilate; the flow of warm blood to the legs increases and excess heat is lost.

Color can also enhance heating or cooling. Black birds absorb much more of the sun's warmth than white birds; thus, black is a thermally adaptive color in cold weather, and white is thermally adaptive in hot weather. However, a number of other factors also influence color—camouflage and mate attraction, for example. As a result the role of color in the regulation of body temperature is often unclear.

Behavioral adaptations. A bird's behavior can also help it cope with cold. It may tuck its bill under the feathers of its back or wing, draw one leg up into its feathers, or fluff its feathers to trap a larger volume of air. It may stay in the sun and position its body to maximize heat absorption or remain in areas sheltered from the wind. Under extreme conditions of cold and lack of food, birds such as the Common Poorwill and some hummingbirds adapt by going into a state of torpor in which metabolism slows and body temperature drops drastically. Some birds have apparently survived for up to three months in this state of dormancy. Hummingbirds commonly seem to spend cold nights in a state of torpor.

Excessive heat also causes behavioral adaptations. One of the most common cooling mechanisms is gular fluttering. Gular fluttering consists of rapidly contracting and relaxing the muscles of the throat. The movement maximizes the flow of air over the moist membranes of the mouth.

Robert A. Tyrrell

Because of their extremely high metabolism, hummingbirds cannot withstand thermal stress due to heat loss. To avoid this problem, Ruby-throated Hummingbirds, such as this female, go into torpor, a condition similar to mammalian hibernation.

Jerome Jackson

Unable to sweat during hot weather, this Killdeer resorts to gular fluttering to keep cool in the same manner that dogs cool themselves by panting. Because the ground temperature may far exceed that required for incubation, the bird must shade its eggs to prevent them from overheating.

The bird is cooled by evaporation from those membranes as a dog is cooled by panting.

Evaporative cooling is crucial to birds because they do not have sweat glands. Birds that nest in open environments in hot climates have a special problem: These birds often have difficulty keeping their eggs cool. Killdeer, Snowy Plovers, and several species of terns stand over their eggs to shade them on warm days. When temperatures rise, some birds fly to the nearest water, soak their breast feathers, and return to the nest to wet their eggs or chicks. Belly-soaking also helps to cool the adult at the nest. Wood Storks and New World vultures use another unusual method of keeping cool: They excrete on their legs and rely on evaporation from the excrement to cool the blood going back to the body.

Precipitation

The places birds prefer to live are largely related to the species and structural diversity of plant communities. The amount and timing of rainfall or snowfall influences plant growth and so affects the distribution and abundance of birds. For example, the extensive irrigation of farmlands in the Great Plains has resulted in the growth of trees in grassland areas. The trees provide habitat for tree-living birds that have expanded their breeding ranges into the area.

Water influences the ecology of birds in other ways too. Spring floods, for instance, can destroy nests. Some species have adapted to reduce such losses. The Pied-billed Grebe builds a floating nest of decaying vegetation and anchors it loosely to aquatic plants in backwaters, ponds, and lakes. As the water level rises, the nest floats upward; when the water level drops, the nest drops. The Clapper Rail nests in coastal marshes that are occasionally flooded by storm tides. If the water rises slowly enough, the rails work frantically to build their nests higher and keep their eggs above water. Of course if the water rises too fast, the nests are swept away.

Snow and ice often cover the foods of northern birds in winter, which is one reason why so many northern birds migrate. When freezing rain coats the tails of roosting birds, their only escape is to leave tail feathers behind. This loss makes the birds more vulnerable to predators and renders flight less efficient at a time when energy demands are already high.

H. Cruickshank/VIREO

H. Cruickshank/VIREO

The floating nest of a Pied-billed Grebe can tolerate the fluctuations in water levels that often occur in its aquatic habitat. Floating nests are common among marsh-nesting birds.

A somewhat less reliable means of coping with fluctuating water levels is adopted by birds like this Clapper Rail, which adds nesting material to the nest when the water level rises. If the water rises too rapidly the nest may become inundated.

Fire

In some ecosystems fire is disastrous. It destroys birds and the habitats they require. In other ecosystems, however, fire plays an important and positive role. Without recurrent fires those ecosystems and some of the species in them could not exist. A natural or prescribed fire maintains the ecosystem in much the same way you maintain your yard by mowing it.

Fire played an important role in the ancient redwood and pine forests of North America. By opening up the forest, eliminating some tree species, and influencing the growth of others, fire created unique habitats for specialized birds such as the White-headed Woodpecker and the Kirtland's Warbler. (For more on the Kirtland's Warbler, see page 91.)

Lightning is the primary source of natural fire in the environment. In North America the highest incidence of thunderstorms occurs in the extreme Southeast, where they occur on more than 80 days per year. It is not surprising, therefore, that the Southeast provides many examples of trees and birds that have special adaptations to survive frequent fires.

The upland areas of the southeastern coastal plain of North America used to be covered with forests of longleaf pines—a tree that is specially adapted to grow in an environment that is burned every two to four years. Thick bark protects the growing tissues of the tree, and as the long needles burn they release moisture that cools the growing tip and allows a spurt of growth after the fire. Hardwood trees that grow in bottomland areas are not at all tolerant of fire; they are eliminated from upland areas when fire sweeps through. On the other hand, hardwood trees are shade-tolerant, and pines are not. Young southern pine seedlings can survive only in the sunlight and thus cannot invade the shady recesses of moist bottomlands where the hardwoods reign. Similarly, if fire is excluded from the uplands by fire-control measures, hardwoods invade, and young pines die in the shade. The parent pines, with crowns in the sun, witness the birth of a new ecosystem and the death of their own. Thus, southern pine forests are fire ecosystems; their existence is dependent on recurrent fire.

Where in the past a fire caused by lightning might burn for a hundred miles across the coastal plain, today natural fires are generally restricted to a few hundred acres. The lesser frequency and limitation of natural fires results in a buildup of dead materials on the ground. When fires do come to such a buildup, they are very hot and destroy much more life than relatively cool fires in areas with limited litter. In addition, southern pines are being crowded out by hardwood trees, and the birds that depend on the open pine forests are disappearing (see page 110).

Forest managers know the value of frequent fire in promoting the growth of fire-adapted species and in preventing infrequent but disastrous fires. Prescribed burning has become a common practice in areas that would have been naturally burned at frequent intervals. Prescribed burning is crucial for the preservation of the birds of the pine forests.

A slash pine forest is burned to destroy the undergrowth. Prescribed burns replace natural fires and are an important management technique that prevents the pine forests from becoming invaded by hardwoods.

Marty Cordano/DRK Photo

Thomas D. Mangelsen

A pair of Whooping Cranes prepares to land near a meltwater pond during spring migration. In 1941 only 23 of these birds existed. Today, through intensive management programs, the wild population totals over 100.

Modern Times

The diversity of birds we enjoy today is in large part due to the diversity of environments. Most birds—even many we have called generalists—are specialists in one way or another; they excel at exploiting a particular element of their habitat. If all birds were generalists, we would have fewer species—competition would eliminate all but the best of them. Fortunately, however, such a situation would not last because birds would most likely compete and evolve back into specialists. The extreme specialists are particularly vulnerable to environmental change, however. Those that are unable to adapt become extinct.

Endangered Bird Life

Changes in vegetation can make a habitat less acceptable or even unacceptable to a species, while at the same time making it more acceptable to a competitor, predator, or parasite. Such changes do occur naturally, but the incidence of such changes and the severity of their effects on bird communities have greatly accelerated in this century due to human influences.

Natural extinctions result from a species' inability to cope with natural environmental change. The changes may be gradual, such as the changes caused by widespread glaciation, or they may be instantaneous, such as the changes caused by a volcanic eruption. A natural extinction may be a result of common occurrences such as competition, predation, or disease.

Thomas D. Mangelsen

The majestic Bald Eagle became dangerously rare during the 1960s and 1970s from preying on fish that were contaminated with DDT. Although banned in North America in 1972, DDT is still used by some Latin American countries. As a result, North American birds that winter in these areas are still exposed to this toxic chemical.

Endangered Species

This list includes species of the continental United States, Hawaii, and Canada. In some cases, the endangered state pertains only to certain subspecies of a particular bird.

Akepa
Akialoa, Kauai
Akiapolaau
Albatross, Short-tailed
Bobwhite, Northern
Condor, California
Coot, American
Crane, Sandhill
Crane, Whooping
Creeper, Hawaii
Creeper, Molokai
Creeper, Oahu
Crow, Hawaiian
Curlew, Eskimo
Duck, Hawaiian
Duck, Laysan
Eagle, Bald
Falcon, Peregrine
Finch, Laysan
Finch, Nihoa
Goose, Canada
Goose, Hawaiian
Hawk, Hawaiian

Honeycreeper, Crested
Kite, Snail
Millerbird
Moorhen, Common
Nukupuu
Oo, Kauai
Ou
Palila
Parrot, Thick-billed
Parrotbill, Maui
Pelican, Brown
Petrel, Dark-rumped
Plover, Piping
Poo-uli
Prairie-Chicken, Greater
Rail, Clapper
Shearwater, Townsend's
Shrike, Loggerhead
Sparrow, Sage
Sparrow, Seaside
Stilt, Black-necked
Stork, Wood
Tern, Least
Thrush, Large Kauai
Thrush, Small Kauai
Warbler, Bachman's
Warbler, Kirtland's
Woodpecker, Ivory-billed
Woodpecker, Red-cockaded

Adapted from "Endangered and Threatened Wildlife and Plants," by the United States Department of the Interior, Fish and Wildlife Service (January 1, 1986).

With only about 10 California Condors left in existence, hope for this species lies in the captive breeding program now being conducted at the San Diego Zoo. Habitat loss and poisoning led to the decline of this bird.

Since the seventeenth century, most cases of extinction have clearly been caused by human actions. In the sixteenth century, nearly half of the in the United States—over 820 million square miles—was forested. Rivers were free flowing, marshes and swamps were undrained. Beaches and gravel bars were not periodically disturbed by dredges or racing dune buggies. Equally important, the air, land, water, and living organisms were not contaminated with pesticides, PCBs (polychlorinated biphenyls), and other by-products of human "progress."

During the past few centuries, advances in technology and a growing human population have enabled us to change the physical and biotic structure of any region—and we are doing so. As we have changed the environment, some species of birds have become more abundant, some have decreased in number, and some have become extinct.

Habitat destruction. By far the most serious threat to birds today is habitat destruction. By 1900 nearly half of the forests of North America were gone. These forests had provided the raw materials for housing, fuel, furniture, and transportation. The supply of wood seemed inexhaustible. Today we know it is not.

A supply of wood for human use in the foreseeable future is assured by the forest industry, which replants after cutting. Modern forests differ substantially from those that greeted the founders of our nation, however. Then the forests consisted primarily of old trees, many hundreds of years old. Young growth replaced them as the old trees fell to disease, wind, or fire. Today's forests are agricultural crops; a grower plants a single, commercially important species and harvests all the trees at the same time.

Commercial forests seldom provide the diversity of ecological niches that many birds require. This 30-year-old slash pine planting will be harvested long before the trees are large enough for the birds that depend on mature forests for their habitat.

Grant Heilman/Grant Heilman Photography

Left: *Previously this contoured farmland was heavily wooded. The advent of agriculture in areas that were once eastern hardwood forests has resulted in many prairie birds expanding their ranges eastward.*

Below: *The planting of windbreaks and hedgerows has opened the prairies to woodland birds. Many eastern species have now expanded their ranges as far west as the foothills of the Rocky Mountains.*

Larry Lefever/Grant Heilman Photography

Grant Heilman/Grant Heilman Photography

A modern, commercial forest is incapable of supporting the diversity of birds that occurs in a forest of mixed trees. Furthermore, commercial forests are often harvested at early ages. Southern pines, for example, are cut for pulp after 20 years and for lumber after 40 years. Southern pines more than one hundred years old are now rare, although their natural potential longevity is in excess of 250 years. The ages of harvest differ for other tree species, but the result is that the birds who depend on older trees suffer.

Management of our forests for commercial purposes is not the only cause of habitat loss. An increasing percentage of land is now used for agriculture, cities, highways, and other human activities. Other habitats have been grossly altered to the detriment of bird life. Prairie-chickens, for example, have disappeared from most of their range because most natural prairie has been replaced by farms and agricultural crops. Wetland species suffer from the draining of our wetlands. The southern end of the San Joaquin Valley in California used to be a marsh that was a winter home for hundreds of thousands of waterfowl. Today the water is channeled into aqueducts and irrigation systems upstream. The valley is now a fertile agricultural region, but it is of little value to the waterfowl that once depended on it. Elsewhere, the channels and dams that we have built have eliminated the sandbars that provided nesting habitat. As a result the Interior Least Tern became an endangered species in 1985.

Habitat losses are serious in North America, but they are not exclusive to it. In the South American tropics, where a large percentage of our North American songbirds spend each winter, habitat destruction results from the cut-and-move-on philosophy prevalent in North America nearly a century ago. Even more unfortunate, the perpetrators of the destruction are using bulldozers and other heavy machinery—machines that, from the ecological perspective, are some of the most destructive of modern technology. In addition to providing wintering grounds for many North American species, the South American tropics boast the greatest diversity of birds anywhere in the world; therefore, the impact of habitat destruction in South America is extremely serious.

Hundreds of Wilson's Phalaropes gather along the shore of a shallow lake. Every year thousands of acres of wetland habitat are drained for agriculture. In some areas, runoff from irrigated fields has dramatically increased the salinity of the water, making it useless for freshwater-seeking birds.

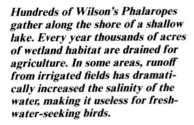

Wardene Weisser/Berg & Associates

H. Cruickshank/VIREO

Introduced in New York City toward the end of the 1800s, the European Starling has spread from coast to coast. Noisy and aggressive, this bird often outcompetes native birds for cavity-nesting sites.

Introduction of exotic species. Habitat destruction may be the worst problem facing birds today, but it is far from the only problem. The introduction of exotic species, particularly the House Sparrow and the European Starling, has wreaked havoc with North American cavity nesting birds such as the Eastern Bluebird. In Hawaii, exotic birds and the diseases introduced with them may have caused the extinction of a number of native species. Although our only native parrot, the Carolina Parakeet, was hunted to extinction, a number of exotic parrots now breed in southern Florida and southern California. It is too soon to evaluate the damage these newcomers may do to our native avifauna, but competition between exotics and native species is likely.

Biomagnification. Development of new pesticides in the 1940s held promise for worldwide control of vectors of human disease and serious crop pests. But some of these pesticides, such as DDT, proved to be persistent in the environment, and a major controversy developed over the possible pesticide residuals in living tissue. It was felt that some of the best avian predators—including the Brown Pelican, the Osprey, the Bald Eagle, and the Peregrine Falcon—might have accumulated DDT at levels higher than that in the environment, a process called biomagnification. Through biomagnification seemingly harmless levels of pesticides may have the potential of becoming harmful. One consequence often attributed to widespread use of DDT was that many birds of prey were laying thin-shelled eggs, which provided less than normal protection to the developing embryos inside.

Many pesticides used today have only an immediate effect—they break down quickly and cannot be concentrated in living tissues. But other chemical pollutants such as PCBs (used in the electrical industry) and lead have also taken a toll. With fewer than a dozen California Condors left in the wild, the death of one from lead poisoning makes the future of the species look bleak. The condors often feed on animals that have been shot, and they eat the lead bullet along with the flesh. Ducks may also eat lead shot that has fallen to the bottom of heavily hunted marshes; they may be unable to distinguish the pellets from the foods they scoop from the water.

Jerome Jackson

The conservation efforts of concerned citizens and wildlife groups have proved invaluable in preserving key habitats for birds. Here Black Skimmers nest in a protected colony next to a busy highway.

Since the North American ban on DDT in 1972, Brown Pelicans have made a surprising comeback and can now be found nesting in areas where the birds were never seen before.

Jerome Jackson

Undoing the Damage

On a more positive note, new public policies and conservation efforts have helped some of the endangered species make a comeback during the past decade. The Brown Pelican in the Southeast is one success story. After several years on the endangered species list, the Brown Pelican is now doing well and has expanded its southeastern nesting range to include areas where it had never been known to nest.

Another success story is that of the Least Tern on the northern Gulf Coast. Populations that were naturally small as a result of predators and a lack of suitable nesting habitat declined even further as coastal environments were developed and exploited. In the early 1970s, following conservation efforts of concerned citizens, protection was given to a small number of nesting birds. By the early 1980s and with public sentiment in the birds' favor, a nesting colony within 30 feet of busy U.S. Highway 90 had grown to over 3,000 pairs—the largest colony of terns in the world. Although California terns and inland tern populations are still on the federal endangered species list, populations have also increased dramatically in coastal Mississippi. Additionally, the Least Tern has enhanced its own chances of survival by beginning to nest on the flat rooftops of shopping malls in the Southeast. Such adaptability and public concern bodes well for the southern populations of the Least Tern.

Not all species will be as lucky, but, in concert with strong public support, state and federal laws can do a great deal to protect quality habitats in North America for resident birds. We can begin by being aware of the health of natural environments around us. Not only do healthy environments support healthy bird populations, they help assure a healthy life for humans. To further conservation efforts and protect natural environments, citizens need to be informed, they must be aware of conservation programs and offer support when possible, and they must voice opinions to the state and national politicians and agencies responsible for protecting environmental resources. International efforts are also desperately needed to assure that the songsters that herald our spring have a place to return from.

The list on the right cites a few of the hundreds of groups in North America that are concerned about birds and the conservation of their habitats. Nearly every state has an ornithological society, and many communities have chapters of some of the listed national organizations. For information about groups in your area, contact your public library, a local natural history museum, or the biology departments at local colleges or universities.

Sharing Our Homes

Birds are more than just coinhabitants of our world. Their colors, their songs, their behavior, their mere presence are sources of pleasure for all of us. An understanding of where they live and nest, how they interact with their environments, and what kinds of foods they prefer provides the key not only to attracting these creatures to our homes but to finding them in natural environments away from our homes.

Avian ecology reminds us of the complexity and diversity of our ecosystems and the role that humans have played in changing them. Over the years, birds have become more valuable to us as indicators of environmental problems. Canaries have been taken into coal mines to test air quality; Bald Eagles and other species have shown us the negative effects of DDT. In the future, a watchful eye on the birds will help us keep our ecosystems flourishing.

Friends of Birds

American Ornithologists'
  Union
National Museum of Natural
  History
Smithsonian Institution
Washington, DC 20560

Cooper Ornithological Society
Museum of Vertebrate
  Zoology
2593 Life Sciences Building
University of California
Berkeley, CA 94720

Defenders of Wildlife
1244 Nineteenth Street, N.W.
Washington, DC 20036

International Council for Bird
  Preservation
645 Pennsylvania Ave., S.E.
Washington, DC 20009

National Audubon Society
645 Pennsylvania Ave., S.E.
Washington, DC 20009

National Wildlife Federation
1412 Sixteenth Street, N.W.
Washington, DC 20036

Sierra Club
730 Polk Street
San Francisco, CA 94109

The Wilderness Society
1400 Eye Street, N.W.
  10th Floor
Washington, DC 20005

The Wildlife Society
5410 Grosvenor Lane
Bethesda, MD 20814

Wilson Ornithological Society
Van Tyne Library
Museum of Zoology
University of Michigan
Ann Arbor, MI 48109

World Wildlife Fund
The Conservation Foundation
1255 Twenty-third St., N.W.
  Suite 200
Washington, DC 20037

J. Dawson '86

The Miracle of Flight

by Susan Roney Drennan

The miracle of flight has fascinated people for thousands of years. Unrestrained, soaring flight of birds has long been a universal symbol of freedom of mind and spirit. Birds in flight are depicted on the walls of ancient caves and in many other Paleolithic works of art. During the Renaissance, Leonardo da Vinci was fascinated with flight and devoted much of his life to studying birds. For years he studied the anatomy and physiology of their wings, their musculature, and their feathers. In a collection of notebooks, "The Codex on the Flight of Birds," da Vinci describes his dreams and inventions for human flight including a pair of self-propelled wings and a mechanical flying machine, both of which have since been used in designing airplanes and helicopters.

In this century we have devised many ingenious flying machines—airplanes, helicopters, hang gliders—in imitation of these feathered creatures, but nothing we have created has ever matched or could ever match the beauty, the grace, the majesty, of a bird in flight.

Hummingbirds beat their wings at a fantastic rate, yet they appear motionless when hovering over a flower. Here, male and female Broad-tailed Hummingbirds feed at skyrocket flowers.

Stephen J. Krasemann/DRK Photo

Gliding low over the water, a Brown Pelican exercises precise control over the air currents around it. Flight has characterized birds for some 140 million years.

From the Ground to the Skies

Though there is much speculation and disagreement about the details of the evolution of flight, it is possible to roughly theorize the course of events. First, there was probably a small, scaly, dinosaurlike reptile that moved on all fours. Through the habit of feeding on objects just above its reach, this reptile raised itself more and more frequently on its hind legs, until these legs became its principal means of support. From running along the ground, it took to the trees, making its way among them by jumping from branch to branch. The first toe changed its position and evolved into a hind claw that gave the reptile a better grip. Then another key change probably occurred: The scales on the forelimbs as well as those on the sides of its tail became longer and formed small planes. This modification continued over the flanks and gradually extended over the entire body. At the same time the scales became frayed at the ends, taking on more of the characteristics of feathers. As the "arms" became increasingly winglike, the animal used them more in gliding from tree to tree. Powerful breast muscles developed, and there was an equally significant modification in the breastbone to accommodate the muscles. The respiratory system became more complex and extremely efficient.

Then, in theory, due to the increased activity of climbing, gliding, and finally flapping, these cold-blooded, sluggish reptiles slowly developed into warm-blooded animals. The newly acquired feathers acted to insulate and protect them from the cold. The "arms" adapted themselves as wings, the long tail became shorter, and many of the bones fused into a compact mass. The animal developed a strong, large heart. Bones throughout the

Avian Evolution

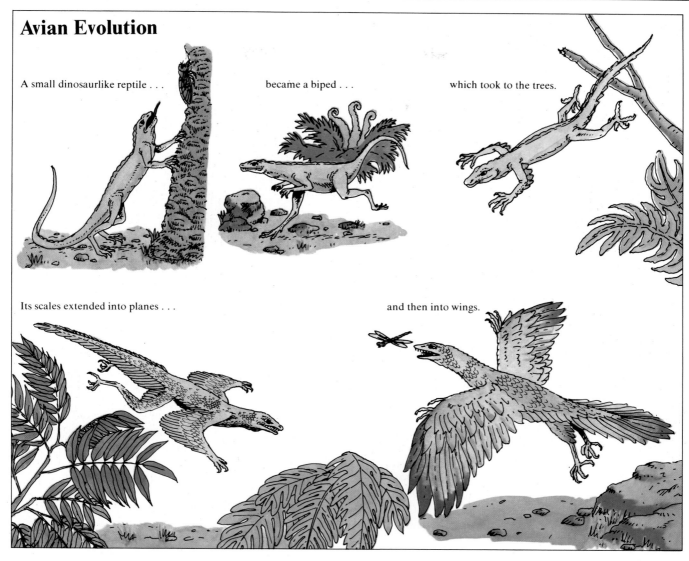

A small dinosaurlike reptile . . .

became a biped . . .

which took to the trees.

Its scales extended into planes . . .

and then into wings.

body became hollow and filled with air, and the air sacs of its lungs expanded. These changes provided an ideal framework for a flying machine. The brain of this creature, compared with that of its ancestor, grew to many times its former size and also became more complex. The scaly, reptilian, centuries-old creature had evolved into something new. At last, approximately 140 million years ago, in the age when the reptiles we know as dinosaurs ruled the land, the earth was populated by the first known bird, Archaeopteryx. (For more information on Archaeopteryx and other ancient birds, see page 26.)

How Do Birds Fly?

Birds have a number of physical characteristics that give them the ability to fly. These qualities—hollow bones; flexible, strong, yet lightweight feathers; huge pectoral muscles; complex, efficient circulatory and respiratory systems—essentially keep their weight low and their power output high. Another practical trait that keeps birds light is that the female has only one ovary, and both sexes have small reproductive organs. During the nonbreeding season birds' reproductive organs decrease in size almost to the point of atrophy.

The Avian Skeleton

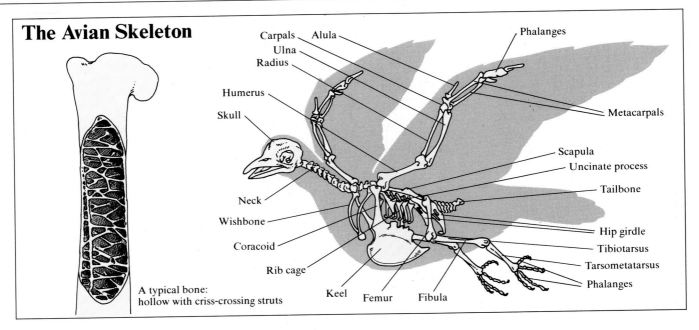

A typical bone:
hollow with criss-crossing struts

Carpals · Alula
Ulna
Radius
Humerus
Skull
Neck
Wishbone
Coracoid
Rib cage
Keel   Femur   Fibula

Phalanges
Metacarpals
Scapula
Uncinate process
Tailbone
Hip girdle
Tibiotarsus
Tarsometatarsus
Phalanges

A Lightweight Skeleton

The fact that a pelican approximately 5 feet long and weighing nearly 20 pounds has a skeleton weighing only 23 ounces indicates how perfectly a bird's skeleton is adapted to its capacity for flight. The reason the skeleton is so lightweight is that many bones in a bird's skeleton are hollow. The hollow bones are honeycombed with air spaces and strengthened by criss-crossing struts. The number of hollow bones varies from species to species, though large gliding and soaring birds tend to have the most. In general, the more efficient fliers seem to have more bones that are hollow.

A bird's streamlining for flight is perhaps best exemplified in the evolution of the skull, which is composed mainly of thin, hollow bones. A bird's skull is extremely light in proportion to the rest of its body due to elimination of a heavy jaw, jaw muscles, and teeth; the job of chewing has largely been replaced by the gizzard. The skull usually represents less than 1 percent of a bird's total body weight.

Although a present-day bird has fewer bones than its ancestors, its skeleton is strong enough for flight due to fusion of many of its bones. Forming rigid girders and platforms, fusion strengthens bones in the skull, chest region, pelvis, wings, and portions of the backbone. Some of the vertebrae in the backbone are fused together for rigidity, and others are not, allowing for mobility. Vertebrae in the lower back are joined, as are the bones of the hip girdle, forming a light but strong plate that rests on the thigh bones and supports the bird when it is on the ground. Overlapping projections (similar to cartilage) near the backbone, called the uncinate processes, add strength to the rib cage. Formed by fusion of the collarbones at their base, the wishbone offers structural support for the wings. In flying birds the breastbone is fused to a deep keel (a longitudinal ridge of bone) that provides an anchor for the powerful flight muscles. Generally, the deeper the keel the more powerful the flight.

In contrast to the rigidity in much of a bird's skeleton, the neck is extremely mobile. This flexible neck is of great value in enabling a bird to see danger approaching from any direction, to catch its prey, and to preen its feathers. Flexibility is increased by the large number of neck vertebrae, which range from about 11 to about 25. In comparison, mammals—even the giraffe—have only 7 neck vertebrae.

M. P. Kahl/DRK Photo

R. Ricklefs/VIREO

Although lightweight and hollow, a bird's bones are extremely strong. Northern Gannets, seen here in a cliffside colony, will—in pursuit of fish—plunge into the water from altitudes of several hundred feet.

Flying requires a streamlined body structure and a low center of gravity. To achieve this, these Caribbean Flamingos must hold their long flexible necks straight to counterbalance the weight of their legs. In flight, both the neck and the legs are held lower than the body.

The Respiratory System

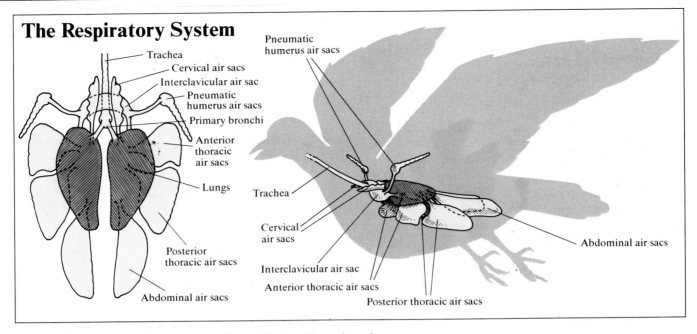

Full-Body Respiration

Ounce for ounce, a bird in flight requires more energy than a terrestrial mammal. Especially when migrating, birds fly at altitudes where oxygen is in such short supply that no mammal could possibly survive. Birds therefore have evolved a respiratory system that is fundamentally different from the mammalian respiratory system.

Like mammals, birds have two symmetrical lungs that are connected to a trachea (windpipe). But here the similarity ends. Mammalian lungs contain many bronchi (tubes), which lead to small sacs called alveoli. Because alveoli have only one opening, air can flow into and out of them, but it can *never* flow through them to the outside of a lung.

In a bird, air flows through the bronchi to several thin-walled air sacs. These air sacs fill a large proportion of the chest and abdominal cavity, and also connect to the air spaces in the bones. Two primary bronchi, leading from the trachea, and a number of secondary bronchi, leading from the primary bronchi, feed air into the *abdominal air sacs*, the largest of the bird's air sacs. Some of the secondary bronchi, which spread over the lower surface of each lung, channel air to the *anterior air sacs*. Also leading from the primary bronchi are between 7 and 10 dorsal bronchi, which spread over the back and sides of each lung, and ventral bronchi, which spread over the front of each lung. Finally there is a network of tertiary bronchi, which connects the ventral bronchi with the dorsal bronchi. Arising directly from the tertiary bronchi are *air capillaries*, which are responsible for the gas exchange between the ventilation system and the blood that transports oxygen to the body cells where it is needed for respiration.

The passage of air through a bird's lungs is similar to water moving through a sponge: Air flows directly through the lungs and into the adjacent air sacs. The theory is that the air sacs might very well function like bellows to drive air through the lungs.

Unlike mammalian lungs, in which the volume of air changes with each inhalation and exhalation, avian lungs maintain a constant volume of air. Because of the air sacs, the lungs inflate but do not deflate to take in more oxygen; they hold air. If its lungs inflated and deflated with every breath, a bird in flight would be continually gaining and losing altitude.

Sharon Chester

As part of the respiratory system, air sacs are important for all flying birds in maintaining a constant buoyancy; they also increase the efficiency of the respiratory system. In some birds the air sacs have become modified to function as a courtship display, as seen in this Magnificent Frigatebird male.

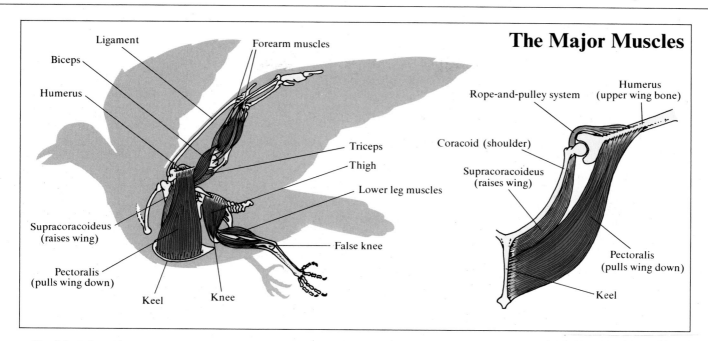

The Major Muscles

Ligament — Forearm muscles
Biceps
Humerus
Triceps
Thigh
Lower leg muscles
Supracoracoideus (raises wing)
Pectoralis (pulls wing down)
Keel — Knee
False knee

Rope-and-pulley system — Humerus (upper wing bone)
Coracoid (shoulder)
Supracoracoideus (raises wing)
Pectoralis (pulls wing down)
Keel

Besides the advantage of keeping them on course, the avian respiratory system enables birds to maintain a higher energy level than mammals, since mammals lose energy just by breathing. Although the rate of respiration varies somewhat with the age of the bird, it is, in general, inversely proportional to body size—the smaller the bird, the faster its breath rate.

Powerful Muscles

A bird has some 175 different muscles controlling the movements of its wings, legs, feet, jaws, tongue, eyes, ears, neck, lungs, sound-producing organs, body wall, and skin. Collectively, the muscles constitute about one half of a bird's total body weight. The bulky muscles are concentrated near a bird's center of gravity, which gives stability in flight.

Largest of all the muscles are the breast muscles, or *pectorals*. These muscles form the bulk of the fleshy mass in the breast and constitute about 15 to 25 percent of a bird's total body weight. They also provide the powerful downstroke of the wing and therefore bear most of the burden of supporting a bird in the air.

The *supracoracoideus*—the muscle that raises the wing—acts as the antagonist to the pectorals. This muscle is located below the pectoral muscles ventrally (on the lower front side). Together, these two muscles constitute about 25 to 35 percent of a bird's body weight. Besides the supracoracoideus there are numerous other small muscles of the wing that allow a bird to control flight.

Other muscles that play a critical role in flight are the skin muscles. The involuntary skin muscles, for example, which are attached to almost every feather follicle, can raise, lower, or move feathers sideways to assist a bird in its flight maneuvers.

The trunk and tail muscles are few, but are extremely mobile and complex. One of these muscles, the *pygostyle*, supports the tail feathers and controls their entire range of movement.

The thin, stringy muscles of the vertebral column control the elaborate lateral and ventral movements of the head and neck. Some of these muscles extend only from one vertebra to the next, and others link the movement of long series of vertebrae.

Alexander Lowry
With the aid of its powerful breast muscles, the Northern Pintail can burst almost vertically from the water and take flight.

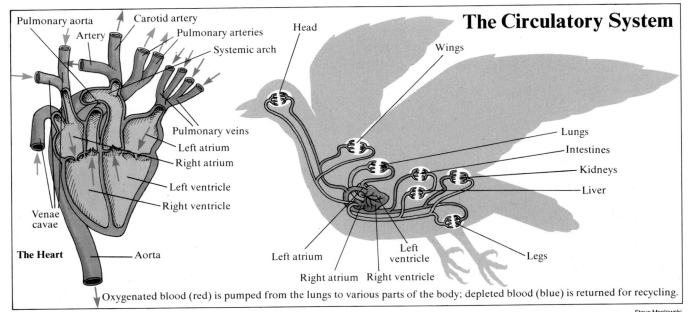

The Circulatory System

Pulmonary aorta
Carotid artery
Artery
Pulmonary arteries
Systemic arch
Pulmonary veins
Left atrium
Right atrium
Left ventricle
Right ventricle
Venae cavae

The Heart
Aorta

Head
Wings
Lungs
Intestines
Kidneys
Liver
Left atrium
Left ventricle
Right atrium
Right ventricle
Legs

Oxygenated blood (red) is pumped from the lungs to various parts of the body; depleted blood (blue) is returned for recycling.

Steve Maslowski

A Ruby-throated Hummingbird sips nectar from a trumpet creeper. The energy-rich food source is necessary if the bird is to maintain its rapid metabolism and a pulse rate of 615 beats per minute.

Fast-Paced Circulation

The avian heart has evolved into a large and powerful organ with rapid muscular contractions. In both birds and mammals it is generally true that the smaller the species, the larger the relative size of the heart and the quicker the heart rate. It is also generally true that birds have hearts that are proportionately larger and faster than those of mammals. In humans, for instance, the heart weight is 0.42 percent of body weight and the pulse rate at rest averages 72 beats per minute. In the House Sparrow the heart is 1.68 percent of body weight and the pulse rate at rest is 460 beats per minute. In the tiny Ruby-throated Hummingbird these figures rise to 2.37 percent and a pulse rate of 615.

A bird's heart consists of four chambers: two receiving vessels called atria, and two synchronized pumping areas called ventricles. Blood that has been depleted of oxygen enters the right atrium through three large veins called the venae cavae. The blood passes into the right ventricle and is then pumped out via the pulmonary aorta. Attached to the pulmonary aorta are two pulmonary arteries, which carry blood to the lungs, where carbon dioxide is exchanged for oxygen. The oxygenated blood is then returned to the heart, not in two blood vessels, as in mammals, but by means of four large pulmonary veins. This oxygenated blood enters the left atrium, then passes into the left ventricle before being pumped out, under high pressure, via the right systemic arch into the arterial system that supplies the whole body. With this highly sophisticated and efficient system, oxygen and other materials are moved rapidly into areas of high metabolic activity, such as working muscles. At the same rapid pace, carbon dioxide and other waste products are removed.

A Variety of Feathers

Feathers have evolved to serve a variety of functions—flight, heat conservation, waterproofing, camouflage, and display. Each feather consists of a tapering shaft bearing a flexible vane on either side. The exposed base of the shaft is called the calamus or quill. If viewed by cross section, the calamus is round and hollow. An opening at the bottom of the calamus, called the lower umbilicus, allows blood to enter the young feather during its short period of growth. When its growth is completed, the feather is sealed off and, although it may be moved by a separate muscle situated in the skin, the feather itself is "dead."

The stiff shaft running through the center of each feather is called a rachis, and the inner and outer vanes carried by the rachis are composed of a row of barbs, arranged side by side. Each barb in turn contains many tiny branches, set side by side, called barbules.

In birds of all sizes there are six commonly recognized types of feathers: contour feathers, semiplumes, filoplumes, down feathers, powder down feathers, and bristle feathers.

Contour feathers. Contour, or vaned, feathers are the most specialized of all feathers. Contour feathers form the outline of the body of a bird, giving it its streamlined look. Included in this group are all of the feathers of the outer body as well as those of the wings and tail. These feathers vary both in length and thickness and range from the large and stiff flight feathers to the much softer and more delicate feathers that cover and shape the body.

When you examine a contour feather you will find that the barbs are stuck together, forming a smooth surface. This is accomplished by tiny hooks on the barbules that interlock with the barbules of the adjoining barb, linking them together. If the barbules are disrupted, the bird can simply pass its bill through the feather to link them once again.

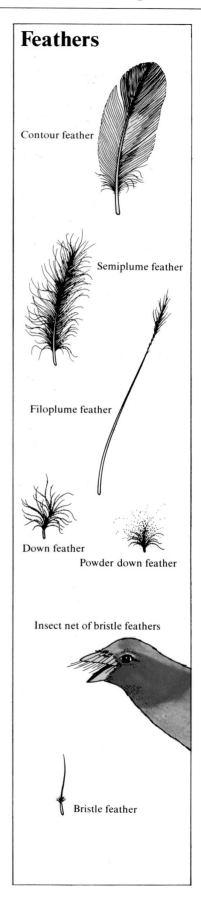

Feathers

Contour feather

Semiplume feather

Filoplume feather

Down feather

Powder down feather

Insect net of bristle feathers

Bristle feather

Flight Feathers

Vanes

Barb

Shaft or rachis

Lower umbilicus

Each row of barbs contains many tiny branches called barbules.

Tail feathers (rectrices)

Tertiaries

Secondaries

Primaries

Flight feathers of the wing (remiges)

Stephen J. Krasemann/DRK Photo

A Common Raven splays its primary feathers to gain maximum control and propulsion. The secondary and tertiary feathers, which are held together, sustain the bird in the air, while the tail feathers act like a rudder.

The contour feathers used for flight are known as *remiges* and *rectrices*. Flight feathers of the wing, or remiges, can be divided into three groups: primaries, secondaries, and tertiaries. The primary feathers propel the bird through the air. They are the largest of the flight feathers and are farthest away from the body, attached to the skin of the wing on the "hand." Primaries are driven through the air by large flight muscles attached to the keel. In most bird species there are about 10 primary feathers on each wing. If these flight feathers are damaged or lost, a bird cannot fly.

The secondary flight feathers run along the "arm" of the wing and sustain the bird in the air, giving it lift. The number of secondary feathers varies a great deal among different species. Birds that perch have 9 or 10 secondaries, but some species of grouse have as many as 20. Experiments have proven that if half of the secondary feathers are removed, a bird will still be able to fly, but some control will be lost.

The tertiaries (or tertials), are the few flight feathers that are attached to the upper part of the "arm." Like secondary feathers, their number varies among species.

The other main group of flight feathers are the tail feathers, or rectrices. The rectrices are mainly concerned with steering and balancing; they are used as a rudder, allowing the bird to twist and turn in flight. In addition, these feathers act as an efficient brake prior to landing. The number of rectrices varies among species, but is usually between 10 and 12.

Semiplume feathers. In appearance, semiplumes fall between contour feathers and down feathers, combining a large rachis with downy vanes. Semiplumes are distinguished from down feathers in that the rachis is longer than the longest barbs. They fill in or smooth out the various contours of a bird's body while insulating it, and they also provide flexibility at constricted areas, such as the base of the wings. Semiplumes are usually hidden beneath the contour feathers and are small and often white.

Filoplume feathers. Filoplumes are always situated beside other feathers. They are simple, hairlike structures that grow in circles around the base of contour or down feathers. They usually stand up like hairs, and are made up of a thin rachis with a few short barbs of barbules at the tip. Filoplumes are generally smaller than semiplumes and are one half to three fourths the length of the covering contour feathers.

Thomas D. Mangelsen

Steve Maslowski

The origin of filoplumes is currently under debate. Some ornithologists disagree with the theory that filoplumes are degenerate contour feathers and believe instead that they are sensitive structures that assist in the movement of the other feathers. Filoplumes do, in fact, have many free nerve endings in the follicle walls that are connected to pressure receptors around the follicle. It is therefore quite possible that filoplumes play a key role in keeping contours in place during preening, display, and flight.

Down feathers. Down feathers make up the underplumage of a bird. They are usually concealed beneath the contour feathers, and their main function appears to be insulation against cold weather. Each down feather has a quill and a soft head of fluffy barbs, but there are no barbules and the barbs are not "zipped" together as they are in contour feathers. These feathers are especially numerous in ducks and other water birds. In some species of water birds the adults pluck down feathers from their breasts and use them to line the nest and keep the eggs warm. Chicks of some species are covered with down when they hatch.

Powder down feathers. Powder down feathers help insulate the bird. Unlike other feathers, powder downs grow continuously. Instead of being molted, their tips disintegrate into a powdery substance. These feathers grow in dense, yellowish patches on the breast, belly, or flanks of herons and bitterns. In other birds powder down feathers are more thinly scattered throughout the plumage. Many ornithologists believe that in water birds the powder serves to soak up water, blood, and slime, thus protecting the feathers and making preening easier.

Bristle feathers. Not all species of birds have bristle feathers. Bristles are specialized feathers that are believed to perform a tactile function. They have a stiff, tapered rachis and few, if any, barbs that appear only at the base of the feather. Bristles are usually found on the head or neck, often around the mouth or on the eyelids. In some insect eaters, bristles found on the face and around the mouth are thought by ornithologists to act as funnels, helping the birds to scoop insects out of the air. Long facial bristles in owls, who tend to be farsighted, are thought to aid the bird in sensing nearby objects. Woodpeckers have bristle feathers over their nostrils, where it is thought that they may act as a filter for the dust produced when they drill holes in trees.

Above left: *A thick layer of down feathers insulates the bodies of these King and Common Eiders from the hostile cold of the Arctic.*

Above: *A Screech Owl peers from the security of a nest cavity. Long bristle feathers surrounding the beak may aid in sensing nearby objects.*

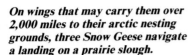

On wings that may carry them over 2,000 miles to their arctic nesting grounds, three Snow Geese navigate a landing on a prairie slough.

Thomas D. Mangelsen

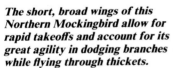

The short, broad wings of this Northern Mockingbird allow for rapid takeoffs and account for its great agility in dodging branches while flying through thickets.

Steve Maslowski

Wings: The Key to Flight

The evolution of wings for moving from one tree to another was, without a doubt, the major turning point in bird development. Wings have allowed birds freer movement over much wider areas than has ever been possible for purely aquatic or terrestrial organisms.

In discussing flight, it is tempting to compare the avian wing with that of an aircraft, but we have to be careful not to take the analogy too far. An aircraft flies because of the airfoil properties of its solid wings; propulsion is provided by the engine. In contrast, birds have feathered wings that are responsible for both propulsion *and* efficient aerodynamics. An airfoil is any stabilizing surface designed to aid in lifting or controlling by making use of the surrounding air currents; in a bird, the airfoil is its wings, individual feathers, or both.

The wing is the basic lifting surface of the bird, and its shape varies according to the type of flight typical of its species. Each feather on a bird's wing functions independently and allows the shape of the wing to be altered during flight, permitting much freedom of movement. The actual size and shape of a wing are determined mainly by the flight feathers. Another significant factor determining wing shape is the length of the wing. A wing is generally considered long when it exceeds the length of a bird's body; a short wing is shorter than the length of the body. Another significant determinant of wing size is *aspect ratio*—the ratio of a wing's length to its width. A wing with a high aspect ratio is long and thin; a wing with a low aspect ratio is short and broad. The *surface loading ratio*—the ratio of body weight to wing surface—is also important: The larger the wing surface is in proportion to weight, the more easily the bird is borne aloft. Finally, a wing also can either be cambered (arched) or flat.

Wing shapes. Different birds have one of six basic wing shapes adapted for different flying styles: short, broad, cupped wings for rapid takeoff and short-distance flight; shorter and broader wings with slotted primary feathers for soaring flight; flat, moderately long, narrow, triangular wings for high-speed flight; large, distinctly arched wings for flapping flight; long, narrow, flat, pointed wings for gliding flight; and pointed, swept-back wings for hovering.

Like everything in a living organism, wing shape has its basis in survival value. For example, birds such as pheasants and grouse that usually inhabit dense cover and need to dodge quickly between obstructions have wings that are good for twisting flight at short distances, and less efficient for sustained high-speed flight. Built for fast takeoff, this type of wing is relatively short but broad and cupped, with flexible tips that can be set at varied angles without twisting the whole wing.

Soaring birds tend to have broad wings, even shorter than those of game birds and others described above. The breadth of this wing type and the arrangement of the slotted primary feathers make it most efficient for soaring over land. (Slotting permits each primary feather to be used as a separate airfoil.) Some birds with this kind of wing are Black and Turkey Vultures, Red-tailed Hawks, Red-shouldered Hawks, Broad-winged Hawks, Northern Harriers, condors, ravens, and some gulls.

Some birds of prey and most other fast-flying birds have developed high-speed wings that offer great maneuverability. These wings are extremely flat, moderately long, narrow, and triangular, and tend to be swept backwards, like the wings of a high-speed jet fighter. This wing type can be found in swifts, swallows, shorebirds, and waterfowl, and other small- to medium-sized birds with rapid flight.

The kind of wing characteristic of slow, flapping flight is large and distinctly arched. Herons, egrets, and ibises have this type of wing, and their style makes them immediately recognizable as belonging to one of those families, even when seen from a distance.

Seabirds, such as shearwaters and albatrosses, have a high-aspect wing, but one that is adapted for long-distance gliding—long, narrow, flat, and pointed, with no slotting of the primary feathers. The longest feathers are

Top left: *The Turkey Vulture has extremely broad wings for soaring.*

Top center: *Sleek, pointed wings give the White Tern high speed and great maneuverability for pursuing fish.*

Top right: *The large, arched wings of this Great Egret are adapted for its slow flapping flight.*

Bottom left: *The Antarctic Giant-Petrel has long and narrow wings for long-distance oceanic soaring.*

Bottom center: *The broad, slotted wings of the Wood Stork enable it to glide long distances between updrafts with minimal loss of altitude.*

Bottom right: *The remarkable maneuverability of the Ruby-throated Hummingbird is achieved by pointed, swept-back wings.*

Taking Off and Landing

Birds always face into the wind when taking off and landing so that they can take advantage of wind speed. (If the wind were at their backs, they would not have the control they have when facing into it.) But differences exist here too: While large birds need a prolonged take-off run to become airborne, small birds can jump straight into the air on takeoff; they can generally achieve lift from zero air speed (no wind). Larger birds can fly at speeds within a minimum and maximum range, but they cannot take flight at zero air speed. Therefore, larger birds need to generate air speed before they can take off. They often run over the ground or water until they reach the minimum air speed needed to take flight.

Large terrestrial birds such as eagles and hawks land on an elevated perch or a hill whenever possible so that they can acquire the necessary minimum takeoff and flying speeds by dropping off of the perch. Seabirds achieve the same result by accelerating down the windward slope of large waves or by paddling over the surface of the water while flapping energetically. Hang gliders operate on a similar principle for takeoff. Because of a hang glider's enormous wingspan and the relatively heavy weight supported by its "wings," the flier must always head into the wind, preferably from a sloped hill or mountaintop, to attain the minimum flying speed for lift.

Large land birds taking off from the ground run with steps that are synchronized to their wingbeats. In a motion that resembles running, most North American water birds use their webbed feet to push themselves forward through the water for takeoff; this motion is also synchronized with the wingbeats.

All birds have in common legs and feet that act as landing gear. This landing gear helps them take flight from a stationary position and cushions them during landing. The extent to which birds are able to use this landing gear, however, varies among species. For example, in the better fliers, such as hummingbirds, swifts, and swallows, the legs are weaker and therefore less useful as landing gear; birds such as roadrunners, grouse, and ptarmigans have strong legs but are not especially skillful fliers.

In landing, birds use their legs and feet both as air brakes and to grasp the perch or surface. Small birds often land by gauging a desired perch and then flying at a speed approaching zero at or slightly above the area; the legs and feet then serve the simple function of grasping the perch. Obliged to land at high speeds, most large birds use a kind of ballistic approach; they dive at a high speed to just below the desired landing site and then pull up into a steep climb, resulting in zero air speed at the landing site. A high landing speed is not a problem for water birds because they can effectively hydroplane to a halt with their large feet. Most large seabirds are adapted to alight on water, but if necessary they can use their landing gear to accomplish adequate, if extremely clumsy, ground landings.

Birds' feet do not have to be webbed to be effective air brakes. The legs of birds of prey are heavy enough to perform this function. The long legs of storks, herons, cranes, and rails are also excellent drag generators when in landing position.

Top: *Tundra Swans rise laboriously from a twilight pond. To lift themselves into the air, these large birds must propel forward over the water to gain flight speed.*

Bottom: *A Great Horned Owl spreads its wings, tail, and feet for maximum braking power as it pulls up for a landing on a dead snag.*

Maslowski Photo

David S. Soliday

Frans Lanting

the outermost primaries (the feathers borne on the "hand"). Pointed wings like these are best suited for long-distance flight over the ocean. Other birds with this type of wing are gulls and frigatebirds, which glide almost endlessly above the sea.

Still another gliding variation is found in the type of wing typical of storks and some vultures, a slotted, high-lifting structure. The wings are broad to provide more wing surface and short to make use of subtle variations in air currents.

Hummingbirds' wings are pointed and swept back, and they rotate at the shoulder, not at the wrist as do those of most other birds. This allows the wing to be turned over in midstroke, so that backward motion cancels forward motion and the bird remains motionlessly poised in the air to sip the nectar of flowers.

Aerodynamics

The dominant aerodynamic forces that affect flight are lift and drag. Lift is produced by differences in the pressure of air above and below a wing. When a wing is held at a slight angle to an air current, air flows faster over the upper surface than it does over the lower surface, thus creating less pressure above the wing than below it and causing lift. At the same time, drag, or resistance to the moving air, drags the wing backward. The combined effect of these two forces is to lift the wing and drag it backwards.

While most of the lift on a bird's wing comes from the low air pressure on its top, a certain amount of lift is generated from beneath by air striking the undersurface of the wing. Air flow in the underside stops at a point close to the wing's front, or *leading edge*, and then gradually speeds up until it is near the back, or *trailing edge*, by which time it has reached the same velocity as the air traveling over its upper surface.

If the front edge of the wing is tilted upward just a little bit and is placed in an air stream, the air will strike the bottom surface more directly, thereby increasing the lifting force on the wing from below. The more the wing is tilted upward, the more lift it will get, but only to a certain point: When the angle of tilt approaches the vertical, the air pressure against the bottom surface begins to push the wing backward rather than upward. If the wing is tilted too much, the lifting force eventually vanishes and the drag is so great that it stops the bird's "buoyancy," or forward movement. This results in what is commonly called a stall, and the bird must regain the proper wing angle and flight speed or it will crash.

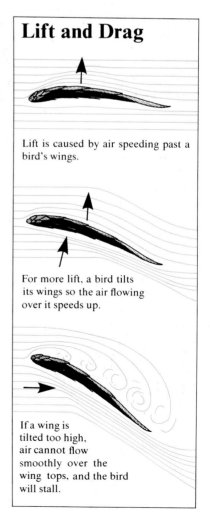

Lift and Drag

Lift is caused by air speeding past a bird's wings.

For more lift, a bird tilts its wings so the air flowing over it speeds up.

If a wing is tilted too high, air cannot flow smoothly over the wing tops, and the bird will stall.

Douglas R. Herr

On outstretched wings, a Golden Eagle hangs effortlessly in the air. By gliding, an eagle may patrol its enormous territory with minimal expenditure of energy.

Types of Flight

Considering the wing variety that exists among birds, it is not surprising that there is much variation in flight styles. Flight styles are as different as the graceful soaring of a condor and the quick darting of a hummingbird. Some birds use primarily one style; other birds trade off between types.

Gliding flight. Gliding flight is possible only when the forces of lift and drag are adjusted to be equal to the weight of the bird. For optimal gliding, a bird's wing must maximize lift and minimize drag.

With the exception of hummingbirds, all birds glide to some extent when flying. As a rule, the smaller the bird, the shorter the distance it can glide and the faster it sinks. For example, a domestic pigeon descends about 33 feet during a glide of approximately 295 feet; a Golden Eagle can glide 558 feet with the same loss in height.

Gliding can be observed particularly well in game birds. A pheasant flushed from the ground ascends like a rocket with whirring wings, then glides for some distance down to the nearby woods. Only when it has too little momentum and is losing too much height does the bird speed up again with a few rapid wingbeats. Long gliding phases and short flapping phases alternate until the pheasant reaches cover. There it glides down to the ground and brakes by flapping against the direction of motion.

During gliding the wings are stretched out stiffly. A good glider travels a long way horizontally with minimal loss of height, but eventually loses altitude due to the pull of gravity. The efficiency of a glider can be measured by calculating the angle between the track of its motion and the horizon. This angle depends not upon the weight of the bird but rather upon the forces of lift and drag, though wing shape does have some influence. The speed of the glide, however, does depend to some degree on the weight of the bird—a heavy bird with small wings will glide quickly, and a light bird with large wings will glide much more slowly. The distance traveled is affected to some extent by the height from which the bird started.

Soaring flight of land birds. Picture the majestic sight of a condor or a Red-tailed Hawk soaring in the spring or fall sky. With quills widely outstretched, it circles round, rising without a single wingbeat, as if lifted by some invisible hand, higher and higher until it disappears from view. The beautiful dance it seems to be performing is known as soaring.

Gliding Flight

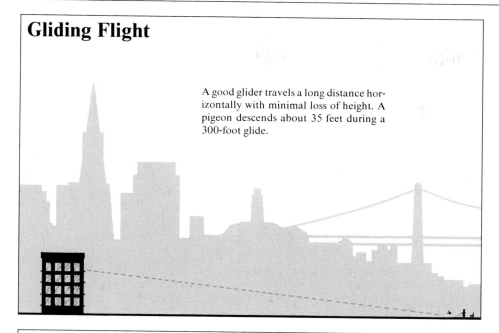

A good glider travels a long distance horizontally with minimal loss of height. A pigeon descends about 35 feet during a 300-foot glide.

Soaring on a warm thermal updraft, this Red-tailed Hawk will reach altitudes in excess of 2,000 feet without a single wingbeat.

Soaring Flight

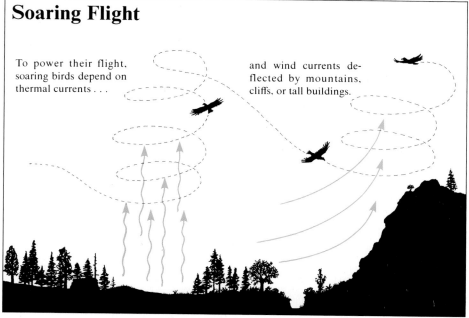

To power their flight, soaring birds depend on thermal currents . . .

and wind currents deflected by mountains, cliffs, or tall buildings.

Soaring differs from gliding flight in that the bird does not lose altitude and sometimes even climbs. When soaring, a bird uses no energy of its own; instead, it depends on external forces called thermal currents—rising masses of warm air that form over areas where the ground warms up rapidly. Thermal currents occur mostly above woodland clearings, cornfields, and even above some large towns.

Thermal currents are caused when warm air moves upward and is replaced by colder air dropping from higher levels in the atmosphere. In temperate climates birds' use of thermal updrafts is somewhat restricted, but they sometimes soar to considerable heights over towns and other regions where hot air rises. Since the production of thermals depends upon solar radiation, these zones of rising air are not equally active at all times of the day and year. This is why soaring birds of prey are usually only seen circling in the air during sunny weather, and also why these birds are not usually seen before 9:30 or 10:00 a.m.; it is only then that thermals become strong enough to bear them aloft. Since extended flapping flight would be far too exhausting for these birds, they remain at their roosts during the first few hours of the morning.

Another kind of wind current soaring birds use in much the same way as they use thermals is called an obstruction current. Obstruction currents are produced when wind currents are deflected by mountains, cliffs, or tall buildings. The resulting updraft of air lifts birds to high altitudes, providing a base for further gliding.

Soaring land birds always have large and broad wings, and the ratio of their body weight to the size of the airfoils (their surface loading ratio) is low. Large airfoils of this type are ideal for soaring flight in thermals or in updrafts near mountainsides, but they are particularly poor for flapping flight. This is why, after takeoff, soaring land birds seek out the nearest updraft zone as quickly as possible and change to soaring flight as soon as they detect the supporting effect of rising air. At a certain height the rate of flow of the thermal current slackens and the bird then switches to gliding flight and travel, losing height until it reaches the next updraft zone, which once more carries it upward. In this manner, soaring land birds can travel great distances without a single wingbeat.

Soaring flight of seabirds. Quite different physical principles underlie the soaring flight of seabirds, such as albatrosses, large petrels, and shearwaters. There are no thermals or updrafts over large bodies of water, only horizontal gusts of wind. The air masses that these gusts drive before them are slowed by friction at the water surface, and their speed is consequently slower there than in higher altitudes. These seabirds have developed a type of soaring and gliding that does not depend upon the presence of either thermal or obstruction currents.

Seabirds use the differential wind velocities that occur over the sea for their soaring flight. Albatrosses, for example, take off against the wind, rising without beating their wings, until they lose momentum in the faster-moving layers of air farther from the water surface, at a height of about 35 to 65 feet. The birds then turn in a curve and shoot back to the water surface in an oblique, gliding path, gaining so much speed that after turning back again they can once more climb against the wind.

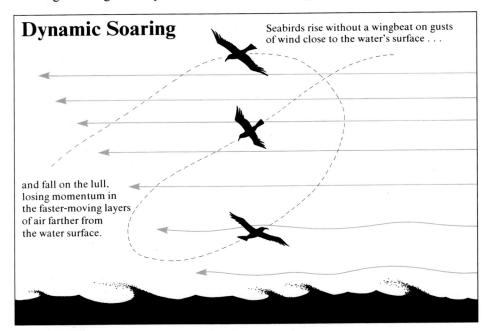

Dynamic Soaring

Seabirds rise without a wingbeat on gusts of wind close to the water's surface . . .

and fall on the lull, losing momentum in the faster-moving layers of air farther from the water surface.

In this way albatrosses can soar for hours and days at a time without ever beating their wings. Ornithologists call this "dynamic soaring" or "gust flying"—rising into the gust and falling on the lull. It is this seemingly endless form of flying that allows the albatross to survive, since albatrosses cannot fly in the absence of wind. This is a significant factor in their latitudinal distribution.

Since soaring flight over the oceans places quite different demands on the physiology of the bird than does soaring in thermals, the wings of soaring seabirds have evolved quite differently from those of soaring land birds. In the continuously fluctuating wind conditions over the sea, with gusts changing in direction from one second to the next, a land bird's wings would be sadly out of place. To utilize the lift from rising air masses, the wings of a soaring land bird need to be broad and to present a large surface area; excessive length would cause difficulties in maneuverability. The large maritime soaring birds have the largest wing spans. First place is taken by the Wandering Albatross, which spans over 11.5 feet from wing tip to wing tip and weighs 17.5 pounds.

Albatrosses are the masters of gust flying. Their wings are quite narrow, the forearm portion is usually long, and the hand portion, by contrast, is relatively short. The entire wing is built for rigidity in the turbulence of sea breezes, and the primary and secondary quills are relatively short and stiff so that their tips will not flutter. Flutter at the wing tips or at the trailing edges (as opposed to the leading edges) of airfoils sets up vortex formation (violent, whirling air masses) and leads to an uncontrollable loss of energy.

The long forearm on the albatross wing bears as many as 37 secondary feathers, but the number of primaries, at 10, is no greater than in other birds. This numerical proportion alone indicates the great extension in length of the forearm, which constitutes the greater part of the airfoil.

Flapping flight. Small birds—the size of an American Crow and downwards—can glide but cannot soar in updrafts on land or gusts over the sea. These birds must generate their own energy for flight that larger, soaring birds receive from air currents. This energy is achieved by beating the wings, which are driven by the strong pectoral muscles in what is called flapping flight.

Frans Lanting

Slipping obliquely through the wind, a Laysan Albatross soars over the ocean, making use of the varying wind velocities between the water surface and higher altitudes.

A young Ring-billed Gull spreads its wings in preparation for takeoff. Smaller birds like this must flap their wings to maintain their flight altitude.

Sharon Chester

Flapping Flight

Smaller birds must generate their own energy for flight by flapping. In the power stroke, the wings move forward and down. The back stroke returns the wings to position for the next power stroke.

Shallow, rapid wingbeats in a forward-backward motion characterize the flight of this Belted Kingfisher as it hovers over a small stream.

Flapping flight consists of two distinct movements: the power stroke and the back stroke. In the power stroke, the wings move forward and down; the back stroke returns the wings to the position from which the next power stroke will commence. During a glide the inner wings (the secondary feathers) and the "hand" regions (the primary feathers) are spread to produce a continuous airfoil. During a flap, however, the two parts of the wing carry out different functions. The inner wings give lift, while the "hands" pull the body forward. During the power stroke the primary feathers are linked together to produce a near-perfect airfoil, giving maximum thrust and minimum drag.

In smaller birds the primary feathers are separated like the slots in a venetian blind on the back stroke, allowing air to pass through and considerably reducing drag. Larger birds, like gulls and the small but long-winged birds of the swallow family, either flex or partially close their wings on the back stroke. With the help of slow-motion photography, scientists have been able to see quite clearly just how this system operates.

Hovering flight. In hovering flight, a bird generates its own lift by means of rapid wingbeats. Holding its body nearly vertical, with its wings firmly flexed at the elbow joint, a hovering bird moves its wing surfaces forward and back in a horizontal plane; each of the two phases of the stroke generates lift. The blur of a hovering bird's wings beating the air like propellers is in sharp contrast to its body, which appears to be suspended.

Kestrels and kingfishers perform amazing maneuvers, hovering over land and sea. But as impressive as the hovering of a kestrel or kingfisher may be, these birds are mere dabblers in this particular talent. It is only in hummingbirds that nature has structured the wings in such a way that when in motion they can act like a perfect lifting rotor. Their pointed wings do not flap and glide as other bird wings do, but propel them through the air by moving up and down, up and down, at a furious rate of 70 times a second. After feeding at a flower they can fly backward, climb vertically, turn at lightning speed, and come to a sudden standstill in mid-air. Hummingbirds have been known to fly up to speeds of 60 miles per hour in a tail wind. No bird of prey even attempts to catch a hummingbird in flight.

Thomas D. Mangelsen

The human eye is incapable of deciphering exactly how a hummingbird's wings beat, since they move so quickly, but slow-motion photography has unveiled the secret: Viewed from the side, the hummingbird beats its wings back and forth in a horizontal figure eight, producing lift on both the forward and backward strokes. (To photograph a "frozen" image of a hummingbird in flight, see page 262.)

Energy consumption during the whirring flight of the hummingbird is, understandably, enormous. The pectoralis minor muscle used for raising the wing is as much as 50 percent heavier than the pectoralis major, which in most other birds is 10 to 20 times heavier than its counterpart. Hummingbirds consume 8 to 12 times as much oxygen as other small birds, and the heart and respiratory systems are proportionately 3 times as large as, for example, those of a pigeon.

The "flight" of flightless birds. Although all birds have feathers and all birds have wings, all birds do not fly. Flightless birds, like penguins and ostriches, use their wings to move in a different way than flying birds. Penguins are adept at using their wings to "fly" under water at high speeds. An ostrich uses its wings to increase its speed when running with the wind by lifting its wings as if they were sails.

The Sky is the Limit

We live in a time when thousands of people fly every day, in crafts ranging from the simple hang glider to the commercial jet to the space shuttle. But the spectacular, natural feats of crossing oceans, skirting deserts, and topping mountains are still possible only for birds, whose feather-powered flight gives them quick and easy access to nearly any spot on earth. The ability to glide with ease over thousands of miles of ocean belongs only to the seabirds; the ability to soar over hundreds of miles of mountain ranges belongs to our beautiful eagles and condors.

In North America we are fortunate to have a huge variety of birds to watch, feed, study, and simply enjoy. The awe, admiration, and childlike wonderment evoked in people of all ages who watch birds in flight are likely to last as long as there are birds that fly.

Hovering Flight

Hummingbirds beat their wings at 70 times per second in a horizontal figure eight motion. Forward and backward strokes both produce lift.

O.S. Pettingill/VIREO

Having traded the sky for the ocean, these Gentoo Penguins prefer to fly through the water with wings that have been modified into paddles.

Migration and Navigation

by Kenneth P. Able

*T*here is frost on the lawn in the mornings, a wind is start-ing to kick up—winter is on its way. The stark, bare-branched trees seem lifeless without the gay song of birds. Where is the Wood Thrush that called in the dawn all sum-mer long? What is the destination of that flock of birds an-gling across a gray sky? A telescope pointed to the full moon on a September night shows winged silhouettes flashing past. Where are the birds going? How do they navigate?

Of the approximately 9,000 species of birds on earth, more than half migrate regularly. Although no one is sure how many individual birds migrate each season, the number is speculated to be in the billions. Migration can be as short and local as a biannual trek up and down a mountainside, or it can be as long as a yearly intercontinental journey. Some species migrate in flocks, others make solitary journeys. Most remarkable is that no matter what distance they have trav-eled, most species return with another change of season to the nesting sites they once fled.

When the bitter cold of winter sets in, tundra species such as Greater White-fronted, Snow, and Canada Geese migrate in spectacular formation, in search of more hospitable regions.

R.J. Shallenberger/VIREO

Twice a year North Americans can mark the change of seasons by the passage of birds, whether the hopeful song of spring's first robin or the distant cackling of geese high overhead on a fall night. Driven by instincts, these Tundra Swans fly more than 2,000 miles across the continent to nest along remote tundra ponds.

Why Migrate?

Food, water, protective cover, and a sheltered place to nest and breed are basic to a bird's survival. But the changing seasons can transform a comfortable environment into an unlivable one—the food and water supply can dwindle or disappear, plant cover can vanish, and competition with other animals can increase.

Most wild animals face the problem of occupying a habitat that is suitable for only a portion of the year. Fortunately, however, nature has provided methods for coping with the situation. One method, known as hibernation, involves entering a dormant state during the winter season. The other method, known as migration, involves escaping the area entirely. Because of their powers of flight, most birds adapt to seasonal changes in the environment by migrating; only a few bird species, such as the Common Poorwill, hibernate.

In North America, the ratio of migratory to nonmigratory birds varies greatly from region to region. In high arctic regions (northern Alaska, northern Canada, and Greenland), where many shorebirds and waterfowl nest, the entire population often consists of migratory birds who are only there during the summers. In the forest and open country of the eastern United States, over 80 percent of the nesting land birds are migratory, spending the winters in more hospitable southern climates. There is a similar high percentage of south-migrating birds in inland areas of the West. However, in areas where the climate is more equable, like the Pacific Coast, more species are nonmigratory; in tropical regions at least 80 percent of the birds are nonmigratory.

D. & M. Zimmerman/VIREO

D. & M. Zimmerman/VIREO

Above left: *During cold winters insects become scarce, forcing many insectivorous birds to fly south. The Common Poorwill overcomes this problem by hibernating when food is in short supply.*

Above: *The annual fall migration of the Townsend's Solitaire may consist merely of descending a few thousand feet from a high mountain forest to the shelter of a wooded valley.*

Left: *The migration of Cedar Waxwings is closely tied to the availability of fruit-bearing trees. Waxwings and many types of finches are said to have eruptive migrations because they often appear unpredictably and in vast numbers.*

A. Cruickshank/VIREO

In the Rockies and Sierras of the West, migration often consists of moving from high to low elevations. Rosy Finches, Townsend's Solitaires, and Mountain Quail perform these movements quite regularly whereas others, such as Clark's Nutcracker, are much more erratic.

Some migration schedules do not always closely follow seasonal changes in the weather. For example, since the vegetative food supply of nomadic species such as the crossbills, redpolls, and Pine Grosbeak fluctuates in abundance from year to year, these birds migrate in some winters and not in others. In contrast, insect-eating birds such as warblers, vireos, and flycatchers that live in the far north have no choice but to migrate from their summer habitats, since their food supply always disappears from sight in winter; their migration therefore tends to involve long distances and regular timing.

The Evolution of Migration

Bird migration is a behavior that has evolved over many thousands of years. Scientists believe that migration began to evolve when individuals that moved from one area to another ultimately produced more young than those that remained in one area. Migratory behavior continues to evolve because of the changing environment in which birds live: If environmental conditions favor migration, the number of birds that migrate increases; if conditions permit the birds to stay in one place, the sedentary type predominates. A good example of such adaptive behavior is a migratory North American bird called the Dark-eyed Junco. It was undoubtedly some of these migrants gone astray that colonized Guadeloupe Island, some 150 miles off the coast of Baja California, where the junco is now established as a sedentary population. Similarly, if less dramatically, populations of White-crowned and Savannah Sparrows along the Pacific Coast of California have abandoned the migratory habit. Just as the power of flight has disappeared when an absence of predators and a stable climate have eliminated the need for it, so has the tendency to migrate disappeared when it is no longer an advantage.

By human standards, evolution is an excruciatingly slow process. Sometimes, however, changes in migratory habits occur so rapidly that we may actually see them in action. In the early 1940s, some House Finches from a nonmigratory population in California were released on Long Island, New York. Once established in the East Coast's far more seasonally variable climate, the birds began to develop a migratory pattern. The eastern House Finch has since become partially migratory and has spread throughout the Northeast. Some individuals are resident the year around, while others regularly migrate back and forth to the Gulf States.

Patterns of Migration

As could be expected, the variety of migration patterns is almost as great as the number of species that migrate. Age, sex, weather, and availability of food, water, and shelter are major influences in migratory behavior. Taking a closer look at some familiar North American birds can provide some insight into just how much variety exists.

Waterfowl

Geese have long life spans and, like many other large water birds, they use regular stopover places along their flyways and return year after year to the same nesting and wintering areas. The migration pattern of the Snow Goose is typical of many of our ducks, geese, and swans. Snow Geese nest in high arctic regions from the North Slope of Alaska, eastward along the coast to northwestern Greenland, and southward along the western and southern shores of the Hudson Bay. They migrate southward during the fall in large flocks, flying both day and night at high altitudes. The time of their flight is dependent upon weather—they prefer to fly in clear skies and with a good tail wind. When conditions are right they can cover many hundreds of miles during a single high-altitude flight. Snow Geese spend the winter on the mid-Atlantic coast, the Louisiana-Texas Gulf coast, and in California and the Southwest.

Shorebirds

Shorebirds, like most of our waterfowl, nest on the arctic tundra and migrate to southern wintering grounds. Yet unlike waterfowl, many shorebirds—sandpipers, plovers, godwits, curlews—migrate beyond the confines of the North American continent.

F.E. Hester/VIREO

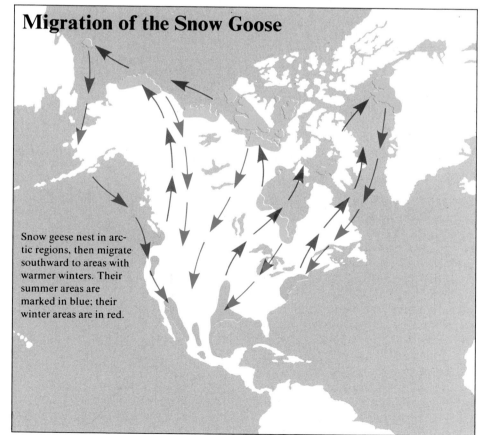

Migration of the Snow Goose

Snow geese nest in arctic regions, then migrate southward to areas with warmer winters. Their summer areas are marked in blue; their winter areas are in red.

Snow Geese arrive at a prairie marsh seeking abundant food to fuel their journey toward arctic nesting grounds. Most species of North American waterfowl winter within the continent and travel traditional routes between their breeding and their winter ranges.

Gary W. Hanlon

The Lesser Golden-Plover breeds in the Arctic and spends the winter in South America. In the fall these and other shorebirds fly nonstop from Labrador to Venezuela, a distance of about 2,800 miles.

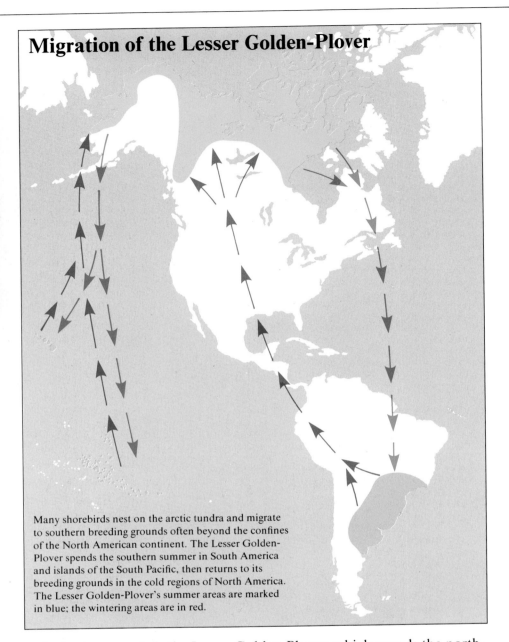

Migration of the Lesser Golden-Plover

Many shorebirds nest on the arctic tundra and migrate to southern breeding grounds often beyond the confines of the North American continent. The Lesser Golden-Plover spends the southern summer in South America and islands of the South Pacific, then returns to its breeding grounds in the cold regions of North America. The Lesser Golden-Plover's summer areas are marked in blue; the wintering areas are in red.

A classic example is the Lesser Golden-Plover, which spends the northern winter on the vast Argentinian grasslands called the pampas. There, along with its fellow migrants—yellowlegs, Hudsonian Godwits, stilts, and Baird's, Pectoral, Upland, and Buff-breasted Sandpipers—the Lesser Golden-Plover spends the southern summer with resident South American shorebirds. In spring the golden-plovers migrate northward in flocks, crossing the Caribbean and Gulf of Mexico. They enter the United States mainly along the Texas and Louisiana coasts, and head up through the interior of North America, stopping to feed on insects in pastures and plowed fields of the agricultural Midwest. These long-distance migrants arrive at their breeding grounds in June, and nest during the long days of the brief northern summer.

Young shorebirds are precocial (see page 80). Little parental care seems to be required in many of these species. In fact, the adult birds depart on their southward migration before summer is over, weeks before their youngsters begin the trip.

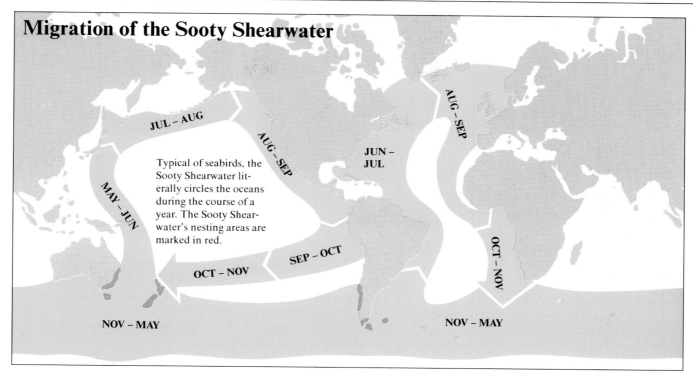

Migration of the Sooty Shearwater

JUL – AUG

AUG – SEP

JUN – JUL

AUG – SEP

MAY – JUN

Typical of seabirds, the Sooty Shearwater literally circles the oceans during the course of a year. The Sooty Shearwater's nesting areas are marked in red.

OCT – NOV

SEP – OCT

OCT – NOV

NOV – MAY

NOV – MAY

Though golden-plovers migrate a bit later, the height of the passage period of many adult shorebirds in the eastern United States occurs from late July through August. In midsummer they reappear, well on their way to the wintering ground. The precocial young birds appear some weeks later, guided southward by their instincts.

Lesser Golden-Plovers are one of a number of species of birds that follow different migration routes in spring and fall. In fall golden-plovers fly southeastward from their nesting areas to the coasts of Labrador and Maritime Canada; from there many initiate a nonstop over-water flight all the way to South America. During the crossing, the golden-plovers ascend to great heights (over 20,000 feet), but it still takes several days and nights of continuous flying before they reach the continent.

Seabirds

Seabirds are marvelously adapted for covering great distances over seemingly trackless oceans and, as migrants go, they hold the records. The fabled Arctic Tern nests as far north as open land exists and travels the length of the oceans to winter at the other end of the world. It is a round trip of some 25,000 miles performed every year of the bird's life.

More truly oceanic are the shearwaters, albatrosses, and storm-petrels, who spend most of their lives out of sight of land, coming ashore only to nest. One of the most numerous species in North American waters is the Sooty Shearwater. Sooty Shearwaters nest on islands deep in the Southern Hemisphere, mostly around New Zealand and the southern tip of South America. Breeding in burrows that they excavate on these islands during the southern summer (October through April), they depart northward after nesting to spend the southern winter at temperate North American latitudes. In late spring and throughout the summer, Sooty Shearwaters appear in large numbers off both American coasts, but they are especially prevalent on the West Coast, where thousands are often viewed from shore. By late summer the shearwaters are on their way back to the other end of the earth, literally circling its oceans in the process.

Arnold Small

Many seabirds migrate vast distances to experience summer seas. The Sooty Shearwater like this one may nest in New Zealand and spend its winter (the North American summer) off the coast of Alaska.

Above: A few North American land birds such as this female Bobolink migrate to South America for the winter. Many of these birds make their passage by flying across the Gulf of Mexico, and others follow the coastline of Central America.

Above center: The Tree Sparrow is typical of many migratory land birds whose migration does not take them out of the continent. Birds that winter within North America frequently have breeding and winter ranges that overlap.

Above right: Common in open woodlands and suburban shade trees in summer, the Northern Oriole spends the winter in tropical forests of Central America and the West Indies.

Land Birds

It is a common misconception that many of our North American summer land birds go to South America in the winter. A few do so—Swainson's and Gray-cheeked Thrushes, Bobolinks, Northern Waterthrushes, and Blackpoll Warblers—but most travel only as far as Mexico, Central America, and the Caribbean. Birds that can eat seeds do not need to migrate even that far because their food is generally more abundant.

Many species of sparrow, junco, towhee, and longspur stay within the United States, migrating only as far as is necessary to find winter weather that is less severe. Most individuals migrate only a few hundred to a thousand miles, and in some cases the northern edge of the winter range overlaps the southern part of the nesting area. When raising young, most of these birds augment their diets by harvesting insects. In winter, however, they feed almost entirely on small seeds.

Unlike water birds, most small land birds do not migrate in compact flocks; they seem more or less to go it alone. In the winter many are found in small flocks, but in summer they nest in dispersed territories, each occupied by a single pair. Most summer land birds migrate at night.

The Northern Oriole, a typical summer land bird, is found across North America wherever deciduous trees predominate. Like most songbirds, the Northern Oriole migrates at night and spends the winter primarily from central Mexico southward to northern South America and the West Indies. Eastern populations fly across the Gulf of Mexico in spring and fall.

The Blackpoll Warbler is a very remarkable traveler. Weighing in at only about 20 grams, this bird performs an over-water flight from New England to the coast of South America, flying at only 25 miles per hour. The bird takes three to four days to make the trip.

Choosing the Route

Each migratory species generally has a route of travel between its nesting and winter range, but for the majority of species these migration routes are quite broad. Waterfowl tend to be confined to somewhat narrower corridors determined by the availability of suitable habitat. In fact, it was once thought that there were distinct, narrow flyways (the Atlantic flyway, Central flyway, and so forth) used exclusively by various populations of waterfowl. The discovery that birds from one nesting area could be found migrating in several different flyways put that concept to rest.

Although entire species might not be confined to narrow corridors during migration, individual birds often exhibit amazing loyalty to places occupied during previous breeding and nonbreeding seasons, as well as stopover points between the two, a phenomenon known as site fidelity.

Migration of the Blackpoll Warbler

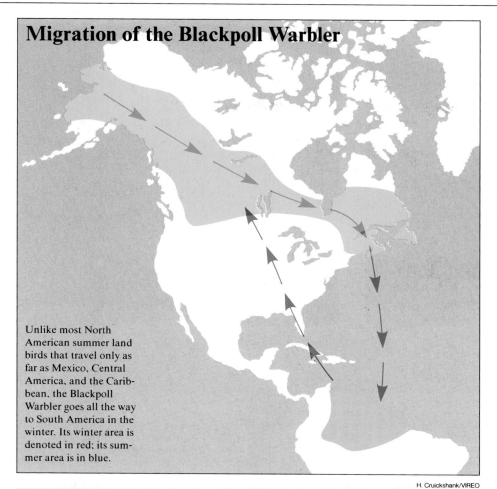

Unlike most North American summer land birds that travel only as far as Mexico, Central America, and the Caribbean, the Blackpoll Warbler goes all the way to South America in the winter. Its winter area is denoted in red; its summer area is in blue.

H. Cruickshank/VIREO

Herbert Clarke

To satisfy its need for abundant quantities of insects, the Blackpoll Warbler flies to a warm climate for the winter. In the fall, from their vast transcontinental breeding ranges, these birds converge on the Atlantic Coast where they depart for northern South America.

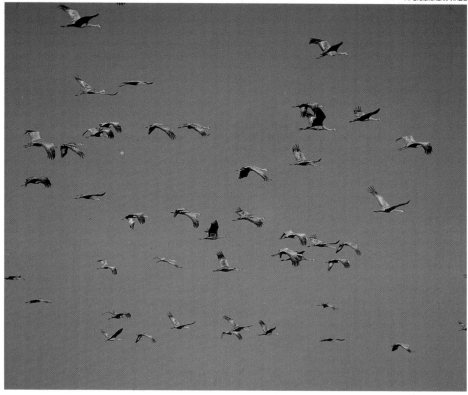

Water birds like these Sandhill Cranes tend to concentrate along narrower migration corridors than do other species. Such corridors often follow major north-south geographic features, such as mountain ranges or river valleys.

Thomas D. Mangelsen

H. Cruickshank/VIREO

Above: *Tree and Barn Swallows are known for their habit of forming large flocks during migration, particularly in the fall when they gather along barbed wires.*

Above right: *The appearance of Red-winged Blackbirds is the first sign of spring for many people. The birds follow a sequential migration: Adult males arrive first, and females come some time later, followed, finally, by juvenile males.*

Right: *The Snowy Owl, like most predatory birds, migrates alone; migrating in flocks would interfere with hunting behavior.*

Thomas D. Mangelsen

The Mechanics of Migration

By employing a diverse array of techniques, we have been able to unlock many of the secrets of bird migration. Though much of it takes place beyond the limits of our sensory capabilities, radar and visual observations (as described in the section "Observing Migration," beginning on page 152) have revealed a great deal about the flight behavior of migratory birds. Using those methods, we have gathered a substantial amount of information about social structure, altitude, speed, and the role that weather conditions play, and we are learning more all the time.

Grouping Together or Going It Alone

Some species of birds are highly social during migration, moving in flocks that may stay together for the whole journey. Flocked migrants are the most conspicuous of migrating birds and are thus the most familiar to us. They are also easiest to watch since they are generally daytime migrants. In at least some cases, flocks of migrating birds consist of family groups. It is thought that young birds learn details of the routes of travel and layover sites from the more experienced adults, though this is surely not the sole reason that these diverse types of birds travel so often in groups.

Flocked migrants include a wide variety of birds. Most of the large water birds travel in flocks, usually of impressive size. Among these are auks and puffins, cormorants, pelicans, ducks and geese, cranes, gulls, terns, sandpipers, and plovers. Often they congregate during migration at a few major stopover or staging areas where food is particularly abundant. Flocking is also common among many land birds, including doves, swifts, swallows, larks, pipits, crows, jays, waxwings, blackbirds, and starlings.

An equally diverse array of species seems to migrate in a more solitary fashion, perhaps occasionally forming more or less chance aggregations with others of their kind, but basically winging it alone. These birds include grebes, most herons, rails, some hawks, owls, nightjars, cuckoos, hummingbirds, kingfishers, woodpeckers, most flycatchers, creepers, wrens, kinglets, thrushes, vireos, wood warblers, and orioles.

Timing It Right

An experienced bird-watcher can mark the seasons in a given locale by the highly predictable times of arrival and departure of familiar migrating birds. Across much of the United States, for example, the first sign of spring is the arrival of flocks of Red-winged Blackbirds. The seasonal timing of migration is closely related to the likelihood that the necessities of life will be available at the time of arrival. Within each family of birds, however, there are great differences in timing among species. For example, among American wood warblers, the Louisiana Waterthrush may arrive at its breeding ground a full two months before the Connecticut Warbler passes through.

Variation also exists in the pace of migratory travel, even among related species. Shorebirds, waterfowl, cranes, and other species that use traditional stopover areas tend to make long flights interrupted by days of layover. Many land birds that are able to enjoy an abundance of resting and feeding habitats, such as warblers, flycatchers, and sparrows, typically fly one night, then rest for two or three nights, depending on the weather. These more leisurely travelers might cover as many as 200 miles in a night's flight, especially if they have a tail wind. Some of these same kinds of birds are capable of making extended flights if, for example, they have to cross a large body of water.

There seems to be a premium on getting to nesting areas as soon as possible. In fact, many kinds of waterfowl begin to move northward as soon as the lakes and ponds are released from the grip of ice. But at the same time there may be a heavy price to pay if the birds arrive too early—weather is less dependable in early spring.

Though it is possible to delineate the migration period of every species, the situation is actually quite complex. In many species, birds of different ages and sexes tend to migrate at somewhat different times. In spring, the males of many species of songbirds precede the females, presumably because it is to a male's advantage to arrive in its breeding area early and stake out its territory before its rivals do. In fall, when a large part of a species' population may be young birds on their first migration, the older and younger birds may migrate at different times. In many shorebirds, for example, the parents abandon their precocial young on the breeding grounds and head south in mid- to late summer. The young follow weeks or months later, so that within the migration period of a given species there is one pulse of adult birds and a second pulse of first-time migrants. These kinds of patterns typify what is known as differential migration of age and sex classes.

Wayne Lankinen/DRK Photo

Many songbirds cross the Gulf of Mexico in the evening and arrive on the northern Gulf Coast sometime the next day. Ruby-throated Hummingbirds like this fair-throated female buzz across this 600-mile water gap without pausing.

Frans Lanting

Canada and Snow Geese stop to feed at a traditional stopover site. Some staging areas have been used by waterfowl for years because they are reliable sources of food and water.

Fueling for the Journey

Flying is strenuous activity, and even though birds are marvelously adapted to their aerial life, with super-efficient hemoglobin, a lung and air-sac system that allows for maximum oxygen intake, and hollow bones, a calorie is still only a calorie, and it takes a lot of them to propel a body through the air over hundreds of miles. As the season of migration approaches, signaled by the changing length of the day (see page 98) as well as by built-in biological clocks (see page 158), a bird's metabolism changes and it begins to deposit stores of fat under its skin. In species that make long, nonstop flights, the amount of fat deposited can be quite impressive, equaling half their normal body weight or more. A single flight exhausts a large proportion of these "fuel tanks," which must then be replenished before the next leg of the journey. For this reason, it is vitally important for migrating birds to find good, stable food supplies during their journey as well as before it. Stopover sites where fat stores can be replenished quickly can therefore be every bit as important to long-distance migrants as suitable nesting and breeding grounds.

Ascending the Heights

Because of reports of planes colliding with birds at very high altitudes and the stories about the Bar-headed Geese that migrate over the Himalayas, cresting above Mount Everest, one could get the impression that bird migration normally occurs at immense heights. With the help of radar, however, we know which altitudes are common and which are unusual.

Birds behave somewhat differently from one species to the next, but most migration takes place at lower altitudes. The bulk of night-migrating songbirds fly at altitudes of less than 5,000 feet, and the majority travel no higher than 2,500 feet. Waterfowl and shorebirds tend to fly higher; it is not unusual to detect them above 10,000 feet or even as high as 20,000 feet, especially when they are making long, over-water flights.

Moody spring and fall skies often mean low cloud ceilings that force migrating birds to fly lower than usual. High-flying birds, such as geese, sometimes ascend through the cloud cover to migrate in the clear skies above.

Frans Lanting

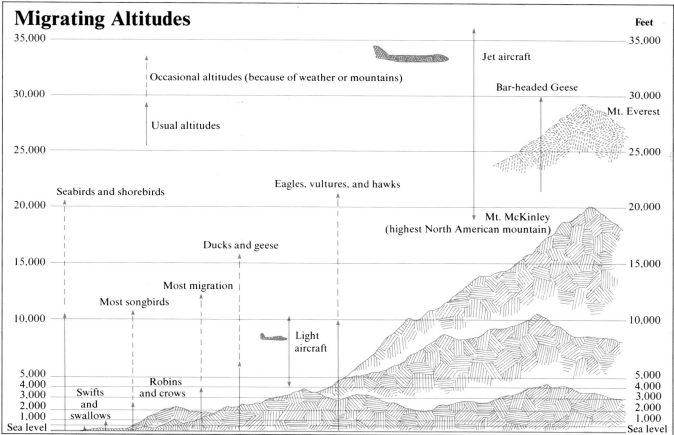

Migrating Altitudes

Feet

The most significant influence on the altitude at which birds fly is the weather, especially cloud cover and wind fields. Birds may fly lower when it is cloudy or, if the overcast is not too thick, they may ascend through it to reach the clear skies above. If favorable tail winds are to be found in certain altitudinal strata, birds often ascend or descend in order to take advantage of them.

H. Cruickshank/VIREO

Above: *Insect-eaters like the Barn Swallow begin to migrate in late summer, well before their food supply is threatened by early frosts. Spring migrants, driven to reach the breeding grounds early, are often caught by late spring storms that cause high mortality.*

Right: *Weather plays an important role in migration. The fog that surrounds these Snow Geese causes poor visibility, which sometimes interferes with the birds' navigational abilities. More turbulent weather may cause birds to stall behind major weather systems; the passage of frontal systems often results in sudden waves of migrants passing through.*

Frans Lanting

Checking the Weather

Just as long-term changes in climate have molded the evolution of bird migration, seasonal and day-to-day changes in weather dramatically influence the timing and course of migration. When the weather conditions are right, the number of birds in flight can reach millions. Not only are the immediate flight conditions important, but the weather at the destination or starting point of the flight may also be critical to a bird's survival. For example, water birds must not arrive at northern latitudes before the ice has melted, and many tend to follow the spring thaw northward; in late fall many linger in the north until freezing temperatures force them to move. For most birds, however, it pays to anticipate seasonal changes in climate and to be gone well before conditions deteriorate. Many warblers, flycatchers, and other insect eaters begin their fall migration in late summer while the days are still warm and the insect life abundant.

During migration, the most critical weather factors are wind direction and changes in temperature. In spring, northbound birds select the warming temperatures and southerly winds that characterize the western sides of high-pressure systems; in fall, they favor the lower temperatures and north winds that occur following the passage of a cold front. Birds also tend to avoid rainy, overcast weather, fog, and high winds, and even stop in the middle of their journey if they encounter deteriorating weather while over land. Recent research has shown that pigeons are quite sensitive to small changes in atmospheric pressure; it is possible that by monitoring changes in air pressure, birds are able to anticipate weather before any overt signs are evident.

The wind factor. At the altitudes at which birds fly, wind speeds often exceed 20 miles per hour. A head wind can halt a bird's forward progress or even blow it backward, whereas a tail wind can easily double its speed. High winds can prevent small birds from migrating. Strong crosswinds can cause birds to drift far off course and may be disastrous for land birds carried over the ocean; such winds are often the reason that birds are sometimes found far outside their normal range.

As in most aspects of bird behavior, there is variation in the speeds at which different species fly. Most small songbirds, for example, fly at air speeds (speed without any influence of wind) of only about 20 miles per hour. Waterfowl, and especially the larger shorebirds, maintain speeds of about 40 miles per hour or even more. Migrating birds, however, generally propel themselves at quite moderate speeds, which means that the wind has an enormous impact on their progress. It is therefore no surprise that birds are supreme interpreters of weather and wind.

Long flights over water or other inhospitable terrain provide the ultimate tests of migratory strategy. In many cases, selecting a departure day on which there are tail winds may make the difference between life and death. In spring, millions of small birds fly northward across the Gulf of Mexico. Most of the time at that latitude, moderate southerly winds blow across the gulf, aiding the migrants. Occasionally, however, a cold front penetrates the gulf from the north. With the northerly winds behind them, these fronts often do not reach Yucatán, a major departure point for the Gulf crossing. Thus, birds can embark on the trip in fine weather with southerly winds only to run into problems out over the water. Trouble will likely come in the form of rain showers and, if the birds penetrate the front, potent head winds. Under these conditions, what would have been a relatively easy trip can turn into a disaster, and birds that would have arrived on the northern Gulf Coast with fat to spare arrive exhausted at the beaches, if they make it at all. Thousands can die of starvation or dehydration while resting on offshore oil rigs or in the water itself, as evidenced by the corpses that sometimes wash up on beaches. Clearly, it pays to be able to judge the weather.

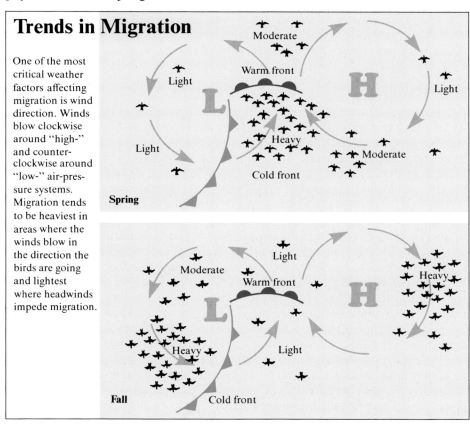

Trends in Migration

One of the most critical weather factors affecting migration is wind direction. Winds blow clockwise around "high-" and counter-clockwise around "low-" air-pressure systems. Migration tends to be heaviest in areas where the winds blow in the direction the birds are going and lightest where headwinds impede migration.

Moderate
Warm front
Light
L
H
Light
Light
Heavy
Moderate
Cold front
Spring

Light
Moderate
Warm front
H
Heavy
L
Heavy
Light
Fall
Cold front

Jonathan Blair/Woodfin Camp & Assoc.

Above: *Trained professionals work quickly to snare and band sandpipers, Red Knots, and others bound for South America. Banding birds has yielded much information on bird behavior and ecology.*

Above right: *Migrating hawks are easily observed from lookout points, usually along ridges or valleys. Other migrants concentrate their flight routes along rivers or the shores of large lakes.*

A. Morris/VIREO

Observing Migration

Over the decades, the dedicated work of the field-glass fraternity has yielded a vast amount of information about bird migration. Dedicated birders have revealed migration patterns of most species in North and Central America and Europe. As a result of these long-term observations, we know which species migrate early in the fall, where they nest and spend the winter, and what routes they travel in between. So detailed is the information on most species that modern field guides contain range maps that are generally accurate to within 50 miles. All over the world, an ever-increasing army of amateur bird-watchers provides state and local clubs with new facts for their files. Summaries of the most important of these observations are published in various state journals and in the magazine *American Birds*, published by the National Audubon Society.

Bird Banding

Answering the more detailed questions about migration requires the ability to recognize individual birds on later encounters and is therefore a somewhat more elaborate procedure than direct observation. Biologists have long employed crude techniques such as attaching bits of colored yarn to individual birds, but with the establishment of large-scale government bird banding programs, major advances became possible.

Since the system was begun in North America in the early 1920s, over 30 million birds have been fitted with tiny aluminum leg bands, each bearing a unique number and the address of the Bird Banding Laboratory of the United States Fish and Wildlife Service. This number is even more remarkable because nearly all of the trapping and banding of birds is done by amateurs who take it on as a hobby. Their meticulous records are transmitted to and logged by the Bird Banding Laboratory. Banded birds, trapped by another bander, recovered by a hunter, or found dead by a conscientious person who sends in the band, have provided an enormous amount of vital information about migration. Banding has also provided our best information on the life span of birds, on the ratios of adult birds to young birds and of males to females, and also on the speed with which migrating birds progress on their journey. (For information on what to do if you find a banded bird, see page 228.)

N.G. Smith/VIREO

Don & Pat Valenti

Above left: *A "kettle" of soaring Broad-winged Hawks takes advantage of rising air currents to gain altitude. Hawk migrations reach peak intensities on warm sunny days when thermal updrafts are well developed.*

Above: *This Canada Goose, with an aluminum band on its leg and a numbered plastic neck collar, can be observed without capturing it. The number and color of the collar identify the bird and can be used to trace its migration routes.*

In the process of handling many thousands of birds, banders have found that in a number of species the youngsters migrate at a different time of the season than the older birds. The patterns are complicated, but where a difference exists, young songbirds born in the summer tend to make their fall migration before the adults, while for many shorebirds, just the opposite is true. Important studies now under way are using banded birds to try to discover patterns of migration distance and winter distribution in relation to the age and sex of the birds.

The most important information we have learned from banded birds is that they regularly return to the same places year after year. Even small songbirds that migrate long distances show a strong tendency to return year after year to the same places to build their nests; similarly, they return again and again to the same winter locality. The first nesting site of most songbirds is close to their place of birth. Before leaving that area on its first fall migration, a young bird does what biologists call imprinting—it learns some characteristics about the place so that it can find the same spot when it returns. A similar process apparently takes place at the wintering ground selected by a young bird on its first migration.

Direct Observation

Sometimes the simplest technique—direct observation—is the best method for learning about birds in migration. All that is required are binoculars, a telescope, an advantageous location, and a good deal of patience.

Several birds, such as hawks, cranes, blackbirds, some waterfowl, and some finches, migrate by day and have concentrated areas of passage. Hawks migrate during the day in order to take advantage of thermal currents (see page 131). Species like Broad-winged, Red-tailed, and Swainson's Hawks are marvelous to watch as they glide from thermal to thermal, effortlessly dipping and rising. They can be seen ascending to great heights without flapping a wing and then losing altitude during the glide between thermals. Hawks use this free ride all year, but tend to depend more on thermals during migration. Because of their dependence on atmospheric structure, hawks are largely confined to migrating over land (thermals rarely develop over water) and can be found in concentrations near ridges and along the shores of large lakes and oceans.

Night Observation

Most species and individual birds that migrate do so under cover of darkness. It is a mystery why so many birds migrate at night. The conventional explanation is that since tiny birds must search for food such as insects on foliage, requiring all the daylight hours just to meet their basic survival requirements, they are left with no alternative but to fly at night. While this explanation may sound reasonable, there is little real evidence to support it. The fact that such a diverse array of birds migrate nocturnally suggests that there may be other, still undiscovered, factors involved.

As could be expected, observing birds at night presents special difficulties. With the help of some telescopic equipment, however, a fascinating world is available for discovery. By training a telescope on the disk of the full moon at certain times of the year, migrating birds can be seen passing in silhouette. Some birds can be seen with 7 × binoculars, but 10 × binoculars or a 20 × to 40 × telescope mounted on a tripod is better. (For more information on spotting equipment, see page 231.)

During the 1950s, two ornithologists at Lousiana State University, George Lowery and Robert Newman, refined the moon-watching method of observing nocturnal migration to calculate the passage rate of migrants and the precise direction of their flight. Large-scale studies using volunteer observers stationed across North America turned up a great amount of data on night migration. Perhaps most important was the confirmation that night-migrating songbirds move on a broad front rather than following narrow corridors or flyways, and often pass over coastlines, river valleys, and mountain ridges without changing course. Also confirmed was the fact that millions of birds regularly cross the Gulf of Mexico.

Moon-watching as a means of studying migration has obvious limitations, the most significant being that observations are confined to clear nights near the time of a full moon. Fairly recently, however, a technique was developed using portable narrow-beam 100-watt ceilometer lights—the kind airports once used for estimating cloud height. Extremely bright

Night Watching

Most birds migrate by night. With a 20× to 40× telescope or 10× binoculars, the birds can be seen passing in silhouette during a full moon.

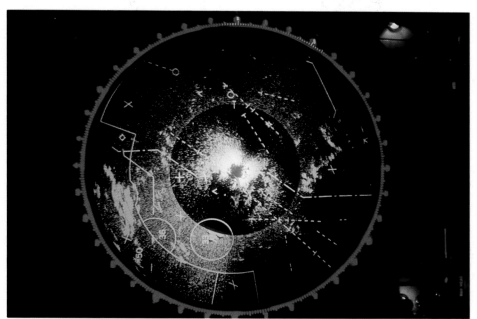

Jonathan Blair/Woodfin Camp & Assoc.

The night exodus of two million songbirds appears as green "continents" on the radar screen at an airport. Radar studies provide information on the effects of weather and geography on nocturnal migration patterns.

ceilometer lights tend to attract migrating birds, but less powerful beams pointed skyward and observed with a pair of binoculars or a telescope can reveal faintly illuminated birds zipping through the field of light. The information obtained—magnitude of migration and direction of flight—is the same as in moon-watching, but the number of nights when data can be gathered is much greater. Moon-watching has also been useful in many parts of the country for studying the orientation (direction-finding) behavior of free-flying birds under a variety of conditions.

Radar Observation

All the methods of observation described so far give the observer the feeling of peeping through a keyhole—if only the door could be opened and the whole room viewed! An accidental discovery made during World War II has allowed us what is probably our best chance to "walk into the room," and has triggered an explosive growth of information on migration over the past 20 years.

During the Second World War, British radar surveillance technicians rather frequently observed echoes on their screens that could not be attributed to aircraft, weather, or ground targets. Because they appeared and disappeared mysteriously and because military personnel could not identify them, the echoes were dubbed "angels," a term still applied to unusual returns on radar scopes. But the appearance and movements of these original angels were not random, and when ornithologists got the opportunity to look at the radar films it became apparent that many of these moving targets were remarkably coincident with known migratory movements of birds. This discovery opened the way for the era of radar ornithology after the war ended.

Radar works much like a searchlight, but instead of a beam of light, a beam of microwave energy is emitted. A minute amount of this energy is reflected back from objects in the air space and is detected as an "echo" by the receiving unit of the radar. Because water is highly reflective of radar wavelength energy, both rain and birds (whose bodies contain water) are readily detected. With the radar used for long-range surveillance and weather monitoring, movements of birds can be seen at ranges of tens and even hundreds of miles.

Charles Walcott

Above: *Homing pigeons are released at an unfamiliar location to test their ability to navigate back to home lofts. Information gathered about birds' homing abilities during long-distance flights derives largely from studies of pigeons.*

Above right: *A Manx Shearwater, when released thousands of miles from its nest, will return within days. In one study, a Manx Shearwater averaged 250 miles per day during a homing flight that lasted 12 days and covered 3,200 miles.*

Adrian Davies/Bruce Coleman, Inc.

Finding the Way Home

The ability of birds to return to a familiar place from any distance is a remarkable feat of nature. For centuries people have taken advantage of this ability in homing pigeons by using them to carry messages from distant points back to familiar sites. Homing pigeons are domesticated non-migratory birds with an instinct to return to their lofts (nesting sites) that is improved with training and by selective breeding. Training is started at short distances from the nesting site; over time, this distance is gradually increased to hundreds of miles. An experienced homing pigeon released hundreds of miles from its loft at a completely unfamiliar location flies in the direction of home within a minute or two of its release. How does this extraordinary behavior work?

Understanding homing behavior is one of the greatest challenges to ornithologists. Fortunately, because they are able to carefully control the conditions under which the pigeons are released, researchers have been able to learn a great deal about how the birds navigate their way home.

Although homing ability has been fostered in pigeons by careful breeding and selecting of stock, it appears that training is not always necessary: Many species of wild birds perform similarly remarkable feats. One such bird is the migratory Manx Shearwater. Built like tiny albatrosses, these seabirds spend most of their lives skimming over the ocean surface far from the sight of land. They come ashore only to nest in burrows, which they dig in the ground on offshore islands in order to be safe from predators. The ease of locating and observing their nests makes shearwaters ideal subjects for homing experiments.

In one such experiment, adult shearwaters taken from nesting burrows off the coast of Wales were flown thousands of miles from their nests to places in Europe and North America that were completely unfamiliar to them. Most of the birds returned to their burrows at astonishing speeds, speeds that would not have been possible had they wandered randomly or searched for the way home over a wide area. Even traveling over what to our eyes appears to be trackless ocean, these birds demonstrated that they knew the precise direction in which they needed to go. Ornithologists believe that similar abilities are responsible for the return of small land birds to previous nesting and wintering places at the ends of long migrations.

Jonathan Blair/Woodfin Camp & Assoc.

From the ink pad on the bottom of this orientation cage, a bird makes tracks to the northeast, a course it would normally fly during spring migration. By rotating visual cues, it is possible to trick the bird into selecting the wrong direction.

In conical cages Indigo Buntings successfully orient under a planetarium sky. By using a planetarium, scientists can alter aspects of the sky to determine their importance as migratory cues.

Jonathan Blair/Woodfin Camp & Assoc.

Charting the Path of Migratory Birds

Charting the path of migratory birds presents some practical problems, since most migratory birds do not lend themselves to experimentation in the way that Manx Shearwaters do. Scientists may be able to determine a bird's migration route in a general way by observing or capturing it somewhere along the way, but it is impossible to pin down its precise destination. Fortunately, as a result of one of those lucky discoveries that often change the course of scientific investigations, controlled experiments can now be performed with migratory birds, even in the wild.

In the 1940s, a German ornithologist named Gustav Kramer studied the behavior of migratory birds by placing them in circular cages. He found that the birds tended to hop in the same direction in which they would have flown had they been free to migrate. This observation led to the development of what are called orientation cages. Orientation cages have enabled scientists to study migration under conditions in which they can control, or even alter, the information available to the bird.

There are several different types of orientation cages, but all of them have in common some means of recording birds' hopping patterns. With the help of these cages, it is now known that species that migrate only at night become restless during the seasons of migration and in those times of year hop and flutter throughout the night. If during the spring one places such a bird outdoors under a clear sky in an orientation cage, the bird hops mainly toward the northward side of the cage; in fall it hops in the opposite direction.

The free-flying world of the migratory bird is much more complex than the confines of an orientation cage. Field studies using radar and visual observation have shown that the direction of the wind often influences the orientation of migrants in dramatic ways. Especially when important visual cues such as the sun and stars are not visible, some migrants have a strong tendency to orient downwind, no matter which direction the wind is blowing. This kind of behavior is partly responsible for the common occurrence of mass migrations in peculiar, often reversed, directions.

The Great Navigators

Many migratory birds are remarkably faithful to previous nesting and overwintering places. Though a bird might be able to come close to these sites merely by flying in a general direction during the course of migration, at some point more sophisticated navigating techniques must take over to guide the bird to its precise destination.

Many animals are able to find their way home. One way of doing this is to directly sense the goal—to see, hear, or smell it. Another way is to memorize the details of the outward journey and then reverse the route based on an integration of that information. Birds, however, apparently rely on a completely different process to find their way.

To understand the nature of the problem, imagine yourself in the following situation: You have been blindfolded and taken by a circuitous and unfamiliar route to a place you have never been before. There, in a forest, without any view of distant landmarks, the blindfold is removed. You are left alone with a compass and a map, and you need to find your way back home. Unfortunately, before you can use the compass for information about direction, you must determine where you are in relation to your goal—you need to find your location on the map so you will know where you are in relation to home. A bird in an unfamiliar setting is quickly able to gain the information it needs to orient itself and navigate its way back home. To explain bird navigation, we have what is known as the "map-and-compass" theory.

The compass component of this theory gives directions—north, south, east, west; the map component tells the bird where it is, or gives locality. Scientists have learned a great deal more about the compass component than they have about mapping. They know that birds have several means of determining compass directions, but, unfortunately, they still have no satisfactory explanation for how birds use biological "maps" to guide them to a precise location from an unfamiliar starting point.

Sun compass. Some observations indicate that birds might use the sun as a visual cue to determine compass directions. Starlings, for example, seem able to negotiate the proper direction only if they have a view of the clear sky and sun; cloud cover seems to induce confusion. In an experiment in which the sun's apparent position was changed with mirrors attached to an orientation cage containing starlings, observers noted that the direction of the starlings' hopping, which earlier had been correlated to the direction they choose to migrate, was shifted accordingly.

Even birds that migrate exclusively at night pay considerable attention to the sun. At first this may seem odd because, after all, the sun is not visible to the nocturnal birds when they are flying. On the other hand, it is a predominant feature in the sky at a time of day (dusk) when birds may well be making decisions about whether to fly that night and in what direction. Radar studies have shown that most night migrants take off during this twilight period.

Like many other animals (including insects, fish, reptiles, and mammals), birds are endowed with a built-in clock that tells them the time of

P. Greenleaf/VIREO

European Starlings, seen here at a morning roost, depend heavily on the sun for orientation. On cloudy days they may restrict their flights to short distances and travel in larger flocks, as if to take advantage of their collective navigational abilities.

day. Using this internal clock, young pigeons, at least, learn the sun's path of movement across the sky. (Many birds are known to have an internal clock, and many are known to have a sun compass, but it is only in pigeons that ornithologists can watch the learning process develop.)

Star compass. As we have mentioned previously, most birds migrate not by day, but by night. Employing the same types of cages, researchers quickly observed that night migrants exhibited hopping behavior similar to that of day migrants and that they oriented themselves in the proper direction under clear, starry skies but became disoriented when it was cloudy. The decisive tests were performed in a planetarium, where star patterns can be manipulated at will. The experiments indicated that night-migrating birds learn and orient by the spatial relationships among the constellations, rather than using information supplied by any single star. More recently, scientists have discovered that birds begin to develop star compass capability when they are quite young, and as experienced adults they can use many parts of the sky to decipher compass directions.

Magnetic compass. A sun compass for migration during the day, a star compass for nocturnal migration—life would be much simpler had this been the end of the story. For a long time there has been a popular theory that birds also have a magnetic compass guiding their navigatory behavior. There is good reason for that speculation—it would be a convenient system to use during overcast days or nights. But many respected biologists assured ornithologists that for birds to sense such a force was almost impossible since the earth's magnetic field is such a weak force. A group of German ornithologists conducted research that provided evidence to the contrary.

Gary R. Zahm/DRK Photo

A flock of ducks, silhouetted by the setting sun, takes flight toward its northern breeding sites. Nocturnal migrants like these may rely on the stars as a means of navigation.

In the study, night migrants that were placed in orientation cages indoors in closed rooms showed weak but consistent and seasonally appropriate hopping directions, which suggested that they did not need the sun or stars to determine direction. By placing the cages within sets of wire coils through which a weak electric current was passed, it was possible to change the configuration of the magnetic field surrounding the birds to determine if they would respond in a predictable way. Although their responses continued to be weak, the birds did respond, and their orientation could be shifted by changing the magnetic directions. Similar results have been obtained with homing pigeons. It therefore appears that in addition to sun and star compasses, at least several kinds of birds possess a magnetic compass, though as yet none of the field studies has found a clear indication of its influence on migratory birds in the wild.

Biological maps. After about three decades of experiments on homing pigeons, scientists currently have two viable hypotheses concerning the "mapping" ability of birds. Although only homing pigeons have been studied, there is good reason to believe that migratory birds also rely on some sort of biological map to find their way back to traditional nesting or wintering sites.

The first hypothesis, conceived and tested primarily by a group of Italian scientists, involves an "odor map." The scientists propose that young pigeons learn this map by smelling different odors that reach their home loft on winds from varying directions. They would, for example, learn that a certain odor arrives on winds blowing from the east. If a pigeon is transported eastward from its loft it should smell that odor more strongly either on the way to or at the release site. That should tell the pigeon that it needs to fly westward to return home. Although it may sound preposterous to some, there is a large amount of evidence supporting this hypothesis. However, even its strongest proponents do not extend the idea to include long-distance migrants.

The second hypothesis proposes that birds may be able to extract latitude and longitude from the earth's magnetic field. Unlike the compasses that are thought to help birds determine direction, this map is believed to help birds determine location. The main support for this hypothesis comes from observations of pigeons released in areas of "magnetic anomalies" (places where the earth's magnetic field is disturbed due to large iron deposits near the surface). When pigeons are first released in these areas, they depart in random directions, but after their initial confusion, most birds are able to correct their course and return home once they escape the influence of the anomaly. Since, in theory, magnetic

Navigating Techniques

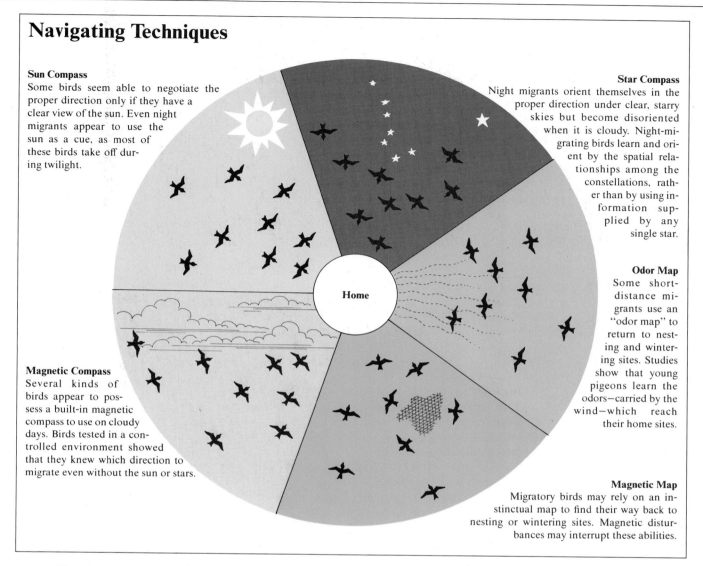

Sun Compass
Some birds seem able to negotiate the proper direction only if they have a clear view of the sun. Even night migrants appear to use the sun as a cue, as most of these birds take off during twilight.

Star Compass
Night migrants orient themselves in the proper direction under clear, starry skies but become disoriented when it is cloudy. Night-migrating birds learn and orient by the spatial relationships among the constellations, rather than by using information supplied by any single star.

Odor Map
Some short-distance migrants use an "odor map" to return to nesting and wintering sites. Studies show that young pigeons learn the odors—carried by the wind—which reach their home sites.

Magnetic Compass
Several kinds of birds appear to possess a built-in magnetic compass to use on cloudy days. Birds tested in a controlled environment showed that they knew which direction to migrate even without the sun or stars.

Magnetic Map
Migratory birds may rely on an instinctual map to find their way back to nesting or wintering sites. Magnetic disturbances may interrupt these abilities.

anomalies are not a strong enough force to affect any of the birds' compasses—magnetic, sun, or star—proponents argue that the fact that the pigeons *are* initially affected indicates the existence of a different aspect of navigation that *is* being affected—hence, the map.

Neither hypothesis has been proven to the satisfaction of all the experts, so new and different experiments continue to be performed. It may turn out that neither of these alternatives is correct, or a synthesis of the two may emerge.

Miles to Go Before We Sleep

Finding not one but several natural compasses in birds has considerably complicated ornithologists' task of trying to understand the processes underlying migratory orientation. Instead of searching for "the answer" to the problem, they have had to try to unravel the relationships among the various known influencing factors. Until we have all the pieces in their proper places, we will not know if others are missing. We have learned a great deal about bird migration over the past two or three decades, but there is much left to be explained and, in all likelihood, some unexpected discoveries await us as we explore this fascinating behavior.

J. Dawson '86

Attracting Birds

by William E. Poole

*B*irds offer us our best chance to observe wild creatures close at hand. Many animals avoid our homes and cities, and those that do happen into our backyards are rarely seen. But birds are all around us, up before we are, and active much of the day. Unless we have retreated to a windowless hole, every day should bring at least a glimpse of a bird.

Those who enjoy the touch of wildness birds bring to their lives often go out of their way to see feathered creatures. According to a recent survey by the United States Department of the Interior, watching and feeding birds ranks second only to gardening as America's favorite pastime. More and more people are buying binoculars and field guides and setting off in search of birds. Many are also taking the opposite approach, making an effort to get the birds to come to them.

Attracting birds can be as simple as hanging a hummingbird feeder on a city balcony or as complex as excavating a backyard duck pond. Wherever you live, winged creatures await your hospitality.

Northern Cardinals, such as this male and female, are easily attracted to suburban gardens for seed. Their bright colors make them a special pleasure to see on bleak winter days.

Thomas D. Mangelsen

By providing the comforts of home, you can turn any backyard into a hotspot for birds like these sparrows, Northern Cardinal, and Blue Jay.

Backyard Habitats

If we want the birds to make their homes near ours, we must provide them with a desirable environment in which to live. Think for a moment about what would attract you to a new home. You would want shelter of the quality to which you were accustomed, nearby facilities to get food and drink, and some promise that your family would be safe and prosperous. Birds look for many of the same things. Food, water, protective cover, and a sheltered place to raise their young are the basic requirements for their survival. To attract nesting birds to your yard, offer as many of these resources as you can within their easy reach.

Many backyards offer birds a landscape familiar enough that they will come to explore, special enough that they will choose to stay. A combination of plants, open space, and buildings, the home landscape offers many parallels to natural habitat. Plants of varying heights, flower beds, and lawns resemble the edge habitat birds find so appealing in the wild.

Our gardens and yards serve many purposes. We use them as picnic grounds and playgrounds. We may dedicate an area to growing food and another to a paved patio for quiet dining or entertainment. We may grow big maples to shade our houses in summer or tight lines of evergreens to deflect winter winds. Birds are able to utilize many parts of this environment. Sparrows flock to glean the crumbs from our picnics. The puddles on our patios after a rain offer birds a drink and a welcome bath. Our trees offer shelter to birds as well as humans, and provide them with seeds, cones, and fat, juicy bugs. Unless your backyard is asphalt from end to end, you probably have a bird habitat of one sort or another.

Chimney Swifts

Chimney Swifts make their nests in chimneys, where they cling to the rocky surface with specially adapted feet.

A Barn Swallow feeds a nest full of young in the shelter of a porch roof. Barn Swallows are dependent almost entirely on artificial structures for nesting sites.

Alexander Lowry

Buildings as Habitats

You might think that houses and other buildings would be unattractive to birds, but nothing could be farther from the truth. Their steep sides present abrupt edges that duplicate the cliff faces and palisades of the natural world. The walls of buildings offer 180-degree protection, and shrubbery or vines used as foundation plantings provide homes for thrushes, finches, cardinals, and many other birds.

Many birds nest in unlikely places around our homes. Hummingbirds may tuck their tiny, cup-shaped nests into the top of a patio light fixture. House Finches and phoebes will nest under the eaves of a house or porch roof. Wrens and other birds have been known to build their nests inside occupied homes. In order to control where birds nest, many people screen off nooks and crannies where birds are not welcome and build nesting shelves or boxes for them.

The rooftops and chimneys of our houses and buildings are often the tallest spots around, which makes them ideal lookouts for birds such as kestrels, mockingbirds, and crows. Starlings sometimes cuddle up to the outside of a warm chimney on a frigid day. During summer in the eastern United States, Chimney Swifts often nest in chimneys where they cling to the sooty walls with long, sharp toes specially adapted for such rocky crevices. If you use your chimney, you will probably want to screen the top to prevent birds from nesting, but if you have a chimney you do not use, you might want to leave it open, since Chimney Swifts can be a pleasure. Their sweeping flight is lovely, and they dedicate their days to the eradication of beetles, flies, ants, termites, and other undesirable insects.

Thomas D. Mangelsen

Above: *American Goldfinches relish thistles. The plant provides soft yet strong nesting material, seeds for the adults, and insects for the young.*

Above right: *A diverse and natural setting, such as this prairie garden, is a sure way of attracting a variety of birds.*

Ortho Photo Library

Creating Attractive Backyard Habitats

The surest way to attract birds is to concentrate the resources they need in one place. Also, the scarcer the resource offered, the more birds you can attract: Offer them something they need and have trouble finding anywhere else. If you live in the deserts of the Southwest, the fastest way to fill your garden with birds is to build a small oasis with water and low shrubs for protection. If you live on the plains, grow trees; if you live in the woods, chop out a clearing.

Consider what your neighbors have done with their yards; the habitat you build in your backyard will be part of a larger one that you share with them. If no one in your neighborhood is offering water, by all means do so. If most local trees drop their leaves and turn to windy skeletons each fall, you might plant evergreens. If no one is growing a pyracantha or other bush with berries that will hold through the winter, consider growing one in your garden. The greater the variety of food, water, and shelter in the neighborhood, the more birds will gather for everyone to enjoy.

Choosing plants. Because they offer food, shelter, and nesting sites, plants are the most important element in any backyard habitat. The chart on page 167 lists plants that are attractive to birds and to gardeners alike. Use it as a guide to ensure that your yard provides the right lighting and space requirements for the plants you choose. Local nurseries and garden centers are excellent sources of plants for your area. Many now tag the plants that attract birds. Garden clubs are another excellent source of inexpensive plants and gardening tips. Many club members are also passionate bird-watchers and willingly share secrets of bird attraction.

If left alone, most plots of ground revert quickly to the native grasses and brush that birds love. If it suits your inclination and neighborhood style, leave a corner of your yard wild to make the birds feel at home.

A yard does not have to be wild, however, to benefit from native plantings. Native plants are an excellent choice for any style of backyard landscaping. Be careful not to waste valuable plants you may already have. When clearing a wild patch, cut around native seedlings and

A Bird's Garden

Annuals
(for flowers and seeds)
Amaranthus [1]
Bachelor Button
Calendula
California Poppy
China Aster
Coreopsis
Cosmos
Gloriosa Daisy [1]
Grasses:
    Crimson Fountain Grass [1]
    Hare's Tail Grass [1]
    Love Grass [1]
    Quaking Grass [1]
    Plains Bristle Grass [1]
Love-in-a-mist [1]
Marigold
Pink
Portulaca
Sea Lavender [1]
Sunflower [1]
Zinnia

Perennials
(for flowers and seeds)
Aster [1]
Black-eyed Susan [1]
Butterfly flower [1]
Chrysanthemum
Columbine
Coreopsis
Goldenrod [1]
Globe Thistle [1]
Grasses:
    Bulbous Oatgrass [1]
    Eulalia Grass [1]
    Little Blue Stem [1]
    Pampas Grass [1]
    Tufted Hair Grass [1]
Pinks
Purple Coneflower [1]
Scabiosa

Showy Stonecrop [1]
Statice [1]
Sunflower [1]

Shrubs
Aromatic Sumac [2]
Bayberry [5]
Blackberry and Raspberry [5]
Blueberry [5]
Boxwood [2, 3, 4, 8]
Cherry Laurel [2, 3, 4, 8]
Currant [5]
Dogwood:
    Bloodtwig Dogwood [2]
    Gray Dogwood [2]
    Red Osier Dogwood [2]
    Silky Dogwood [2]
    Taterian Dogwood [2]
Elderberry [2, 5]
Elaeagnus [5]
Euonymus:
    Winged Euonymus [2]
    Wintercreeper [2]
Firethorn [3, 5, 8]
Holly:
    Chinese Holly [2, 3, 4, 5, 8]
    Common Winterberry [2, 3, 5]
    Japanese Holly [2, 3, 4, 8]
    Possumhaw [2, 3, 5]
    Yaupon [3, 4, 8]
Honeysuckle:
    Amur Honeysuckle [5]
    Box Honeysuckle [8]
    Morrow Honeysuckle [5]
    Tatarian Honeysuckle [3, 5]
    Winter Honeysuckle [5]
Japanese Barberry [8]
Juniper [3, 4, 8]
Mugo Pine [3, 4]
Myrtle [3, 4, 8]
Privet:
    Amur Privet [2, 8]
    Border Privet [2, 8]

California Privet [2, 8]
Rose [5]
Serviceberry:
    Pacific Serviceberry [2, 3, 5]
    Running Serviceberry [2, 3, 5]
Shrub Bushclover [3]
Silverberry [8]
Spicebush [2, 5]
Viburnum:
    American Cranberrybush [2, 3, 5]
    Arrowwood Viburnum [2, 5]
    Doublefile Viburnum [5]
    European Cranberrybush [3, 5]
    Hobblebush [2]
    Linden Viburnum [5]
    Sargent Viburnum [5]
    Siebold Viburnum [5]
    Tea Viburnum [5]
    Wayfaringtree Viburnum [2]
Wintercreeper [8]
Witchhazel:
    Chinese Witchhazel [2]
    Common Witchhazel [2]
    Japanese Witchhazel [2]
    Vernal Witchhazel [2, 3]
Yew [2, 3, 4, 8]

Trees
Alder:
    Black Alder [6]
    Italian Alder [6]
Birch [6]
Cherry and Plum [5]
Crabapple [3, 5]
Dogwood:
    Flowering Dogwood [2, 3, 5]
    Kousa Dogwood [2, 5]
    Red Osier Dogwood [5]
Eastern Hemlock [2]
Eastern White Pine [6]
Green Ash [6]
Hackberry:
    Common Hackberry [6]

Sugar Hackberry [6]
Hawthorn [3, 5]
Holly:
    American Holly [2, 3, 5]
    English Holly [2, 3, 5]
    Longstalk Holly [2, 3, 5]
Honeylocust [6]
Hornbeam [3]
Japanese Maple [2]
Japanese Privet [2]
Maple:
    Amur Maple [3]
    Japanese Maple [3, 4]
    Red Maple [6]
Mountain Ash [5]
Oak:
    Pin Oak [6]
    Red Oak [6]
Poplar, Aspen [6]
Serviceberry:
    Allegheny Serviceberry [2, 3, 5]
    Apple Serviceberry [2, 3, 5]
    Downy Serviceberry [2, 3, 5]
Sumac:
    Flameleaf Sumac [5, 6]
    Staghorn Sumac [5, 6]
Sweet Gum [6]
Tuliptree [6]

Vines
Bittersweet:
    American Bittersweet
    Oriental Bittersweet
English Ivy [7]
Fiveleaf Akebia
Grape
Honeysuckle:
    Everblooming Honeysuckle
    Japanese Honeysuckle
    Trumpet Honeysuckle
Porcelain Ampelopsis
Virginia Creeper [7]
Wintercreeper [7]

Key
[1] Especially beautiful in seed.
[2] Shade-tolerant; good for woodland understory.
[3] Good for small places.
[4] Good in containers.
[5] Fruiting type for full sun.
[6] Fast growing; good for small groves.
[7] Attaches to rough surfaces without a trellis.
[8] Shrubs for hedges.

Consult your local nursery or garden center for more bird-attracting plants.

nurture them into trees or shrubs. Many are as beautiful as those that come from nurseries, and a plant you own is always cheaper than one you buy. Collect your own wild plant seeds, too. The period between August and November is generally best for collecting the seeds. Never transplant from parks or other public lands or from any natural area that is not about to be destroyed. Removing wild plants is illegal in many states and only acceptable when the area is about to be leveled and developed. Even then, be sure to ask the landowner for permission before you dig.

You can supplement the wild plants in your yard without spending too much money. Arboretums and native plant societies sometimes have fund-raising plant sales, and many nurseries carry native plants and seeds.

Ortho Photo Library

A well-planned hedge like this one provides plenty of food, cover, and nesting sites for birds.

Cedar Waxwings are easily attracted to fruit-bearing trees or shrubs for food and tend to nest in areas where such plantings are available.

D. & M. Zimmerman

Whether you get your plants from a friend, rescue them from a construction site, or purchase them at the corner garden center, keep the following suggestions in mind as you make your choices:

• Choose a variety of vegetational types. Remember, birds favor areas where different kinds of vegetation come together. Trees, shrubs, flowers, grasses, and vines offer different advantages to birds.

• Choose plants that birds can use for a variety of purposes. Plants that supply shelter but are without edible berries or seeds only work half-time for the birds in your yard.

• Provide as great a mixture of food as you can. Plant cone-bearing evergreens for finches and crossbills, and grasses and grains for seed-eating birds. Offer berries for waxwings and mockingbirds and acorns and other nuts for jays and woodpeckers.

• Select plants that will bear food in different seasons. Some trees and shrubs bear fruit in the summer; others bear in the fall. Summer berries, like raspberries and blueberries, are high in sugar and must be eaten quickly before they spoil. Many fall berries, such as pyracantha, hawthorns, and chokecherries, are lower in sugar and fats so they do not decay, but stay on their branches through the winter as food for birds. Variety is important when it comes to backyard plantings—it is your guarantee that the birds will find enough resources in your yard to make them stay around.

Placement of backyard plants. You will not be able to enjoy the birds if you cannot see them. Whether you are creating a new landscape or making changes in the one you already have, try to attract the birds to areas where they are visible from a window. In general, put taller trees and shrubs farther from the house, and shorter shrubs, flower beds, and lawns closer to the house. Make sure you can see every planting from the house so you get the most pleasure when birds visit.

Shrubbery is the most versatile vegetation in a backyard bird habitat. One medium-sized bush can provide cover, food, and nesting sites for many birds. Most birds prefer to locate their nests between 5 and 8 feet

A Diverse Backyard Habitat

A yard that combines trees, shrubs, flowers, grasses, and vines with food and water is especially appealing to birds.

off the ground. Whenever possible, plant shrubs along the walls of buildings to take advantage of the extra protection the walls provide. Do not keep plantings too closely cropped—most birds prefer shaggy shrubbery.

Because shrubs and evergreens provide much of the middle-height cover in a backyard habitat, situate them close to food sources. Few birds are comfortable feeding in the open for very long; most prefer to have cover nearby in the event that some unexpected danger necessitates quick retreat. Place bird feeders and baths so the birds can reach shrubbery in a moment's flight but not so close that a cat or other predator could pounce from hiding.

Ivies, creepers, and other vines along the wall of a building greatly enhance the cover it provides. Many vines offer berries as well and are favorite nesting sites. Protect your home from dampness by growing vines on trellises a few inches out from the walls. Vines also provide ground cover in the garden where they furnish food and shelter for thrushes, Fox Sparrows, and other birds of the forest floor.

B. Lebaron

Above: *Cavity-nesting birds, such as this Northern Flicker, depend on strong dead trees and will return to favorable sites year after year.*

Above right: *This wooded backyard shows a good mixture of coniferous and deciduous trees. Native underbrush merges gently with a centralized clearing.*

Ortho Photo Library

Improving a wooded garden. A wooded garden will attract more birds if you create the edge habitat they find so inviting. Start by taking an inventory of your biggest plants. Do you have both evergreen and deciduous trees? The best bird habitat contains a mixture of the two types of trees. Trees with evergreen needles—pines, hemlocks, firs, spruces, yews, and junipers—provide crucial cover for birds in cold or stormy climates. Gardens that consist entirely of evergreens often seem dark and closed in, however. An eye-pleasing combination of deciduous and evergreen trees contains about 10 percent evergreens.

If your whole yard is in shade, decide whether you really need all those trees. A little sunlight encourages the growth of smaller plants and makes it easier to grow shrubs in your yard. Before removing any dead trees, however, consider that they provide a feast for woodpeckers and are a natural home to many cavity-nesting birds. If the roots of a dead tree seem secure, trim any branches that might fall into the yard and leave the trunk for the birds.

After you have cut clearings in your wooded habitat, you have a choice. If you are of the school of natural landscaping, simply put away the pruning shears; in a year or two you should have a rich growth of brushy vegetation thick with sparrows. If you are a more traditional gardener, select shrubs, vines, and ground cover for your woodland habitat, and keep the wilder growth cut back. Many people choose an option between the two extremes. They leave a wild corner here and there or use native plants in a formal style.

If your garden has a dark corner in which nothing can grow, leave it alone. Let the leaves from surrounding trees accumulate for a year or two. The plant material keeps the soil from washing away and provides cover for a feast of grubs and insects for ground-feeding forest birds like Wood Thrushes, Fox Sparrows, and towhees. Vines and ivies also work well as ground cover in dark areas, and they provide the same benefits to birds of the forest floor.

George H. Harrison

By creating islands of vegetation, the attractiveness of a garden can be increased. This island of trees, shrubs, flowers, and a birdbath can provide birds with a wealth of food, water, and cover.

Improving an open garden. If your yard is part of a sunny, open habitat, it probably already attracts many open-country birds, such as mockingbirds, quail, and goldfinches. Increasing the number and variety of birds in such a place is a matter of building edges and adding varied habitat.

Inventory your yard or garden. Unless you have dedicated all of your land to manicured lawn, you probably have an assortment of small trees, shrubs, and flower beds scattered about. Keep these spots, and plant around them to increase the diversity of the vegetation. If you have a tree standing alone, for example, resist the temptation to mow all the way to its trunk. Let the native grasses and hardwood brush fill in or dig around the tree and plant shade-loving shrubs of your choosing. Plant borders along one side of your flower beds, and big trees beside your shrubs. In each case the goal is the same—an island of complex vegetation where there was once a single feature.

If you are starting from scratch, get the trees in first—they take the longest to grow. This is a good time to break the rule about planting for mature spacing. Planting a cluster of trees provides much-needed cover and a focal point for some shrubs or native grasses. As the trees grow too large for the cluster, transplant as needed to create space or to start other islands around the yard. Fast-growing trees like alders, birches, and hackberries are most appropriate for this venture. (Hackberries produce sweet, purple fruit that lasts through the winter.) In winter put feeders, birdbaths, and other water sources near these plantings. Most birds prefer to approach water from cover and appreciate perches nearby for drying off.

Also take advantage of the house itself. Plant the walls with ivy and the foundations with pyracantha, yew, or another dense shrub. Be sure to plant far enough back from the edges of the windows to allow clear lines of sight to your bird feeders. Take advantage of the cover your house provides by adding one or two fruit-bearing trees nearby. Remember, the attractiveness of both food and cover are doubled by their proximity to one another.

Flowers growing in big, sunny garden plots attract birds. They provide nectar and insects for warblers, kinglets, and many other species. Later in the season they also provide seeds for doves, quail, finches, sparrows, and other seed-eaters.

Pick out a sunny spot toward the back of your property for a special bird-food garden. The core of this garden should be as many sunflower plants as you have space for. Sunflower seeds are a great favorite with many seed-eating birds, and they are an excellent source of protein. Leave them to dry on the stalks, where birds can find them during fall and winter. Along with your sunflowers, plant millet and other cereal grains and some shocks of corn. Come harvest time your bird-food garden will be a favorite spot. After the natural food is gone, scatter cracked corn or other seed among the old stalks, and the birds will stay until spring.

Water for Backyard Birds

Birds need water every day in order to survive. Much of their water comes from surface sources—streams, ponds, puddles, raindrops on leaves, or dew on the grass—but they also get water from the foods they eat. Birds that live on fat, juicy insects, for example, need less than those that live on seeds, nuts, and grains. Some desert birds live for weeks on water they obtain from the insects and succulent plants in their diet.

Birds have evolved waste systems that absorb and concentrate fluids for reuse by the body; these systems reduce the amount of water birds need. On the other hand, birds lose much water during respiration, when the dry air they inhale steals it from moist lung tissue. Birds have no sweat glands and must cool their bodies by breathing more rapidly to increase evaporation in the lungs. As a result birds—especially small birds—are prone to dehydration on hot days. Water is tremendously important to birds in summer and is the one infallible bird lure in hot desert regions.

Clean, fresh water is an extremely attractive feature in a backyard habitat. It is far scarcer than food in most environments, and birds often fly several miles to obtain it. Many species of birds that would not otherwise visit a backyard will do so if there is water.

Below: *Bathing in water not only helps this American Robin to keep its feathers clean but also helps it to stay cool. Birds that shun feeders will often frequent a birdbath.*

Below right: *In drier areas of their ranges, birds like this Plain Titmouse must depend on the water that they obtain from insects to prevent dehydration.*

George H. Harrison

Herbert Clarke

Birds in the City

Cities are home to a surprising number of birds. Some are "city" species, like Rock Doves (pigeons) and House Sparrows, which are especially comfortable living close to humans. Others are wilder birds that have found a location that provides the resources they need to live and raise their young. The Peregrine Falcon is such a bird. Adapted to nesting on abrupt cliffs, small numbers of this endangered species now balance their homes on the ledges of tall city buildings.

The Importance of Plants

Because green areas represent a scarce and essential resource, they are often crowded with birds, especially in the spring and fall, when migrants descend in search of a place to rest. These travelers see the land covered with city from one horizon to the other and head for the nearest spot of green. Birdwatchers in Central Park in New York City counted 101 different species in one day.

In general, the number of birds living in a city depends on how many parks, cemeteries, golf courses, and other green spaces are in the area. This does not mean that you must live near a big park to have birds; the pattern of green in a neighborhood may be as important as the overall amount. Small backyards, single trees, even potted plants on a balcony attract a bird that can see nothing else but concrete. A cluster of resources on a balcony or at a window feeder may tempt them to stop. Many birds found in suburban or rural locations can be tempted to a city yard at some time during the year.

Attracting City Birds

Birds are birds wherever they live, and the rules for attracting them are as valid in the city as anywhere else: Offer them food, water, and as complex an array of vegetation as you can provide. But attracting birds in the city does require special techniques and present unusual problems. The most common limiting factor is space. No one will deny that a 3-foot window box attracts fewer birds than a spacious backyard, but creative use of a small space and other resources will attract a number of birds.

Following is a list of tips to help city dwellers increase the number of birds outside their windows:

• Grow trees, shrubs, flowers, and vines in containers on balconies, patios, and in small backyards. The staff at your local garden center should be able to tell you which plants will grow well in your area. Choose your plants with variety in mind: an evergreen for shelter; a bright, flowering vine for nectar; a berry bush for food.

• When space is at a premium, make every resource do double duty. If you have a potted evergreen on a balcony, turn it into a bird feeder by hanging strings of popcorn or berries from its branches. Grow brightly colored hummingbird flowers in a summer window box; when winter comes, smooth out the soil and sprinkle it daily with birdseed to create a platform feeder.

• Do not forget fresh water. Large saucers like the ones used under flowerpots make compact, balcony-sized birdbaths. A hanging bath outside a window may attract the attention of birds, especially if there is a tree nearby on which they can preen after they have finished bathing.

• Remember that many city birds are ground feeders. Start your feeding program by offering a small amount of seed in a dish or in a flower box. Begin slowly until you see what kinds of birds show up. If pigeons become a problem, switch to a hanging feeder. Pigeons cannot balance on any type of hanging feeder and, since the seed cannot be spread around, there is less mess.

• Keep the area clean. This eliminates the danger of attracting rodents. Offer seed daily, so you know how much is being eaten and where it is going. Sweep up spilled seed frequently. If you offer sunflower seeds, you may want to provide the hulled variety. If you offer suet, check frequently to be sure it is not attracting insects.

Frans Lanting

Peregrine Falcons have been released in major cities across North America where they feed on pigeons. Many of these birds have stayed as permanent residents, adding a touch of wilderness to city skies.

Bathing

Many birds scout a source of water because they are looking for a drink. Once they have found it, they will probably take a bath as well. Bathing is part of an intricate grooming behavior that keeps the feathers clean, waterproof, and in good working condition. Birds spend many hours each day maintaining their feathers. After bathing, most birds seek out a perch on which to preen; they run their bills through the ranks of feathers and spread oil across them from a gland located at the base of the tail. The oiled feathers provide crucial insulation during cold and wet weather.

Birds bathe wherever water accumulates. From the smallest warblers to the largest hawks and eagles, birds of all sizes splash about in shallow pools at the edges of rivers or streams. Other natural birdbaths include ponds, rain puddles, and even the water-filled tops of hollow tree stumps. Some smaller birds flutter in the foliage of trees and shrubs after a rain in order to take a leafy shower. Garden birds like robins, towhees, and hummingbirds often bathe in the fine spray of a lawn sprinkler. Birds sometimes bathe in nothing more than the morning dew.

Most small birds bathe rapidly, standing up in shallow water. They dunk their heads quickly, showering their backs with the vigorous splashing of their wings. This basic bathing motion is innate—young birds who have never bathed before make dunking and splashing motions on dry ground if they spot another bird using a pool or birdbath.

Birds that spend most of their time in flight, such as swifts and swallows, bathe on the wing by dive-bombing quickly in and out of a lake or pond. Flycatchers swoop to bathe from waterside perches and return to preen in the sun. Birds also "bathe" in dust, sifting and shaking it through their feathers. Experts believe that dust baths improve feather alignment and discourage fleas, lice, and other parasites.

Stephen J. Krasemann/DRK Photo

A Cactus Wren preens its feathers to maintain their aerodynamic properties. Oil from a gland near the tail conditions the feathers against drying and fraying.

A Gambel's Quail bathes furiously in dust to enhance the quality of its feathers and to discourage parasites.

Stephen J. Krasemann/DRK Photo

A Natural Birdbath

You can create an attractive natural birdbath by filling a shallow depression in the soil that will hold water. To avoid losing too much water to evaporation on hot days, refill it as you would any birdbath. Add rocks and branches so the birds can perch both in the shallow water and at the edge of the bath. Enhance your landscape and make the bath more appealing to birds at the same time by planting flowering bulbs and low shrubs near the water. You can even add some fish to the bath.

Birdbaths

The most popular way of offering water to backyard birds is with a birdbath. Ready-made birdbaths are available in a variety of sizes and materials, or you can make one from many common household items. All birdbaths are not created equal, however. Here are some things to consider as you buy or build your birdbath:

• The bigger the birdbath, the more birds use it. Anything less than a foot in diameter may provide valuable drinking water, but probably will not be used for bathing. A bath twice that size will be big enough to allow more than one bird to bathe at a time. Most commercially available baths measure 24 to 36 inches in diameter, big enough for birds to bathe in flocks, as some do.

• The slope of the birdbath is more important than the size. Most songbirds are afraid of deep water and rarely submerge when bathing; they prefer to keep a solid footing at all times. To be useful for bathing, backyard water should be no deeper than 3 inches in the center, with a gradual slope to the edge so that every bird can wade to a suitable depth.

• The bottom of a pool or birdbath should be textured to provide a sure grip for little feet. Many commercial birdbaths are made of concrete, a material that provides excellent footing. Make smooth surfaces more attractive to birds by covering them with pebbles, sand, or the safety footing sold for the bottom of bathtubs.

• The bottom of a birdbath should be a light color, to provide contrast and to reassure birds that the water is shallow enough for bathing.

Commercial Birdbaths

Birds are easily attracted to a yard where there is water for drinking or bathing.

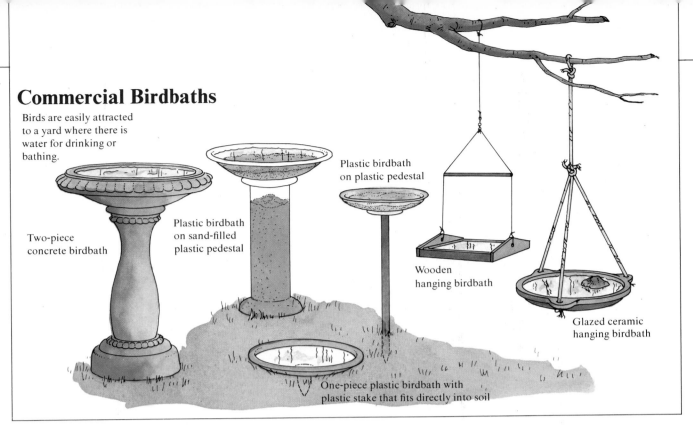

Two-piece concrete birdbath

Plastic birdbath on sand-filled plastic pedestal

Plastic birdbath on plastic pedestal

Wooden hanging birdbath

Glazed ceramic hanging birdbath

One-piece plastic birdbath with plastic stake that fits directly into soil

Commercial birdbaths. Commercial birdbaths are available in many different materials and in two basic styles: supported on a pedestal or suspended in some way from ropes or chains. Pedestal baths are usually sold in two pieces for convenience of manufacture and ease of shipment. Their dishes can be used either with or without the accompanying pedestal. Hanging birdbaths are available in many materials, and are often designed to hang beneath overhead cover. When selecting a commercial birdbath, be sure it meets the birds' needs for gradual slope and texture underfoot. Consider the following when comparing baths of various materials:

• Terra-cotta and glazed ceramic birdbaths are available in a variety of colors and designs. These baths are lovely and easy to handle; place them on a patio or near a window where you can enjoy them. Filled terra-cotta and ceramic baths are prone to cracking in freezing weather and are therefore not always recommended for winter use.

• Wooden birdbaths are also attractive and very well accepted by birds, but are difficult to keep clean. Even baths made of water-resistant redwood or cedar do not last as long as baths made of other materials.

• Plastic birdbaths are impervious to all weather. If you buy one, however, be prepared to modify it to offer a more textured surface underfoot. Plastic baths are lighter in weight and easier to handle than birdbaths of other materials, but this will not seem like an advantage when you are trying to set one firmly in place against the elements. Some plastic birdbaths come with hollow pedestals that you can fill with sand to provide extra weight. Others are a single unit that is pointed on the bottom; the point sets in the ground like a stake.

• The most popular birdbaths are made of concrete. Concrete is similar to natural stone in weight and texture, and the birds find the surface of these baths familiar underfoot. Concrete baths are heavy to handle, but once in place they stay put in strong winds. Although concrete baths are more expensive than plastic, their ruggedness probably makes them cheaper in the long run. Cement birdbaths are also popular because they have a smoother texture than concrete, but are usually not as strong.

Homemade Birdbaths

With some creativity you can design appealing birdbaths from objects found around the yard or house.

Aluminum or tin pie plate on window ledge

Garbage can lid mounted on drainage tile with a small rock suspended on a rope to steady lid

Ceramic saucer on tree stump

Hollowed top of tree stump

Rock with natural depression

Homemade birdbaths. The world is full of free birdbaths. Some day after a heavy rain search your backyard for water-filled depressions in stone or wood. If you refill them daily, these natural pools can serve as water sources for birds. If your backyard does not contain natural birdbaths, try to acquire some. Rocky streambeds and mountainsides often yield stones of the right size and shape. While this may seem more difficult than buying a bath at the local garden center, it can be worth the effort.

If there is a tree stump in your yard, hollow out the top to cradle a large saucer of the type used under a potted plant. The saucer may not even be necessary if the stump is a close-grained wood such as oak or hickory that will hold water without it. Stumps also make good pedestals for commercial birdbaths. If you do not have a stump, simulate one by finding a fat log and squaring it off on both ends.

Birdbath materials are all around the house. Garbage-can lids can be rigged onto a pedestal made of a single ceramic drainage tile, or drilled around the lip and suspended on chains beneath a tree branch. Depending on the lid, you may have to add sand or pebbles to correct the slope and add traction underfoot. The footing material also adds weight to the bath, so that it will not be upset by the first high wind.

Peter M. La Tourrette

The pebbled surface and gentle slope of this birdbath provide a good grip and shallow water for this House Sparrow. By providing a variety of water depths and a large enough area, it is possible to accommodate the needs of many kinds of birds.

Many items retired from use in the kitchen are the correct shape for small birdbaths. Cooking-pot lids, disposable aluminum pie plates, and casserole dishes that once contained frozen foods are useful as small windowsill baths. In the winter, fill the aluminum trays with warm water and put them out at about the same time each day. The birds quickly learn when and where to come for a hot bath.

Once you have seen the life that birdbaths can add to your backyard, you may find yourself intrigued by the possibility of filling bigger containers with water. That old barrel or the bathtub that has been hanging around for months may start to look like a birdbath or garden pool. Bury these containers to form a pool or leave them above ground and surround them with shrubs and ground cover. Many larger containers are deep enough for growing aquatic plants and can become lovely accent pieces in the garden.

Placing birdbaths in the yard. Birds are attracted to brushy cover near birdbaths because they are particularly fond of perches on which to preen. Placing birdbaths too close to heavy cover offers deadly opportunities to the family cat, however. A wet bird is especially vulnerable—wet feathers make for slow takeoff—and nearby cover often gives a cat just the edge it needs to secure an otherwise elusive catch. If cats prowl your yard, do not place ground-level birdbaths within 15 feet of heavy cover. Raised baths, such as the traditional 3-foot-high pedestal type, are safer and can usually be placed closer to heavy cover. In general, the closer a birdbath is to the ground, the more open space should be around it.

Another solution to the cat problem is to make use of any trees you have in your yard. Set your birdbath in an open spot beneath an overhanging branch. The absence of low cover allows birds ample warning against sneaky cats, and the branches offer inviting perches.

Once you have tested a few spots and decided on the best location for your backyard birdbath, you will probably want to dig a drainage pad around it. A bathing bird can kick up quite a spray, and a flock of bathing birds can rapidly turn the area around a birdbath into a swamp. For a 30-inch birdbath, remove 4 inches of soil from an area 4 feet square and add gravel in its place. Garden centers sell many types of natural and decorative gravels.

George H. Harrison

A garden pool can enhance your landscape as well as entice more birds to your yard. The natural setting of a backyard pool provides a quiet place for this Northern Mockingbird to bathe.

Garden Pools

The easiest way to add a pool to your backyard is to bury a birdbath basin. This can be done in an afternoon with an hour or two left over for you to sit and enjoy your work.

You can use any of the many birdbaths and birdbath-shaped objects already discussed as an inset pool for birds. Simply dig a depression big enough so that the lip of the basin will protrude a couple of inches above ground level, and set it in. Never set the basin completely into the ground; it will fill with debris after the first rain. For a more finished look, dig out the earth 12 to 15 inches from the lip of the pool and replace it with gravel to a depth of 3 to 4 inches. You may want to put some low plants or flowers along one side, but be sure to add nothing dense enough to hide a cat. If you want something bigger than the average birdbath or one with a slightly different shape, preformed garden pools are available at many garden centers and nurseries. The installation procedure is the same as for birdbaths, except that the hole must be bigger and shaped like the pool. These pools are usually made of plastic or fiberglass. The heavier they are, the longer they last.

Most prefabricated garden pools are not designed specifically for birds. In many the bottom slopes too steeply rather than offering the gradual slope that birds need to bathe. Customize these pools for birds by adding rocks on which they can land. If the surface of the rock slopes gradually into the water, all the better. Place rocks just below the surface as well—the tops offer different water depths to accommodate different-sized birds. Arrange dead branches so that they extend over the surface of the pool to provide perches on which birds can rest.

Elaborate garden pools. Of course backyard pools can be bigger and more complicated. The larger the pool, the more likely it is that you will want such conveniences as drains and plumbing. Digging, pouring, and plumbing a concrete pool large enough for fish or water lilies could take the greater part of a month. If you are going to attempt such a project, you need a good book on the subject, some special tools, and perhaps the help of a professional. The results will undoubtedly be a lovely addition to your garden, and if the water in your pool is clean and accessible, it will attract the birds as well.

One kind of large backyard pool that is easy to build and relatively inexpensive is a pool made with polyethylene sheeting. The size of a polyethylene pool is limited by the width of sheeting available. Polyethylene pools usually need to be rebuilt every few years because weather degrades the plastic, but once the initial hole is dug, rebuilding is simple.

Dig a hole of the desired size and shape. As you dig, form a mound of earth that is about 6 inches high and stretches back about 12 inches from the edge of the hole all the way around. This mound forms the lip of the pool. Tamp down the soil in the hole and on the mound thoroughly. Remove sharp roots and rocks that might puncture the polyethylene. As you tamp, excavate a small trench in the mound about 4 inches deep and halfway back from the edge of the hole. Line the hole with the polyethylene and trim it so that it extends a foot beyond the mound in all directions. Fold this overlap into the trench, weight it well with gravel, and fill the pool with water.

Like other pools, a polyethylene pool can use some dressing up. Add sand or gravel on the bottom to disguise the underlying plastic and to supply texture for birds' feet. If your pool does not have a gradually sloping side, add rocks or branches to make it accessible to the birds.

Choosing a location. Many of the rules for the placement of birdbaths hold true for pools as well—they should be free of cover by the water's edge but should be within a short flight of shrubbery or a big tree. If you build a large pool, be sure to choose the right spot. After a day or two of digging, it is unpleasant to decide that the hole belongs somewhere else.

For ease in filling and cleaning, make sure that you can reach the pool with a hose. To empty the pool bail out water with buckets, or use an electrically powered pump or siphon.

Place the pool in a high spot in your yard to prevent leaves, debris, and garden chemicals from collecting in it. Plant underwater greenery such as ancharis, cabomba, or vallisneria to inhibit the growth of algae. Some types of fish will also eat any algae that may form. Do not treat the water with chemicals that may be hazardous to birds.

Prefabricated Garden Pools

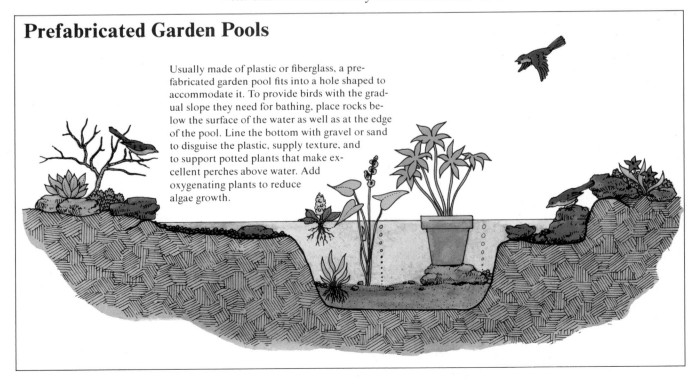

Usually made of plastic or fiberglass, a prefabricated garden pool fits into a hole shaped to accommodate it. To provide birds with the gradual slope they need for bathing, place rocks below the surface of the water as well as at the edge of the pool. Line the bottom with gravel or sand to disguise the plastic, supply texture, and to support potted plants that make excellent perches above water. Add oxygenating plants to reduce algae growth.

George H. Harrison

The sound of gently running water has drawn an Evening Grosbeak to a fountain for a drink. Many birds prefer running water to still water.

Adding Running Water

Birds are strongly attracted to the sound of running water. Those that might otherwise pass a yard without a visit may change course for a dripping birdbath or gently gurgling fountain. Many backyard bird-watchers first discover birds' attraction to moving water while watering their lawns or gardens. Hummingbirds in particular enjoy a shower and show up to play in the mist of soaker hoses or sprinklers.

When it comes to running water in a backyard habitat, bigger is not better. Thundering waterfalls and large, spurting fountains frighten birds more than they attract them. If you are planning a fountain with seven tiers, let the water drop from one to another with the tinkle of a little brook, not the roar of the great Niagara.

A few easy methods. The easiest way to add light sounds of water is to hang a dripping bucket several feet above the surface of a birdbath. Punch a hole in the side of a bucket, about ½ inch from the bottom. (Do not punch it in the bottom—it will clog with tiny particles of debris before the bucket is half empty.) Start with a very small hole. Count the drops per minute; 10 or 20 drops a minute means the hole is the right size. Remember, the faster the bucket empties, the more often you must refill it. Keeping the bucket covered helps keep the hole from clogging. Hang the bucket about 2 to 3 feet above the birdbath—high enough so the water makes a good, solid plop but not so high that the wind blows the water off course before it hits the target.

Create many other attractive elaborations on the drip-into-the-birdbath trick. Clear plastic tubing provides one alternative. Attach the tubing to the end of your garden hose with a connector and run it inconspicuously up a tree and out a branch overhanging the birdbath. An adjustable clamp on the tubing allows you to regulate the flow. Another alternative is to connect tubing to a spigot on the bottom of a large bucket or some other container. Conceal the bucket behind the branch of a tree or in the shrubbery. As long as the bucket is higher than the tubing above the birdbath, the water flows. Use the spigot to regulate the drops.

Offering Running Water

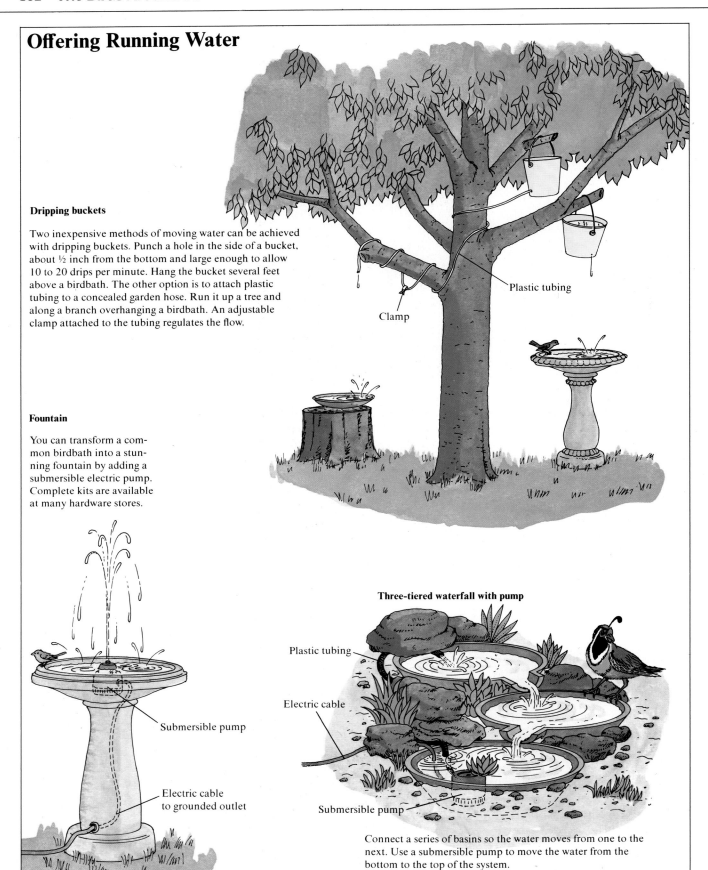

Dripping buckets

Two inexpensive methods of moving water can be achieved with dripping buckets. Punch a hole in the side of a bucket, about ½ inch from the bottom and large enough to allow 10 to 20 drips per minute. Hang the bucket several feet above a birdbath. The other option is to attach plastic tubing to a concealed garden hose. Run it up a tree and along a branch overhanging a birdbath. An adjustable clamp attached to the tubing regulates the flow.

Plastic tubing

Clamp

Fountain

You can transform a common birdbath into a stunning fountain by adding a submersible electric pump. Complete kits are available at many hardware stores.

Submersible pump

Electric cable to grounded outlet

Three-tiered waterfall with pump

Plastic tubing

Electric cable

Submersible pump

Connect a series of basins so the water moves from one to the next. Use a submersible pump to move the water from the bottom to the top of the system.

If you want to schedule special showers for birds, set the nozzle of your garden hose on mist spray and drape it over a tree branch or other elevated support. Turning on the water at the same time each day draws a regular clientele.

More complex systems of moving water usually employ electric pumps with power fountains or waterfalls. Some birdbaths have jet sprays that produce a shower in the center of the basin. To construct a simple waterfall, connect a series of ready-made basins so that water will drop from one to the next; use a submersible pump to move water from the bottom to the top of the system. Check your local hardware store for fountain-ring sets—complete kits with instructions that show you how to turn a birdbath or pool into a fountain or waterfall.

Water for Winter Birds

In cold climates, winter birds can obtain drinking water from snow but are hard put to find open pools for bathing. It is not essential to keep birdbaths and pools open in freezing weather; wild birds get by without bathing for long periods. Birds seem to enjoy winter bathing, however, and many backyard bird-watchers enjoy providing water in winter. Never use chemical antifreeze to keep backyard water from freezing; keep the birdbath open by filling it with boiling water several times a day. If you find this task too time-consuming, and would rather stay indoors out of the cold, you may want to buy a submersible water heater specially designed for backyard use. The best have built-in thermostats that turn off the heat when the water temperature reaches about 50° F.

Care with electricity. Treat submersible heaters for winter birdbaths and recirculating pumps for fountains and waterfalls with great respect. The appliances usually come with a three-wire grounded electrical cord appropriate for use in wet conditions. If you use them with an extension cord, be sure that you choose one that is grounded as well. The extension cord should be as heavy and well made as the appliance it powers.

It is a bad idea, however, to use extension cords of any kind as permanent garden fixtures. In many areas it is against the law. Play it safe; have an electrician install an underground power line. With a dedicated power line each backyard appliance has a separate fuse inside the house and a switch so you can turn it off when not in use. Bury electrical lines away from potential sites of future excavation and deep enough so that yearly garden chores do not disturb them.

Fresh Water

Water is always more attractive to birds if it is fresh and clean. Wash out and re-fill birdbaths often, and check larger pools frequently, especially in hot weather. Never place chemicals of any kind in water intended for birds, and be careful that chemicals used elsewhere around the garden do not make their way into fountains or birdbaths. When you are forced to spray for troublesome insects, make sure that the wind does not blow chemicals into pools or other water sources.

Birds like this Northern Flicker may learn to depend on a birdbath for clean, healthy water.

Mary Clay/Cornell Lab. of Orn./VIREO

Feeding the Birds

Feeding birds preceded the development of the commercial bird feeder by thousands of years. Since the earliest days of human history, birds have been hanging around our homes hoping to clean up the crumbs. Think of the unplanned bird feeding that went on around the family farms that once dotted the countryside—sparrows snatching feed in the chicken yards, finches scavenging grain behind the threshers.

Many people who never erect a bird feeder or buy an ounce of seed find that casting their crusts of bread and scraps of pastry to the birds is more rewarding than feeding the great mechanical mouth of the garbage disposer. But most people who get excited about feeding birds quickly run out of scraps and are soon shopping for birdseed. Before long they are thinking about bird feeders—what to buy or what to build. By 1980 over 60 million people in the United States had made the transition from casual to serious bird feeding, which makes it one of the most popular hobbies of all time.

Winter Feeding

Feeding birds can be a useful and entertaining activity throughout the year, but for many Americans bird feeding is mostly a winter sport. This is especially true in colder parts of the country, where flocks of feeding birds may lend the only movement or color to an otherwise stark landscape. In cold climates winter birds remind us that nature is alive and well in the midst of the deep freeze.

Winter feeding attracts more birds than summer feeding, and for a good reason. In the summertime most garden birds disperse and establish nesting territories, which they do not leave as long as the young are in the nest. The only birds likely to come to a summer feeder are those that happen to be nesting in the backyard. In the winter most garden birds abandon their nesting territories and are more likely to be found in flocks.

Winter brings a change in food supply as well. In cold climates many insects become dormant during the winter and are unavailable as food for birds. Woodpeckers, nuthatches, and other insect eaters that brave the northern winter feed by prying grubs and hibernating beetles from under

Snow and cold weather cause many birds to join nomadic flocks in search of energy-rich patches of food. Arctic birds, like these Snow Buntings, invade more southerly latitudes during winter months.

Thomas D. Mangelsen

Maslowski Photo

Attracted by a backyard feeder, Northern Cardinals brighten a winter scene. Because these and other species may learn to depend on feeders for their winter food, it is important that the food is available continuously.

tree bark, and they often supplement their intake with seeds, nuts, and berries. Some wintering birds, like cardinals, grosbeaks, finches, and siskins, are equipped with stout bills for cracking the seeds and nuts that are plentiful in the winter environment.

The birds who do stay around in cold weather are faced with a special problem. They must eat large quantities of food to keep warm, but some of that food can disappear under a pile of snow at any moment. No longer tied to their breeding territories, most winter birds do a very sensible thing—they cluster in places where nourishment and shelter are plentiful and sit out the bad weather. Turn your yard into such a place.

When we put out bird feeders we are asking birds to trade whatever other food they might find for the food we provide. Some argue that feeding the birds tampers with the natural system and might be harmful. Might the presence of artificial feeding stations disrupt the migratory urge of some birds, leaving them victims of cold weather they cannot handle? This does not seem likely. Birds migrate in response to signals of the approaching winter. This is a complex process, and many of the cues birds use occur in early fall, when natural food is still abundant and many backyard feeders are still in the basement. (For a discussion of migration cues, see the text beginning on page 98.)

Several nonmigratory species come to depend on food you offer during the winter, and if you are the only person in your neighborhood that feeds birds, it is a good idea to keep feeding them until spring has come to stay. This is especially true during bad weather, when birds might not locate a new source of food quickly enough to stay alive.

Protecting Your Crops

A quick look at the list of bird foods on page 193 reveals that many of the fruits and berries that birds love are human favorites as well. What do you do if you want to attract birds but do not want them eating the crops you grow for your own table? The most reliable way to protect fruit trees and berry bushes is to cover them with a fine mesh fabric called bird netting, which is available from many garden-supply stores. Throw the netting directly over trees and large shrubs or support it on stakes above berry bushes and other low plants. Be sure to position the netting early in the spring; many birds nip buds off trees and shrubs, a practice that can seriously reduce your crop before it gets started.

Birds can also damage newly planted seed and sprouted seedlings. To prevent this, place netting directly on the ground over the planted seed, and take it off as soon as the plants begin to grow. For smaller seedbeds, use heavy wire-mesh cages with or without wooden supporting frames. Leave the cages in place until the plants are well established.

Many other techniques have been tried over the years to keep birds from the garden or berry patch. Try dangling pie plates, coffee-can lids, and other shiny objects from strings or wires above vulnerable plants. As they turn in the wind, they catch the sunlight and frighten the birds. The more wind and sunlight you have, the better they work. Scarecrows and stuffed owls are sometimes set up to frighten birds. These may work for a day or two, but birds stay alive by sorting real dangers from false alarms, and they soon learn that stuffed predators present little threat.

Try diverting birds from crops by offering them a treat elsewhere in the yard. During the week or two that your seeds are in the ground, for example, be sure the birds know there is a little pile of cracked corn on the other side of the house. You may not be able to protect your whole crop with this technique, so plant more seeds than you think you need. Think of gardening as a cooperative venture between yourself and the birds; they share in your crop and in return keep the garden free of insects.

Easy Ways to Protect Backyard Plants

Cover trees or bushes with bird netting, a fine mesh fabric available at many garden-supply stores.

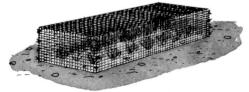

A heavy wire-mesh cage, screen cage, or ¼-inch hardware cloth stitched at the corners with short pieces of wire protects seedlings or low-growing plants.

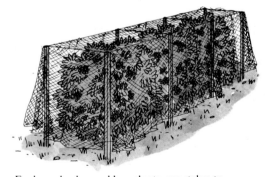

For berry bushes and low plants, use stakes to support bird netting.

Hang light, shiny objects such as pie plates or coffee-can lids above vulnerable plants.

Summer Feeding

The North American summer is rich in insects, seeds, nuts, worms, nectar, and many other bird delicacies. This is, after all, why the birds come here to nest in the first place. Birds with young to feed seek out the richest food sources they can find. A bird feeder may convince a winter resident to nest nearby rather than take its chances somewhere else.

Summer birds will consume all the foods you offered through the winter, but do not expect your seed to disappear as quickly in July as it did in December; now you are feeding pairs of birds, not flocks. Here are some things to keep in mind when feeding birds in warm weather:

• Food spoils more quickly as the temperature rises. Even seed can get soft and moldy in hot, humid weather. Offer small quantities and clean feeders often, including after a rainstorm. If you offer suet (see page 191), cut it into little pieces and put out a small amount at a time or use hard commercial cakes. Take the same precaution with baked goods.

• Summer is the season for treats. Nuts and other expensive goodies that you would hesitate to provide for hungry flocks of winter birds are affordable for the scattered nesting pairs of summer. Use a simple feeder (see text beginning on page 195) to offer small amounts of food. Chopped walnuts and pecans find ready takers.

• Many of our brightest and most colorful birds—orioles, tanagers, and Rose-breasted Grosbeaks—are only present in summer. The best way to attract these birds is with offerings of fresh fruit. Orioles seem to have a special love for fresh oranges but will only come for them in spring and early summer. Halve the oranges and impale them on a nail or small stick. Apples, cherries, raisins, bananas, and many other fruits are also popular at summer feeders. Other fruits attractive to birds are noted on page 193.

Alexander Lowry

An Altamira Oriole finds an orange half to be a welcome supplement to its normal diet.

A Varied Diet

When you consider the energy requirements of a bird, it is easy to understand why it consumes a proportionally greater quantity of food than a human does to survive. Besides having high metabolic rates, birds require extra energy for their daily flights as well as for migration. In general, the smaller the bird, the greater amount of food in proportion to its body weight it needs to consume each day. Garden songbirds, for example, usually consume between 30 and 80 percent of their body weight in food each day. A person weighing 150 pounds would have to eat 75 pounds of food a day to keep up with the average warbler.

Birds eat a wide variety of foods, including many kinds of plants, animals, and insects. For all this diversity, the foods that birds favor have in common a lot of nutritional value wrapped in a small package.

The best way to tell what kind of food a bird eats is to look at its bill. If it is short, heavy, and powerful, it is a good bet the bill is used to crack seeds and cones. Cardinals, juncos, sparrows, finches, and siskins all have this type of bill. Crossbills have a further modification of the basic seed-cracking bill: The tips of their bills curve and overlap each other to help them open stubborn evergreen cones.

Narrower bills are frequently used for eating insects. Long, narrow bills, such as those of creepers, thrashers, and nuthatches, are used to probe for bugs beneath the bark of trees or in the litter on the forest floor. Short, pointed bills, like those of the warblers and other leaf gleaners, are sometimes used for picking thrips and aphids from the underside of foliage. Woodpeckers and sapsuckers have sharp, chisel-shaped bills for carving nest holes and digging out burrowing grubs and borers.

O.S. Pettingill, Jr./VIREO

Although the sharp, slender bill of this House Wren is adapted for capturing insects, the right food can entice such specialists to a feeder.

While most of our common garden birds have bills that are specialized to some degree for a certain food, many switch back and forth according to their nutritional needs and the availability of food. Anyone who has watched a nuthatch hammering its way into a sunflower seed with its pointed, insect-eater's bill has seen an example of this adaptability. Many birds gladly gorge themselves on fruits and berries if the opportunity arises. This flexibility of diet is a boon for bird lovers; it means that many garden birds can be lured closer by one delicacy or another.

Seeds

Birdseed is the mainstay of any winter feeding program. Not only are seeds nutritious and widely accepted by most wintering birds, they are also inexpensive, easily stored, and convenient to use.

For many years, no one knew which commonly offered seeds birds really preferred. People with backyard feeders were aware that some seeds disappeared quickly and others never disappeared at all, but no one really understood which species favored what. In 1980, Dr. A. D. Geis of the U.S. Fish and Wildlife Service published the results of a series of feeding experiments. Because of this work we now have a list of common seeds and their relative attractiveness to many backyard species. The chart of birds' seed preferences that appears on page 190 is compiled from Dr. Geis's figures. For information on offering seed, see pages 195 to 199.

Sunflower seeds. As the chart on page 190 shows, some seeds are significantly more popular than others. Sunflower seeds are very popular. Ounce for ounce, sunflower seeds contain as much protein as ground beef. There are three kinds of sunflower seeds for birds: black oil, black striped, and gray striped. The small black-oil seeds generally attract the largest number of birds, but all three types are great favorites.

The one drawback to sunflower seeds is that the shells are inedible and quickly pile up beneath the feeder. The husks can, however, be raked up, or the shelled variety may be provided. Shelled sunflower seeds are more expensive, but because they are smaller and do not need to be cracked, more birds can eat them.

Small seeds. The majority of birds that usually eat small seeds prefer white proso millet. These birds also eat cracked corn and milo, but generally choose the white millet when it is available. Peanut hearts, which are often used in seed mixes and are similar to sunflower seeds in nutritional value, have the disadvantage of being attractive to starlings, whose aggressive behavior can often frighten shy birds away from feeders. Peanut hearts are also relatively expensive. Niger seed (sometimes mistakenly called thistle seed) is a tiny black seed high in protein and calories that goldfinches and several other species seem to prize. Niger seed is expensive and requires a special feeder to prevent waste.

Commercial birdseed mixtures. Bird feeding has become such a popular winter pastime that bags of commercial birdseed show up on many supermarket shelves at about the same time as the Halloween candy. Commercial mixtures are widely available, convenient, and an easy way for a beginner to become involved. Buyers should be aware, however, that some mixtures are stretched with wheat, oats, flaxseed, and other ingredients that are relatively unattractive to birds. Birds often toss these less desirable seeds to the winds as they search out the best seeds in the batch. Sometimes ground-feeding birds clean up beneath the feeders; sometimes leftover seed sprouts in spring rains to yield a lush crop of wheat, milo, or flax. Because of this problem, many commercial birdseed producers offer premium mixtures with higher proportions of favored seeds.

Mixtures designed to suit the preferences of birds in your area may be available from the local chapter of the Audubon Society and from nature centers. Remember, however, that you can always doctor commercial seed mix at home to make it more attractive. The easiest way to do this is to add extra sunflower seeds. If you add twice the number of sunflower seeds as were in a mixture when you bought it, the birds will have to search half as long to find one, and you will achieve a corresponding reduction in the amount that ends up on the ground during the hunt.

George H. Harrison   Eileen Schlagenhaft/Duncraft

Far left: *American Goldfinches find a bountiful harvest at a niger-seed feeder. Niger feeders often attract the small winter finches that have trouble competing at conventional platform feeders.*

Left: *The combination of suet and seed in this feeder has attracted a Tufted Titmouse.*

Seed Preferences of Common Backyard Birds

	Buckwheat	Canary Seed	Cracked Corn—Fine	Flaxseed	Millet—German ("Golden")	Millet—Red Proso	Millet—White Proso ("White")	Milo (Sorghum)	Niger	Oats—Hulled (Groats)	Oats (Whole)	Peanuts—Hearts	Peanuts—Kernels	Rice (Cooked)	Rape Seed	Safflower Seed	Sunflower Seed—Black-Oil Type	Sunflower Seed—Black Striped	Sunflower Seed—Gray Striped	Sunflower Seed—Hulled	Wheat
Cardinal, Northern	1	1	1	1	1	1	2	1	1	1	1	1	1	1	1	2	3	3	3	2	1
Chickadee, Black-capped	1	1	1	1	1	1	1	1	1	1	1	1	2	1	1	1	3	3	3	2	1
Dove, Mourning	2	3	2	1	3	3	3	2	2	1	1	2	1	1	1	2	3	2	2	2	2
Finch, House	1	2	1	2	1	1	2	1	3	1	1	2	2	1	2	1	3	3	2	3	2
Finch, Purple	1	2	1	1	1	1	1	1	2	1	1	1	1	1	1	1	3	3	3	2	1
Goldfinch, American	1	1	1	1	1	1	1	1	3	1	1	1	1	1	1	1	3	3	2	3	1
Grackle, Common	1	1	3	1	1	1	1	1	1	1	2	2	2	1	1	1	3	3	3	3	1
Grosbeak, Evening	1	1	1	1	1	1	1	1	1	1	1	1	1	1	1	1	3	3	3	2	1
Jay, Blue	1	1	2	1	1	1	1	1	1	1	1	1	3	1	1	1	2	3	3	1	1
Jay, Scrub	1	1	1	1	1	1	1	1	1	1	1	1	3	1	1	1	3	3	3	1	1
Sparrow, House	1	2	2	1	2	2	3	1	1	1	1	1	1	1	1	1	2	2	2	2	2
Sparrow, Song	1	3	1	1	3	3	3	1	1	1	1	2	1	1	1	2	2	2	2	2	1
Sparrow, White-crowned	1	2	2	2	2	3	3	2	1	1	2	3	3	1	1	1	3	3	2	3	1
Sparrow, White-throated	1	2	3	1	3	3	3	2	1	2	2	2	3	1	1	2	3	3	2	3	2
Titmouse, Tufted	1	1	1	1	1	1	1	1	1	1	1	1	3	1	1	1	3	3	3	1	1

Key: 1 = Low attractiveness   2 = Moderate attractiveness   3 = High attractiveness

Homemade blends. A good alternative to suit your birds' preferences is to combine individual seeds to make your own mixture. Cracked corn, peanut hearts, millet, and other popular seeds are available from feed stores and by mail from businesses that cater to bird-watchers. Use the list on this page to determine which seeds the birds in your backyard like best or, if you feel more adventurous, design an experiment to discover the tastes of your personal collection of birds. Build a feeding tray like the one illustrated on the top of page 195, with individual compartments for each kind of seed. Keep a record of which seeds disappear the quickest and use four or five of the preferred seeds to make your mixture. Do not be surprised if the most highly desired seeds are also the most expensive. Some compromise may be necessary to keep your expenses down.

For a birdseed mix that should appeal to a wide variety of seed-eating birds, use 1 part cracked corn (fine or medium), 2 parts white proso millet, and 3 parts sunflower seeds (the unhulled black-oil type).

Avoiding waste. The best solution to the problem of waste is to offer a narrower choice of seed. We often assume that because humans enjoy a variety of food, birds do as well. Experience shows just the opposite. Birds eat their favorite of whatever is around until it is gone and then move on to something else. A feeding program need not offer wide variety; it will attract just as many birds if it offers only one or two popular kinds of seed. Here is a feeding plan that should minimize waste:

• Offer some inexpensive "scratch seed," such as millet, cracked corn, and buckwheat, directly on the ground or on a low raised platform. Ground-feeding birds such as sparrows and doves favor this kind of seed.

• Offer sunflower seeds in a feeder that selects, in one way or another, for the kind of birds you want to attract—usually chickadees, finches, titmice, and the like. (See "Bird Feeders," page 195.) The purpose of the feeder is to keep expensive seed dry and away from the voracious mouths of squirrels and jays.

• Use a different feeder for each type of seed you offer.

Fats

Not all the birds at winter feeders are seed eaters. Nuthatches, woodpeckers, and chickadees, for example, are equipped with the pointed bills of dedicated insect specialists. These insect-eating birds survive the northern winter on a diet of hibernating insects dug from under the bark of trees, supplemented by nuts, seeds, fruit, and berries. The plant foods, however, are poor substitutes for the rich, juicy insects of summer.

Although we cannot easily offer insects to birds, we can supply them with food in the form of suet or other animal fat. Animal fat is the single most concentrated source of energy we can offer.

Animal fats. Bacon drippings and meat fats rendered from cooking (as long as they are not heavily spiced) seem to work fairly well in cold weather, although they never set firmly enough to be offered in a bag or wire feeder. Mix the fat with cornmeal, seed, or other bird food in the same manner as suet (see below), or smear the fat directly into holes in tree trunks or hole-style suet feeders (see page 200). Birds also eat the fat trimmed from the outside of a ham. Ham fat hangs together well; present it in the same manner as suet. Remember, animal fat becomes soft and rancid in warm weather; offer it only until the mercury starts to climb.

Suet. Beef suet is the tastiest and most readily available source of animal fats for birds. The best suet is trimmed from the inside of a beef carcass in the vicinity of the kidney. This fat is harder than that from the outside of the carcass and is less likely to soften in warm weather. It can be purchased intact or ground like hamburger if you intend to melt and reform it before feeding. As with any meat, it should look and smell fresh when you buy it. Keep in mind that suet begins to melt at about 70° F and quickly becomes rancid. Offer it with caution during hot weather.

To make suet cakes, place ground suet in a double boiler, and heat it until it becomes liquid. Pour the liquid into muffin forms, orange-juice cans, or whatever you are using to shape your cakes. When the suet is hard, put it out for the birds. Cooling and reheating the suet twice produces a harder cake that stands up better in warm weather. Many people add seeds, nuts, small fruits, and other delicacies to cooling suet just before it sets. The addition of dog food or ground dog biscuits adds protein.

Suet cakes, with or without added treats, are also available commercially for not much more than what you would pay for the materials to make them. These cakes, especially the hard commercial kind, seem to stand up better in warm weather than raw suet. The type of cake with embedded delicacies may attract more birds simply because it contains a greater variety of food. For more on how to serve suet, see page 201.

Nuts

Nuts are an excellent bird food. They are high in nutrition and are quite popular with birds. Unfortunately, however, they are also expensive. Birds are happy to eat whatever nuts you can afford to feed them. Walnuts and pecans are both great favorites. Serve them on the half-shell—birds can pick out the meats more efficiently than you can. If you do offer expensive nuts at your feeders, watch to be sure the birds are getting them—nuts are great favorites with squirrels as well.

Ben Goldstein/Valenti Photo

A female Red-bellied Woodpecker finds this suet feeder to be an easy source of high-energy food.

Right: *A suspended log with peanut butter in its holes provides winter food for a Downy Woodpecker. Peanut butter, favored by woodpeckers, nuthatches, and chickadees, can be offered in a variety of ways.*

Far right: *A shish kebab feeder is used to present a variety of food items at the same time. Some lucky bird will get to choose between peanuts, oranges, doughnuts, apples, and pieces of animal fat.*

Michael Hopiak/Cornell Lab. of Orn./VIREO   George H. Harrison

Peanuts are the most reasonably priced nut we can offer, and peanut-butter concoctions have long been staples at winter feeders. Jays are quite fond of peanut kernels and, with some training, come to the hand for whole peanuts in the shell. For information on ways to offer nuts, see page 198.

Peanut butter. Peanuts are most frequently offered in the form of peanut butter, which is often mixed with suet, seeds, and other ingredients to produce homemade bird food. Peanut butter and peanut-butter mixtures can be smeared like suet and animal fat into the holes in trees or hole-style feeders. One of the most attractive ways of presenting peanut butter is to pack it into the spaces of an evergreen cone.

Some people believe that peanut butter is too gooey for birds—that it can clog their nostrils or cause them to choke. For this reason they mix it with cornmeal to give it a drier consistency. No real evidence proves, however, that peanut butter poses this danger. For information on offering peanut butter, see "Recipes for Backyard Birds" on page 194.

Baked Goods

Birds accept stale bread, doughnuts, pie crust, corn bread, and other baked goods gladly. Because birds can spot them from a distance, white bread crumbs are particularly useful in starting a feeding program. Doughnuts—either crumbled and tossed on the ground or dangled by thread from the branch of a tree—are also great favorites.

Because they spoil quickly, scatter baked goods on the ground or offer them on platforms; do not mix them into birdseed feeders. Do not put out more than birds can eat in a day or two, for what was bird food rapidly becomes garbage. Bread and pastry are particularly attractive to House Sparrows and starlings. If you do not already have these birds and do not want them, keep your baked goods in the kitchen.

Fruit

Many birds eat fruit, which is not surprising since part of the function of many fruits is to attract birds, who then scatter their seed over a wide area. Fruit is particularly attractive to summer birds, but do not hesitate to offer it in winter as well. Put out orange and grapefruit rinds, and watch the birds pick them clean of what you have left behind. Finches appreciate halved apples, and mockingbirds enjoy raisins. Collect bayberries and other natural fruits on winter outings, and distribute them at the backyard feeding station. Other fruits that attract birds are listed on page 193.

Food Preferences of Common Backyard Birds

Blackbird, Red-winged [19]
Bluebirds [1, 5, 9, 16, 19, 20, 25]
Bunting, Indigo [3, 19]
Bunting, Lark [23a]
Bunting, Snow [6, 8]
Catbird, Gray [3, 7, 9, 10, 13, 16, 18, 19, 20, 21, 25, 26]
Chat, Yellow-breasted [2, 3]
Chickadees [4, 6, 19, 20, 23c, 23d]
Cowbird, Brown-headed [19]
Crossbill, Red [11]
Crow, American [21]
Dove, Mourning [22, 24]
Finch, House [2, 3, 16, 23a, 27]
Finch, Purple [12, 19]
Goldfinches [19]
Grackles [6, 20, 21]
Grosbeaks [27]
Grosbeak, Black-headed [16, 25]
Grosbeak, Pine [13]
Grosbeak, Rose-breasted [16, 18, 25]
Ground-Doves [19]
Grouse, Ruffed [24]
Jays [19]
Jay, Blue [2, 6, 7, 14, 21]
Jay, Gray [3, 7, 16]
Juncos [19]
Junco, Dark-eyed (Slate-colored) [6, 17, 20, 23c, 23d]
Kinglet, Ruby-crowned [19]
Lark, Horned [6, 8]
Longspur, Lapland [6, 8]
Martin, Purple [14]
Meadowlarks [24]
Mockingbirds [2, 3, 16, 18, 25, 27]
Nuthatch, Red-breasted [23b]
Nuthatch, White-breasted [6, 23b, 23c, 23d]
Orioles [2, 27]
Oriole, Hooded [16]
Oriole, Northern (Baltimore) [15, 16, 18, 20]
Oriole, Scott's [16]

Pheasants [24]
Pigeon, Band-tailed [17]
Pyrrhuloxia [26]
Robin, American [1, 2, 5, 9, 10, 12, 13, 16, 19, 25]
Quails [8, 24]
Quail, Bobwhite [22, 25]
Sapsucker, Yellow-bellied [15]
Siskin, Pine [17, 19]
Sparrow, American Tree [6, 8, 23c]
Sparrow, Black-throated [23a]
Sparrow, Chipping [7]
Sparrow, Field [19]
Sparrow, House [7, 23b]
Sparrow, White-crowned [2, 19, 22, 23a, 26]
Starlings [3, 6, 10, 13, 20, 21]
Tanagers [10]
Tanager, Scarlet [18, 20]
Tanager, Summer [18, 20]
Tanager, Western [3, 16, 18]
Thrasher, Brown [18]
Thrasher, California [16]
Thrasher, Curve-billed [2, 17, 21]
Thrushes [10]
Thrush, Hermit [2, 19]
Thrush, Swainson's [16]
Titmouse, Tufted [7, 19, 20]
Towhees [16]
Towhee, Green-tailed [23a]
Warblers [16, 27]
Warbler, Orange-crowned [2]
Warbler, Tennessee [3, 26]
Warbler, Yellow-rumped (Myrtle) [4, 15, 18, 23c]
Waxwing, Cedar [2, 10, 12, 16]
Woodpeckers [19]
Woodpecker, Acorn [16]
Woodpecker, Hairy [2, 3]
Woodpecker, Red-bellied [18]
Wren, Cactus [2, 21]
Wren, Carolina [3, 9, 19]
Wren, House [19, 20]

Key

[1] Apples (baked)
[2] Apples (raw)
[3] Bananas
[4] Bayberries
[5] Biscuits (baking powder)
[6] Biscuits (dog)
[7] Cake, cracker, and cookie crumbs
[8] Chaff (barn floor sweepings)
[9] Cheese (cottage or pot)
[10] Cherries (canned or fresh)
[11] Corn bread
[12] Crabapples (frozen)
[13] Cranberries (canned or fresh)
[14] Eggshells of poultry (crushed)
[15] Grape jelly
[16] Grapes
[17] Oats (rolled)
[18] Oranges
[19] Pecan meats (broken or ground)
[20] Pie crust (dry)
[21] Potatoes (fried, mashed, or baked)
[22] Rice
[23] Seeds
  [23a] Barrel cactus seeds (in Southwest)
  [23b] Cantaloupe seeds
  [23c] Pumpkin seeds (ground)
  [23d] Squash seeds (broken)
[24] Soybeans
[25] Strawberries
[26] Tomatoes (fresh)
[27] Watermelon (pulp or rind)

Adapted from "Food List for Birds" from *Songbirds in Your Garden* by John K. Terres (Thomas Y. Crowell) ©1953, ©1968 by John K. Terres. Reprinted by permission of Harper and Row, Publishers, Inc.

Grit

Humans who lose their teeth must restrict their diet to foods with the consistency of oatmeal. How then can birds—who have no teeth to begin with—spend their days devouring seeds, nuts, beetles, and other hard foods? Their secret is a tough, muscular digestive organ called a gizzard that grinds up food with strong, regular contractions.

Sand, gravel, and other gritty substances enhance the grinding action of the gizzard. Birds swallow and retain this grit in the gizzard and tend not to be particular—any substance of the right size and shape seems to suffice. Quartz, granite, chert, broken glass, coal, and cinders have all been found in bird gizzards. Experts believe that birds acquire at least some of the minerals they need from the grit they ingest, and some varieties of grit are richer in minerals than others.

Offering grit at a feeder is not absolutely necessary because birds can retain grit in their gizzards for weeks and sometimes months at a time. But if you want to offer grit, mix it in with the seed at a ratio of 20 parts birdseed to 1 part grit, or put it out as a side dish. Coarse sand or the ground shells of oysters, clams, or eggs serve as excellent grit. Eggshells have the added advantage of providing calcium, a valuable dietary mineral.

Recipes for Backyard Birds

Many people enjoy mixing different ingredients to create food for birds. The goal is to create irresistible items that are packed with the protein, calories, vitamins, and minerals that birds need. Here are just a few of the many recipes available. Use your imagination to create your own.

Basic Bird Cakes

Bird cakes can be offered whole in a mesh bag or suet feeder, or crumbled and scattered on the ground.

> 2 cups suet
> 2 cups peanut butter
> 12 cups cornmeal

1. Melt the suet in a saucepan.
2. Mix in the peanut butter and cornmeal.
3. Spoon the mixture into muffin cups and cool.

Fruit Cup

This is a special treat for summer birds. Chop up and mix an assortment of fresh and dried fruits and berries. Put the mixture out for the birds in an empty grapefruit or orange half. Birds seem to particularly enjoy apples, bananas, figs, dates, raisins, blueberries, strawberries, and cherries. For a special treat, serve the fruit in a halved coconut. Use your imagination.

Peanut Butter–Suet Mixture

The peanut butter adds protein and the cornmeal adds carbohydrate to this easy-to-make offering. The mixture can stay fairly hard in warm weather.

> 2 cups suet
> 1 cup peanut butter
> 2 cups cornmeal
> 2 cups finely cracked corn,
>   millet, or other small seed

1. Melt the suet. Allow it to cool thoroughly, then reheat it.
2. Add the peanut butter, stirring until melted and well blended.
3. Add the cornmeal and cracked corn and blend well.
4. Pour into forms or suet feeders and cool until hardened.

Bird-Food Shish Kebabs

Assemble an assortment of foods that can be threaded on a string. Chunks of suet, apple slices, cranberries, raisins, dates, and stale bread or doughnuts are only a few of the items that work well. Make shish kebabs of convenient lengths, and drape them in your trees or in any other suitable place.

Simple Pine Cone Mixture

Pine cones are an attractive way to offer soft foods.

> 1 cup suet
> 1 cup peanut butter
> 3½ cups ground dog
>   biscuits or cornmeal

1. Melt the suet in a saucepan.
2. Add the peanut butter, stirring until melted and well blended.
3. Add the ground biscuits to the cooling mixture, and blend into a dough.
4. Pack the dough into the crevices of large pine cones.

Bird Feeders

How you present food to birds depends on what types of foods you offer and on what kinds of birds you want to attract. For instance, if you only want to attract ground-feeding birds, you will need no more than a simple platform feeder in your backyard. If you want to offer Niger seed, you will need a small-holed, tube-shaped feeder designed for this purpose.

An Array of Feeders

The variety of bird feeders is dizzying. There are expensive, solidly built feeders that can outlast their owners and become heirlooms; there are reasonably priced, respectably built feeders that endure the seasons; and there are homemade versions made of everything from milk cartons to the finest redwood.

Most beginners buy or build an inexpensive bird feeder, then spend several months making a list of the features they wish it had. As they add feeders to their backyards, they become increasingly sophisticated about selection and construction. When they buy or build a heavy-duty, long-lasting feeder, they are prepared.

To a certain extent, everyone must go through a trial-and-error process when they start feeding birds. A knowledge of feeders and their special features can, however, speed up success.

Platform feeders. The most basic style of bird feeder is a board with a little lip around it to keep the seed from falling off. Such a platform feeder is particularly helpful in beginning a backyard feeding program. Birds have to learn that food is available in your yard, and the best way to teach them is to put it out where they can see it. A platform feeder is also a good way to offer mixed seed, since birds can review the entire menu and pick and choose what they want. For this reason, one platform feeder attracts a greater variety of birds than a single feeder of any other type.

Platform feeders have two drawbacks: They offer the seed no protection from the elements, and they are completely unselective in both the creatures they feed and the rate at which the food is offered. A pair of jays or flock of grosbeaks, for example, can empty one in a matter of hours, at no small expense to you. Almost all refinements in bird-feeder design have arisen from an attempt to solve one or both of these problems.

The most obvious way to improve a platform feeder is to put a roof on it to keep rain and snow out. Round and bowl-shaped feeders often have a cover shaped like a bell, which can be raised and lowered to admit birds of different sizes. Screened feeders admit small birds but not large ones.

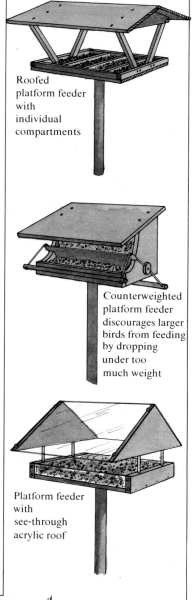

Roofed platform feeder with individual compartments

Counterweighted platform feeder discourages larger birds from feeding by dropping under too much weight

Platform feeder with see-through acrylic roof

Feeders

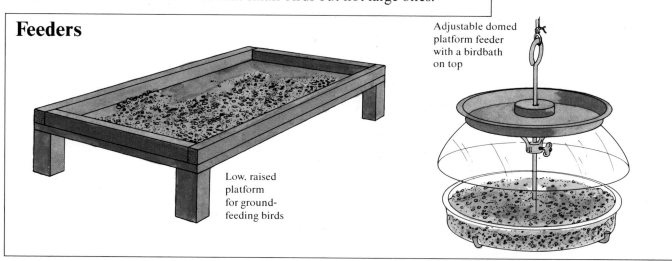

Low, raised platform for ground-feeding birds

Adjustable domed platform feeder with a birdbath on top

Hopper Feeders

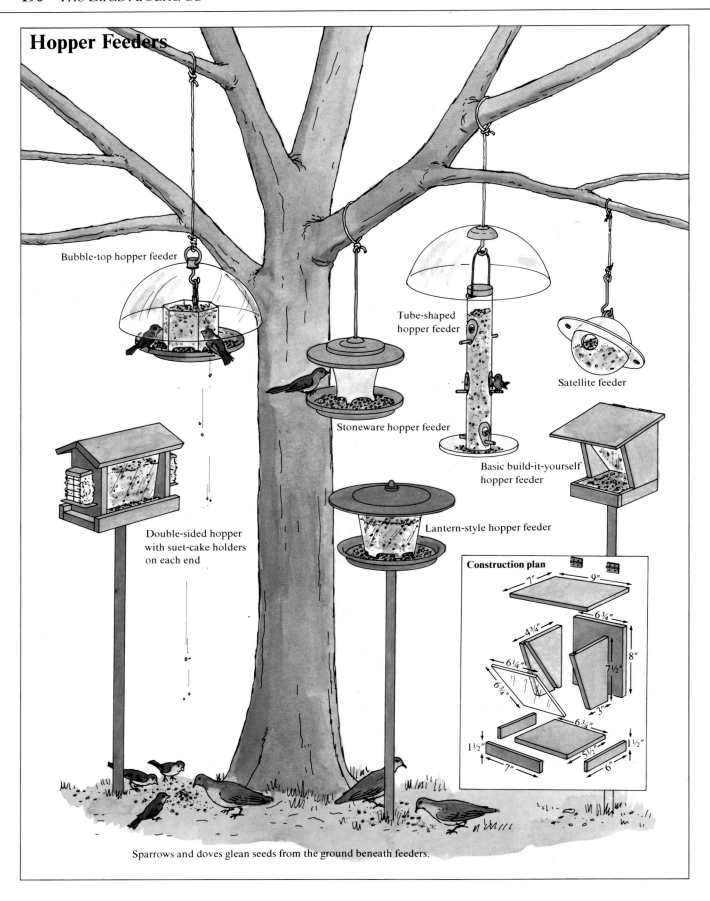

Bubble-top hopper feeder

Double-sided hopper with suet-cake holders on each end

Stoneware hopper feeder

Tube-shaped hopper feeder

Satellite feeder

Basic build-it-yourself hopper feeder

Lantern-style hopper feeder

Construction plan

7" 9"

4¾"

6¾"

6¼"

6¾"

7½"

8"

3"

1½" 6¾" 1½"

7" 5½" 6"

Sparrows and doves glean seeds from the ground beneath feeders.

Hopper-style feeders. One of the most popular bird-feeder designs is a roofed platform to which walls are added; the walls turn the center of the feeder into a small hopper. The seed is delivered by gravity to birds perched on the edges of the feeder. Hopper-style feeders protect seed from the weather more fully than simple roofed platforms and have to be filled less often because they have greater storage capacity.

Hopper-style feeders are available in many shapes and sizes. They may be round, square, rectangular, or tube shaped, and are usually made of glass, plastic, metal, wood, or acrylic. Whatever the style, they all work on the same principle; they offer seed to birds from openings somewhere on the hopper. Many release seed from the bottom; others, like the popular acrylic tubular feeders, have portholes where birds can take seed at several levels on the hopper.

Modifications to hopper-style feeders can make them more selective in the birds they attract. It is possible to vary the size of the feeding hole or the perch beside it to discourage larger birds, for example. A feeder without perches allows only chickadees, nuthatches, and other small, clinging birds to feed. Some feeders have counterweighted access doors that open only when a bird of a particular size lands on the perch.

No matter what the design, hopper-style feeders share one flaw: If they are used to offer mixed seed, birds litter the ground with seeds they do not want in hopes that the hopper will eventually deliver one they do want. Minimize the problem by adjusting the seed mixture to match the tastes of your birds or by using these feeders to offer only one type of seed.

Mayonnaise or peanut butter jar feeders. Using a pair of pliers or vise grips, wrap one end of a straightened wire coat hanger around the threads of an empty mayonnaise or peanut butter jar and twist it tight. Form a hook at the other end of the coat hanger and suspend the jar from a tree limb. The jar should be approximately horizontal when empty. Add seed so that the jar is about half full. The weight of the seed should pull the bottom of the jar down slightly.

Salad bowl feeders. Select two wooden salad bowls—one about 12 inches in diameter, the other about 9 inches. (Other sizes may be used as well, as long as one bowl is somewhat larger than the other to provide an overhang for the roof.) You will also need several yards of waterproof cord or monofilament fishline—anything over 12-pound test should do. Cut three 14-inch pieces of the cord and reserve the rest.

Treat the bowls inside and out with several applications of mineral oil to protect them from weather. Drill three equidistant holes around the rim of the smaller bowl using a drill bit just slightly larger than the diameter of the cord. Place the smaller bowl (open side down) inside the larger bowl (open side up). Mark three spots on the inside of the larger bowl to correspond to the holes you have drilled in the rim of the smaller bowl. Remove the smaller bowl and drill holes at the locations you have marked in the larger one. Drill a hole in the bottom center of the larger bowl.

Using the three 14-inch pieces of cord, string the two bowls together at each of the sets of holes. On the smaller bowl, the cords can be threaded through the holes and tied around the lip. On the larger bowl, the cords should be threaded through the holes and knotted several times on the outside to prevent them from pulling back through. The bowls should be about 6 inches apart, though if you wish to restrict your feeder to smaller birds they can be closer.

Thread the remaining piece of cord through the hole in the center of the larger (now the upper) bowl and knot it several times on the inside so that it will not pull back through. Use this cord to suspend your bird feeder. Fill the bottom bowl with seed.

Jar Feeder

In less than 10 minutes you can make an attractive feeder from a wide-mouthed jar. Wrap one end of a straightened wire coat hanger around the jar and the other end around a tree limb. Fill half-full with seed.

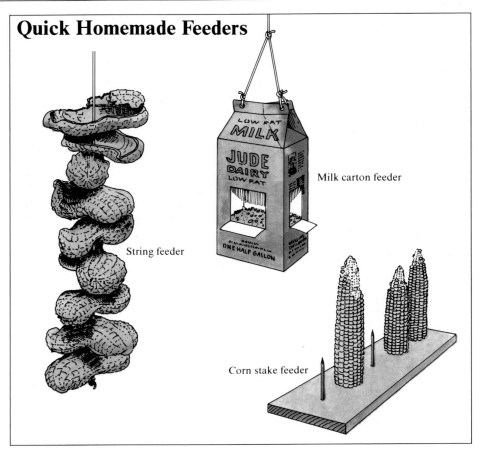

Quick Homemade Feeders

String feeder

Milk carton feeder

Corn stake feeder

String feeders. Using a heavy needle, thread unshelled peanuts onto a length of stout thread or monofilament fishline. Using finer threads, this method also works well for cranberries and popcorn.

Corn stake feeders. Pound 8 or 10 penny nails through a board so that they protrude, straight up, 3 to 4 inches apart. Offer whole ears of dried corn skewered on these nails.

Milk carton feeders. Ten minutes is all the time it takes to make a bird feeder from a half-gallon milk carton. Starting 2½ inches up from the bottom, cut out windows on all sides. The windows should be about 2½ inches wide and 3 inches high—small enough to leave a supporting column on each corner to hold the bottom of the feeder to the top. Next cut a slit ½ inch down at the bottom corners of each feeding window and fold this half-inch ledge out to make a perch for the birds. Poke a half dozen holes in the bottom of the feeder to allow water to drain out and a hole at each end of the peak of the roof. Thread the roof holes with string. Fill your feeder with seed and hang it in a sheltered location.

Window feeders. If you are like most people, you probably want a few feeders as close to your home as possible. Window feeders bring birds closer than other types, and allow you to tend them from inside where it is warm. Because the birds remain in full view, uncovered platforms make popular window feeders. A gauze curtain will screen the birds from your activity but allow you to watch theirs.

Lure shy birds closer gradually by attaching a feeder to a trolley and reeling it in a little each day. As it nears the house, the birds transfer to the window feeder, and you can dispense with the trolley feeder altogether. Birds are more comfortable at a window feeder if there is brushy cover nearby in the form of shrubbery or foundation plantings.

A Black-capped Chickadee takes sunflower seeds from a window feeder, which easily fastens, via suction cups, onto a window. Window feeders allow observation of wild birds at remarkably close ranges.

Window Feeders

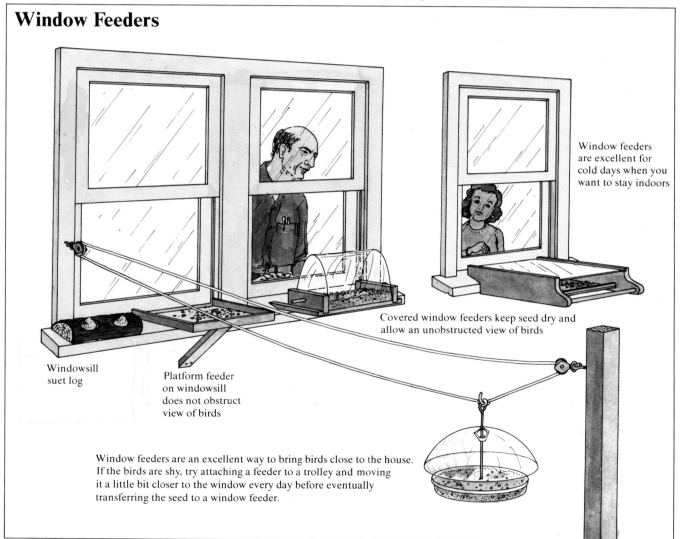

Window feeders are excellent for cold days when you want to stay indoors

Covered window feeders keep seed dry and allow an unobstructed view of birds

Windowsill suet log

Platform feeder on windowsill does not obstruct view of birds

Window feeders are an excellent way to bring birds close to the house. If the birds are shy, try attaching a feeder to a trolley and moving it a little bit closer to the window every day before eventually transferring the seed to a window feeder.

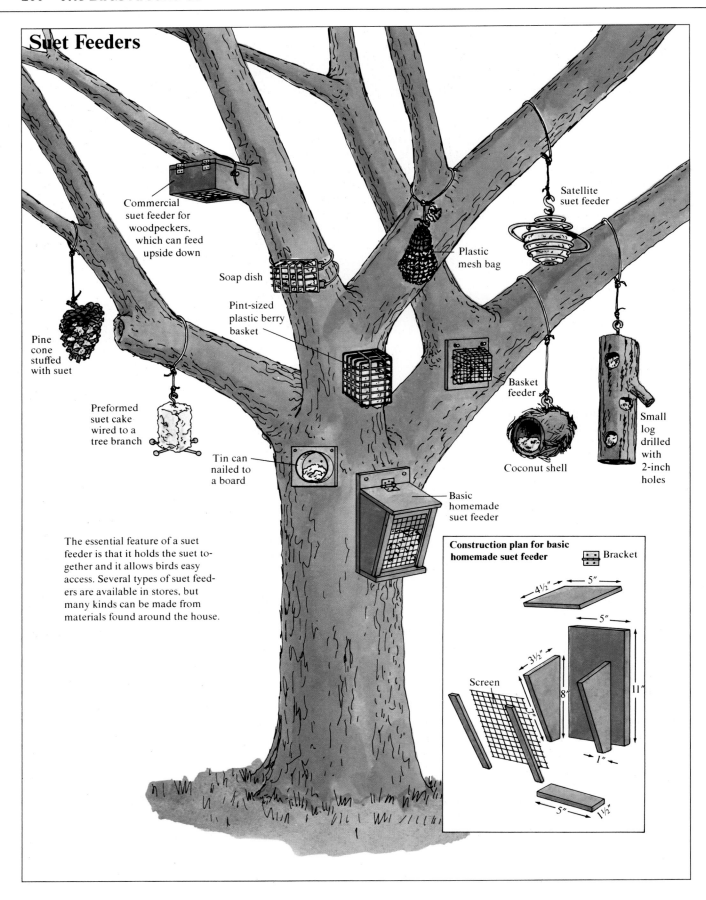

Suet Feeders

Commercial suet feeder for woodpeckers, which can feed upside down

Pine cone stuffed with suet

Preformed suet cake wired to a tree branch

Soap dish

Pint-sized plastic berry basket

Tin can nailed to a board

Plastic mesh bag

Satellite suet feeder

Basket feeder

Coconut shell

Small log drilled with 2-inch holes

Basic homemade suet feeder

The essential feature of a suet feeder is that it holds the suet together and it allows birds easy access. Several types of suet feeders are available in stores, but many kinds can be made from materials found around the house.

Construction plan for basic homemade suet feeder

Bracket

Screen

4½"
5"
5"
3½"
8"
11"
1"
5"
1½"

Suet feeders. A suet feeder is simply a container that holds the suet together and allows birds access to it. Many commercial seed feeders incorporate a suet basket, and wire baskets are also available that hold the popular sizes of suet cakes. The best commercial suet feeders are built with a slight slant to the front, so that the suet falls forward against the screen and is always within reach.

Suet feeders are so easy to build that many people never purchase one. Plastic mesh bags, like those supermarkets sometimes use to sell bulk fruit and vegetables, make efficient suet feeders. Tighten the bag around the suet every few days so that the birds can reach it from all sides. As an alternative, stuff suet into a pint-sized plastic berry basket and fasten it, open side in, to the branch or trunk of a tree. Two rubberized wire soap dishes fastened together make a hanging suet feeder when filled with a mixture of suet and seed. Construct yet another type by drilling holes about 2 inches deep and 2 inches wide into a log and packing them with soft suet. Simpler still, stuff suet into natural holes or cracks in a tree or wire it directly to a branch.

Fasten suet feeders to the trunks and branches of trees where insect-eating birds usually find food. If you place a feeder on the underside of a branch, woodpeckers and other birds adapted to feeding upside down are able to use it, but starlings are not. Place feeders at about eye level; they should not be too high for you to reach easily.

Suet can become soft and rancid in warm weather. If you are going to offer it to woodpeckers and other birds that will accept it through the summer, put out small portions at a time and check your feeders frequently. You may also want to refill your suet feeders after a prolonged midwinter thaw. Suet does not require any type of special protection from rain or snow.

A suet feeder is easy to make but must be kept clean and fresh. A Black-capped Chickadee visits this feeder for a mixture of suet and seed.

Placing Feeders in the Backyard

Birds eventually find feeders no matter where you put them, but feeders attract a greater number and variety of birds if they are placed at logical locations around your backyard. Experiment with different spots before choosing one. Once you find locations that seem to work, stick with them through the winter—birds like their food sources to be predictable. Here are some suggestions for placing feeders around your yard:

• Group three or four feeders together in stations scattered around the yard. Space the stations about 50 feet apart. Offer as many feeding stations as you have the inclination and space for. Put different types of seed or mixtures of seed in each feeder, and include a suet feeder or two for your insect-eating birds. Multiple feeding stations make it difficult for aggressive birds to dominate all of the feeders in the yard at once. (For information on hummingbird feeders, see page 212.)

• Place feeding stations within an easy flight to cover and perches. Birds feeding out in the open are particularly vulnerable to hawks, shrikes, and other avian predators. Many birds like to dart quickly to a feeder, grab a few seeds, and return to the safety of a tree or bush.

• Locate your feeders in sheltered spots where they are not exposed to the full force of winter winds. Suspended plastic feeders swaying in high winds discourage birds and scatter seed. Because cold winds rapidly rob small birds of their warmth, the south side of a house is usually the best place for feeders. Large tree trunks and heavy shrubs also provide a sheltered feeding site.

• Place your feeders at varying distances from the house. This attracts most of the birds to where you can see them and provides the shyer species with a place to feed.

• Do not forget ground-feeding birds. Sparrows, doves, and other ground feeders usually eat small seeds. If you are offering mixed seed in your feeders, you may find that these birds have plenty to eat just by cleaning up what other birds spill. If this does not seem to be the case, scatter a little millet or cracked corn in sheltered spots around the yard—under a picnic table is a good spot. Take the same precautions you would when offering ground-level water—avoid sites that provide shrubbery or other cover that could hide a cat.

Problems at Feeders

Cleanliness is important inside bird feeders as well as outside them. Few feeders are truly waterproof, and wet birdseed—especially cracked cereal grains—spoils quickly. Moldy birdseed is distasteful at best; at worst it makes birds sick. Check your feeders after a storm to be sure the seed is clean and dry. Even under the most favorable conditions it is a good idea to clean feeders thoroughly several times each season to ensure that the seed you offer is as healthful as the seeds the birds would find in nature.

Along with keeping a bird feeder clean, you may need to watch out for various types of pests.

Nuisance birds. House Sparrows, Blue Jays, and starlings are highly successful because they are adaptable and aggressive; it is their aggression that causes the most problems at winter feeders.

Some people are more adamant than others in their dislike for these birds. For example, many people are fond of Blue Jays for their quick intelligence and bright plumage, and city dwellers who sometimes have trouble attracting less-common native species welcome the chance to observe any birds—even those scorned by suburban and rural bird lovers. If you find them disruptive, here are ways to discourage their presence:

• Avoid offering foods that attract these birds. House Sparrows favor millet, cracked corn, and other "scratch" seeds. Starlings are suet eaters. Both species are exceptionally fond of baked goods and table scraps. Watch for a while to see what foods are the favorites of the problem birds in your yard, then cut back on them. (The drawback of this method is obvious—other species must be deprived to rid yourself of problem birds, and the method cannot be used at all for Blue Jays, who eat anything.)

Don Enger

Although it is attractive in plumage, the Blue Jay's aggressive nature causes other birds to shy away from feeders. Blue Jays can be directed away from a main feeder by erecting additional feeders elsewhere.

• Set up a decoy feeding station at the corner of your yard and stock it with baked goods, table scraps, and the other favorite foods of problem birds. This allows the more timid birds access to your other feeders.

• Maintain a number of feeding stations at different locations around the yard. Again, the idea is to prevent the problem birds from monopolizing all the feeders at once.

• Use feeders that discourage problem birds. House Sparrows usually avoid hanging feeders. Starlings cannot use suet feeders mounted on the underside of a branch. Blue Jays are shut out of many feeders designed for small birds.

• Fill your feeders when problem birds are not around. Different birds feed at different times of the day. By planning carefully you can feed the birds you want without feeding the ones you do not want. In some areas, for example, Blue Jays and starlings begin feeding later in the day and quit feeding earlier than most smaller birds. If you fill your feeders in mid-afternoon, small birds can feed alone for several hours before retiring and get a head start the next morning before the bigger birds arrive.

Squirrels. Squirrels are remarkably adept at emptying bird feeders as quickly as they can be filled. This is fine entertainment for a while, but soon proves too expensive to endure. Many veterans of the squirrel wars maintain that if these creatures want to get to a feeder badly enough they will. Others claim victory, and brag of squirrel-proof feeders they have purchased or designed. The truth lies somewhere in between. Here are some things you should know if you want to foil some of the squirrels some of the time:

• Baffles are the first line of defense against squirrels. Baffles are platter-shaped or conical objects placed between the feeder and the squirrel in the hope that the squirrel does not find a way around them. Aluminum pie plates and old phonograph records are often used as homemade baffles. Baffles strung on a line can be separated and spaced by lengths of old hose. Some commercial feeders come with dome-style roofs designed to double as baffles. Sometimes they work, sometimes they do not. (For an illustration of various baffles, see page 204.)

• Feeders in trees are the most difficult to protect from squirrels since they are located on the enemy's home ground. Trim nearby branches from which a squirrel might leap. Feeders on a line stretched between two trees or posts are somewhat more secure than feeders suspended from branches. Applying grease to the line may help to prevent high-wire acrobatics. Place baffles on the line on both sides of the feeder.

• Pole-mounted feeders are probably the most secure. Commercial squirrel-proof feeders often have a cone-shaped baffle mounted on the post below the feeder. Homemade baffles that you add yourself may be just as effective. Mount baffles at least 4 feet above the ground to keep the squirrel from leaping over them. The pole should be smooth to prevent climbing. Try wrapping a wooden pole with sheets of lightweight aluminum (called metal flashing), which are available in most building supply stores.

• Build a special feeding station to divert squirrels from feeders you cannot protect. A wire basket filled with ears of dried corn helps save more expensive seed. This alternative is for people who enjoy the entertainment and touch of wildness that squirrels bring to their yards, but not enough to forfeit expensive bird food.

• The more difficult solution to the squirrel problem is to live-trap the beasts in the fall and move them to another location, preferably some distance from the nearest bird feeder. This should help for a while, but do not be surprised if another squirrel shows up sooner or later.

F.E. Hester/VIREO

The Gray Squirrel is a wily pest that is difficult to keep away from all bird feeders.

Rats. Not all rodents are as furry and personable as squirrels. Uneaten seed under your feeders may attract rats, especially if feeders are located close to the house where the relative warmth along the foundation and the bounty of food from the feeder offer them ideal conditions. Prevent this problem by giving birds no more seed than they can eat in a few days, and clean up what is left over.

Rats can be tenacious enemies; eliminating them usually requires the use of poisoned baits that can harm other wildlife. Follow the suggestions for avoiding seed waste on page 190 to prevent the accumulation of seed under your feeders.

Protecting Backyard Feeders

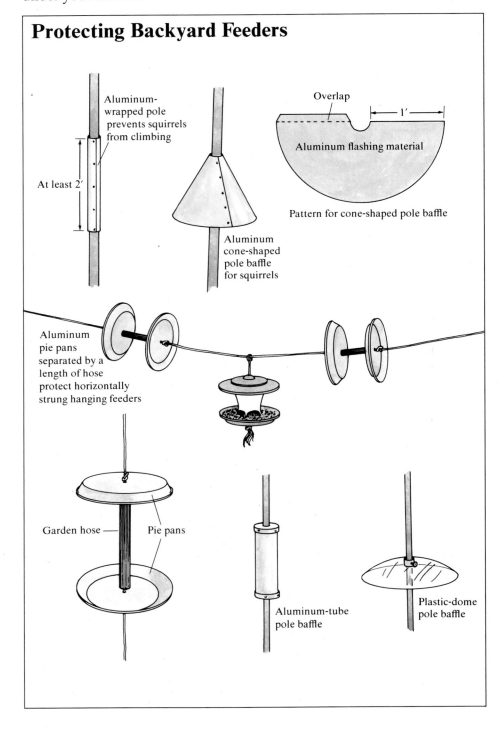

Aluminum-wrapped pole prevents squirrels from climbing

At least 2′

Aluminum cone-shaped pole baffle for squirrels

Overlap

1′

Aluminum flashing material

Pattern for cone-shaped pole baffle

Aluminum pie pans separated by a length of hose protect horizontally strung hanging feeders

Garden hose — Pie pans

Aluminum-tube pole baffle

Plastic-dome pole baffle

Karl H. Maslowski

The Kentucky Warbler is extremely selective in its choice of nesting habitat. This ground nester places a well-hidden nest of leaves under a dense thicket, far away from disturbances.

Nesting Time

Summer can be a quiet time for many bird-watchers. Winter birds no longer flock to garden feeders, and the bright variety of the spring migration is past. With the birds dispersed across the land, their nests carefully hidden in the dense green of summer foliage, many bird enthusiasts simply wash out the bird feeders and hang up the binoculars until fall. But while summer is a quieter time for a backyard bird-watcher, it need be no less exciting. Summer provides a wider variety of birds, and it is the only season when we can attract and study nesting pairs and their young.

A bird's nest can be anything from a simple pile of sticks to an intricately woven feat of engineering. Nests are temporary quarters built for the single purpose of protecting eggs and young birds. Generally, the more helpless the young of a species at birth, the more protection a nest must provide. Most common garden birds hatch naked, helpless young, and their nests are often carefully made and cleverly hidden.

Garden birds rarely build nests on the ground. Most songbirds place their cuplike nests firmly in the upright crotch of a tree or shrub or at the fork in a branch. Other nests, such as those of the Northern Oriole, are pendulous pouches anchored to branches with strongly woven plant fibers. Barn Swallows use mud to glue their nests under the eaves of buildings or on the rafters of old barns.

Many garden birds build cup- or bowl-shaped nests. They start with a framework of twigs and add layers of other materials including grass, leaves, plant-down, strips of bark, spiderwebs, moss, feathers, and animal hair. When these natural items are in short supply, birds construct their nests from an improbable array of synthetic products including barbed wire, thumbtacks, rubber bands, and assorted office supplies.

Attracting Birds at Nesting Time

Offering just the right habitat is the key to attracting summer birds. Enticing birds to your yard instead of the yard next door or the park down the street is a matter of offering protective cover, water, nesting sites, and perhaps some supplemental food. While winter feeders may tempt goldfinches from the fields and chickadees from the forests, these species only nest where conditions are ideal for raising their young. Many birds find suburban backyards ideal for nesting; many others nest in backyards if they adjoin other habitats, such as forests or open fields.

If you want to attract birds in summer, you must have plants: birds do not nest in a bare yard. Many garden birds rely on the thick foliage of trees and shrubs to shield their eggs and nestlings from wind, rain, and the eyes of hungry predators. The American Robin, for example, often builds its first nest each year among the dense branches of an evergreen; by the time it builds its second, the deciduous trees have come into leaf, and it chooses a maple, oak, or elm. Remember, the greater the variety of vegetation in a backyard, the more birds of different kinds it will attract.

The size of a yard is a significant factor in attracting different kinds of birds as well. Nesting territories are specific to species. While a pair of chickadees and a pair of vireos may share the same half-acre yard, two pairs of either bird will probably not. Some species have larger nesting territories than others. A large yard, for example, may support several pairs of nesting robins; their territories are frequently smaller than half an acre. Two pairs of Downy Woodpeckers would be another matter; each pair of these birds often defends over five acres. Nevertheless, there are a number of ways of encouraging birds to nest in even the smallest backyard.

Territorial Sizes in Some North American Birds

Species	Locality	Size (acres or sq. mi.) for each pair
Bunting, Snow	Greenland	0.5 to 7.0 acres
Chickadee, Black-capped	New York	8.4 to 17.1 acres
Eagle, Bald	Florida	2 to 3 sq. mi.
Eagle, Golden	California	19 to 59 sq. mi.
Eagle, Golden	Utah	25.4 to 35.5 sq. mi.
Flycatcher, Least	Michigan	0.37 to 0.50 acres
Hawk, Red-tailed	California	320 acres (avg.)
Longspur, Chestnut-collared	Saskatchewan	1 to 2 acres
Meadowlarks, Eastern and Western	Wisconsin	3 to 15 acres
Mockingbird, Northern	California	0.1 to 1.5 acres
Ovenbird	Michigan	0.5 to 4.5 acres
Robin, American	Wisconsin	0.11 to 0.6 acres
Sapsucker, Yellow-bellied	Ontario	5.1 to 5.4 acres
Sparrow, Song	Ohio	0.5 to 1.5 acres
Vireo, Red-eyed	Ontario	1.4 to 2.1 acres
Warbler, Prothonotary	Michigan	1.9 to 6.38 acres
Woodpecker, Downy	Ontario	5 to 8 acres
Woodpecker, Hairy	Ontario	6 to 8 acres
Wren, House	Ohio	0.25 to 3.6 acres

Adapted from *The Audubon Society Encyclopedia of North American Birds* by John K. Terres (New York: Alfred A. Knopf). Copyright © 1980 by John K. Terres.

Herbert Clarke

Ground-nesting Dark-eyed Juncos build their nests from dried grasses and line them with soft hair. Like many other birds, they readily accept offerings of good nesting material.

Offering Nesting Materials

Progress has not been kind to the birds that nest in our backyards. The power lawn mower with a grass catcher chops, sweeps up, and discards much potential nesting material. In this, as in so many aspects of a backyard, the neat, clean look does not suit the birds. They may pass over some gardens that offer nesting sites, food, and water because of a scarcity of nesting materials.

The obvious solution to a shortage of natural nesting material is to augment the supply with offerings of your own. A wide array of common products are similar to natural nesting material and are readily accepted by the birds. A partial list appears in the box at right, but use your imagination. Birds eagerly accept almost any material that is soft and can be easily woven. Of course, all materials that may end up in a bird's nest should be clean and dry.

String, yarn, and bits of cloth make good offerings to nesting birds. Cut the material into 6- to 8-inch pieces; birds have been known to tangle more lengthy portions around their necks and die of strangulation. Hair of any kind is also a great favorite for nest building. Birds are often so eager to obtain it that they may pluck it from the heads and bodies of live animals, including humans. Save that ball of fuzz caught in the brush after grooming your dog or cat, and set it aside to offer to the birds during the spring and summer.

When offering materials for nesting, remember that whenever birds leave the safety of trees, they risk exposure to cats and other predators. Since birds painstakingly gather several thousand bits of material one piece at a time, it is safer for them if you put nesting materials close to the nest site so the trip is as short as possible.

Instead of leaving nesting materials in the middle of a lawn, dangle them over the branches of your shrubbery, or offer them in special containers. Wire baskets fastened to the trunks of trees work well, as do the containers used to offer suet in winter. Put an assortment of nesting materials in a mesh bag so the birds can choose what they want through the holes in the sack. (See page 208.)

Materials to Offer Nesting Birds

Bits of fur
Bristles from old paint brush
Cotton
Dental floss
Dried grass
Dried sphagnum moss
Excelsior (wood shavings)
Feathers
Hair (cleaned from hairbrush)
Horsehair
Kapok
Knitting yarn
Pieces of soft cloth
Raveled burlap
Raveled rope
Spanish moss
String
Stuffing from old furniture
Thread
Wool

Adapted from *The New Handbook of Attracting Birds*, Second Edition, by Thomas P. McElroy, Jr. (New York: Alfred A. Knopf). Copyright ©1960 by Alfred A. Knopf, Inc.

How to Offer Nesting Materials

Nesting shelf placed near a window for easy viewing

Induce more birds to nest in your yard by augmenting their supply of natural nesting materials. Offer materials close to the nest site in accessible containers or dangled over shrubbery.

Mesh bag

Bush

Winter suet holder

Bicycle basket

Half-buried pan filled with mud

Construction plan for nesting shelf

8½″   8½″

8½″

10½″

1½″

7″

8″

7″   7″

Don & Pat Valenti

The American Robin requires a supply of wet mud to build a firm nest. Other birds, particularly swallows, also use wet mud in constructing their nests.

Offering mud. Robins, Barn Swallows, and several other common backyard birds need mud to build their nests. Most neighborhoods provide plenty of mud through the early part of each nesting season—melting snow and spring rains often leave an overabundance of it. As the season progresses and the birds build their second and possibly their third nests, however, the land begins to dry up and mud becomes scarcer.

Many backyard bird-watchers provide mud for birds. One Wisconsin farmer with a hatred of flying insects encouraged several thousand Cliff Swallows to nest in his barn by maintaining a large mud wallow. If you are going to offer mud to the birds, a little pan or birdbath buried in one corner of the yard does well. Add enough water each day to keep things sticky. Clay in the soil helps to hold the mixture together.

Offering nesting shelves. A few birds accustomed to nesting close to people accept artificial nesting shelves. If you live near a lake, river, or pond, you may attract Eastern Phoebes by installing shelves tucked under the overhanging eaves of your home. Barn Swallows often make trouble by nesting in porch or patio lighting fixtures; divert them to shelves nearby. Place nesting shelves for robins in a protected spot near a window so you can glimpse nesting drama close at hand.

Nesting shelves are easy to build. For size specifications, see the box below. Lumber, hardware, and construction methods are the same as those used for birdhouses (see pages 214 to 218), although you may want to waterproof the inside surfaces of your nesting shelves.

Dimensions of Nesting Shelves

Bird	Floor of Shelf	Depth of Shelf	Height Above Ground
Phoebe, Eastern	6″ × 6″	6″	8′ to 12′
Robin, American	6″ × 8″	8″	6′ to 15′
Sparrow, Song	6″ × 6″	6″	1′ to 3′
Swallow, Barn	6″ × 6″	6″	8′ to 12′

Adapted from *Homes for Birds*, Department of the Interior, U.S. Fish and Wildlife Service.

A Special Bird for Summer Gardens

Seeing a hummingbird in flight brings goose bumps to adults and children alike. A tiny, bright patch of color darts through the air at a remarkable speed then suddenly stops, braking in an instant to hover at the throat of a colorful bloom, its body still, its wings a blur of motion. It probes the flower for a moment or two with its long bill, and is quickly gone.

North American Hummingbirds

Hummingbirds originated in equatorial South America, and the great majority are still there, where flowers are abundant and in bloom the year around. A few species come north to raise their families in summer gardens; a very few remain in southern sections of the United States throughout the year. The number of North American hummingbirds decreases as you move north and east. Of the 320 known species, 21 make it to U.S. soil, most of them clustering in the states along the Mexican border. Eight species are more widely found in the West; four make it as far north as Canada; and one, the Rufous Hummingbird, makes a trip of 2,000 miles to nest in the southern part of Alaska. Only the Ruby-throated Hummingbird inhabits territory east of the Mississippi.

Flight. Hummingbirds evolved their style of helicopter flight over thousands of years. They can fly straight up, straight down, sideways, and backward; they can stop in an instant from a speed of 60 miles per hour in a tail wind; and they can hover in midair, their bodies motionless. Where other nectar-eating birds must cling to blossoms while they feed, hummingbirds can approach flowers head-on, dipping nectar directly from the bloom with their long bills and tongues.

Hummingbirds propel themselves through the air with a constant reciprocating motion of their wings—back and forth, back and forth, 70 times a second. Their wings are pointed and swept back, like those of a jet fighter, and they rotate at the shoulder rather than at the wrist like those of most birds. This shoulder rotation allows the wing to turn over in midstroke, so that backward motion cancels forward motion and the bird remains poised in the air. For more on the flight of hummingbirds, see page 134.

Color. With names like Ruby-throated Hummingbird, Violet-crowned Hummingbird, Blue-throated Hummingbird, and Cuban Emerald, it is not hard to guess that hummingbirds are colorful. Color variations often occur on feathers of the head and along the front of the neck. The neck area is known as the gorget because it resembles a piece of medieval armor by that name that protected the throat. The hummingbird's gorget feathers are iridescent and scatter rays of light into bright greens, purples, and reds. As the birds turn this way and that, they appear to change color before your eyes.

Size. Hummingbirds and shrews are the smallest warm-blooded animals theoretically possible; anything smaller could not eat quickly enough to maintain its temperature or fuel activity. The Ruby-throated Hummingbird is about 3 inches long, and most of that is feathers; its body is no bigger than the end joint of a person's thumb. The smallest hummingbird, the Calliope Hummingbird, weighs a tenth of an ounce—little more than the eraser on the end of a pencil. One Caribbean hummingbird is the size of a large bee.

Food. Hummingbirds must refuel almost constantly to stoke their furnaces for their frenetic activity. Nectar is their basic food—a sweet, high-calorie, ready-to-burn fuel. But nectar supplies only energy; for their protein the birds depend on insects, which they pluck from the hearts of colorful flowers as they feed. Hummingbirds also visit the holes drilled in trees by sapsuckers to sample sap and feast on the bugs attracted to it.

Most North American hummingbirds migrate long distances to winter in the Caribbean or the forests of Central and South America. Most species simply follow the flowers north in the spring and retreat as the flowers die off in late summer.

Revered for their vivid colors and incredible mobility, hummingbirds, like this male Allen's Hummingbird, feature prominently in the folklore of many pre-Columbian cultures.

Mike Yuschenkoff

Robert A. Tyrrell

An Anna's Hummingbird uses its long bill to reach nectar at the base of tubular flowers.

Ruby-throated Hummingbirds migrate 600 miles across the Gulf of Mexico, a journey of 20 hours; during this time they are unable to feed. Before the crossing, they stop off in Florida and Georgia and gorge themselves on nectar, adding 50 percent of their body weight as fat to sustain them through the journey.

The Flower Bird

The relationship between hummingbirds and flowers offers advantages to both organisms. The bird is lured to the flower by the nectar, which is secreted by glands called nectares located deep within the bloom. In the process of feeding, the bird gathers a fine dusting of pollen, which it carries to the next plant. Pollination allows the plant to reproduce. (Other birds and insects, especially bees, also share the work pollinating plants.)

Hummingbirds are such efficient pollinators that many plants have evolved flowers specially built to make use of them. These "hummingbird flowers" have long tubular blooms and particularly deep-seated nectares. The birds and flowers probably evolved together, each to take advantage of resources offered by the other: The birds have a guaranteed food supply for which they do not have to compete; the flowers receive the special attention of high-class professional pollinators.

The color of a flower is as important in attracting hummingbirds as its shape. While the birds feed from flowers of any hue, the brighter colors usually receive the most attention. Because red is the color complement of the surrounding green foliage, red flowers tend to stand out most strongly. Ruby-throated Hummingbirds are so attracted to red that they have been known to hover hungrily before a crimson necktie or hair ribbon. Hummingbirds also feed at orange, pink, yellow, blue, and purple flowers. They quickly learn which flowers in the neighborhood reward them with food and seek out others of that color. Apparently, hummingbirds cannot distinguish one flower from another by its smell.

Attracting Hummingbirds

Hummingbirds live where there are flowers. They are especially attracted to edge habitats—parks, gardens, backyards. To bring hummingbirds into your garden or backyard, there is no substitute for filling it with bloom. Select flowers, trees, and shrubs that complement each other so that there are blossoms throughout the season. Because hummingbirds often arrive early in the year, the garden with spring-blooming plants has a head start on securing the birds for the summer.

Flowers are more eye-catching if they are clustered by variety in blocks of color. You may want to plant a garden of hummingbird favorites: honeysuckle or morning glories on a trellis, hollyhocks or gladiolus in the center, and short bedding flowers like begonias in the front. Ask a local nursery or garden club when these species bloom in your area. When you select trees and shrubs for your yard, keep hummingbirds in mind; if you can satisfy your needs with flowering varieties they enjoy, so much the better.

Hummingbird Feeders

While masses of colorful flowers are obviously the easiest way to attract hummingbirds, they can often be tempted without a bud or blossom in sight by taking advantage of their strong affinity for bright colors. A hummingbird feeder is nothing more than a container of artificial nectar dressed up to look like a flower. Inexpensive feeders are available commercially; any small container that holds water serves as the basis for the homemade variety.

Commercial hummingbird feeders are sometimes quite ornate, with half a dozen or more feeding holes. This extra feeding space is sometimes wasted on hummingbirds, who are quite territorial and frequently defend a feeder against other birds, or even try to defend two feeders at once. A soft-drink or fruit-juice bottle with a red ribbon wrapped around the mouth to simulate a bloom makes a fine hummingbird feeder when filled with sugar water. As an alternative, put sugar water in an 8-ounce milk carton. Punch a small hole on either side of the sloping top and, using a bright color, draw the petals of a flower around each hole. Like the red ribbon, the drawings attract the birds initially; once they know the food is there, you can dispense with them.

Making your own nectar. Commercial nectars are available, some with dietary supplements to provide extra nutrients for the hummingbirds. But a simple sugar-water solution is easy to make at home: Use 1 part granulated sugar to 4 parts boiling water, stir to dissolve, and let it cool. Store what you do not use in the refrigerator. Never use honey; it ferments and can make the birds sick. Every two or three days, wash the feeder in hot water and refill. This cleaning of the feeder is important in order to prevent passing a fungal infection to the birds.

Ortho Photo Library

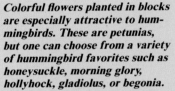

Colorful flowers planted in blocks are especially attractive to hummingbirds. These are petunias, but one can choose from a variety of hummingbird favorites such as honeysuckle, morning glory, hollyhock, gladiolus, or begonia.

Hummingbird Feeders

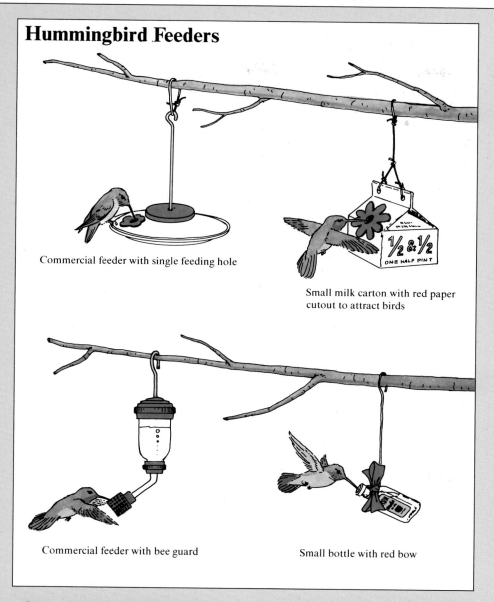

Commercial feeder with single feeding hole

Small milk carton with red paper cutout to attract birds

Commercial feeder with bee guard

Small bottle with red bow

Insects at hummingbird feeders. Sugar water can also attract troublemakers like ants and yellow-jacket wasps. Discourage ants by coating the hangers from which feeders are suspended with petroleum jelly. A fine spray of water on a feeder washes off spilled sugar water and keeps away flying insects—at least while it is turned on—and birds love the shower. Do not be tempted to use pesticides on or around hummingbird feeders; the annoyance of the bugs is not worth the danger to the birds.

Nesting

Once hummingbirds are established in your yard, they will probably stay all summer. Hummingbirds are feisty creatures. Their territorial battles are often dramatic, full of bluffing and chasing, fervent attacks, and swooping aerial acrobatics. The males establish and defend feeding territories; the females settle nesting territories, which they defend against intruders of all sizes, including other hummingbirds.

Female hummingbirds assume all nesting chores. The nest is about the size of a fifty-cent piece and carefully constructed of downy plant fibers held together with scavenged bits of a tent-caterpillar nest or spiderweb. The white, pea-sized eggs are usually laid in pairs, and the female incubates them for two to three weeks. After the featherless, helpless chicks hatch, the mother feeds them for 25 days, then they must leave the nest permanently to survive on their own.

Top: *The Red-bellied Woodpecker relies on standing dead trees as food sources and places to nest. Good trees are dry, well-cured, and solid.*

Bottom: *The Eastern Bluebird, a cavity-nesting species, relies on holes that have been carved out by other birds. These birds readily take to birdhouses.*

Attracting Cavity Nesters

Many backyard birds are not fond of open-air homesteading. Woodpeckers, wrens, titmice, chickadees, and bluebirds are only a few of the birds that prefer to hide their nests in cavities, usually in trees. Some of them—mostly woodpeckers—carve their own nesting holes. Others reuse abandoned woodpecker holes or nest in naturally occurring cavities. In either case, the advantage to the bird is clear. Nests that are fully enclosed and out of sight are safer from predators and the weather than those balanced on outside branches.

A hundred years ago, cavity-nesting birds in this country were enjoying good times. The woodlots and orchards of the nineteenth-century family farm provided a rich source of nesting sites. Miles of fence were strung across the land, and every 10 to 20 feet a wooden fence post waited to become a birdhouse. The Eastern Bluebird—that loveliest of cavity nesters—was a common sight; its hunched form decorated wires and fence rails from the Atlantic to the Rocky Mountains. Now the Eastern Bluebird as a species is in trouble; many Americans will never see one.

The twentieth century has not been kind to cavity-loving birds. Acre after acre of old farmland has been bulldozed and seeded into tightly landscaped suburban backyards. Across much of the country, "clean practice" in landscaping, forestry, and fruit growing has eliminated the dead trees and old snags in which many cavity nesters made their homes. Where farms and ranches remain, most of the old wooden fence posts are gone, long since replaced by the longer-lasting metal variety.

Two practices ensure that cavity-loving birds find places to nest in your yard: Save the natural spots you have, and supplement them with artificial ones. Saving what you have is easy—simply put away the chain saw. If there is a dead tree on your property, cut the branches that could fall into the yard, and leave the hulk as a home for birds. Remove dead limbs from a live tree only if they pose a danger.

Birdhouses

Supplying cavity nesters with artificial homes is more involved than retaining natural cavities. It is an unusual backyard that is blessed with standing dead wood. Most backyard birders must supply artificial cavities for cavity-nesting birds. The easiest way to do this is with a birdhouse (sometimes called a bird box). A birdhouse is a simple structure consisting of four walls, a floor, a roof, and a hole in the front for the bird to enter and exit.

Thousands of birdhouses are built every year and thousands of ready-made birdhouses are bought in stores or from displays in roadside yards. Unfortunately, many never house the birds for which they were intended. Many birdhouses end up stuffed with problem birds such as starlings or House Sparrows; many are warped beyond recognition after the weather of one season. But this needn't be so. Properly placed birdhouses find suitable occupants; properly built birdhouses last for many years.

Commercially made birdhouses are designed in a variety of dimensions to suit the needs of particular birds. The person who sells you a birdhouse should be able to tell you what type of bird you may expect to attract. If you are building a birdhouse, see the chart on page 216 to learn the best size for the birds you wish to attract.

Although birdhouses are not used by nesting birds until spring, the best time to erect them is in autumn. The house will season and become more attractive to birds as it weathers. If you put up birdhouses before the trees are bare, you can see how much sun or shade they will have through the nesting season.

Kit Harrison

George H. Harrison

The basic birdhouse. The way a birdhouse looks on the outside means nothing to birds. Birdhouses that are best looked upon as lawn decorations may or may not ever house birds. It is the inside that interests them, and the inside is, after all, only a cavity. In general, therefore, the simpler the design, the better.

To offer a birdhouse that birds will use, consider the following:

• The most critical dimension on any birdhouse is the diameter of the entrance hole. If you want a house for chickadees, the diameter must be at least 1⅛ inches; if you make it 1¼ inches, the house will fill up with sparrows. Wrens, bluebirds, and several species of swallows all use houses with 1½-inch entrance holes; anything bigger will admit starlings.

• The area below the entrance hole inside the house should be a bit rough so that birds can get a grip when climbing out. If this area seems too smooth in a purchased birdhouse, roughen it with a rasp before you assemble the pieces. When building a birdhouse from rough-sawn lumber, put the rough side facing in.

• A birdhouse should not have a perch in front of the entrance hole—they are unnecessary and encourage problem birds like House Sparrows to sit outside and torment the occupants.

• Include ventilation holes in the top of the walls and holes in the floor for drainage in case water gets in. The roof of a birdhouse should extend well over the front and sides to keep water away from the entrance and ventilation holes. A shallow groove midway between the front of the roof and where it meets the body of the house prevents water from "walking" down the underside of the roof into the entrance hole.

• Be sure the roof extends over the back of the box. In many birdhouses the back extends beyond the roof line to form a mounting plate, leaving a crack between the roof and back for water to get in. Mounting boards should be screwed or nailed to a completed birdhouse so the roof fits tightly over all four sides.

• One piece of any birdhouse should be hinged in some way to allow for cleaning. Hinging the front or one of the sides allows the most complete access, but a removable roof also works.

• With the exception of wrens, birds do not tolerate swaying bird-houses. Birdhouses should be firmly anchored to a post, a tree, or the side of a building. (If you plan to take your birdhouses indoors each winter, be sure to mount them with screws or nuts and bolts so they may be easily taken up and down.) Lengths of pipe make excellent birdhouse supports. Drive the pipe into the ground, then to its threaded upper end, attach a pipe flange of the same size that has been fastened to the bottom of the house. The size pipe you choose depends upon the weight of the bird-house. If the house is especially heavy, you may need to set the pipe in concrete. No matter how birdhouses are erected, they should be as level as possible and should face away from the prevailing wind.

Materials. With the exception of specially designed houses for Purple Martins (see page 222), metal birdhouses are dangerous, better for baking birds than for housing them. Plastic birdhouses are also poor insulators and do not "breathe," causing moisture to build up inside the house. Wood is by far the best material for building birdhouses: No other substance insulates and protects birds as well.

Wood has advantages for the home hobbyist too: It is easy to work with and readily obtained. By far the best kinds of wood for birdhouses are red-wood, cypress, and cedar, which are high in natural resins and stand up against the weather for many years. Pine, fir, and other soft woods are widely available and tend to be more reasonably priced.

It is not necessary to use top-grade lumber, but the wood should always be thoroughly dry before it is worked. Use ¾-inch wood for birdhouses. If possible, it should be rough-sawn on at least one side to provide better traction for the birds' feet. Construct houses of slab wood with the bark side out for nuthatches and several other birds listed below.

Dimensions of Various Birdhouses

Bird	Floor of House	Depth of House	Diameter of Entrance Hole	Height of Entrance Above Floor	Height Above Ground
Bluebirds	5" × 5"	8"	1½"	6"	5' to 10'
Chickadees	4" × 4"	8" to 10"	1⅛"	6" to 8"	6' to 15'
Finch, House	6" × 6"	6"	2"	4"	8' to 12'
Flicker, Northern	7" × 7"	16" to 18"	2½"	14" to 16"	6' to 20'
Kestrel, American	8" × 8"	12" to 15"	3"	9" to 12"	10' to 30'
Nuthatches	4" × 4"	8" to 10"	1¼"	6" to 8"	12' to 20'
Screech-Owls	8" × 8"	12" to 15"	3"	9" to 12"	10' to 30'
Starlings	6" × 6"	16" to 18"	2"	14" to 16"	10' to 25'
Swallow, Tree	5" × 5"	6"	1½"	1" to 5"	10' to 15'
Titmice	4" × 4"	8" to 10"	1¼"	6" to 8"	6' to 15'
Woodpecker, Downy	4" × 4"	8" to 10"	1¼"	6" to 8"	6' to 20'
Woodpecker, Red-bellied	6" × 6"	12" to 15"	2½"	9" to 12"	12' to 20'
Woodpecker, Red-headed	6" × 6"	12" to 15"	2"	9" to 12"	12' to 20'
Wren, Carolina	4" × 4"	6" to 8"	1½"	4" to 6"	6' to 10'
Wren, House	4" × 4"	6" to 8"	1" to 1¼"	4" to 6"	6' to 10'
Wren, Winter	4" × 4"	6" to 8"	1" to 1¼"	4" to 6"	6' to 10'

Adapted from *Homes for Birds*, Department of the Interior, U.S. Fish and Wildlife Service.

Birdhouses

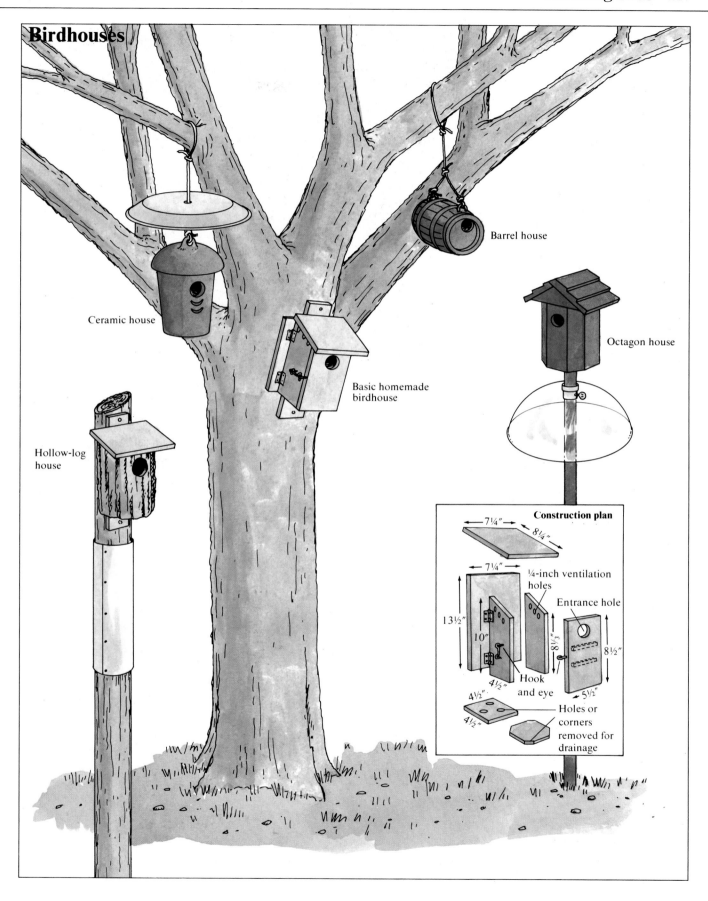

Barrel house

Ceramic house

Octagon house

Basic homemade
birdhouse

Hollow-log
house

Construction plan

7¼"

8¼"

7¼"

¼-inch ventilation
holes

Entrance hole

13½"

10"

8½"

8½"

Hook
and eye

4½"

4½"

5½"

4½"

Holes or
corners
removed for
drainage

Karl H. Maslowski

A simple design and sturdy construction are all that the House Wren needs to hold its nest.

Give any birdhouse or the lumber to build one a sniff test. If you detect an odor of creosote or other chemicals, or if the wood is the least bit sticky, it is unsuitable for birds. Do not treat the inside surface of a birdhouse with chemicals of any kind. Never use green, copper-based wood preservatives, or lumber that has been treated with them, because they are toxic. It is best to avoid paint as well—it cracks and chips and is generally a nuisance. If you do choose to paint the box, use drab, natural colors, but avoid dark colors like black and dark brown because they will absorb heat. Do not paint the inside. A martin house is an exception to the no-paint rule. Martin houses should be in direct sun, and a coat of white paint will reflect the heat.

Treat birdhouses that need waterproofing with clear mineral wax, marine varnish, or any other product that will not become sticky when the temperature climbs. If you mount the house against a tree or wall, give the back an extra coat of waterproofing—the back will be the last part to dry out after a storm.

The hardware that holds a birdhouse together is almost as important as what the house is made of. Most birdhouses fall apart because inadequate fasteners give way. Hardware should be zinc coated, galvanized, or made of aluminum or other weather-resistant material. Use the type of nails with ridges in them (ring-shank nails) so they will not pull out. The best—and usually the most expensive—houses are held together with brass, galvanized, or stainless steel screws.

Use the guidelines on page 216 to build a house for any bird you want to attract.

Nighttime Shelter for Winter Birds

During most of the year birds find adequate shelter in the vegetation of their habitats. In the depths of winter, however, even the thickest evergreen tree may not provide enough shelter to keep a bird from perishing in the cold.

Birds are most vulnerable to the elements at night, when temperatures plunge and darkness keeps them from finding food to provide the fuel they need to keep warm. Most birds sleep at night, roosting in the same kinds of places in which they build their nests in spring and summer. Cavity-nesting birds, such as chickadees, nuthatches, and titmice, look for hollow spaces in which to roost—either natural cavities or summer birdhouses left open through the winter months. Frequently there is not enough space for the flocks of birds that gather near bird feeders or other concentrations of food.

Roosting boxes are artificial cavities designed as communal bedrooms for winter birds. They are easy to build out of the same sort of lumber and hardware as that used for nesting boxes (see "Materials" on page 216). Some stores that sell bird feeders also sell roosting boxes. Follow these guidelines for buying, building, or placing roosting boxes:

• Roosting boxes should contain perches. Boxes intended for larger birds, which roost alone, should have a single perch. Small birds, which roost communally, need several perches or one long perch. Communal roosting gives small birds the advantage of sharing body heat. Make perches out of ¼- or ⅜-inch dowel. Before assembling your box, clamp the side pieces together and drill the holes where the dowels will go. Fasten them with glue or small nails.

• The overall size of a roosting box is not crucial; the bigger the box, the more birds it holds. Roosting boxes are usually about 14 to 18 inches wide and several feet tall. Boxes designed to hold single-roosting larger birds should be smaller.

• The entrance hole on a roosting box should be located near the floor. If it were higher, rising heat would escape to the open air. The size of the bird for which the box is intended dictates the size of the entrance hole. The chart on page 216 includes hole dimensions. You do not need to provide a box for each species; one for smaller birds and one for somewhat bigger birds should do.

• Unlike nesting boxes, boxes intended for roosting should have no ventilation or drainage holes. Construction should be as tight as possible all the way around. The front of the box should be hinged or removable to allow easy cleaning. (Do not hinge the top—the perches get in the way when you try to clean the bottom of the box.) Clean boxes thoroughly each season and close them for the summer so they do not fill up with sparrows or mice.

• Place roosting boxes in the most sheltered spot you can find. The south side of a building or large tree is often a good location.

Vertical roosting box

¼" or ⅜" dowels

18"

Entrance hole

9"

Hinged side

Mounting board

Roosting Boxes

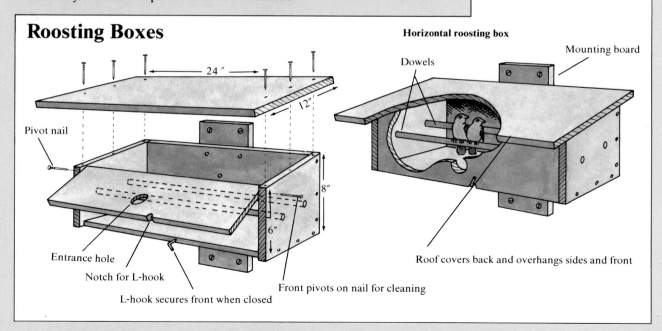

24"

12"

Pivot nail

Entrance hole

Notch for L-hook

L-hook secures front when closed

8"

6"

Front pivots on nail for cleaning

Horizontal roosting box

Dowels

Mounting board

Roof covers back and overhangs sides and front

George H. Harrison

The male House Wren requires several potential nest sites to attract a female. This and other wren species build decoy nests, which seem to function in both self-defense—as a means of confusing predators—and in courtship.

Location. Birdhouses often remain unoccupied because they are in the wrong location. Consider the kind of nesting conditions the birdhouse is meant to duplicate. Natural nesting cavities are in dead trees and branches, which are typically out of cover in bright sun. Most birdhouses end up in just the opposite kinds of locations, tucked among the lush branches of big trees. Some birds like heavily shaded houses, but many would rather be in sunny areas.

It is impossible to know precisely which birds you may attract to your birdhouse—a quick glimpse of the chart on page 216 shows that nuthatches, chickadees, and titmice, for example, all use houses of similar size. If you can provide the right habitat, however, three small birdhouses may well gain you a pair of birds of each species. Similarly, larger houses may attract swallows, bluebirds, and Carolina Wrens; houses that are larger still attract woodpeckers. In general, the best way to increase the number of cavity nesters in your yard is to put out several houses of different sizes.

Nesting birds are territorial, and instinct determines their location and density in a landscape. Some birds nest much closer together than others. For example, one birdhouse on a half-acre lot is sufficient for one pair of chickadees. Purple Martins nest in colonies (see "The Apartment-House Bird" on page 222). Tree Swallows maintain small territories—their houses can be placed as close as 30 feet from one another. Two pairs of tree swallows will sometimes occupy boxes in the same tree.

Territoriality between different species of birds is not nearly as strong as that between two individuals of the same species. Even so, only a few species will nest right next to another species. For best results, spread your birdhouses out as much as conditions permit.

Birdhouses for House Wrens. Many people maintain a number of small nesting boxes in the hope of attracting House Wrens. These delightful little birds are careful housing shoppers and like to have more than one site from which to choose. The male arrives first in the spring and busily builds as many as a dozen nests. When the female arrives, the male escorts its mate from one nest to another until she makes her choice. House Wrens maintain territories of ¼ to 3½ acres, so large yards may attract two or even three pairs. More important, erecting several wren houses increases the chances of attracting one pair, since the male must have several nesting sites to attract a female. Once House Wrens find a home, they return to nest year after year.

Birdhouse maintenance. Like other animals, birds can host an assortment of lice, mites, and other pests. While these pests pose no danger to humans, their effects range from making life uncomfortable for the birds to causing significant nestling mortality.

Many birds discourage parasites by refusing to use the same nest twice. But even if birds are willing to reuse old nests, do not let them do it. Watch your birdhouses. Each time a brood is fledged, open up the house, sweep out the old nest, and wash the house with water. If you see evidence of lice or mites, dust the interior with a commercial miticide. Leave the birdhouse open until it is thoroughly dry, then close it up so the birds can get started on their next brood.

After the last brood in the fall, clean out birdhouses as described above and discourage mice or squirrels from nesting in them by sealing the entrance holes. This also prevents starlings and House Sparrows from taking early possession of the house in the spring. Slip plastic bags over the tops of the houses to keep out the worst of the winter weather, or take them from their mounts and store them indoors. Be sure to put them back up, clean and ready for birds, by late February or early March.

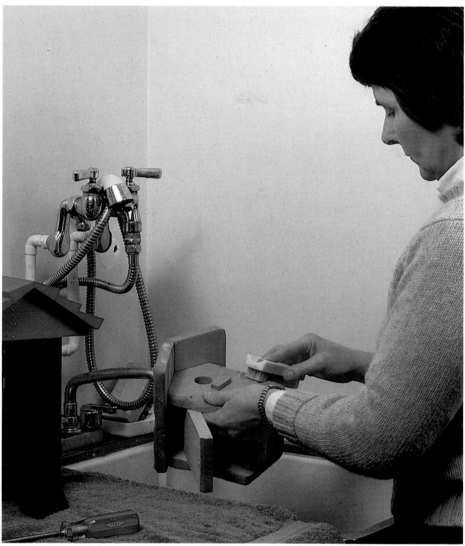

Cleaning a birdhouse is important because many birds will not return to one that is not properly cleaned. Scrub it well, and be sure it has dried completely before closing it up.

Many people leave their birdhouses open through the winter to provide shelter for cold-weather birds. Some winter birds that are cavity nesters in summer—and a few that are not—crowd into birdhouses on cold nights. The houses provide shelter from the wind and capture the heat given off by the birds' bodies. But nesting boxes can only shelter a limited number of birds, and some people build special roosting boxes for winter use (see "Nighttime Shelter for Winter Birds" on page 219). If birdhouses are left open through the winter, make sure you clean them out in February to prepare for nesting birds.

Discouraging unwanted guests. House Sparrows and starlings are cavity nesters and are aggressive about acquiring and holding nesting sites. The only sure way to prevent starlings and House Sparrows from seizing every birdhouse in your yard is to throw the nests out as the birds set up housekeeping. This requires some vigilance in late winter and early spring. House Sparrows do not migrate and are often happily settled in a box by the time wrens and other birds arrive.

As the discussion of winter feeding points out, some people are more tolerant than others of European Starlings and House Sparrows. Starlings in particular are a mixed blessing in a summer backyard—common and noisy, to be sure, but also ardent consumers of large numbers of insects.

The Apartment-House Bird

No one knows exactly how long Americans have been offering housing to Purple Martins. Long before the arrival of Europeans, native peoples used hollowed dried gourds to attract these large, dark swallows. Other settlers were quick to adopt the custom. Traveling the country in the early 1840s, John James Audubon remarked, "Almost every country tavern has a Martin box on the upper part of its signboard; and I have observed that the handsomer the box, the better does the inn generally prove to be."

It is not hard to see why Purple Martins have such loyal fans. These birds have an intricate and fascinating social behavior, a breathtaking flight, and a passion for mosquitoes and other flying insects. Martins are not territorial birds; they prefer to nest in colonies that grow from year to year as new members are added. Martin fanciers take advantage of the birds' colonial urges by offering them intricate avian apartment houses designed to hold from half a dozen to fifty or more birds.

Martin houses can be time-consuming to build and expensive to buy—the kind of investment that warrants preparatory research. If you are interested in starting a martin colony, first find out if the birds already nest in your area; new colonies are almost always settled by birds from older colonies nearby. Your local Audubon Society chapter should be able to give you this information. Next, evaluate your habitat. Martins only establish colonies near broad, open areas—beside a field or meadow, for example, or at the edge of a lake. They are aerial feeders and must have unobstructed air space in which to freely soar.

Even if you have martin colonies nearby and can offer them the perfect habitat, do not spend a lot of time or money on a large martin house without some guarantee that you will attract the birds. Many people try for years without success and, without martins, even the most elegant martin house is doomed to become a hotel for House Sparrows.

Start small; some commercial martin houses have as few as six compartments and are expandable. Alternately, build yourself three or four properly sized birdhouses and mount them together, or build your first martin houses out of gourds as the Indians did. Whatever approach you take, keep your initial investment small. (See the sample house at right.)

If you do attract martins, rejoice; you have probably got them for life. The birds

are loyal to their colonies year after year. Then start thinking about adding more room. If you started with an expandable martin house, add another section. If you began with single-unit housing, add more units or build a special martin house.

The decision to buy or build a martin house depends on your resources and skill at construction. As a rule, metal birdhouses are a bad idea, but martin houses are an exception. The designs of most commercial aluminum martin houses provide adequate ventilation and are treated with light-colored, reflective paints to keep them cool inside. They are also significantly lighter in weight than homemade wooden houses, an important consideration when it comes to taking them down for cleaning or storage. Homemade martin houses continue to be a popular and economical alternative to the commercial variety, however. For a basic martin house, see illustration at right.

Every martin house should incorporate the following important characteristics:

• Individual nesting compartments should be built to the dimensions given in the illustration. Note that the compartments have a large entrance hole located a short distance above the floor. The low sill allows young birds easy access to the exercise ledges outside. Quality martin houses often provide railings around the ledges to keep young birds from falling.

• Martin houses are usually built in tiers, and each tier contains six or eight apartments. Most homemade houses and some of the commercial ones are expandable; you can add tiers as a colony grows. If you buy a martin house, be sure it is expandable or already contains as many apartments as you want. Otherwise, you will need to buy a new house every time you want to expand your colony.

• Since martin houses must be in full sun, features that reduce overheating are essential. Each compartment should have ventilation holes both to the outside and to a central air shaft that passes from top to bottom through the heart of the house. The air shaft goes through the ceiling of the topmost tier and into a ventilated attic. Martin houses should be painted white or some other highly reflective color.

• The best martin houses include perches, which are often on the roof or arrayed on the mounting pole below it. Martins welcome nearby telephone poles or electrical wires because of the open perches these features provide. Martins do not perch in trees and will rarely use a birdhouse within 30 feet of one.

• Martin houses should be easy to clean and store. Aluminum houses often have

Most people enjoy Purple Martins because the birds consume large numbers of insects. Purple Martins nesting in suspended gourds form an attractive, expandable colony.

Jerome Jackson

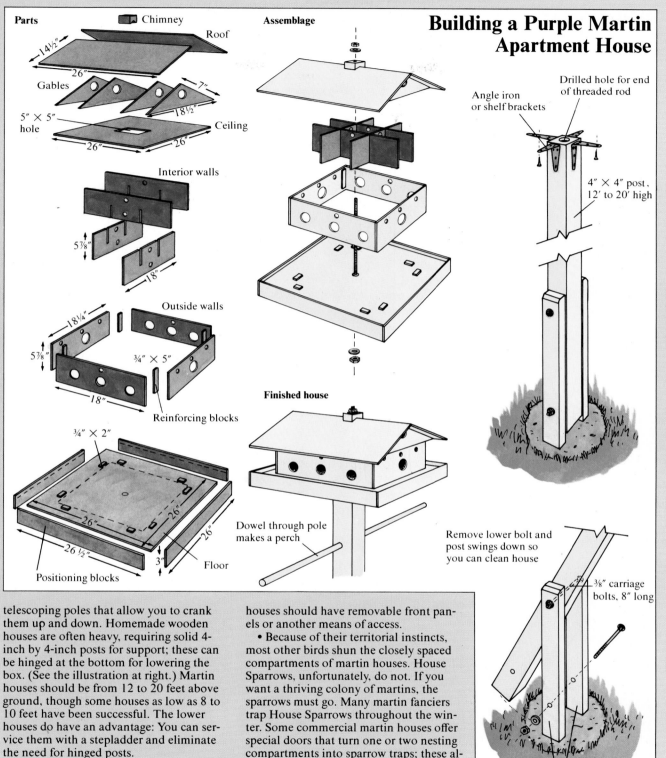

Parts

Chimney

Roof

14½"

26"

Gables

7"

5" × 5" hole

18½"

Ceiling

26"   26"

Interior walls

5⅞"

18"

Outside walls

18¼"

5⅞"

¾" × 5"

18"

Reinforcing blocks

¾" × 2"

26"

26½"

26"

3"

Positioning blocks

Floor

Assemblage

Finished house

Dowel through pole makes a perch

Building a Purple Martin Apartment House

Angle iron or shelf brackets

Drilled hole for end of threaded rod

4" × 4" post, 12' to 20' high

Remove lower bolt and post swings down so you can clean house

⅜" carriage bolts, 8" long

2 × 4s, 5' long, 3' above ground, set in concrete

telescoping poles that allow you to crank them up and down. Homemade wooden houses are often heavy, requiring solid 4-inch by 4-inch posts for support; these can be hinged at the bottom for lowering the box. (See the illustration at right.) Martin houses should be from 12 to 20 feet above ground, though some houses as low as 8 to 10 feet have been successful. The lower houses do have an advantage: You can service them with a stepladder and eliminate the need for hinged posts.

• Nesting compartments in any martin house should be accessible for cleaning. Do not use nails or screws to fasten a homemade house; use hooks and eyes or a long, threaded rod for easy disassembly. Compartments of commercial aluminum

houses should have removable front panels or another means of access.

• Because of their territorial instincts, most other birds shun the closely spaced compartments of martin houses. House Sparrows, unfortunately, do not. If you want a thriving colony of martins, the sparrows must go. Many martin fanciers trap House Sparrows throughout the winter. Some commercial martin houses offer special doors that turn one or two nesting compartments into sparrow traps; these allow you to remove the sparrows throughout the nesting season. The best method is to store martin houses during the winter. If you do not store them, block off the nesting compartments to prevent sparrows from getting an early start in the spring.

Safety in the Backyard Habitat

While many songbirds live 10 to 12 years, most die of trauma or predation long before. Some robins, for example, have been banded and recaptured after nearly 12 years, but the life span of the average robin is only 14 months. Ornithologists estimate that almost three fourths of all songbirds die during their first year.

With so many birds dying all the time, we can expect that some of them will inevitably do so in our yards. We cannot rewrite the laws of nature. We can, however, make an effort to minimize danger to birds, especially when it arises from changes we have made in the ecosystem.

Protecting Backyard Birds

The greatest danger to birds in any backyard is the family pet. Young birds constitute a large part of the diet of wild or vagrant cats in spring and summer. Dogs also catch and eat birds, although they usually escape detection because they do not carry their prey around in their mouths the way cats do.

Squirrels attracted by winter birdseed may remain through the summer, gnawing their way into nesting boxes to eat eggs and young birds. In rural areas raccoons, opossums, and snakes present a threat. Small birds can also be threatened from the air by kestrels and shrikes, a particular problem when birds cluster around winter feeders. Help these birds by creating a brush pile out of branches (especially evergreen) in which they can hide.

The best way to deal with a predator is to remove it altogether. This is impossible if the offender is a larger bird, and difficult if it is a pet cat or dog—either yours or the neighbor's. Squirrels, raccoons, opossums, and other small mammals can be live-trapped and relocated.

Consider removing roving cats and dogs. Never trap and relocate them—they will simply prey on native wildlife somewhere else. Contact your local Society for the Prevention of Cruelty to Animals (SPCA) or animal control officer for help in removing them from your yard.

Removing pet cats and dogs is more difficult. The best solution is to keep your cats in the house and your dogs on a line, especially during the nesting season. Whether you can persuade your neighbors to restrain their animals is another matter. A fence around your yard might exclude dogs, but will probably not be effective against cats.

Below: *A Gray Squirrel can easily chew the entrance of a birdhouse to suit its own dimensions. Squirrels that claim birdhouses for their own use often destroy the nests and young of the previous owners.*

Below right: *The predacious behavior of dogs and cats poses a serious threat to small birds such as the Black Phoebe.*

George H. Harrison

Peter M. La Tourrette

If you cannot remove cats, dogs, and other predators, the next best thing is to give the birds some protection. Often all birds need is an early warning to avoid becoming some other creature's meal. Some pet owners attach bells to their cat's collar in hope of providing birds with early knowledge of approaching felines. Bells are not much help to ground-nesting birds with young in the nest, however. For information about the best locations for birdbaths, see page 180; for information about placing food, see page 201.

Predators at nesting time. Nestlings and fledglings are particularly helpless against predators. Sometimes people unwittingly increase this danger by searching out nests in the hope of seeing young birds. Predators are sometimes led to the nest by following the human trail. Human visits can also prompt a nervous parent to abandon a nest and eggs to try its luck in a quieter location.

During the nesting season, birdhouses are a great temptation to predators; they almost guarantee a meal of eggs or young birds. Parent birds can be trapped in a box by a cat or other predator lurking outside. In general, post-mounted nesting boxes are safer from predators than those fastened to trees. Many predators find pipes particularly difficult to climb, and a pipe smeared with grease provides extra protection. Use the same type of predator guard to protect nesting boxes as you would to protect winter feeders (see pages 203 and 204). Conical baffles work well, provided they are high enough off the ground to prevent a cat from jumping over them. A sheet-metal sleeve placed around a tree or wooden post also discourages predators. If you place metal sleeves or baffles around a living tree, loosen them several times a year to allow the tree to grow.

Orphaned Birds

If birds are nesting in your backyard, you may occasionally discover an "orphan"—a nestling that has become separated from its parents. Wherever an orphan comes from, it can present a problem for the person who discovers it, especially if there is a child in the house. Our natural tendency is to save, cuddle, and nurture helpless creatures; it is a tendency responsible for the deaths of many birds each year.

Young birds are almost always better off in the wild than they are in a cardboard box under human care. Bringing a young bird through the first weeks of life is an extremely chancy business, even for a mother bird, who has all the right tools and instincts for the job; people without special training and equipment have little hope of raising a young bird. As another incentive to leave the birds alone, federal statute prohibits any unlicensed person from keeping protected wildlife—a category that includes nearly all backyard birds.

Many birds assumed to be orphans are not. Parents are frequently nearby, deliberately apart from their young in an effort to lure potential predators away. Even a bird brought home by a dog or cat probably has a distressed parent nearby. If you find an unaccompanied nestling and cannot spot a nest from which it has fallen, do what you can to protect it from predators and leave it alone.

Replacing nests and nestlings. If you find a bird that has obviously fallen from a nest, replace it—parent birds are unable to do so. There is no truth to the old tale that nestlings handled by humans are rejected by parents. If an entire nest has fallen, place the young birds in it and put it back in the tree as near to the location of the old nest as possible. If the nest needs additional support, fashion a cup from wire cloth or a small wire basket and fasten it to the branch to hold the nest. If an entire branch has come down in a storm, wire or tie it to the tree until the birds hatch.

Only a trained professional has the knowledge—or the time—to care for lost or injured birds that have fallen from their nests, such as this young Anna's Hummingbird. Many young birds eat twice their body weight in food per day and must be fed continually.

Seemingly orphaned young birds, such as this sparrow, are better off left alone since the parent birds are usually close by. If a young bird is unprotected from harsh weather or predators, create a safe place for it until the danger has passed.

Marin Wildlife Center

Kent MacKenzie/Marin Wildlife Center

If a nest has been thoroughly soaked or shattered, build the birds a new one. Again, use wire cloth or a little wire basket as a platform. Fill it with dry grass and leaves, replace the nestlings, and put it back in the tree. Never use cardboard or wooden boxes to hold a nest, and never use green vegetation to line one—both encourage dampness and mold.

Work as quickly as possible. Most songbirds are born featherless and cold; their mother's wings warm them through the first days of life. They become chilled and die if exposed for too long. Warm very young birds by placing them in a small box with a nest of tissue and a container filled with warm water. This is a *temporary* measure; keep the birds only until the branch is wired or the nest replaced. The goal is always to replace nestlings quickly, so parents can find them and take over.

Injured Birds

Caring for injured wildlife demands considerable training and experience. Most of us are unprepared to decide if treating an injured creature gives it a reasonable chance of survival or simply causes it extended pain and suffering. This is one of the reasons that it is illegal for untrained private citizens to keep wild animals. The government licenses facilities that can provide competent care.

Most birds captured by cats or dogs die of internal injury and stress, even if they are rescued before they die. Other birds may suffer a broken wing or leg but be unharmed otherwise. Stress and shock complicate all injuries. When you find an injured bird, put it in a warm, dark spot and reach for the telephone. Many communities have wildlife conservation officers, humane societies, and bird clubs that know the local licensed facilities that treat injured wildlife. Do not try to nurse the bird while waiting for help; a wild bird is unaccustomed to being touched, and excessive handling may add enough extra stress to kill it. Never offer food or water to an animal under stress.

Marin Wildlife Center

Repairing the leg of this two-month-old Great Horned Owl is a job for an expert. The hollow bones of birds require special attention and the powerful talons of raptors are particularly dangerous.

William E. Grenfell, Jr.

Birds frequently crash into big reflective windows. To prevent window accidents, hang colored streamers outside the glass or apply decals of hawk silhouettes or other shapes directly onto the windowpane.

This Song Sparrow has one aluminum and three colored bands on its legs. The colored bands are used in ecological studies and can be observed without requiring capture of the bird. The bands reveal information about the bird's sex, age, and sometimes even the location of its natal nest site.

A. Morris/VIREO

Window accidents. Big windows and glass doors are the most frequent causes of bird injury around the house. Under the right lighting conditions, birds apparently glimpse an image of the backyard reflected in the glass and react to it as empty space. The result is a collision that sometimes dazes and often kills the bird. To prevent this type of accident, hang colored streamers outside the glass, or tape large paper shapes to the glass.

Most birds that hit windows simply bounce off, sit around groggily for a while, then fly away. If a bird is noticeably dazed, place a large kitchen colander upside down over the bird to protect it from predators while it regains its wits. If it is a warm day, leave the bird where it sits; if it is cold, bring the creature into the house and place it in a small, dark box or under a colander on a sheet of newspaper. Avoid handling the bird as much as possible—excessive touching can be as traumatic as the accident itself. When the bird begins to chirp or move around, it no longer needs your protection—release it.

Banded birds. Much of the information we have on bird range, migration, and life span comes from banding studies (see page 152). If you find a dead or injured bird with a small plastic or metal ring on its leg, you have a chance to participate in such a study. To do this you must file a report with the federal agency that coordinates bird-banding studies. The agency staff will want to know the following: (1) the type of bird or a detailed description, (2) all numbers and letters on the band, (3) the date you found the bird, (4) where you found the bird (the state, county, and direction and distance from the nearest town), and (5) what the bird was doing and its condition when you found it. If the bird is dead, send along the band as well. Never remove a band from a living bird. Send your report to: Migratory Bird Research Laboratory, U.S. Fish and Wildlife Service, Laurel, MD 20811.

Be sure to send along your name and address when you submit the report; the Fish and Wildlife Service will let you know when and where the bird was banded. The service also forwards your report to the agency that banded the bird. The two of you will have advanced our knowledge of birds another step.

Supplies and Resources

Identifying birds was a good deal more difficult a hundred years ago than it is today. Except for common or well-known species, positive identification could only be made "in the hand," after birds had been collected with shotguns. Bird-identification books did not become generally available until the 1890s. Most people could only name the few birds that came closest to their backyards.

The development of high-quality binoculars and systematic field guides has changed all that. Today anyone can learn to identify birds. All it takes is patience, a few carefully chosen tools, and a little practice.

Bird identification is an excellent hobby. It is inexpensive, relaxing, and it can be fascinating for a lifetime. Many homeowners who started by hanging winter feeders are now full-fledged bird-watchers who explore far beyond their backyards in search of birds.

Binoculars

Some of what you should know about a pair of binoculars is stamped in a kind of code near the eyepiece. These three or four numbers are the technical specifications of the binoculars. They tell you a great deal about what you see when you put them to your eyes.

A typical pair of bird-watching binoculars might have these specifications: 7 × 35, 400 feet at 1,000 yards. The first number (7) tells the magnification, or power, of the binoculars. (× is an abbreviation for power.) Birds seen through this pair of binoculars appear 7 times larger than they do with the naked eye. The second number (35) indicates the diameter of the objective lens (the lens farthest from the eye) in millimeters. The last set of numbers (400 feet at 1,000 yards) expresses the field of view of the binoculars: the user is able to see an image that is up to 400 feet wide at a distance of 1,000 yards.

David S. Soliday

Binoculars are the most popular and versatile tool for both professional and amateur bird-watchers. A variety of models with varying degrees of magnification are available.

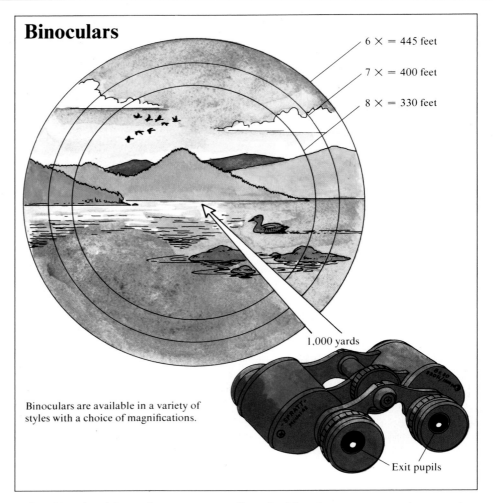

Binoculars

6 × = 445 feet

7 × = 400 feet

8 × = 330 feet

1,000 yards

Binoculars are available in a variety of styles with a choice of magnifications.

Exit pupils

In choosing binoculars you must first decide what you want them to do, then determine what specifications they should have. After that you can choose which pair of binoculars with those specifications is right for you. This is not always easy. Binoculars with identical specifications may be available at a bewildering array of prices. Learn which features are worth paying for and which you might be able to do without. The following information will help you decide what to look for.

Greater power is not necessarily better in binoculars. Seven- and eight-power binoculars are popular for bird-watching; they offer good magnification and reasonable cost, and they are light in weight. Do not consider binoculars that are less powerful. More powerful ones are heavier and often more expensive. Binoculars of greater than 10 × are difficult to hold steady and are usually considered too heavy for general field use.

The more light that enters a pair of binoculars, the brighter the image appears. This is something to consider if you are bird-watching at dawn or dusk or in heavily shaded areas. To compare the light-gathering capacity of binoculars, divide the power into the size of the objective lens. The resulting number is expressed in millimeters and is called the exit pupil. Binoculars with specifications 7 × 35 and 8 × 40 each have exit pupils of 5 millimeters and gather the same amount of light. Either would be fine for bird-watching. Brighter binoculars—those with larger objective lenses for the same power—give clearer images in dim light, but are heavier and more expensive.

Not all of the light entering a binocular's objective lens makes it through to the eyepiece; some light is lost when it bounces off internal glass. The best binoculars have lenses and prisms coated with magnesium fluoride to reduce light loss, and are usually labeled as having "fully coated optics."

A pair of binoculars with a wide field of view can be helpful to the beginning bird-watcher because they make it easier to find the bird. The field of view of a pair of binoculars is determined by their power: The greater the power, the narrower the field. "Wide-angle" binoculars are designed to provide a wider than standard field of view. Because they contain more glass, wide-angle binoculars are usually heavy and expensive. Check inexpensive models carefully; be certain that the image is sharp to the edges of the field.

Specialty binoculars usually sacrifice one characteristic or another to gain some alternate advantage. "Miniature" or pocket-sized binoculars have become increasingly available. They are light and compact, and the better-quality models yield images that are every bit as sharp as full-sized models. Because the objective lens must be small, however, miniature binoculars generally gather less light than larger models and are best suited to bright viewing conditions. Zoom binoculars may be tempting because of the variety of powers they provide, but they frequently sacrifice some image quality and angle of view to provide the zoom feature.

Unfortunately, no technical specification expresses image sharpness, an important characteristic. Sharpness, usually called resolution, depends on the quality of the glass and the lens alignment. Test resolution by focusing on newspaper-sized print at about 25 feet. Good-quality binoculars provide an image that is as sharp on the edges as it is in the center.

When shopping for binoculars, check to make sure that the two barrels are firmly and accurately aligned; misalignment can cause eyestrain. Try the binoculars over a variety of distances, preferably outside. Focus on an unbroken horizontal line, like the roof of a building; make certain that it appears continuous from one end to the other. Focus should be smooth throughout the range, with no double or overlapping images.

Eyeglass wearers should be particularly careful when buying binoculars. Eye cups on some models can put eyeglass wearers so far from the rear lenses that the field of view is markedly decreased. Some manufacturers solve this problem by supplying retractable eye cups; some models have rubber cups that fold back over the barrel of the lens.

If the specifications and features of two pairs of binoculars seem identical, price is probably a good index of relative quality. Prices range from about to $100 for a decent pair to about $400 for high-quality glasses. Buy the best binoculars you can afford. Many important qualities, such as firm alignment and ruggedness of construction, become evident only after long and repeated use.

Spotting Scopes

Above 10 × magnification, binoculars become too heavy and cumbersome for practical use. When bird-watchers need more powerful optics, they sometimes use spotting scopes. A spotting scope is basically half a pair of binoculars that you look through with one eye. Some scopes come with an internal zoom mechanism; others have interchangeable eyepieces, which the buyer usually purchases separately. Both systems offer a variety of image magnifications. The higher the magnification, the greater the loss in brightness, image sharpness, and field of view. Many people find 20 × an ideal power for scopes. Images of 60 × and more are often subject to considerable distortion by heat waves in the atmosphere.

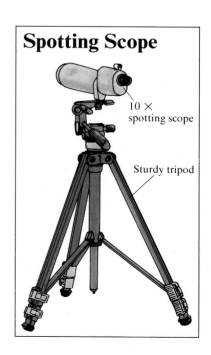

Spotting Scope

10 ×
spotting scope

Sturdy tripod

Stefan Hames

David S. Soliday

Above : *A field guide is an important asset and a birder's constant companion. After some use in the field, the tattered pages and taped binding will attest to your pursuit as a seasoned bird-watcher.*

Above right: *Spotting scopes have high magnification and good optics, but require a tripod and work best when the subject is relatively stationary.*

Because of their weight and tendency to magnify the slightest movement, spotting scopes are most useful when mounted on sturdy tripods. Many backyard bird-watchers leave their scopes on the tripod and focused out a back window.

Spotting scopes contain expensive, highly polished glass and cost several hundred dollars. Good scopes are rugged and last many years. As with binoculars, shop for features, not price, and buy the best one you can afford. Consider weight, size, and the power you want. Never buy a spotting scope without setting it up and trying it out. Experiment with the different powers until you understand the trade-offs between magnification, image quality, and field of view. Be sure the scope focuses closely enough to be useful in the backyard—the higher the power the less likely this is.

After spending a lot of money on a spotting scope, it is tempting to economize on a tripod. Do not make this mistake. A sturdy, easily adjustable tripod markedly increases the usefulness of a spotting scope, especially if it is used in the field. Many people feel that flip-lock legs on a tripod are faster and more convenient than legs that rotate to lock.

Field Guides

"The Gallery of Birds," beginning on page 269, can help you identify the birds you see in your backyard. You may also want to get a field guide—a comprehensive guide, specifically designed to aid identification. Several good field guides are available, each with a slightly different approach:

• Field guides organize the birds in different ways. Many group birds by family, which has the advantage of teaching the bird-watcher the relationships between the species. Other guides group birds by similarity of appearance or color, a method that beginning bird-watchers sometimes find helpful.

• Field guides present birds either in photographs or in drawings. Many beginning bird-watchers prefer photographs. Veteran bird-watchers often purchase several field guides—some with illustrations for use first and others with photographs for reference.

• Some guides place descriptive information about each bird next to the photograph or drawing; others place the description in a separate section. The first kind of guide requires far less back-and-forth paging.

• Some guides cite ranges in descriptions or with maps. Some render a bird's voice in a diagram called a sonogram; others describe it with words. Some illustrate birds in different plumages or from different angles.

You may want to consider these field guides: *A Field Guide to the Birds East of the Rockies* by Roger Tory Peterson (Houghton Mifflin, Boston, 1980); *A Field Guide to Western Birds* by Roger Tory Peterson (Houghton Mifflin, Boston, 1961); *Birds of North America* by Chandler S. Robbins, Bertel Bruun, and Herbert S. Zim (Golden Press, New York, 1983); *Field Guide to the Birds of North America* by The National Geographic Society, Washington, DC (1983); *The Audubon Society Field Guide to North American Birds: Eastern Region* by John Bull and John Farrand, Jr. (Alfred A. Knopf, New York, 1977); *The Audubon Society Field Guide to North American Birds: Western Region* by Miklos D. F. Udvardy (Alfred A. Knopf, New York, 1977).

Periodicals

The periodicals listed here are designed specifically for backyard bird-watchers. In addition to articles about birds, these periodicals contain articles about bird feeders, birdhouses, birdbaths, and many of the other subjects covered in this chapter.

Bird Watcher's Digest
Box 110
Marietta, OH 45705

Nature Society News
The Nature Society
Purple Martin Junction
Griggsville, IL 62340

Clubs and Organizations

One of the best ways to expand your involvement in bird-watching is to join a bird club. Bird club members are usually experts on the birds of their area and delight in sharing their knowledge with others. There are more than 800 local bird clubs in the United States, many of which are affiliated with a state Audubon Society or with the National Audubon Society. These clubs often sponsor field trips and informative programs. For information on local organizations, check the white pages of the telephone directory under "Audubon," or contact the national headquarters: National Audubon Society, 645 Pennsylvania Avenue, S.E., Washington, DC 20009.

Another way to expand your activity in bird-watching is to join the National Wildlife Federation and participate in their Backyard Wildlife Program. This program is designed for all backyard bird-watchers, including those with even the smallest backyards. Applicants who agree to provide certain minimum requirements of food, water, and shelter receive a Backyard Wildlife Registration Certificate, an annual newsletter, and a list of publications on a variety of subjects published by the federation. For further information about their activities write: Backyard Wildlife Habitat Program, National Wildlife Federation, 1412 Sixteenth Street, N.W., Washington, DC 20036.

A Guide to Equipment Suppliers

Most of the supplies needed for a backyard habitat are available close to home. It is a rare community that is without some source of bird feeders, birdbaths, seed, plants, and the like. Garden centers, feed stores, and hardware stores are good places to shop for these items. Binoculars and spotting scopes are often available at camera stores and many department stores. Building-supply outlets will have what you need to construct feeders, birdhouses, and garden pools.

But some items are harder to come by. Martin houses, birdbath heaters, recirculating pumps, and unmixed seed are not always available in every community. These items and other bird-attraction supplies are available by mail from the outlets listed at right.

Equipment for Bird-Watching

Audubon Workshop
1501 Paddock Drive
Northbrook, IL 60062

Bower Bird Feeders
Box 92
Elkhart, IN 46515

The Crow's Nest Book Shop
Cornell Laboratory of
 Ornithology
Sapsucker Woods
Ithaca, NY 14850

Duncraft
25 South Main Street
Penacook, NH 03303

Droll Yankees Bird Feeders
Mill Road
Foster, RI 02825

Hummingbird Heaven
1255 Carmel Drive
Simi Valley, CA 93065

Hyde Bird Feeder Co.
56 Felton Street
Box 168
Waltham, MA 02254

Massachusetts Audubon
 Society
South Great Road
Lincoln, MA 01773

National Audubon Society
Wild Bird Food
Box 207
Bristol, IL 60512

Postmart
RFD #1, Box 232
Keene, NH 03431
(birdbath heaters only)

Wild Bird Supplies
4815 Oak Street
Crystal Lake, IL 60014

Wildlife Refuge
3341 Coleman Road
Lansing, MI 48912

Photographing Birds

by J.P. Myers and Robert F. Cardillo

Why photograph birds? For some, bird photography is a hobby that offers relaxation and excitement; for others it is an artistic medium for discovering form and color in nature. Some devote many hours of every week to bird photography as part of their profession, and use the pictures as a research tool. Many advances in the scientific study of birds have resulted from facts recorded with a camera.

Photography gives us the unique opportunity to capture the beauty of birds in flight. It allows us to record their habits and document their distribution. Above all, bird photography lets us savor and share what we would otherwise glimpse for only a fleeting moment.

In turn, birds offer photographers endless challenges. How do you photograph birds at a feeder? How do you capture a parent bird caring for its young without disturbing the nest? How do you photograph ducks at eye level or take pictures of small birds moving through the forest? These challenges make bird photography the rewarding pursuit that it is.

American Robins are common ground-feeding birds in most of North America. Capturing the image of a bird at its eye level means getting close to the ground, but the effort is worthwhile.

Frans Lanting

Above: *Photographing birds is a means of preserving an appreciation for the beauty of birds. This White Tern with its chick provides an appealing subject for a well-composed picture.*

Above right: *A close-up shot of a Northern Cardinal reveals the intricacy of its plumage and coloration. Patience and practice can turn anyone into a skilled photographer.*

Bob Gossington/Tom Stack & Associates

Bird Photography Comes of Age

In 1839 Louis Daguerre began the first experiments in photography. Unfortunately for bird enthusiasts his daguerreotype camera required an exposure time of over one-half hour for each image; it could not produce a satisfactory image of even the slowest-moving bird. The only bird that sits still for half an hour is a taxidermic specimen. A number of photographers resorted to this taxidermic trickery in the early days of bird photography, but not many viewers were fooled.

Not long thereafter, however, technological advances enabled photographers to capture the images of living birds on film. In 1878 Eadweard Muybridge photographed captive pigeons, eagles, and other birds using cameras with guillotine shutters. These shutters dropped a small hole rapidly past the film; the hole allowed light to reach the film for a brief moment. Muybridge's work became famous as studies of motion because he answered, for the first time, many questions about how animals move. His photographs offered brilliant examples of how the camera could be used to study animals' lives.

Early field cameras were enormous—they weighed as much as 160 pounds. As photographic equipment became smaller and more portable, photographers began experimenting with ways to get close to animals. In the late 1800s the Kearton brothers of England followed the traditional practices of hunters by using blinds to get close to animals in the field. These two developments—lighter equipment and a method for getting close—played a significant role in stimulating interest in bird photography in the late nineteenth century.

The first half of this century brought further developments. The 35-mm camera and its lenses, color film, improved portable flash units, and stroboscopic lights (strobes) are twentieth-century inventions that contribute to photography in all applications. In fact, bird photography stimulated some of these improvements. Strobe lights—electronically controlled bulbs that flash brilliantly for a short duration—were invented to freeze the motion of a hummingbird's wingbeat. A hummingbird beats its wings about 500 times per second; to freeze that motion for a photograph, the strobe flashed for about 1/5,000 of a second.

Bird photography did not come of age until the mid-twentieth century. In America photographers such as Allan and Helen Cruickshank, Crawford H. Greenewalt, Eliot Porter, Frederick Kent Truslow, and

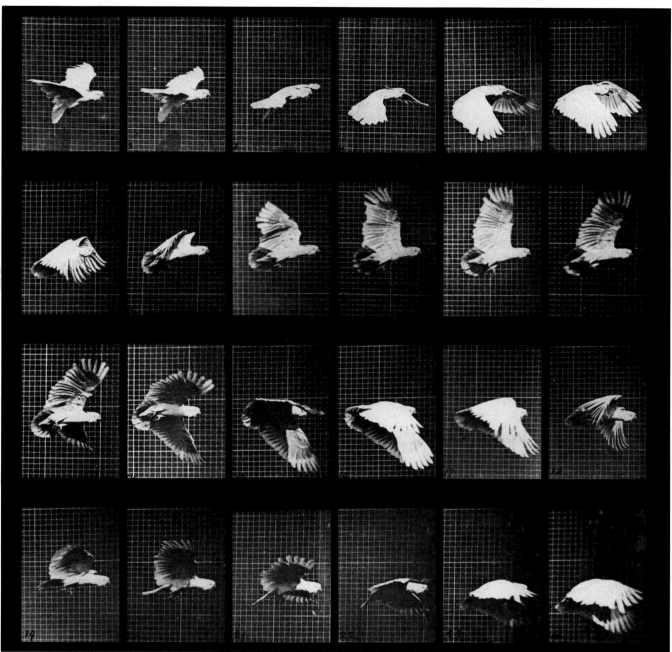

E. Muybridge/VIREO

M. Philip Kahl achieved public recognition for their work, and their photographs fueled interest in images of birds on film. Color film improved to the point where bird photographers took it from the studio into the field under natural lighting conditions. Good equipment became so widely available and affordable that all a photographer needed was patience, cleverness, and a knowledge of birds.

This classic series of photographs represents the early developments of bird photography by Eadweard Muybridge. Here the mechanics of flight are revealed in a Lesser Sulpher-crested Cockatoo.

Developing Your Photographic Eye

Even though there are specific techniques to photographing birds, much of the process involves the same basic principles as photographing most other subjects. To take the best photos of birds, you must understand these photographic principles before picking up a camera.

Photography embraces two fundamentals: composition and exposure. Composition brings the shapes, lines, and colors of an image together in a pleasing whole; exposure translates the photographer's concept to reality on film. The challenge of bird photography is applying these principles in that fleeting moment when a bird pauses in the range of the viewfinder.

Composition

Successful bird photography leaves nothing to chance. The photographer has a desired image in mind before attempting to photograph. Planning an image is what photographic composition is about—manipulating all the pieces available to evoke a strong response in the viewer. When photographing birds, however, manipulating the pieces is never easy. A bird is rarely a cooperative subject; it does not wait for you to take out the camera, change the lens, move to another side, or experiment with distance or lighting. You can neither control its behavior nor always select its posture or background. What powers do you have? By learning to act quickly you can place your subject in different sections of the viewfinder, alter the depth of field, vary the angle of view, freeze the action, or retain the blur of motion. Following a few basic rules of good composition will help you develop your photographic eye.

Elements of good composition. When composing an image pay attention to the time-tested elements of good composition: simplicity, shape, size, lines, pattern, and texture. The image of a bird can get lost against a complicated background. Use bold, simple, familiar shapes such as circles, triangles, squares, and ellipses against plain backgrounds. For example, the arch of raised wings silhouetted against a clear blue sky is a strong image; the photograph would have less impact if the background were a complicated urban landscape or a mosaic of sharply contrasting tree branches.

Clean curves and straight lines should connect the strong elements of a photograph and lead the viewer to the subject of focus. Look for these natural lines when composing a frame; build an image around the natural lines in anticipation of the way the viewer will scan it. Another way to enhance your photographs is by highlighting patterns. Repeating elements within the photograph reinforces the image and adds rhythm to what otherwise might be a static picture. A flock of birds, for example, often contains repetitive patterns that direct the viewer's focus from individual birds within the group to the whole flock.

When considering image size, keep in mind that because birds are so difficult to approach, filling the frame can be one of the hardest tasks. On the other hand bigger is not always better. The image size you choose should support the message you wish to convey. You cannot, for example,

Below: *The arched wings of this Laysan Albatross contrast with the backdrop of a clear blue sky and accentuate the elements of shape. Backgrounds are an important consideration when composing a photograph.*

Below right: *In this picture of roosting Wood Storks, a repeated pattern of shapes superimposed on the twisted form of a dead tree develops the mood. Look for natural patterns to create well-balanced shots.*

Frans Lanting

H. Cruickshank/VIREO

R. Cardillo/VIREO

R. Cardillo/VIREO

Far left: *Proper framing enhances the balance of these silhouetted geese and a gallinule taken at dusk.*

Left: *By drawing in the imaginary lines, it is possible to see how the balance in this picture was achieved. Notice that the trees in the background fall along the line between the top third and the bottom two thirds of the photograph. The goose in the foreground stands out because of its location in the lower left side of the picture.*

show a bird within its habitat in a close-up. The emotional impact of many successful photographs comes about precisely because the bird occupies only a small part of the image. Empty space is often a powerful element in frame composition.

Framing. Placing the subject directly in the center of the viewfinder may be the easiest way to focus, but the result is usually not as interesting as when the subject is somewhat offset. The rule of thirds can help you create a more interesting photograph.

Divide the frame into horizontal and vertical thirds by drawing four imaginary lines—two horizontal and two vertical—across the viewfinder. From the visual perspective the four points of intersection are the strong positions. By placing a distinctive element near one of these points—the bird's head, its nest, its eye—you add appeal to your photograph.

Your decisions about subject placement and the four intersections also play an important part in creating visual mood. Placing a subject at one intersection adds tension and drama to the image; placing key elements at opposite intersections creates a balance that imparts a sense of harmony.

In addition, the imaginary horizontal lines are effective guides in determining where to place the horizon. Inexperienced photographers tend to place the horizon in the middle of the viewfinder. Placing the horizon one-third of the way from the top or bottom of the viewfinder creates a far more dynamic image. Another hint: Keep the horizon—as well as other strong horizontal or vertical lines—from intersecting the subject unless your intent is to use the lines to draw the eye to the subject.

When placing your subject in the frame, try to capture it facing the center of the image instead of looking off to the side. Viewers examine a photograph by following the bird's direction of focus; if it is peering toward the edge of the frame, the viewer's eyes will drift off your photograph and perhaps onto someone else's.

Birds generally lend themselves well to the horizontal format of a 35-mm camera, but if the subject is a woodpecker on a tree or a heron in marsh grass, for example, the vertical format is usually the better choice. Examine the lines of the subject and background within your viewfinder and select the format that enhances them most effectively.

B. Gadsby/VIREO

R.J. Shallenberger/VIREO

M.P. Kahl/VIREO

Above: *Front lighting, where light originates from behind the photographer, brings out all the detail in the plumage of these Greater White-fronted Geese. Lighting of this sort often results in pictures that lack depth.*

Above center: *Side lighting brings out the surface texture of this Snowy Egret and helps to add depth to the photograph.*

Above right: *Backlighting eliminates detail altogether but can create a feeling of intense drama, as in this picture of Marabou Storks at a sparse treetop.*

Natural lighting. Most photographers follow the time-tested rule of keeping the sun behind their shoulders. Light from this angle ensures even lighting on your subject, but it can lead to a flat-looking picture. Because direct light eliminates subtle shadows on the subject's surface, it robs your eye of information about depth.

Experiment with lighting from different angles. Light from the side brings out the surface texture of the bird and emphasizes its depth. Backlit photos—ones taken with the camera facing the sun—often suffer from lack of detail. Backlighting can also yield images of high drama by emphasizing a bird's silhouette and displaying the feathers against a glow.

Natural light has characteristics that affect the quality and mood of a photograph. Study the subtleties of natural light even when you are not photographing. Notice how the light can be hard and contrasting on clear days and soft and muted when overcast. The colors of the rays differ during the day—they are warm and rich at dawn and sunset and cool and blue at noon. Birds are most active in the early morning and the late afternoon. Although this kind of light is best for enhancing texture, it is not as bright, which makes taking exposures at slower shutter speeds a challenge.

Color. When shooting with color film the photographs that are usually most pleasing emphasize a few closely related hues. A bright bird of primary colors against a neutral background also photographs well. When photographing a pitch black raven or pure white swan, you may want to include elements in the background to add color. Keep in mind, however, that having many contrasting colors within the same photograph creates clutter, which affects mood. The key—as always in bird photography—is to keep it simple.

Exposure

Making sure the right amount of light reaches your film is fundamental to good bird photography. With the sophisticated cameras and light meters that exist today, selecting a "proper" exposure can be simple, but a proper exposure is not necessarily the most effective exposure. In any given lighting many different combinations of shutter speed and aperture expose film adequately; however, the resulting depth of field, the degree

Stephen J. Krasemann/DRK Photo

This picture achieves a good exposure of the nesting Willow Flycatcher, considering the bird is tucked into the surrounding vegetation. Some light meters average the readings from light and dark areas, and unless this is compensated for, dark recesses such as this nest will turn out underexposed.

of contrast, the amount of detail retained in shadows, and the pictorial highlights differ with each combination. The best exposure is the one that matches the subject's lighting conditions with the photographer's concept. To understand why this is so and to make the best choice, you must understand how light, film, shutter speed, motion, aperture, and depth of field contribute to the final image.

Shutter speed and aperture. When light strikes unexposed film, it causes a latent image, which is brought out in developing. The amount of light that strikes the film when you press the shutter release determines the intensity of these chemical reactions and the quality of the exposure.

Light is to film as water is to a bathtub: To fill up the tub you can turn on the spigot full blast for a short time or allow a slow trickle to flow for a long time. To "fill up" the film with the appropriate amount of light, you vary the shutter speed and the aperture. Shutter speed is the length of time the shutter is open. The faster the shutter speed, the shorter the time that the film is exposed to light. The width that the shutter opens to allow light to pass is known as the aperture size or *f*-stop.

Cameras with adjustable shutter speeds and apertures are preferable to those that are not adjustable. The shutter speeds of some cameras can be adjusted to 1/4,000 of a second, but most cameras adjust from speeds of 1/1,000 of a second to 1 second. Good telephoto work of birds at shutter speeds slower than 1/250 is only possible in a few circumstances: when photographing slow-moving birds, when creating special effects such as intentionally blurred wings, or when using a tripod. With slow shutter speeds and large lenses, any movement will produce a blurred image.

The *f*-stop is expressed by a number equal to the focal length of a lens divided by the width of the aperture. The lower the *f*-stop number, the wider the aperture and the more light that enters the lens. The *f*-stops range from *f*-1.2 to *f*-64 (see chart at right) and are adjusted by opening or closing the diaphragm on your lens.

Aperture Widths

F-stops follow a standard mathematical sequence. Moving from *f*-1.4 to *f*-2 or from *f*-8 to *f*-11 cuts the light entering the camera's lens in half.

Wide apertures	=	More light entering lens
	f-1.4	
	f-2	
	f-2.8	
	f-4	
	f-5.6	
	f-8	
	f-11	
	f-16	
	f-22	
	f-32	
	f-44	
	f-64	
Narrow apertures	=	Less light entering lens

Right: *These Trumpeter Swans were photographed at dawn. At this time of day, as well as at dusk, the low angle of the sun adds a golden hue to illuminated objects.*

Far right: *Careful use of depth of field helps bring attention to this Green-backed Heron by softening the background and reducing clutter.*

Chip Isenhart/Tom Stack & Associates

Don & Pat Valenti

Reciprocity. The trade-off between shutter speed and aperture is known as reciprocity. Reciprocity allows you to achieve a proper exposure for a particular film with many different combinations of *f*-stops and shutter speeds. Imagine that your light meter indicates that a shutter speed of 1/125 of a second at an aperture of *f*-11 would do the trick. If you are using a telephoto lens, however, 1/125 would be too slow. If you change to a shutter speed of 1/250, you have to open the aperture up to *f*-8, or twice as wide as *f*-11, to bring the same amount of light to your film.

Reciprocity imposes a special hardship on bird photographers. Most bird photographers work in natural light and use telephoto lenses to produce frame-filling, crystal-sharp images. With long lenses, stopping all motion requires fast shutter speeds. Fast shutter speeds mean less time for light to expose the film, and the reciprocal requirement of a wider aperture. Unfortunately for the bird photographer, telephoto lenses usually do not have wide apertures. In many times and places—at dawn or dusk, in a forest, or on a cloudy day—there is simply not enough light to use a particular lens. Under these circumstances you have three choices: switch your lens, change your film, or give up the picture.

Depth of field. Depth of field is the range over which the image can be focused. When you focus on a bird, you focus on a thin vertical plane that "cuts through" the bird and runs parallel to the film. Manipulating the depth of field expands your creative control. Wide apertures create a shallow depth of field—the subject is in focus and the background is blurred; narrow apertures deepen the depth of field so that both subject and background are in focus. Poor lighting conditions—which are common out in the field—often dictate the use of a wide aperture. The need to limit depth of field as a result of a low level of light can be a source of frustration for the bird photographer. For example, narrowing the depth of field to photograph an owl in a darkened forest may mean that the eyes are in focus while the beak is not.

Every lighting situation presents numerous combinations of shutter speeds and apertures from which to choose. Each combination alters the apparent motion and depth of field. Slow shutter speeds and narrow apertures mean blurred motion and a large depth of field; fast shutter speeds stop the motion but leave you with a narrow depth of field. Developing an awareness of this trade-off helps develop your photographic instinct.

Measuring light. To determine the best shutter speed and aperture, a photographer must measure the available light with a light meter (see pages 246 to 247). Unfortunately, blindly following the indications of a light meter can produce some bad exposures. The challenge is to understand and anticipate the exceptions.

The root of the problem lies in how a light meter works. Light meters are designed to produce an exposure that has a neutral gray intensity. Imagine a range of grays between black and white; halfway between black and white is neutral gray. Light meters treat color in an image just as they treat black-and-white film—it is not the hue of color that matters but the amount of light. If you point your camera at a completely neutral gray object and expose according to the light meter, the resulting image will be neutral gray, exactly as you (and the light meter) expect. This approach does not usually present problems; the light meter cues appropriate exposures most of the time. But if you point your camera at a white ptarmigan perched on a snowbank, and use the exposure your light meter indicates, the image will be gray instead of white; if you accept the recommendation of the light meter when photographing a black raven in a cave, it will produce a gray bird and a gray background.

A number of solutions apply to these tricky situations. One is to use an incident light meter (see page 247). Another solution is to take a reflected light reading off a neutral gray object that receives the same amount of light as the white ptarmigan. Though foliage and dry tree bark are not gray, they are middle tones that reflect about the same amount of light as neutral gray. If you take your meter reading from surrounding foliage, you will probably avoid the gray-scale trap. Many photographers carry what is known as a gray card—a card of a technically perfect middle tone. (Gray cards are available in photography stores.) If you take your meter reading with a gray card, beware of any glare from it.

Bracketing. The practice of bracketing increases the chance of producing at least one good exposure; it is especially useful for the beginner and when those rare, once-in-a-lifetime photographic opportunities arise. To bracket your exposures take one shot at the exposure you think is correct, then take two more—one at one *f*-stop lower (an overexposure) and the other at one *f*-stop higher (an underexposure). If you are working in bright light around water, and especially when photographing backlit subjects, you may want to bracket two *f*-stops toward overexposure until you have experience with this lighting situation. It might seem like an expensive form of insurance, but after all, will that Ivory-billed Woodpecker ever be in your viewfinder again? A useful rule if you are unsure of the exposure is that it is better to underexpose than to overexpose. Darkroom techniques will allow you to recover some detail in the underexposed areas when you make a duplicate slide or print.

Kent & Donna Dannen

By using a gray card or an incident light meter, it is possible to obtain a more accurate light reading when photographing white objects against white backgrounds or black objects against black backgrounds. Compensation of this sort enhances the white plumage of the White-tailed Ptarmigan in this photograph.

Between true black and white is a range of grays, with neutral gray at the midpoint. To avoid overexposure of a white bird on a snowbank or underexposure of a black bird in a cave, take a reflected light reading off a neutral gray object that receives the same amount of light as your subject.

Frans Lanting   C.H. Greenewalt/VIREO

Focusing: Traditional to Unusual

For decades bird photographers have struggled to freeze motion on film. A blurred image doomed a photograph to the wastebasket, or at least relegated it to the second-best category. As lenses improved, film speeds became faster, and flash offered more versatility, the perfect image became more and more feasible. Now, with practice and patience, the image of almost any bird can be frozen in mid-flight or at the apex of its display with every feather in crystal-sharp focus.

Though it is now possible to obtain perfect focus and frozen motion, blurred lines are often desirable as a means of conveying motion and mood. Frans Lanting, a Dutch photographer who lives in the United States, has experimented with long lenses and slow exposures to create impressionistic visions of birds in flight. Instead of offending the image, the blurred lines of Lanting's photographs convey motion with exceptional elegance. If you attempt similar pictures, do not expect success the first time out. For a start, try a 400-mm lens with shutter speeds between 1/15 and 1/60, and pan with the motion of your subjects.

Top: *A rapid shutter speed and a flash help to freeze the wings of this Barn Swallow.*
Bottom: *The blurred image of this Brown Pelican creates the impression of motion and may be used to impart mood to the picture.*

Guidelines for Success

Bird photography calls on all of your photographic and artistic skills in that critical moment when a bird darts out from some underbrush or when a Bald Eagle soars into view overhead. There is often only one chance to capture the image you desire. To make the most of that chance, keep the following in mind:

Be prepared. As you await the perfect photographic opportunity, practice. Learn to think photographically. Combine your knowledge of birds with familiarity of the camera. Study how other photographers treat a given species or theme, and plan how you would treat a similar situation.

Experiment. When a cooperative bird remains in your viewfinder, take advantage of the moment. Try photographing from different angles and heights. Move so that light is coming in from another direction. Change your lens, use a flash, or alter the depth of field and shutter speed. Do not be concerned that every photograph be a masterpiece; you do not have to show the unsuccessful shots to anyone. If you cannot afford to be liberal with color film, use black-and-white film. You can even practice with an empty camera.

Johnny Johnson/DRK Photo

A well-composed shot, such as this Bald Eagle in flight, requires preparation and quick thinking. It is often possible to have the proper exposure set on the camera even before the bird is encountered. This can eliminate the need to make these adjustments during the short time that the bird is in the field of view.

This photograph of an American Bittern bends some photographic rules, yet it is balanced, well focused, well exposed, and also helps to illustrate the bird's habitat. Although partly obscured in vegetation, the off-center placement of the bird helps draw attention toward it.

Douglas R. Herr

Anticipate. Enter a photographic situation knowing what you want to accomplish. Have the proper film in the camera and the appropriate lenses on hand. Study the light from various angles before you approach a bird. Look at the background from afar. Before the bird takes off, decide if you want a smooth blur of motion or a frozen flash of wing. Above all become familiar with the haunts and behaviors of your subjects before you begin to photograph.

Adapt the rules. The rules of good composition (see page 238) are practical guidelines, but any rule in photography can be broken if the resulting effect helps convey the mood you want in your image. A successful bird photographer uses the rules instinctively and breaks them in a conscious and controlled fashion. If you know the rules and know when you can break them, you can direct the emotional impact of your photograph.

Basic Equipment

Before you begin to photograph birds, you must have the proper equipment. A professional bird photographer will probably own every piece of equipment discussed below, but a beginner can start with a few basic pieces and expand as needs grow.

Cameras. Although professional photographers may use large cameras with high-quality resolution, and nonprofessionals may prefer compact cameras that are easy to operate, a 35-mm camera is the best compromise for bird photography because of its manageable size and versatility.

Look for a camera that will adapt to your future needs. Excellent cameras are available, from "no frills" manual models to those with automated features. Serious bird photographers should be aware that a completely automated camera is a disadvantage because of the fast-moving subjects and difficult lighting situations, which are better controlled manually.

Film. The type of film you select depends on the lighting conditions in which you will use it, your particular photographic style, and your preference of color rendition. A film's sensitivity to light is known as its speed, indicated by an ISO rating from 25 to 1,600. A slow film (ISO 50 or under) is less sensitive to light than a fast film (ISO 200 or above). Fast film tends to be more useful for bird photography because it is far more versatile in varied lighting situations; the drawback is that it is quite grainy and gives poorer contrast and color rendition than slow film. In general, the best sharpness and image quality comes with the slowest film possible for the lighting conditions.

Jonathan Blair/Woodfin Camp & Assoc.

As this bird photographer illustrates, old clothes—preferably cotton and in subdued, natural colors—are most suitable. Although the photographer may be prone to getting dirty, particular care must be made to ensure that photographic equipment stays clean and dry.

Most bird photographers prefer color film, but there is a time for black-and-white film in bird photography. Birds lacking colorful plumage, like shorebirds, are often better captured with black-and-white film, particularly when you want to emphasize their shapes and motions.

Lenses. For frame-filling portraits of birds, the standard 50-mm lens typically sold with most camera bodies is insufficient. The most practical lens is a telephoto—a 400-mm, or for greater versatility, a 200- or 300-mm lens combined with a teleconverter (see below). For close-ups of birds in nests, ponds, or at feeders, the lens must be at least a 200-mm. If you must work at a greater distance from your subject, you will need a longer lens—a 300-, 400-, 1,000-, or 1,200-mm.

For close-ups of fine detail with high-image magnification—showing the delicate surface texture of a feather, for example—a macro lens is the answer. Some macros can focus out to infinity, but a 50-mm macro is most effective when shooting at a distance of just a few feet.

Opportunities for wide-angle lenses rarely arise in bird photography, but when they do—a prairie bird with miles of field behind it, for example—the results can be stunning. You have all the advantages of a short-focal-length lens at your disposal with exceptional depth of field, fast speed, low weight, and enormous compositional control. In addition, instead of struggling to bring separate elements of the subject into focus at once, as with a 400-mm telephoto lens, the whole frame is in crystal-sharp focus. A 28-mm is a good size to use, though wide-angle lenses are also available in 30- and 35-mm sizes.

Zoom lenses are highly versatile because you can adjust them from 35- to 200-mm, for example, at a flick of the wrist. A drawback to using them for bird photography is that—although they eliminate the need for carrying many lenses of different focal lengths—they do not extend beyond 300-mm. Macro zoom lenses are also available.

Lens attachments. Extension tubes and teleconverters fit between the camera body and the lens to achieve a larger image. Extension tubes reduce the minimum focusing distance of a lens. Thus, you can photograph small birds as close as 6 or 7 feet away instead of 20 feet, the typical focusing distance of a 400-mm lens. Teleconverters—sometimes called multipliers or doublers—magnify the image by means of a multiplication factor determined by their sizes: a 200-mm lens with a 2× teleconverter becomes a 400-mm lens; a 300-mm lens with a 1.4× teleconverter becomes a 420-mm lens.

Light meters. *Incident meters* measure the light falling on the subject. To use one, you hold it so the light falling on it is the same as (or at least similar to) the light falling on your subject. This obviously can be tricky if the bird is in a dark hollow and you are in the sunshine. Fortunately most 35-mm cameras have built-in meters that measure the light reflected off the subject. These built-in *reflectance meters* come in two types: spot and averaging. Spot meters, which measure only a small portion of the field of view, give precise measurements of the lighting characteristics of key parts of your image. Averaging meters take the lighting conditions of the whole scene into account.

Flashes. A flash can be used at night or to supplement natural ambient light, eliminating shadows and creating new highlights. Many flashes are automated to produce light, measure it as it bounces off the subject, and turn off once the exposure is good. Powerful flashes—those with high guide numbers, such as GN 120 or GN 190—are an advantage because they permit work at greater distances.

In some cases, such as photographing at nests, it is helpful to use a *slave*, a small electronic device attached to an auxiliary flash placed near the subject. Triggered by the first flash, the slave fires the second flash almost instantaneously.

Camera supports. A tripod is an essential component of bird photography, because of the fast-moving subjects and the long lenses required. Tripods steady a camera, preventing camera shake. For most bird work, a good maximum height of a tripod is no higher than waist or midchest; a good minimum height is near or beneath eye level when you are kneeling or crouching. Choose a tripod with a head that smoothly pans, tilts, raises, and lowers; legs that are sturdy, durable and lock by levers rather than collar rings; and a dull color to make it less obvious to birds.

A shoulder stock is no match for a tripod in stability, but it is far superior to hand holding a camera. Essential for photographing birds in flight, a shoulder stock permits you to adjust the mounting position of the camera along a bar and, thus, to vary the distance between your eye and the lens. Some allow several adjustments in addition to lens position, including the angle of the barrel relative to your shoulder. This flexibility leads to a more comfortable fit and a steadier shot.

Monopods—one-legged tripods—offer reasonable support for their weight and bulk. Because they do not require a fancy head (they simply lean to one side or another), monopods are exceptionally light.

Herbert Clarke

Birds are wary of humans, hence anything that disguises the human form can be helpful. Here, a simple blind is made by draping the photographer and camera with a camouflage blanket.

Simple hand-holding of a camera can always be improved upon by using any stable object—car hood, roof, fallen log, driftwood. A bean bag makes a great accessory because it will fit virtually any surface and will dampen most vibrations.

Camera attachments. When you have only a moment to photograph a bird, every second counts. Advancing film manually often wastes those precious seconds. A motor drive can expose two to six frames per second. (Slower winders are also available.) Motor drives are particularly useful for photographing birds in flight or capturing a pose at the peak of display. Before using a winder, try to determine whether its mechanical noise will be more disturbing to your subject than the movements of your hand and arm when you manually advance the film.

An attachment that is frequently useful—though usually employed in conjunction with a tripod or other support—is a cable release. Cable releases diminish the vibration that occurs in a camera when the shutter is released. The cable attaches directly to the shutter-release button and is available in a variety of lengths.

Blinds. Blinds are used to conceal the photographer and equipment from the subject so that it will not be disturbed. Among other features, a good blind is easy to transport, is waterproof, has adequate ventilation, and allows photography from different angles. Blinds can be anything from a cardboard box or a large piece of cloth or canvas, to a ready-made one available in sporting-goods stores. To get close to water birds, you can place a blind atop a boat or use hip waders and a floating blind made of an inner tube and a canvas seat. (For more on using blinds, see page 250.)

G. Nuechterlein/VIREO

With careful study, a photographer can anticipate the more outstanding aspects of a subject, such as the courtship display of these Western Grebes.

Know Your Subjects

The correct equipment, patience and practice, and the development of your photographic eye are essential basics for any photographer. But there is more to bird photography than that. To achieve high-quality photographs, the bird photographer must also be armed with an understanding of the birds themselves.

A key step to successful bird photography is knowing your subject well enough to anticipate its actions. Without this understanding of bird behavior, chances are you will wind up with a slide collection full of barely recognizable dots against a huge background, bird backs, and selected views of just-abandoned branches.

Understanding birds and learning how to anticipate their behavior allow you to influence your subject's behavior to your advantage. Sometimes small modifications make a great difference. For example, a feeder brings birds closer to your window; birdbaths entice more birds into your yard. There are, of course, some limits to what you can do—no Peregrine Falcon will ever come to eat sunflower seeds outside the kitchen window. (For a thorough discussion of bird behavior, see the chapter beginning on page 43.)

Observing Before You Photograph

Before you photograph a bird you must watch it patiently. When observing your subject you learn what kinds of things—squeeks, pishes, subtle hand motions—alter the bird's behavior. You will notice behavioral patterns that allow you to anticipate its next action. Before shooting consider the following:

• Why is a bird in a particular environment? Is it feeding, roosting, or displaying? Feeding birds, especially if they are hungry, are often quite tolerant of people. If they are feeding at a spot with a good supply of food, they often return after a disturbance. If they return repeatedly, take advantage of a temporary withdrawl to improve your position, change a lens, or remove a distracting element (such as a carelessly discarded tin can). Roosting birds require a somewhat different approach. Since they can easily rest somewhere else, they are more likely to fly from the area. Displaying birds, in contrast, may be almost oblivious to your approach.

• How does the bird react to you and to other birds? Its reaction determines whether you can get close. Sometimes anticipating how birds will interact with each other can lead you to a perfect photograph: Will it attack, fly, display, or ignore the other one? Be poised for the moment.

• What might disturb the bird during your work? Anticipate the bird's behavior in relation to what is going in the environment. Are people likely to be walking past? If so, perhaps you can use them to "push" your subject toward you, or perhaps you had better hurry and expose the last frame before they get too close. Your choice usually depends upon the type of bird being photographed. If you have become familiar with the species you may be able to judge how it will respond.

• What can the bird do to improve the picture, and how can you encourage it to do just that? Often you can enhance your photograph by gently coaxing a bird into a slightly different position or perhaps to a nearby perch. Try circling around for another angle and coming in just a bit closer, thereby encouraging a skittish bird to hop to a better spot.

Getting Close to Birds

To capture exquisite, frame-filling images there is no substitute for getting close to your subject. The closer you get, the more photographic options you have—a greater variety of lenses, a wider selection of film, and a wider range of exposures. Though long lenses help, they have their limits. There are a number of strategies that allow you to get close to birds.

First and foremost, win your subject's confidence. When you watch a bird, be sure that if it can see you, it is also watching you. The longer you remain in its presence without threatening it, the more accustomed to you a bird will become. Winning confidence does not work with all birds, and it takes time, but even a minor effort on your part will contribute significantly to your success. With time an undisturbed bird will tolerate extraordinary intrusions, including a long lens staring at it from only a few feet away.

A tried and true method is to choose locations where birds are sure to come, such as feeders and nests. Another technique is to watch for customary roosting sites. This works especially well with shorebirds because they use traditional sites at predictable times. Learn where the birds roost and in what point of the tidal cycle they fly, then go there before they begin to roost and remain quiet while their numbers build. With patience you will find yourself surrounded by hundreds of willing subjects who are almost oblivious to your presence.

Concealing yourself is sometimes the best strategy. Depending on the bird you are photographing, your options include photographing from a car, using a blind, or taking pictures through a window. Even partial concealment is helpful. By lying down, sitting, crouching, or stooping, you improve your chances of appearing smaller as well as less human to the birds. Another way to appear less human is to wear a hat with a brim; the brim breaks up the lines of your face.

Be inconspicuous. Wear subdued dark-colored clothing. Avoid shiny equipment; paint it with dull, nonreflective paint if necessary. A word of caution: Do not forget about hunting season. When hunters are afield, being conspicuous and obviously human has its virtues. Try to take photographs somewhere where hunting is prohibited.

Finally, seize opportunities when they arise. Most birds will not let you get very near when you are walking through a forest, but every so often you will happen across one that does, or you may approach a bird unawares. Remember, though, that the method of chance encounter is not ideal; it produces many frustrating near successes.

To obtain this picture of a Pectoral Sandpiper, the photographer spent many hours watching the habits of this individual. After several days, the bird became so accustomed to the presence of the photographer that he was able to take this picture from a distance of less than 2 feet.

J. P. Myers/VIREO

Blinds. If you do not want to be seen by birds, a blind provides excellent concealment. Innovative photographers have used everything from cow skins to cardboard boxes with holes cut for the lens, from trees or bales of hay to high platforms built on top of steel scaffolding.

Whatever type of blind you choose, the key to using it is patience. Long, tedious hours inside a tiny enclosure may yield only a few moments of an eagle eating fish or a Sage Grouse booming on its lek. Those with the patience to use blinds gain not only exquisite photographs, but the opportunity to perceive nature anew. Many hours of anticipation in a small blind with only one or two peepholes alters your perception, heightening your awareness of small, quiet patterns and details in nature. These new perceptions enhance photographic skills and sensitivity.

In selecting a blind, first evaluate how you want to use it. Will you photograph birds at eye-level, on the ground, or near a tree-top nest? Does it need to be portable? Do you want to stand in it, sit in it, or lie prone? Is it waterproof? Will your silhouette be visible in strong sunlight? Does it flap in the wind? Is there ventilation? Are there enough holes for different viewing positions? Can you afford to leave it unguarded for a period so that birds will adapt to it?

Ready-made blinds are available at some sporting goods stores. For a simple homemade blind, spread out a tarp or camouflage net over an aluminum or wood framework; this design allows you freedom of movement while concealing you from your subject. The frame should extend out in front far enough to cover the camera with your arms extended; in back it should spread out beyond your legs.

Large cardboard boxes (like those used for refrigerators) make quick and easy blinds. Cover the top with plastic for some protection against rain. Cut a hole in the front and cover it with two pieces of overlapping material so the lens can protrude without attracting too much attention. A cardboard box blind should be anchored in open, windy areas lest it and the erstwhile photographer wind up tumbling across the field.

Do not overlook natural blinds. Log piles, hay bales, snow banks, brushy areas, and hollows can all serve as blinds, especially if dressed with a tarp or cut vegetation. On many natural preserves it is illegal to cut vegetation, so be sure to inquire beforehand.

One of the best ways to get close to birds is by using a blind. Inexpensive and simple to build, blinds work best when the materials used are of natural colors. This one is constructed of cloth stretched over a metal frame.

Herbert Clarke

Field Ethics

Bird photographers have a special responsibility to their subjects. Always keep one guideline in mind: Your efforts at getting a good photograph should not put the birds in jeopardy. When working at a nest, for example, remember that the parent bird needs to feed its young without disruption and that the birds need the surrounding vegetation to provide concealment from predators or shade from the sun. Do not remain too long at a nest if the parent refuses to come while you are there. If you push aside the vegetation to improve the image, make sure it returns to the original position after you are done. Also, have some sympathy for roosting birds. Birds, like humans, need rest, and the constant attention of a harrassing photographer sometimes interferes.

Young birds, like these baby Mourning Doves, require constant attention from the parent birds and prolonged disruptions can be detrimental.

Herbert Clarke

Backyard Photography

Backyard bird photography is more than challenging and satisfying—it is also convenient. After all it is far more comfortable changing film in the warmth of your kitchen than in a canvas blind on the banks of a river in early spring.

Since food, water, shelter, and nesting materials make a backyard more attractive to birds, backyards offer many opportunities for bird photography. Even an urban apartment dweller without a yard can draw a half dozen species to a well-stocked window feeder, especially in winter when other food sources dwindle or disappear. (For more about attracting birds to the backyard, see the chapter beginning on page 163.)

Photographing at Feeders

Photographing at a feeder involves three important elements: choosing the best location from which to take the photograph, attracting the birds, and taking the picture. Some ambitious photographers go so far as to move the feeder to suit the photograph.

Choose a location that will make the best use of the feeder. Take the lighting, background, and surroundings into consideration; these variables are often the most difficult to adjust, so take care of them first. Avoid a site with too much foot traffic; you will have enough to keep you busy without constant disruptions from people and pets.

Photographing through a window from inside a house is ideal under most circumstances because you gain the benefits of a superb blind—the house. When shooting through a window, keep in mind that it needs to be of high-quality distortion-free glass if you are to reap the benefits of an expensive lens. As soon as the birds frequent your backyard feeding location without hesitation, darken the room and place the lens as close as possible to the glass to avoid reflections; a rubber lens hood can help bring the lens as close as possible to the window.

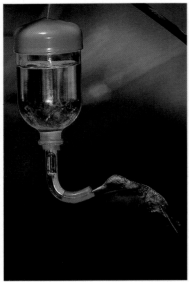

Wayne Lankinen/DRK Photo

Above: *Hummingbirds, like this Broad-billed Hummingbird, can easily be attracted to feeders. Hummingbirds provide excellent subjects for photography and offer an opportunity to see what shutter speeds are required to stop motion or keep the motion as a soft blur.*

Above right: *Feeders can attract a variety of birds to within camera range. An attractive feeder with an uncluttered neutral background provides the best pictures. Here a pair of Evening Grosbeaks feeds on sunflower seeds.*

Maslowski Photo

Surroundings. Good light is essential—morning sun from the side or from behind you is best. The ideal background is natural shrubbery rather than angular objects. If you cannot avoid the corner of a neighbor's house or a fence post, move the feeder as far away from the offending objects and as close to your camera as possible. Minimize the impact of angular background objects by using apertures with shallow depths of field.

Improving composition. Before settling on the spot, get behind your camera and think about composition. If you can move the feeder, how close can you get it to your home? The closer the feeder is to your home, the better. At first the birds may not be willing to come to a feeder that is close to your house. Encourage them by gradually moving a feeder from a site they accept to a site you require. Start with a simple tray feeder on a pole. Place the feeder in an area with protective cover nearby to allow birds quick approach and rapid escape.

Over a week bring the feeder closer and closer to the window. In the meantime mask the window with paper, but leave a hole through which the lens can peer. Cut another hole in the mask and tape your flash onto the glass. You will need a synch cord to attach the flash to the camera.

Next, consider whether suitable perches near the feeder make attractive photographic settings. If not, create some—provide a dead branch, some potted plants. These additions provide perches for the birds and opportunities for you to photograph them before their beaks are full of birdseed. But, to make the setting more attractive to birds, offer small quanitites of food in unobtrusive places.

Consider next whether the site is flexible. Can you alter it to create different settings? Some backyard bird photographers go to great lengths to compose the scenery. In spring you might clamp some forsythia or apple blossoms to the feeder; birds waiting to feed will pose atop the flowers. Foresight is essential or you will be locked into a single setting.

Photographing at ground level increases the intimacy of your work. Use a basement window to go eye to eye with ground-feeding birds such as Mourning Doves and Dark-eyed Juncos.

Water Sources

Birdbaths, fountains, and other backyard sources of water make excellent sites for bird photography. This is especially true in regions where water is in short supply during the hot summer. You can be particularly creative with birdbaths because they attract many species that never come to feeders, such as thrushes and warblers.

When installing a a birdbath or pool in your yard, think about photographic composition. Give birds a pleasing, flowered background. Smooth any harsh corners of the water source, and make sure any water hoses are out of sight. If you are depending on natural light, choose a site that is completely in sunlight or in light shade; you do not want sharp differences in the light conditions to cause excessive contrast in your photo. A little foresight will give you years of pleasureful photography.

Gardens

Gardens and plantings offer a range of photographic opportunities. Berry bushes, in particular, are a focus of bird activity during the season when they bear fruit. The bearing season varies with the crop—you can have blueberries and cherries in summer, apples in early fall, pyracantha in fall and winter. A stand of pyracantha in good light near your photography window will provide many seasons of enjoyable shooting as well as food for hungry birds. Berry eaters such as robins, thrushes, and waxwings will pose for you with beaks full of berries. A mockingbird may establish its territory in the same fruit tree each winter and offer you numerous opportunities to photograph its territorial displays.

Equipment for Backyard Photography

Backyard bird photography allows you to take frame-filling portraits without a monstrous lens. Macro zooms are ideal because they allow sharp, close focus with variable magnification. If your feeder is close to the window, a short telephoto macro or a telephoto lens with an extension tube is useful. Do not forget to use a tripod.

If you want to use flash, try using several at once; a single flash produces harsh shadows and a black background. Set up a slave-initiated flash (see pages 246 to 247) in order to light your subject without disturbing it by getting close. Clamp additional flashes onto supports in the yard, such as a feeder. Cover the flash units with a clear plastic bag if the weather is damp and use an AC adapter—especially in the cold—because batteries lose their power rapidly.

J.R. Woodward/VIREO

Create specialized perches for birds to use that are in line with your camera set-up. This picture of a House Finch among flowers was set up by attaching a branch with blossoms to a feeding station.

Fruit-bearing trees and shrubs are attractive to birds like this American Robin, here feeding on mountain ash. Carefully arranged trees of this sort can add to the diversity of backyard photography.

Thomas D. Mangelsen

S. Lipschutz/VIREO

J.P. Myers/VIREO

Sharon Chester

Above: *Zoos provide a variety of colorful and cooperative subjects. This shot, taken at a zoo, shows a Guianian Cock of the Rock.*

Above center: *Zoos can also attract a variety of native birds like this Black-crowned Night-Heron. Native birds at zoos are often easily approached.*

Above right: *Careful framing and selection of the right backdrop can give zoo pictures a very natural appearance. This Rainbow Lorikeet, photographed in a zoo, appears just as it would in the wild.*

Photographing in Zoos and Aviaries

Your local zoo or aviary is a little farther away than your backyard, but it is probably much richer in bird life. Zoos are marvelous places to practice the arts of anticipation, composition, and exposure. Thousands of exotic species offer countless opportunities to aspiring bird photographers. In many zoos the birds fly freely in walk-in aviaries, large open rooms without wire or glass separating them from you.

Wild birds also thrive in the park-like environments around zoos. They become accustomed to people and dependent on feeding schedules at the zoo. The next time you watch seals being fed, Black-crowned Night-Herons may be waiting for an overlooked fish. Red-winged Blackbirds often feed around the elephants; sparrows flit through shrubbery.

Before making the excursion to photograph birds at a zoo, consider timing. Go on weekdays and early mornings when zoos are less crowded. You will have fewer disruptions and more opportunities to compose carefully. In addition, the light is more attractive early in the morning, and the inhabitants of the zoo are more active.

Eliminating Signs of "Zooness"

Because the animals are captive and accustomed to people, zoos give you time to think and anticipate before shooting. Set up your camera on a tripod, study the scene, and carefully examine the background before committing the image to film. Often you can eliminate the worst offenses by simply moving a bit to one side or another.

The main challenge of bird photography in zoos is keeping the "zooness" out of your photographs. Zoos mean cages, and cages mean bars, fences, or some other material. Zoos also mean backgrounds polluted with signs of the zoo environment—a water pipe, a building, a pile of hay, or a cement floor.

Many smaller birds are kept in areas fenced with fine vertically strung piano wire; cages for larger birds are usually made from chain-link fences. Neither type of fencing is attractive in photographs, and the visual effects of both can be mitigated by using a shallow depth of field. Place your lens directly against the chain-link fence. Even if a link crosses the lens, it may be only barely visible when you use a long lens. Before you shoot, go through the motions and practice with various depths of field.

Use flash selectively to light portions of the image. When photographing at a fence, be careful not to illuminate the part of the fence in the viewfinder; you will not discover the flash highlights until after the film is developed—at that point you see an offensive white bar across the edge of your slide. Instead of mounting your flash directly on the camera, connect the camera and flash with a flexible cable that allows you to move the two around. Find just the right position to avoid flash highlights.

Avoiding reflections. Reflections from glass enclosures can spoil an image. In natural light you will see these reflections before you photograph. Minimize reflections by changing angles or by using a polarizing filter.

To reduce the reflections directly in front of your camera, make a mask that fits over the lens. Use a large square of black cardboard with a hole in the middle for the lens. A small cardboard box offers even better control. Cut a lens hole in the bottom, paint the inside flat black, and attach the box to your lens with tape or rubber bands. By keeping the open end of the box in contact with the glass you can photograph without reflection.

Flash reflections are not obvious until the slides are developed. To minimize them use a mask or box, as described above, and keep the flash as close as possible to the glass, as you would if you were photographing a feeder through a window (see page 251). Another technique is to shoot at an angle to the glass.

The lighting in zoos is never designed for photographers. Dim tungsten and fluorescent lights prevail indoors, so you must use filters and flash to achieve a good exposure and a natural color balance.

Equipment for Zoo Photography

One of the benefits of bird photography in zoos is that the equipment you need is simple. Because the birds cannot fly too far away and because they are accustomed to people, a long lens is generally unnecessary.

For photographing in zoos an 80- to 200-mm lens will provide all the versatility you need. For detailed close-ups a 105-mm macro lens might also come in handy. The other essential piece of equipment is a flash, because lighting inside zoos is not adequate for slow, fine-grained film. Some zoo photographers use up to three flashes at once. In these multi-flash set-ups the main flash on the camera usually triggers two slave units.

C. Volpe/VIREO

This Tawny Frogmouth was photographed through plate glass. The right camera angle, a mask around the lens, or a polarizing filter are all techniques that can be used to eliminate reflections on glass.

Frans Lanting

To photograph a family of Laysan Albatrosses like this one, it is necessary to travel to the remote islands where they nest. Green patches both in and around cities are good places to find birds that may not frequent your backyard.

Photographing in the Field

Whether a veteran or a novice, a bird photographer's first challenge is selecting a location. For the beginner the safest and most practical way to begin field photography is to concentrate on locations where birds are accustomed to people, such as in city parks, at city ponds, wharves and piers, national wildlife refuges, and public beaches. Some islands are renowned for the tameness of resident birds. On the Galápagos Islands, for example, almost every bird will let you approach within camera range. Whether exotic or close to home, locations where the birds are not skittish enable you to hone your photographic skills while improving your ability to work with wild birds in the field.

You will have fewer frustrations if you begin working with wild birds in a location with good visibility and excellent light. Open-country and edge habitats are good places to start. Photographing in a dense forest is difficult because of a cluttered view and poor light. It is hard enough to see birds in a spruce forest, much less photograph them well.

A beginner should specialize: Learn the intricacies of one habitat, one group of birds, and one location. If the site is rich in birds, exhausting the photographic opportunities will seem impossible even if you specialize. Explore light, behaviors, and angles. The benefit of working continuously with one group of birds is that you will truly know your subjects.

Stalking a Bird

The single most vexing and constant frustration for a bird photographer working in the field is distance. Since most birds react to people as they react to predators, the key to frame-filling images is to get close to your subject without scaring it away.

Always move slowly and cautiously. Watch the bird's reaction to your approach. If it twitches nervously, slow your advance. Wait 5 to 10 minutes in your current position before going ahead. Take advantage of these waiting periods to photograph. In fact, by taking photographs from several vantage points as you approach, you assure yourself of at least one good picture, and you build a collection of habitat shots to match bird portraits. These shots can be valuable for documentation and study.

Do not move directly toward the bird. Imagine you are a sailboat and the bird is directly upwind. Tack off to one side, then another. You will get much closer this way than if you were to head straight toward the subject. When photographing on the beach, lie down and inch toward the bird using your elbows and knees for propulsion.

The best photographs are usually those taken when the bird is moving toward you, rather than you toward the bird. Be alert to approaching birds. If you see a robin coming along the lawn, wait for it to approach. Get down on the ground and work at its eye level. Observe your subjects' behavior, then move to the site that you think they are approaching.

Sometimes two photographers can collaborate quite effectively in stalking birds in the field. First one gently works a bird or flock toward the other, then the collaboraters trade roles. In the process of being repeatedly urged in one direction then another, the birds become accustomed to the humans. In many cases a flock will eventually feed quietly just a few feet away from both photographers.

When you can, use natural blinds to minimize your visibility. Do not, however, rush from one tree to another. Slow, deliberate movements are far more effective even if they leave you visible for longer periods.

Luring a Bird

Playing a recording of a species' song is an excellent means of inducing an unwilling subject to pose for the camera. Birders have learned that many secretive species become quite exhibitionistic when they hear a recording of their song in their territory. Sometimes it is the only way to find an uncommonly shy species. During breeding season small perching birds respond best to this approach. Many local bookstores carry tapes of North American species.

Some birds also approach when they hear an imitation of the harsh sound that chickadees, titmice, and other small forest residents make when they mob a larger predator. Loudly repeat "*p-sh-wsh-wsh*" when you hear the noises of a winter flock of these species, and you may find yourself surrounded by a flock of small birds coming within a few feet. You have to work quickly under these conditions, but if the light is right you usually end up with a good sequence.

Keith H. Murakami/Tom Stack & Associates

By staying low in the dense vegetation that often borders mudflats, you may get a good shot at a Black-necked Stilt; this one was photographed at ground level. Patience and slow, even movements can help you to approach many species.

C. Servheen/Raptor Information Center/VIREO

This Great Gray Owl was photographed by luring it toward the photographer with a mouse in a cage. For most birds, food provides the best lure.

In some situations food can be an excellent lure. Carry a sack of birdseed in the car on trips to encourage park and camp residents into camera range. It usually does not take much training to get them in close because they are accustomed to people. Try lacing a pine cone with peanut butter, or smearing peanut butter on the back of a branch. The birds will find it quickly and pose for you while enjoying the food.

Small animals in cages often lure birds to a viewfinder. During eastern winters, for example, a small live mouse in a wire cage easily attracts northern owls like Snowy and Great Gray Owls. Put the cage out on the ground in view of the owl and it will quickly swoop down to investigate— even if you are only a few feet away.

Photographing from Your Car

Birds are more tolerant of the close approach of cars than they are of people walking. This is especially true in places like National Wildlife Refuges or in parks where cars are common.

To use your car for effective field photography, find a place where cars can get close to birds and where there is little road traffic. The dike roads of many wildlife refuges are often ideal. Another excellent site for car photography is along beaches that permit vehicles. On a beach it is possible to go back and forth and experiment with many different angles. Within 10 or 15 minutes the birds will behave as if the car is not there.

Wherever you use a car, drive slowly and gently. If the road and traffic permit, tack as you would on foot rather than driving directly toward your subject. Turn off the engine as you draw near and coast to a stop. Avoid using a car with squeaky brakes or a sputtering idle.

Turning off the engine is vital; the bird and the camera are less disturbed. Vibrations from the engine, however subtle, can be a serious problem. A ball-and-socket head that holds the camera to the window will reduce vibrations. Ask passengers to hold still while you shoot.

The other drawback to car photography is that you rarely can shoot at a bird's eye level, and the photos may lack intimacy. In addition, do not forget that you must return from the area in which you are shooting. Sand along beaches can be treacherous even if you are careful. Be especially watchful of incoming tides and sleeper waves.

Peter M. La Tourrette

By framing this Turkey Vulture at the left side of the picture, the motion of the flight is captured and viewers are less likely to find their eyes wandering off the picture.

Compositional Challenges

Composition possibilities in the field are endless because you are in the natural world, but the guidelines that apply in more controlled settings are still relevant. Experiment with placement of the subject within the frame; for example, move the viewfinder so that a bird flying from left to right in the image is placed on the left half of the frame.

Compositional and photographic challenges intensify when you have more than one bird in the frame. Should both be in focus or just the bird in front? Should both be parallel in the image or slightly out of line? The answer to any compositional question depends upon what you want to say with your photograph.

What lighting conditions should you seek? Dramatic, well-lit photographs are often the result of the bright sun of early morning or late afternoon, when the quality of light warms and the angle of the sun deepens. Mid-day sun in winter or in the Arctic also offers some of these qualities.

Dark, overcast days reduce contrast, decrease the brilliance of color, and lessen the total amount of light. Exposures tend to be more difficult, and the results are less saturated with color. Overcast conditions often require flash-fill—a flash combined with natural lighting—to yield successful exposure.

Equipment for Field Photography

A long lens, a tripod or shoulder stock, and a cable release are essentials for field work. Wherever you work, make sure to put more than enough film in your camera bag; nothing is more aggravating than having worked carefully for an hour or more to gain just the right view to discover you have only a few frames left. A 50-mm macro, which enables you to switch from telephoto work to close-ups or general habitat photographs, is also useful. Extension tubes should go into the camera bag early, especially if your subjects are small birds.

Beyond these basic recommendations, the choice of equipment will depend on the occasion. What species is your quarry? Does it live in caves or on beaches? Will you be floating up to grebe nests in a marsh or waiting beside a wild cherry tree in the forest?

Sharon Chester

This is a free-form shot of an Arctic Tern in flight. The presence of the young bird makes the flight path of the adult somewhat predictable and allows a photographer to prepare for the picture.

Photographing Birds in Flight

To photograph birds in flight you can use one of two radically different approaches. Many photographers take their chances while others strive for total control. While a little good luck never hurts, the secrets to success in either approach are careful planning, patient work, and many exposures.

Free-form. In free-form flight photography you take whatever photographic opportunities come your way and make the most of them. This photographic style depends on anticipation, fast reflexes, timing, instinctive knowledge of exposure and composition, and repeated attempts.

Look for a place where birds in flight frequently pass close by. Windy cliffs with soaring birds or a wharf with seagulls and terns offer good opportunities. If the birds are flying against the wind, they move more slowly. On your next ferry ride sit near the stern as people feed trailing gulls. The birds will be intent on getting the bread and oblivious to your lenses. Another excellent place to work is beside a duck pond or in a field where geese come to feed. Photograph as they approach or depart. Heron rookeries also offer excellent possibilities. In fact any bird breeding site is a choice location, but remember—it is the bird photographer's responsibility to be sensitive to the needs of the birds and their young.

Free-form photography of birds in flight calls for a steady hand and smooth motions. Sit down and brace your elbows on your knees. Loosen the controls on your tripod or use a shoulder stock (see pages 246 to 247); shoulder stocks allow you to follow the birds quickly and with smoother motions. If you have selected a site that birds pass regularly, focus in advance on a place in their path. Choose one bird as it approaches, follow it smoothly to the point of focus, and expose. Be sure to follow through with your motions after the exposure; otherwise, you may unconsciously jerk at the moment of exposure and blur the image.

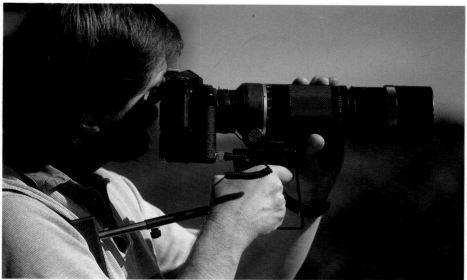

George D. Lepp

Anthony Mercieca/Tom Stack & Associates

R. Hansen/VIREO

Above left: *This photographer is using a shoulder stock to steady his hands and allow for smooth panning. Shoulder stocks are especially helpful when using long lenses.*

Above: *Using electronic equipment, one can obtain sharp, clear pictures of birds frozen in flight, such as with this Acorn Woodpecker. By using a strobe light and a motor drive, sequential shots can also be made.*

Left: *By limiting the number of approaches to a feeding station or by carefully placing perches, it is possible to control the flight paths of birds. Here, a Tufted Titmouse is caught as it prepares to land on a perch.*

Total control. Careful planning, construction, and a touch of technology will allow you to direct a bird's flight to your advantage. This is easier than you might think. Increase your control of flight patterns around your bird feeder by simply limiting the number of approaches and placing a perch along the flight path. Many birds will land first on the perch, then fly to the feeder. Prefocusing at a spot between the perch and the feeder facilitates photos of birds in flight. To simplify focusing, direct the bird to fly parallel to your window between the perch and the feeder.

Use the same principles to set up your equipment along the flight paths to nests and birdhouses. Use a cable release so you do not disturb the bird when you take the picture.

Electronics have been a boon to bird photography; they narrow the gap between the speed of a bird and the speed of the photographer's reflexes. For years bird photographers have used light-triggered circuits—devices that generate a pulse of electricity when a bird's shadow passes over them. These circuits rely on a photocell, which senses changes in light intensity. The photocell signals the camera to release the shutter, and the two devices take the picture more rapidly and reliably than the fastest finger.

Freezing the Flight of Hummingbirds

Hummingbirds seem almost fearless in their search for nectar; they approach almost any bright red object. They quickly learn to use a feeder filled with sugar water, and as they hover sipping from the feeder, they become a perfect subject for bird photography.

If you want to stop the motion of their wings, electronic flash is essential. The wing motion of hummingbirds is so fast that even the fastest shutter speed is insufficient. Place the camera and flash on a tripod near a hummingbird feeder (see page 212) and prefocus a short telephoto lens—about 200-mm—on one of the feeding tubes. A long pneumatic cable release or some other remote triggering device will enable you to sit comfortably a few yards away, clicking away. A motor drive will make the task even simpler; you will not have to get up to advance the film after each exposure.

If you want the photograph to appear natural, camouflage the feeder tube with flowers and shrubbery. Hummingbirds adjust to such arrangements, and the results will be more pleasing.

With an electronic flash, it was possible to stop the motion in the wings of this Calliope Hummingbird.

Robert Tyrrell

Composition. Birds in flight offer wonderful opportunities for composition. However, flying birds move quickly and force rapid decision making on the photographer. If you are working a flight line, think ahead about where in the flight path you wish to expose the next photograph.

In flight photography you have a choice: Do you want frozen or blurred motion in your image? To create an image in which each feather is etched sharply, use fast shutter speeds of 1/500 to 1/1,000. For hummingbirds you must shoot much faster, up to 1/10,000 of a second. To accentuate motion by blurring the details of the wing or body, use shutter speeds of 1/15 or 1/30 with a 300-mm or 400-mm lens.

Equipment for Flight Photography

To capture images of flying birds, use a 300-mm or 400-mm lens. A smaller lens sometimes works for large (egret-sized) birds close by. A shoulder stock or tripod with a ball head will help you follow the motion of the bird without losing much steadiness. Use the slowest and finest-grained film possible for the lighting conditions. If the level of light is low, move to high-speed film of ISO 400 or more.

Flight photography is one area where a motor drive really pays off (see pages 246 to 247). Though it is no panacea, a motor drive can help you produce more focused shots than you would have without one.

Black-and-white film is often preferable for photographing birds in flight, especially for beginners. It is less expensive per frame than color and lets you experiment as you work toward that perfect image.

Douglas R. Herr

J.D. Young/VIREO

Photographing at Nests

Photographers are at an advantage in nest photography. Even with intermittent disruption, parent birds follow their strong instincts to protect and feed their young. They keep returning, hour after hour, and provide endless opportunities for fine adjustments to photographic technique.

Some knowledge of the species is particularly helpful when photographing around the nest. For example, the young of many ground-nesting species are precocial—they leave the nest within hours of hatching to forage for themselves. The best time to set up your equipment to photograph these species is several days before the eggs hatch. (See the box on page 265 about using caution around nests.)

Before beginning, learn the nesting cycle of the species you choose to photograph. How long does it take to build the nest or incubate eggs? How many days will the young remain there before flying off on their own? These simple facts will help schedule your photography. The breeding cycles of most species are listed in Arthur Cleveland Bent's series of life histories of North American birds.

Finding Nests

Nests lie where you least suspect them. In summer they are enshrouded in foliage, safe from a predator's piercing gaze. During winter when trees are bare, nests from the previous summer are in plain sight. Few birds use the same nest year after year, but most return to similar habitats—adjacent to water, in the same species of tree, or in deep forest. Noting nest sites in winter will help you find new sites in the next nesting season. The edges of woods and groves of backyard trees are likely nest sites.

During the nesting season, watching the way birds behave provides the best clues about nest sites. A male's territorial song marks the general area. Look for birds flying by with bits of nest-building materials, food, or fecal sacs—the feces of their young, which adults carry from the nest to keep the nest site inconspicuous—then concentrate your search where you see them going. Many birds do not fly directly to their nests but land nearby and go unobtrusively the rest of the way.

Above left: *A recently hatched Killdeer rests near an egg. To obtain pictures of young precocial birds, it is best to set up photographic equipment several days before the eggs hatch. Since precocial birds wander away from the nest after hatching, it is essential to be present during hatching.*

Above: *This Brown Thrasher with its young is an example of a well-composed nest photograph. Timing is important. Disturbances at the nest too early may cause the nest to be deserted by parents; disturbing the young too early may cause them to leave the nest before they are able to fly.*

Above: *Nests used in previous years are easily located in the winter and generally indicate the presence of breeding pairs that will return the next summer. A number of books illustrate the nests of North American birds and can be used to identify these old nests.*

Above right: *Here a Chestnut-sided Warbler removes a fecal sac from its nest. By carefully watching birds during the breeding season, nests are often easily located.*

Once you have located the general area of a nest, back away until you can barely see the parents and leave them undisturbed for several minutes. Approach once again, prepared to detect the adults flying off the nest. You may have to approach and withdraw several times, but gradually you will discern the focus of their activity and find the nest.

Once you find the nest, mark the location so you can find it when you next return. Use an inconspicuous mark since predators learn cues with frightening speed. Tie a ribbon on a branch, or plant a stake in the ground a standard distance and direction from the location, such as 5 to 10 yards to the north.

Getting Close to a Nest

When approaching a nest for photographing, always consider the birds' safety first. By moving in too quickly or at the wrong time in the nesting cycle, a well-meaning photographer can seriously jeopardize the success of the nest.

As a rule, do not approach the nest during the nest-building and early incubation periods. Wait until a few days after the eggs hatch and the parent birds have a strong investment in their nest before you begin to photograph.

Equipment with a dull color and finish is more suitable than bright, shiny gear for work close to a nest. To help nesting birds adapt to your equipment, fashion a dummy camera, flash, and tripod by attaching a tin can to a black cardboard box and placing it on top of three sticks. Set up this rig 15 to 20 yards away from the nest. The birds will not take long to become accustomed to the shapes of your equipment. Move the dummy closer to the nest over a period of a few days. Once in the desired position, replace the dummy with your real camera outfit.

Although a little "gardening" near the nest site is often necessary, do not cut or trample the foliage. The nest must remain concealed from predators. Simply tie back any intruding twigs or grasses, and rearrange them at the end of each photo session. Also remember that many bird predators can be attracted to the nest site via scent. Use gloves while handling vegetation, and handle it as little as possible.

Using Caution Around Nests

It is imperative that the photographer exercise patience and care to minimize impact on the young birds in nests. Nest desertion will occur with excessive and continuous disruption. In most cases photography should not begin until a few days after hatching. Until then the young need regular incubation to stay warm; intrusions will place them in peril. After the young hatch, the adults become more committed to the nest and are less likely to desert.

Take special care when photographing raptors. They abandon their nests with only a minor disturbance and they can be quite dangerous. Their talons easily pierce clothing and their blows can be strong enough to throw you off balance. When photographing raptors, wear heavy clothing, a helmet, and safety goggles. Mount a yardstick in your backpack so that it projects above your head to deflect attacks.

Colonial seabirds are best photographed offshore or from an overlooking cliff. A single human visit to a colony can have a disastrous effect. An entire colony of terns may take flight, exposing eggs and young to predators.

Frans Lanting

Colonial nesting birds, like these Sooty Terns, may desert colonies with frequent disturbances.

Equipment and Techniques for Nest Photography

Photography at a nest site requires the same basic equipment as in the field, but because nests are usually in poor light, flash is frequently necessary. Attach flashes to tree branches with clamps or supports that screw into the tree. If no branches are suitable, use a small light stand. Keep the path of light from flash to nest clear of any foliage.

For remote-control photography—which is quite useful at nests—you need a tripod and a remote-release device. The simplest is a pneumatic cable—a rubber bulb attached to a long vinyl tube with a plunger on the opposite end. A motor drive or automatic winder permits film advance from afar. Automatic exposure control allows the camera to adjust for changing light conditions and reduces the number of times the photographer must approach the nest.

Most birds have little tolerance of intruders during the nest-building and incubation stages; during these times use remote releases and blinds. A blind will allow you to get closer to the nest and its inhabitants without frightening the birds (see page 250).

A medium telephoto lens (100-mm to 200-mm) is ideal for photographing around a nest. Do not frame too tightly, or you may cut off the tail or beak in the photos. Use the guide on your lens to determine the depth of field.

If a flash is the major light source, position it to the side for a more dramatic effect. If you use flash only to fill shadows, leave the flash on top of the camera—as long as the camera is not too far from the nest. Like the pleasing result when used at feeders, using several flashes at once can enhance your work at a nest site.

L.P. Brown/Cornell Lab. of Orn./VIREO

Perhaps the best way to photograph birds at their nests is by using a blind. These Yellow Warblers, photographed from a blind, appear natural and undisturbed.

This is an elaborate, elevated blind, such as might be necessary when photographing treetop nests. The best shots are taken when birds and photographer are at the same height.

Karl Maslowski

Photographic methods. You can choose from three basic approaches to photographing at nests: free-form, remote control, and camouflage. With a free-form approach you need tolerant birds that will remain on the nest despite your presence. There are a few unusually tolerant birds around—individual birds of varying species that for unknown reasons allow a human to come near the nest. In more remote areas these individuals become more common. Sandpipers in the Arctic and Red-footed Boobies on the Galápagos Islands seem to have no fear of humans. If you are lucky enough to have such cooperative subjects, move slowly and smoothly so you do not startle them. Take their portrait, be grateful for their cooperation, and be gone. The less time you spend at their side, the better.

Remote-control photography at nests is particularly useful when conditions do not permit the use of a blind. Consider remote control if the nest is high above the ground in trees or if a blind is too valuable to be left unattended. The chief drawback to remote-control work is that you have less control over your composition. Once you leave the camera in place, the composition is set; from afar you cannot adjust the angle of view as the birds move about.

In contrast, using blinds at nests can be extraordinarily effective. From a blind you can adjust each photograph as the birds change positions or as the moving sun shifts the highlights across the image. If your blind is large and immobile, set it up piece by piece over several days to minimize your disturbance near the nest. Move in mobile blinds gradually so birds get used to them. For more hints on using blinds, see page 250.

Whatever method you use, above all, take care not to disturb the birds and cause them to abandon their efforts during this time (see page 265).

Bird Photography: A Satisfying Pursuit

Bird photography challenges devotees with a special blend of natural history, technology, and artistry. The natural history comes with observation, with the need to learn where and when to find subjects and how they will react to your presence. The technology comes in the form of special equipment—long lenses, capable cameras, electronic flashes, and exposure controls. With an eye for exciting composition—and a great deal of patience—the successful bird photographer combines knowledge and technology to translate an idea into a photographic image. Filled as it is with opportunity for creative new approaches, it is no wonder bird photography becomes a compelling habit for practitioners.

Frans Lanting

This detailed picture showing the texture of a Northern Pintail's feathers was taken with a macro lens and illustrates a more artistic approach to bird photography.

The Gallery of Birds

by Kit and George Harrison

B irds seem more visible than any other kind of wildlife in North America. On any sunny day, during any season, in any region, birds can be seen on the ground, in trees, and in the sky. That is why North America is considered The Bird Continent.

Ornithologists estimate that the continent is home to more than 700 species. This gallery features 125 of the most common North American species and includes birds from all geographic regions of the continent. The gallery lists species in the accepted taxonomic order—that is, in the sequence in which experts believe they evolved. For each species, you will find a description of appearance, voice, habitat, habits, food, nest, and eggs. In addition to a color photograph of each species, a map shows the bird's breeding range in pink and the winter range in blue. If the species is a year-round resident, the map shows the permanent range in gray.

With this information and a keen eye, you can identify nearly any bird that appears in the backyard.

From one end of the continent to the other, North America is rich in an exciting diversity of bird families. The more you know about a bird, the more likely you will find and recognize it.

Brown Pelican

A. Cruickshank/VIREO

Brown Pelican
(Pelecanus occidentalis)

"A wonderful bird is the pelican, his bill will hold more than his belican." This famous limerick by Dixon Lanier Merritt characterizes both the Brown and White Pelicans. Indeed, the huge, naked skin pouch that hangs from the pelican's lower bill does hold more than its belly can—two or three times as much, according to one scientist. The pelican uses its pouch to catch and briefly hold fish. As soon as the water drains from the pouch, the bird swallows its catch. In hot weather, the membrane of the pouch helps keep the bird cool. Though Brown Pelican populations were drastically reduced by the effects of pesticides, they are now recovering because of the ban on DDT and similar chemicals.

Description. The Brown Pelican is a large (3½ to 4½ feet) bird with short legs, webbed feet, a long bill, a deep pouch, and a 6½- to 7½-foot wingspan. The adult has a white head with yellow crest, a red-brown neck, and a gray back. The immature bird has a brown head and back and is light below.

Voice. Adults are usually silent, but occasionally utter a low croak. The young squeal and hiss.

Habitat. Home for the Brown Pelican is on coastlines, oceans, saltwater bays, and islands along most U.S. coasts.

Habits. A graceful flier, the Brown Pelican often skims over the crests of waves in formations with other pelicans. When it spots a fish while in flight, it folds its wings, closes its bill, and dives into the water head first, sometimes to the depth of 1 or 2 feet. Air pockets under the skin cushion the impact as the bird hits the water from heights of up to 50 feet. Once in the water, the pelican opens its bill and scoops the fish into its pouch. To become airborne without the aid of a brisk wind, the pelican must run on top of the water while beating its wings. The Brown Pelican is the state bird of Louisiana.

Nest and eggs. A colonial bird, the Brown Pelican builds its bulky nest of sticks and grass in trees along lagoons or on the ground on coastal islands. The 3 white, oval, blood-stained eggs are incubated by both parents for 30 days. Young birds fly at 9 weeks.

White Pelican

H. Cruickshank/VIREO

Food. The Brown Pelican eats fish almost exclusively, with menhaden forming up to 95 percent of food intake in the bird's southern range.

White Pelican
(Pelecanus erythrorhynchos)

Flying White Pelicans remind some observers of military formations as they flap and glide in perfect unison. White Pelicans have similarly synchronized behavior when sunning on a sandbar: They face the same direction, bills pointed skyward, and flutter their pouches to keep cool. John James Audubon wrote, "Should one chance to gape, all, as if in sympathy, in succession open their . . . mandibles, yawning lazily and ludicrously." This

sociability extends to these birds' cooperative feeding behavior and colonial nesting habits.

Description. One of the largest birds in North America, the White Pelican has a wingspan of up to 9½ feet, rivaling that of the California Condor. It is white with black wing tips, a yellow to orange bill, a pouch, and webbed feet. Juveniles have gray bills and streaked dark crowns. A vertical horny fin decorates the top of the bill through the breeding season.

Voice. In colonies, White Pelicans utter low groans; the young whine and grunt.

Habitat. Unlike the oceanic Brown Pelican, the White Pelican is common along the inland lakes, marshes, ponds, and freshwater islands in the north-central and northwestern United States and in south-central and southwestern Canada. During winter, it migrates to areas along the Pacific and Gulf Coasts.

Great Egret

B. Schorre/VIREO

Snowy Egret

H. Cruickshank/VIREO

Great Egret

B. Schorre/VIREO

Snowy Egret

H. Cruickshank/VIREO

Description. The daintiest of all wading birds, the Snowy Egret is a rather small, slim white heron that sports a slender black bill with a patch of yellow skin at the base, black legs, and bright yellow feet. Immature birds have pale green legs and feet.

Voice. Snowy Egrets are noisy; they fill their colonies with a bubbling *wulla-wulla-wulla*. They also sound off with a low croak.

Habitat. Snowy Egrets live in the edges and shallows of both fresh- and saltwater wetlands as well as on beaches and tidal flats.

Habits. Known for its active feeding behavior, the Snowy Egret often rushes about the shallows, wings partly extended, stirring up and shuffling the water with its feet to frighten prey into the open. The Snowy Egret also feeds in concert with puddle ducks, which help stir up prey.

Nest and eggs. Snowy Egrets usually nest in colonies, which sometimes contain thousands of birds, but they may also nest alone at the periphery of their range. The nest of loosely woven twigs and heavy sticks is built 5 to 10 feet above ground in a shrub or tree. Both sexes build the nest and defend the site, and both incubate the 4 or 5 oval, pale greenish blue eggs for the 18 days required for hatching. The parents produce only one brood a year; young birds leave the nest in about 3 weeks.

Food. The Snowy Egret subsists on a variety of fish, frogs, shrimp, crabs, crayfish, aquatic insects, and a few small reptiles.

Canada Goose

H. Cruickshank/VIREO

Canada Goose
(Branta canadensis)

The Canada Goose has become so numerous in some parts of its range that it is a nuisance on golf courses, city reservoirs, and recreational lakes. The burgeoning population is in part due to the successful management efforts of state and federal wildlife agencies that have created refuges and feeding areas for the honkers along their traditional migration routes. In many cases, the refuges have altered the birds' habits by causing them to remain in feeding areas throughout much of the year.

Description. The Canada Goose is large—from 22 to 40 inches long. The 11 subspecies range in size from the small Cackling Canada Goose of 3 to 4 pounds to the Giant Canada Goose, which weighs up to 24 pounds. The species has a brown-gray back and is lighter below; black bill, legs, and webbed feet; a black stockinglike neck; and a distinct white chin strap. The sexes look alike.

Voice. Their famous call, a clarion, musical, honking *ka-ronk*, is one of the most haunting sounds in all of nature. When defending its nest, the Canada Goose hisses at intruders.

Habitat. The Canada Goose is at home in a variety of wetlands close to grasslands or agricultural areas where it can graze. National wildlife refuges, which use a flying goose as their logo, are particularly favored by breeding and migrating honkers.

Habits. The well-known V-formations of flying geese consist of a family or group of families led by an adult. One- and two-year-olds stay with their parents to form a family unit of about nine birds. Geese are mated until one of the pair dies. Canada geese roost on water.

Nest and eggs. Canada geese usually build their nests near water on low stumps, mounds, or muskrat houses using sticks, reeds, and grasses. Their 5 or 6 creamy-to dirty-white eggs are incubated by the female (the goose) for 28 days while the gander stands guard nearby. The young can fly 42 days after hatching.

Food. Canada geese are grazers. They particularly relish the fresh green sprouts of winter wheat, a characteristic that makes them unpopular among farmers. They also eat waste grain and a great variety of aquatic vegetation, wetland grasses, and clovers.

Mallard

Mallard
(Anas platyrhynchos)

The Mallard is the best known and most common wild duck in the Northern Hemisphere. Also known as greenheads, Mallards are the prize quarry of the duck hunter each fall, as huge flocks of Mallards swarm south from breeding areas across Canada and the northern United States.

Description. The male Mallard is recognizable by its glossy green head, yellow bill, white collar, and chestnut breast on a gray body. The male's dapper, curly, black upper tail feathers are one of its trademarks. The hen, with its plain brown mottled body, is sometimes confused with the darker American Black Duck. The male and the female both have a violet-blue wing patch.

Voice. Male Mallards utter a *yeeb* and a low *kwek*; the female calls a boisterous series of quacks.

Habitat. The prairie pothole country of the Great Plains is famous for an abundance of Mallards. The ducks also are found on freshwater lakes, ponds, sloughs, and reservoirs, and in backyards close to water.

Habits. Typical puddle ducks, Mallards tip up in the water when feeding, showing only their rumps as they glean aquatic vegetation from shallow wetlands. Though they do not usually nest near houses, homeowners have sometimes found nests in backyard shrubbery, in rooftop gutters, in vines on stone walls, and in window wells.

Nest and eggs. Mallards usually conceal their nests on the ground in tall grass or thick reeds. The female lines the nest of grasses or reeds with down and feathers from its own breast. One lightgreenish buff egg is laid each day for 8 to 12 days, at which point the female settles into the 26-day incubation period. Mallards sometimes lay eggs in the nests of other ducks.

Food. A Mallard's diet consists of aquatic vegetation, from shallow wetlands, as well as seeds, waste grain, and—in agricultural areas—tender green shoots.

Blue-winged Teal

Blue-winged Teal
(Anas discors)

A small but swift duck, the Blue-winged Teal spends little time on its breeding grounds. It is the last migrant northward in the spring and the first to leave its breeding grounds in the fall. For that reason, this is the first migrant to be greeted by duck hunters.

Description. A common, shy, small (14 to 16 inches) puddle duck, the drake has a white crescent on the face and a large chalky blue patch on the forewing. The hen is a mottled drab brown and has a similar blue patch on its forewing.

Voice. The drake's peeping sound has been described as *tseeel, tseeel, tseeel*; the hen quacks softly.

Habitat. Primarily a duck of the prairie pothole regions of the north-central United States and south-central Canada, the Blue-winged Teal also inhabits small ponds, swamps, sloughs, cattail marshes, and grassy fields.

Habits. This duck is a fast flier in tight formations with others of its kind. It passes the winter in large flocks in Cuba, Mexico, and Central and South America.

Nest and eggs. A well-built basketlike nest of cattails and fine dry grasses is well hidden on dry ground. The female finishes the nest with down from its own breast, then lays one egg a day for 10 to 13 days. When the last egg is laid, the female begins to incubate the clutch and sits on the nest for the 23 or 24 days required for hatching. Young birds can fly 35 to 44 days after hatching.

Food. The bulk of the Blue-winged Teal's diet is aquatic seeds and vegetation from ponds, lakes, swamps, mud flats, and grassy marshes. They also eat waste grains.

Wood Duck
(Aix sponsa)

The drake Wood Duck is one of the most beautiful birds in the world. Traditional descriptions of the drake compare it to a bridegroom. In 1882 naturalist Elliott Coues described the drake Wood Duck as "arrayed for bridal." Its species name, *sponsa*, is Latin for "betrothed" or "promised one." Near extinction in 1918 due to habitat loss and hunting, the Wood Duck is one of the first successes of wildlife management. Due to protection and habitat preservation, the Wood Duck is one of the most common ducks in the eastern United States today.

Description. The male Wood Duck bears dramatic patterns. It is a medium-sized duck (17 to 20½ inches) with a flamboyant iridescent head and a facial pattern of white stripes. It has a multiple-colored bill, orange-red eye, long swept-back crest, burgundy neck and breast, iridescent back, flecked buff flanks, and white belly. The hen's gray, black, and white plumage is dull by comparison, but its crest and its bold white, pear-shaped eye patch add a bit of flair.

Voice. The calls of the Wood Duck vary from a loud *whoo-eek* when flushed to a sharp *cr-r-ek, cr-r-ek* when alarmed. The drake's usual call is a high-pitched, sparrowlike *jeeeee*.

Habitat. The Wood Duck was so named because it prefers wooded swamps, river forests, woodlots, and wooded lake and pond borders, and because it nests in tree holes.

Wood Duck

Orville Andrews

Turkey Vulture

Gary W. Hanlon

Habits. Wood Ducks usually court and pair on their southern wintering grounds. They are early spring migrants, arriving on their northern breeding grounds soon after the thaw. The female remembers where it was hatched and leads its mate to the same tree. If the nesting cavity is occupied, the female selects a nesting site nearby.

Nest and eggs. This tree duck nests 3 to 60 feet above ground in a natural cavity or nesting box. The drake accompanies the hen to the nest each day while the hen lays 10 to 15 creamy- to dull-white eggs. The male's interest diminishes by hatching time, however. The female alone incubates the eggs for the 28 to 31 days before

they hatch. Ducklings jump out of the nest hours after hatching, then follow the hen to nearby cover and food. They can fly after 63 days.

Food. The Wood Duck's diet is almost completely vegetation. It is fond of duckweed, wild rice, and other aquatic vegetation. It also eats acorns, beechnuts, hickory nuts, and wild grapes.

Red-tailed Hawk

Frans Lanting

Turkey Vulture
(Cathartes aura)

The American Vulture family name Cathartidae is Greek for "cleanser." Vultures are indeed cleansers in that they feed on dead and decaying animal matter. The Turkey Vulture is the most common buzzard throughout most of its range.

Description. This large, nearly eagle-sized (26 to 32 inches) soaring bird has a wingspan of 6 feet. From below, its wings are a blackish two-tone. The adult Turkey Vulture's head is small, naked, and red; the young have black heads. Turkey Vultures have long tails, and the sexes look alike.

Voice. Turkey Vultures are usually silent. They occasionally make a hissing sound or raucous growl when disturbed or fighting over an animal carcass.

Habitat. This shy scavenger seeks remote areas that are inaccessible to predators and humans. Cliffs, caves, and forests of dead trees are its preferred habitat.

Habits. Soaring to heights of 200 feet or more is common for this bird that spends much of its day searching for carrion. A master of the thermal air currents, the Turkey Vulture often travels many miles without so much as a flap of its shallow, V-shaped wings. On the ground, the bird is ungainly; it hops about clumsily with its great wings folded against its slim body.

Nest and eggs. Due to the strong odor of the carrion that nestlings eat, Turkey Vultures must conceal their eggs and young from predators who could find the site by the smell. Even though there is little or no nest for the 2 elliptical, dull white eggs splotched with brown, they are well hidden on a cliff, on the ground, or in logs or stumps. Both parents incubate the eggs for the nearly 40 days required for them to hatch. The young can fly 60 to 70 days after hatching.

Food. Turkey Vultures feed almost exclusively on carrion. The fact that their food is often badly decomposed appears not to matter to them. Once food is located, other Turkey Vultures gather and vie for the food.

Red-tailed Hawk
(Buteo jamaicensis)

The common roadside *Buteo* of North America, the Red-tailed Hawk is the most widely distributed of our birds of prey. Like other raptors, many of these hawks died from careless pesticide use during the 1950s and 1960s. Since the banning of DDT, this big hawk has recovered and is once again seen perched regally on dead trees and fence posts throughout much of the continent.

Description. This large 19- to 25-inch raptor has a wingspan of 46 to 58 inches. The Red-tailed Hawk has a brown back and a dark-banded whitish belly. Its round tail is reddish on top. Juveniles have fine barring on their brown tails. Subspecies of this hawk occur in both lighter and darker phases.

Voice. While soaring, this hawk produces an asthmatic-sounding, rasping scream like escaping steam: *p-s-s-s.* They also emit a piglike squealing *kree-e-e-e.*

Habitat. A bird of dry woodlands, farm woodlots, hilly woods, and large stands of oak and white pine, the Red-tailed Hawk adapts to a great variety of natural habitats and is thriving in most of them.

Habits. This majestic *Buteo* is usually seen either soaring in wide circles or keeping a keen lookout for small mammal activity from a perch in a dead tree along the highway. In the northern extremities of its range, the bird migrates during the coldest months but returns to its nesting territory in early spring. Pairs are mated for life, or until one dies, at which time the surviving bird takes a new mate. They return to the same nest territory year after year, usually to the same nest, which they sometimes repair in fall.

Nest and eggs. Red-tailed Hawks build their large, flat, shallow nests of twigs and sticks 35 to 90 feet above the ground in trees. The nest is lined with bark, cedar, and moss. The hawks constantly renew the lining of evergreen sprigs. The 2 or 3 brown-spotted, bluish white eggs are incubated by the female for 28 to 32 days. The male brings food to the nest for its mate during the incubation period. The young fly when they are about 45 days old.

Food. The diet of the Red-tailed Hawk consists of about 85 percent rodents and other small mammals. The balance is made up of insects, birds, amphibians, and reptiles. Most are captured in the air.

Red-shouldered Hawk

O.S. Pettingill, Jr./VIREO

Red-shouldered Hawk
(Buteo lineatus)

Though closely related to the better known and more common Red-tailed Hawk, the Red-shouldered Hawk is a less conspicuous, more secretive raptor. It also occupies a somewhat different niche. The Red-tailed Hawk inhabits open woodlands; the Red-shouldered Hawk confines its activities to moist bottomlands. Nevertheless, both are dramatically marked, stately birds of prey that provide natural controls on many harmful rodents.

Description. This large *Buteo* has broad wings and heavy white bands on both sides of its dark tail. The hawk is named for its reddish brown shoulder patches. Its heavily barred robin-red breast gives it an added touch of beauty.

Juveniles look like adults but do not have red on their shoulders and breasts. In flight, this bird shows a translucent patch, or "window," at the base of the primary wing feathers.

Voice. A nesting pair of Red-shouldered Hawks is extremely noisy. They repeatedly call a musical *kee-you, kee-you, kee-you.* Some Blue Jays can imitate the call and may use it to frighten other birds from feeding stations.

Habitat. The Red-shouldered Hawk prefers moist woodlands, river timber, open pine woods, and the borders of swamps.

Habits. In contrast to the Red-tailed Hawk, the Red-shouldered Hawk soars less and prefers to perch hidden in the cover of trees. The bird returns to its nesting territory year after year. In Massachusetts, where the hawk is migratory, either the same pair or succeeding generations were known to occupy the same nesting territory for 26 consecutive years. In another site the hawk returned for 45 years. In the South, the Red-shouldered Hawk is a year-round resident.

Golden Eagle

D. & M. Zimmerman/VIREO

Nest and eggs. The well-built stick-and-twig nest of the Red-shouldered Hawk is usually placed from 20 to 60 feet above ground near the trunk of a tree. After lining the nest with fine bark, leaves, sprigs of evergreen, feathers, and down, both parents incubate the 3 dull white or pale bluish spotted eggs during the 28 days it takes for them to hatch. The young are able to fly when they are 35 to 42 days old.

Food. This hawk eats rodents and other small mammals, plus a few insects, spiders, earthworms, snails, birds, amphibians, and reptiles.

Golden Eagle
(Aquila chrysaetos)

Because the Golden Eagle is one of the most powerful hunters among birds of prey, it has earned a bad reputation with ranchers and sheep herders. In 1962, research proving that the bird was not responsible for destroying livestock led to the protection of the species. Though similar in appearance to immature Bald Eagles, the two species are not closely related.

Bald Eagle

Stephen J. Krasemann/DRK Photo

Nest and eggs. Golden Eagles build huge nests in trees or on rocky cliffs. They use sticks, brush, roots, and rubbish as building materials, and they add to their nests over the years. Western Kingbirds and American Kestrels occasionally nest in the lower parts of Golden Eagle aeries. The female assumes responsibility for most of the 45-day incubation, which begins as soon as the first of the 2 dull, creamy-buff, splotched eggs is laid. The young hatch several days apart, and the older eaglet sometimes kills its younger nest mate. A Golden Eagle makes its first flight when it is about 65 days old.

Food. The Golden Eagle has an undeserved reputation for killing livestock. Its usual food is rabbits, marmots, ground squirrels, prairie dogs, and an occasional grouse. Only rarely will this bird attack prey as large as deer.

Bald Eagle
(Haliaeetus leucocephalus)

Despite its distinction as the symbol of the United States, the Bald Eagle did not receive legislative protection until June 1940. Even with protection, however, the species declined. During the last 30 years or so, Bald Eagles suffered greatly from loss of nesting habitat and from the toxic effects of DDT and other pesticides. During the 1960s and early 1970s, the species was threatened with extinction in the lower 48 states, particularly in the Southeast. It is now recovering in most of its range. Wildlife managers have helped Bald Eagles recover by replacing infertile eggs with healthy eggs taken from eagles' nests in other regions of the country.

Description. The head of the adult Bald Eagle is not actually without feathers; the word *bald* describes the all-white head. Other distinguishing features of this large raptor with a 7½-foot wingspan are the white tail and the bright yellow beak, eyes, and feet. The balance of the plumage is brownish black. Until they reach maturity as four- or five-year-olds, young Bald Eagles are entirely dark brown with whitish wing linings.

Voice. The call of the Bald Eagle is a harsh, squealing cackle.

Habitat. Bald Eagles live in open areas of forests and mountains, typically near lakes, rivers, and seashores.

Habits. Mated for life or until one of the pair dies, Bald Eagles may live for nearly 50 years. In gliding or soaring, the Bald Eagle keeps its broad wings flat. It winters over much of its nesting range and is rarely seen far from water—sea coasts, rivers, lakes.

Nest and eggs. A Bald Eagle's nest is usually built in the fork of a giant tree. The birds deposit immense piles of sticks and branches, which, after years of reuse, sometimes grow to measure 7 to 8 feet across and 12 feet deep. A nest often weighs as much as 2 tons. The 2 dull white eggs are incubated by both parents for about 35 days. Eaglets make their first flight 72 to 75 days after hatching.

Food. The diet of Bald Eagles consists largely of fish, which they catch themselves or steal from Ospreys. Bald Eagles also chase and catch injured or wounded waterfowl and eat small mammals and carrion.

Bald Eagle

Description. When gliding and soaring, the Golden Eagle flattens its wings, which have a span of 7½ feet. It is a large, majestic brown bird with yellow feet. The golden-brown wash on the adult's neck and crown is visible when the bird wheels in flight. Juveniles show a white wash at the base of their tails and wings when they fly. With the exception that females are larger (as is the case with all birds of prey), both sexes look alike.

Voice. Though it is rare for a Golden Eagle to make sounds, it has been heard yelping, mewing, and whistling.

Habitat. Inhabiting mountains and remote rangelands and forests, a Golden Eagle pair may have a territory of 70 square miles.

Habits. One of the most impressive fliers in the bird world, the Golden Eagle soars for hours, riding the thermals to amazing heights. Observers have clocked hunting and playing eagles at 150 to 200 miles per hour. Pairs are assumed to be mated for life.

Northern Harrier

Frans Lanting

Northern Harrier
(Circus cyaneus)

Also known as the marsh hawk, the Northern Harrier lives on prairies and marshlands. It is most often seen gliding gracefully and buoyantly over grasslands with its head bowed in search of mice and other small prey. The decline of marshlands and the toxic effects of pesticides have resulted in the general decline of this species.

Description. Northern Harriers are slim raptors with long, pointed wings and owllike faces. Though the distinguishing mark of both sexes is a white rump patch, males are pale gray and females are streaked brown. Immature birds have rich russet breasts.

Voice. The call of the Northern Harrier is a shrill, nasal whistle that is common to both sexes.

Habitat. Northern Harriers prefer wet meadows, fresh- or saltwater marshes, and prairie grasslands.

Habits. The hunting routine of the Northern Harrier involves a thorough inspection of the hunting ground, performed by alternately soaring and flapping its wings. The species has been reported to be polygamous. One male sometimes defends the nests of two females in the same area.

Nest and eggs. The female usually builds the nest of sticks, straw, and grasses on or near the ground. The nest materials are often gathered by the male. The 4 to 6 dull white or pale bluish white eggs are incubated mostly by the female for about 24 days. Incubation often begins immediately after the first egg is laid. Young Northern Harriers can fly about 30 to 35 days after hatching.

Food. Though it feeds mainly on field mice, the Northern Harrier also consumes frogs, snakes, and crayfish. A male feeds its mate in midair by dropping food to the female, who flies up from the ground to catch it.

American Kestrel
(Falco sparverius)

The American Kestrel, formerly called the sparrow hawk, could be the most familiar bird of prey in North America. No other raptor is more visible to motorists, for one of its favorite perches is on roadside telephone poles. From this lofty lookout, the little falcon scans the countryside in search of food. Suddenly it strikes out on powerful wings, veering one way and then another. It faces the wind and hovers, body tilted upward, wings beating

American Kestrel

M. Hebard, Jr./VIREO

Ruffed Grouse

Don & Pat Valenti

lightly—food has been sighted. The hawk swoops to the ground to grasp its quarry. Back on the pole, the kestrel grips its prey in sharp talons and tears it apart with its hooked bill.

Description. The American Kestrel is barely larger than a robin—9 to 10 inches long. It is a colorful raptor, with a reddish back and tail, and a black-and-white patterned face. The male's long, pointed wings are blue-gray; the female's wings are a reddish color.

Voice. The call is a shrill, ringing *killy, killy, killy.*

Habitat. The American Kestrel prefers open areas: farmland, edges, roadsides.

Habits. This small falcon often perches on telephone poles or wires, especially at the edge of a field or roadside, where it searches for prey. It is often seen hovering on rapidly beating wings.

Nest and eggs. The breeding season begins as early as March in the far South and as late as May in southern Canada. The American Kestrel typically nests in a natural tree cavity, an abandoned woodpecker hole, or a hand-crafted nesting box. The birds use little or no nesting material. A clutch commonly contains 4 or 5 eggs, which are white covered with small spots of brown. The female undertakes most of the 30-day incubation. This is the only North American falcon that readily nests in a bird box. If you provide one, place it in a tree or tall cactus from 10 to 30 feet above the ground next to an open area.

Food. Insects (especially grasshoppers), mice and other small mammals, frogs, and an occasional small songbird make up the diet of the American Kestrel.

Ruffed Grouse
(Bonasa umbellus)

One of North America's most respected game birds and the state bird of Pennsylvania, the Ruffed Grouse is a smart, wary, and elusive target. Only a skilled grouse hunter takes home one bird for every three shots fired.

Description. The Ruffed Grouse is a red-brown to gray-brown chicken-like bird with a barred, fan-shaped tail; a crest; and black triangular patches or ruffs on each side of its neck. The sexes look alike, though adult males are larger and heavier.

Voice. The Ruffed Grouse is well known for the drumming sounds the male produces to establish territory and attract mates. The bird stands on a log and beats the air with its wings, producing a thumping sound. The beating is slow at first, but ends with

a rapid whirring. Aside from this drumming sound, both sexes utter short clucking calls. A female with its brood gives a loud squeal or whine when surprised.

Habitat. Ruffed Grouse are found in coniferous, deciduous, and mixed woodlands.

Habits. When an alarmed Ruffed Grouse flushes from a woodland, it may make a loud booming noise intended to momentarily shock a potential predator. Anyone who has been surprised by a Ruffed Grouse taking flight with such a roar of wings can attest to the effectiveness of the sound.

Nest and eggs. On the ground in thick woods and dense cover, the female Ruffed Grouse creates a hollow for its nest at the base of a tree, rock, or root; under a log; or in dense brush. On a bed of dry leaves or pine needles it lays 9 to 12 buff eggs—a few of them speckled with brown—at the rate of one a day. The female incubates the eggs for 21 to 24 days. The precocial young can fly to perches a foot above the ground 7 days after hatching.

Food. The chick eats insects, including caterpillars, beetles, grasshoppers, and ants. The adult's diet includes berries, buds, fruit, and seeds.

Northern Bobwhite   Herbert Clarke

Northern Bobwhite
(Colinus virginianus)

No North American game bird is better known and cherished than the Northern Bobwhite, a member of the pheasant family. Hunters in the North call it quail; southern hunters go partridge hunting. In spring this lovely bird endears itself as the well-known happy call of the male's *bob-white* rings across brushy pastures. At that time of year, this wild game bird becomes tamer, often coming into gardens, yards, and nearby fields. Coveys break up into pairs seeking solitary territories for courtship, nest-building, and raising a family.

In the fall, after domestic duties are complete, the birds form coveys of 10 to 15 birds, sometimes more. These coveys typically encompass an extended family group or members of two or three families.

Description. The Northern Bobwhite is medium-sized (8½ to 10½ inches long) and reddish brown above with a short gray tail. The male has a white throat and eye line; the female is buff in these areas.

Voice. This bird calls its name with a clear, whistled *bob-WHITE* or *bob-bob-WHITE.*

Habits. During the nesting season, pairs defend individual territories, but in fall and winter these ground-inhabiting birds feed and roost in flocks. On cold nights coveys roost in circular, heat-conserving groups; birds face outward with tails touching in the center. If a covey is flushed, the birds scatter in all

directions and reassemble later in answer to a gather call uttered by individuals. If undisturbed, the covey may return to the same roosting spot for several weeks.

Nest and eggs. Both sexes contribute to the construction of the bobwhite's well-hidden and well-camouflaged nest, although the female does most of the work. The birds line a hollow in the ground with grasses and usually arch grasses over the top as well. The female lays from 12 to 20 eggs; a typical clutch contains 14 to 16 eggs. The eggs are dull or creamy white and without spots. They are unusually pointed on the small end and fit together closely in the nest. The male and female share incubation duties over the 23- to 24-day period. Each pair raises at least two broods a year; pairs in the South raise more.

Food. The Northern Bobwhite's diet consists of grass and forb seeds, berries, wild fruit, legumes, small insects, and spiders. Bobwhites often come to backyard feeding stations in winter.

California Quail   Peter M. La Tourrette

California Quail
(Callipepla californica)

The California Quail, sometimes called the valley quail, is a common backyard and garden bird that survives and flourishes in climates ranging from arid deserts to cool, wet coastal areas. It is California's most important upland game bird. In years past, the California Quail was remarkably abundant, and reports of 100,000 birds killed for market in a single day were not unusual. Unlike Northern Bobwhites, their eastern counterpart, California Quail are not strictly ground-inhabiting birds. In coveys during the winter and in pairs during the summer, they roost side by side in trees. Winter coveys of 10 to 200 birds break up in late April, and the pairs begin courting. The monogamous males defend their mates, but generally do not defend territories.

Gambel's Quail

Herbert Clarke

Description. The California Quail is blue-gray and brown. The female is duller in color and has a shorter plume than the male. The black plume, which curves forward from the crown over the forehead, is the California Quail's most conspicuous identifying feature. Females are marked with white on the flanks; males have a white stripe across their foreheads and a white necklacelike border on a black throat. Both sexes have a scaled belly.

Voice. The male's spring song is a loud *kah-ah.* The assembly call is three slurred notes: *qus-quer-go,* sometimes interpreted as *come right here.*

Habitat. The California Quail is generally found where winters are mild and precipitation is moderate. Although the bird usually lives close to a permanent water supply, it can forage in many habitats because it eats a variety of seeds and legumes.

Look for flocks in gardens, backyards, and city parks as well as in woodlands, brushy foothills, and stream valleys.

Habits. You are most likely to see California Quail as a small flock of gaily plumed birds making off through chaparral as fast as their swift little legs will carry them. If surprised, a covey may take flight with a loud whir. When forced to fly, they take to the air for only a short distance, then set their wings and glide to the ground.

Nest and eggs. The grassy nests of California Quail have been found from January to October under brush piles; beside rocks, logs, clumps of grass or cactus; and in rocky crannies. For 21 to 23 days, the female incubates 10 to 15 dull white eggs that are splotched with brown.

Food. California Quail eat some insects, but their diet is mostly seeds, acorns, wild berries, and, in spring, the tips of buds.

Gambel's Quail
(Callipepla gambelii)

A bird of the arid regions of the Southwest, the Gambel's Quail was named by Thomas Nuttall in 1843 in honor of his friend William Gambel, an ornithologist who collected birds in southern California. It resembles the California Quail with its jaunty, black plume tipped with a comma or teardrop. The primary difference between the appearance of the two species is the Gambel's black belly patch.

Description. This grayish quail of the southwestern deserts is 10 to 11 inches long and carries a curious topknot plume on its forehead. The male has a black-and-white face, forehead, and throat pattern, plus a black patch on its light, unscaled belly. Both sexes have chestnut flanks broadly streaked with white.

Voice. A single Gambel's Quail sounds a loud, three- or four-note *chi-kwair-cut-cut,* a call similar to the California Quail's. A covey may utter a series of low chuckles or piglike grunts.

Habitat. Gambel's Quail are most often found in desert thickets near water.

Habits. A runner, the Gambel's Quail does not hide in cover like its eastern cousin, the Northern Bobwhite. When flushed, it is a fast flier. Families join together in the fall to form coveys of 12 to 50 birds. They roost in trees, but drop to the ground in the early morning to begin feeding.

Nest and eggs. A nest constructed of grasses is formed in a small depression in the ground known as a scrape, which is usually under a desert tree or shrub. The 10 to 12 slightly glossy pale white or pale buff eggs are incubated by the hen for 21 to 24 days. Often two or more hens lay eggs in the same nest. A Gambel's Quail occasionally takes over an abandoned roadrunner's nest.

Food. Almost any seed, fruit, or green plant in their arid habitat is food for Gambel's Quail, including fruits of cacti. These birds may be attracted to desert backyards with birdseed .

Ring-necked Pheasant

Leonard Lee Rue III

Ring-necked Pheasant
(Phasianus colchicus)

Though the Ring-necked Pheasant is America's leading game bird, it is not a native. The species was successfully introduced in 1881 when 30 birds from China were released in Oregon. Since then, the species has been reintroduced many times in many parts of the continent, and has thrived in the farm areas of southern Canada and across the northern United States.

Description. The male Ring-necked Pheasant is a large bird; it is 30 to 35 inches long with a long, pointed tail and a 32-inch wingspan. The colors of the male are brilliant, from its scarlet wattled face, green head, and white neck ring to the iridescent green-blue and purple feathers that cover the remainder of its body. In contrast, the hen is a dull mottled brown bird with a shorter tail.

Voice. The male's loud, roosterlike crowing, *kork-kok*, is followed by a brief whir of its wings. When flushed, both sexes emit harsh cackles. Hens utter *queep, queep, queep* as an alarm call.

Habitat. Ring-necked Pheasants inhabit grain-growing farmlands where hedges and windbreaks offer additional cover and protection.

Habits. A cunning prey for hunters, a Ring-necked Pheasant prefers to run through standing crops and high grasses until forced to fly. When it does fly, it usually rises abruptly at a severe angle—nearly straight up. This pheasant enjoys dust-bathing at the entrances to woodchuck and fox burrows in the exposed soil.

Nest and eggs. On the ground and usually in the open, a hen Ring-necked Pheasant lines a hollow or scrape with weed stalks, grasses, and leaves to form its nest. The male is polygamous, and leaves the hen to incubate the 10 to 12 brownish olive to buff eggs for 23 to 25 days after the last egg is laid. The precocial chicks can fly to low branches after only 7 days.

Food. Ring-necked Pheasants are fond of any kind of waste grain such as corn, wheat, barley, and oats. They also eat a variety of weed seeds, acorns, and wild berries. In the spring and summer, chicks and adults relish green plants as well as grasshoppers, beetles, caterpillars, and numerous other insects. These pheasants may be coaxed to backyard bird feeders with cracked corn and other birdseeds.

Killdeer
(Charadrius vociferus)

The best known and most widely distributed of all American shorebirds, the Killdeer calls its own name. Not only is it the farmer's constant summer companion, the Killdeer is also the farmer's benefactor; about 98 percent of its diet consists of insects removed from farm fields.

Description. This 9- to 11-inch plover has a white neck ring and two black bands across a white breast. This color scheme, an example of disruptive coloration, allows the bird to blend with its surroundings. Its reddish

Killdeer

J.D. Young/VIREO

rump and upper tail feathers are conspicuous only when displaying or in flight. Its red eye-ring is visible only at close range. Male and female look alike.

Voice. A noisy bird, the Killdeer calls *kill-deeah* and repeats *dee-dee-dee* as it wings across its rural habitat.

Habitat. Often far from water, Killdeer are at home on lawns, in cemeteries, parking lots, cultivated fields, and golf courses.

Habits. When a potential enemy approaches a nesting Killdeer or a pair with young, the birds call loudly and feign broken wings to distract attention from the nest or brood. It is one of the first birds to migrate in the fall and to return to its breeding grounds in early spring.

Nest and eggs. Killdeer do not build nests. They simply lay 4 eggs in a depression or scrape in a field of gravel, pebbles, or grass. Their eggs are pointed and heavily marked with brown spots, scrawls, and blotches; the eggs blend with their surroundings and are almost invisible to the passing human. The pair takes turns incubating for 24 to 26 days until the

eggs hatch. Young are precocial, leaving the nest as soon as they are dry. They fly about 25 days after hatching. Killdeer often raise two broods in one breeding season.

Food. When feeding, a Killdeer alternates between running and standing as it searches for food. Though nearly all of its diet consists of insects gleaned from the fields and lawns where it lives, it also consumes earthworms, crayfish, and weed seeds.

Herring Gull
(Larus argentatus)

The Herring Gull was named for the herring that is part of its varied diet. It is the most abundant and widespread of the gulls of North America, breeding on both coasts and along inland lakes and rivers. These scavengers feed at garbage dumps, wharves, around fishing boats, and behind farm plows.

Herring Gull

O.S. Pettingill, Jr./VIREO

Description. The Herring Gull is a large white bird with a silver back and black wing tips with white spots. It is 22 to 26 inches long with a 54-inch wingspan. Its yellow bill with an orange spot and its flesh-colored legs distinguish the Herring Gull from other large gray-backed gulls in its range. Immatures are a dusky gray-brown during their first year. They become whiter during their second year.

Voice. The Herring Gull's loud, buglelike alarm cries—*hyah . . . hiyah . . . hiyah-hyah* or *yuk-yuk-yuk-yukle-yukle*—carry across great distances. A quieter mewing and plaintive wailing, as well as squeaks, caws, and cries, are also common gull utterances.

Habitat. Coastal islands and shorelines, lakes, rivers, garbage dumps, and salt marshes are the preferred habitats of this gull.

Habits. The flight of the Herring Gull as it soars in search of food is beautiful and graceful. It returns to com-

munal roosts at sunset or lives in a loose flock that moves inland during bad weather. A breeding pair is monogamous and usually mated for life, returning to the same nesting site each year.

Nest and eggs. Herring Gulls nest in colonies anywhere on or near the ground. They build nests of grasses and debris lined with finer grasses and feathers. Their 3 olive drab, heavily marked eggs are incubated by both sexes for 24 to 28 days, a period that starts with the laying of the first egg. The young can fly after about 45 days but require 3 years to mature.

Food. These omnivorous birds eat small fish and glean food from the sewage at boats, waterfronts, and garbage dumps. They crack shellfish by dropping them onto rocks or highways. They also prey on one another's eggs and young as well as those of other species. Inland, they follow farm plows to glean grubs and worms from freshly turned soil.

Laughing Gull

H. Cruickshank/VIREO

Common Tern

O.S. Pettingill, Jr./VIREO

Laughing Gull
(Larus atricilla)

Named for its laughing, wailing calls, the Laughing Gull is a common small gull that summers along the Atlantic and Gulf coasts. Laughing Gulls frequently winter along the Pacific Coast as far south as Mexico.

Description. This coastal gull is small—15 to 17 inches long—with a wingspan of about 42 inches. The Laughing Gull has a black head in summer and a white head with dark smudges in winter. Its back and wings are dark gray with white trailing edges and black wing tips. During their first year, immature Laughing Gulls are very dark with a white rump and black band on their tails. The sexes look alike.

Voice. As its name implies, the Laughing Gull emits a *hs-ha-ha-ha-ha-hash-haah-hsah* as well as a variety of low chuckles.

Habitat. These gulls are usually found along coasts, estuaries, and salt marshes where they feed and nest.

Habits. Never far from water, this gull keeps the company of Brown Pelicans and sometimes steals fish from their pouches. The tables are turned when Laughing Gulls are chased by jaegers and frigatebirds, who force the gulls to surrender food.

Nest and eggs. Laughing Gulls breed in large colonies that can contain thousands of nests. They sometimes share sandy breeding grounds with a colony of terns. The gulls select a site where beach grass or other vegetation conceals their bulky, grassy nests. Three olive brown, spotted eggs are incubated by both sexes for about 20 days.

Food. Laughing Gulls catch small fish near the surface and take others from the pouches of Brown Pelicans. Though not a scavenger like the Herring Gull, a Laughing Gull follows boats in search of food scraps. The Laughing Gull eats the eggs and downy young of other birds. Conversely, other species of gulls pose the greatest threat to the eggs and young of the Laughing Gull. Summer high tides also take a toll when water inundates nesting colonies.

Common Tern
(Sterna hirundo)

The Common Tern inhabits the coasts of North America throughout the warm months. Because these birds are attracted to small fish driven to the surface by larger species, people fishing often look for concentrations of Common Terns as indicators of fertile fishing waters.

Description. Of the four terns that look alike—the Arctic, Forster's, Roseate, and Common—the Common Tern is the most abundant. This bird has noticeably darker wing tips, a shorter tail, and a black tip on its red bill. Its breeding plumage includes a black cap, white rump, gray back and wings, and a pure white tail that is dark along the outer edges. Adults in winter and immature birds have a cap that is only partially black. The Common Tern's legs and feet are as red as its bill.

Rock Dove

Herbert Clarke

Voice. This bird's harsh *kee-arr* has a downward inflection. It also calls *kik-kik-kik* and *kirri-kirri*.

Habitat. Common Terns frequent sand and shell beaches as well as grassy uplands, marshes, and lakes. In some areas they have resorted to nesting on mounds or banks of excavated soil or on piles of synthetic material at construction sites.

Habits. Hovering above the water, Common Terns fold their wings and dart straight down when they sight a small fish. The Common Tern is no different from other terns in its vigorous defense of its nesting colony. But its nesting habitat has been shrinking and its future depends largely on the availability of suitable breeding sites.

Nest and eggs. Common Terns nest in large colonies with other species of terns, skimmers, and gulls. Usually no nest is built; the bird simply hollows a place in sand, shells, or pebbles to support the 3 pale buff to cinnamon-brown spotted eggs. Both sexes incubate the eggs until they hatch at 24 to 26 days. The young can fly about 28 days after hatching.

Food. Common Terns are partial to mackerel, menhaden, and pipefish. They also eat some crustaceans.

Rock Dove
(Columba livia)

The Rock Dove, known throughout North America as the pigeon, was probably the first domesticated bird. About 4500 B.C. humans began to use its meat for food and its homing instinct to carry messages. The Rock Dove was introduced in Virginia and Massachusetts in the early 1600s and is now established in most U.S. cities, towns, and farms. Rock Doves have highly developed instincts and mapping capabilities that help them return to home lofts even if released at great distances from them.

White-winged Dove

Peter M. La Tourrette

Rock Doves are a resilient species. One reason for their resiliency is that their breeding season continues throughout the year.

Description. Selective breeding of Rock Doves in captivity has produced many variations in color, but wild birds retain the ancestral gray with white bars on the wings, white rump, and dark tail tips. Feathers on the sides of the neck are typically iridescent.

Voice. They sing a cooing *co-roo-coo*.

Habitat. Wild Rock Doves originally sought high cliffs and ledges as their homes, but today the birds use tall city buildings for home sites. Rock Doves are common in city streets, parks, gardens, and on farmlands.

Habits. This semi-domesticated bird is often seen on streets and sidewalks pattering busily among pigeon lovers who delight in offering handouts. They also visit backyard feeding stations. Unlike most birds, pigeons and doves can drink without raising their heads.

Nest and eggs. Rock Doves nest either in colonies or singly. Some wild birds nest on cliffs and in caves; as human structures have replaced natural structures, however, most have adopted the ledges of buildings, the undersides of highway bridges, and the

rafters of barns as nest sites. The nest is a shallow, flimsy platform of carelessly arranged grasses, straw, and debris. The pair usually share the incubation of the 2 glossy white eggs for 17 to 19 days. Several broods are raised annually.

Food. In addition to handouts in city parks and at feeding stations, Rock Doves eat waste grain and berries and seeds from grasses and forbs.

White-winged Dove
(Zenaida asiatica)

For the White-winged Dove of the arid Southwest, the quest for water is as important as the quest for food. Some fly more than 25 miles to water in irrigation canals, streams, stock tanks, or backyard water areas. In years when there is an abundance of a favorite food, such as doveweed or sorghum, White-winged Doves descend upon the fields where it grows in flocks of up to a million birds.

Description. The White-winged Dove looks very much like a heavy Mourning Dove but the large white patches on its wings distinguish it. The rounded tail is tipped with large white spots on all but the central feathers. When the bird is in flight, the spots look like a white band across the tail.

Voice. This dove's voice has been likened to a rooster's crow, the Barred Owl's call, a harsh cooing, or notes that might be translated as *Who cooks for you?* Some say that the call is delivered with rather insulting emphasis.

Habitat. The White-winged Dove is a bird of the cactus deserts and mesquite regions. It is also found in oak woodlands, thickets, chaparral, citrus groves, and towns.

Habits. The whirring of the wings of a White-winged Dove in flight distinguishes this southwestern bird. They are gregarious birds, feeding and roosting in flocks, especially after the nesting season. Most of the White-winged Doves that nest in the United States are migratory. The birds may travel up to 1,000 miles to wintering grounds in Mexico and Central America.

Nest and eggs. Often located in a colony with other White-winged Doves, the nesting area is chosen by the male, who coos to attract a mate. After the female has selected a nest site, the male brings twigs over a period of 2 to 4 days, which the female works into a frail platform. The birds share the 14-day incubation of their 2 creamy buff eggs; the male sits on the eggs most of the day, then the female takes over in mid- to late afternoon and stays on the nest until morning. The eggs hatch 24 hours apart.

Food. Seeds and fruit make up the White-winged Dove's diet. Among the preferred foods are the seeds of doveweed and wild sunflowers. They also flock to fields of sorghum and other grains and eat the fruits and seeds of several cacti.

Mourning Dove

J.R. Woodward/VIREO

Mourning Dove
(Zenaida macroura)

Controversy arises often over the Mourning Dove's status in America. Is it a songbird or is it a game bird? Advocates of the former identification favor complete protection of this common and widespread native, which is also known as the turtle dove. But the bird's flight speed—anywhere from 30 to 55 miles per hour—has convinced hunters; the laws in more than 30 states classify the Mourning Dove as a game bird. The fact that the birds are individualists has saved this species from wholesale killing and extinction. Mourning Doves flock to some extent while searching for food in winter, but each pair nests in its own private territory. In contrast, its close relative, the Passenger Pigeon, is now extinct because it could not adapt to human predation—its enormous nesting colonies were accessible to hunters who supplied the market.

Description. The Mourning Dove is gray-brown with a small head, a long, narrow, pointed tail bordered with white, and a wingspan of 17 to 19 inches. The female Mourning Dove is smaller and duller than its mate.

Voice. The Mourning Dove's name comes from its song, a slow, moaning *coo-ah-coo, coo, coo.*

Habitat. This dove is adaptable and lives successfully throughout the United States in open woods, evergreen plantations, orchards, roadside trees, farms, arid mesquite areas and prairies of the West, and mountainous areas of the Southwest.

Habits. After nesting, the birds tend to congregate, often on utility wires, in areas where food, grit, and water are readily available. Their wings produce a whistling sound in flight.

Nest and eggs. A Mourning Dove nest is a platform of sticks, usually 10 to 25 feet above ground in a tree, a shrub, or in vines. The birds line their nests with a sparse scattering of grass, forbs, and rootlets. Two white eggs are incubated by both parents for 13 to 14 days.

Food. This dove eats seeds almost exclusively and searches for weed seeds in meadows and harvested fields. Adults feed nestlings by regurgitating a glandular fluid called pigeon milk. This liquid food is pumped into the mouths of the young from the throats of the parents.

Common Ground-Dove
(Columbina passerina)

The Common Ground-Dove, the smallest dove in North America, is often seen in backyards. Looking very much like a miniature Mourning Dove, it is relatively tame and gleans seeds from under bird feeders. It walks quickly on short legs with head nodding gracefully.

Common Ground-Dove

Description. This dainty little bird is about the size of a sparrow—6 to 6½ inches long. The male's upper body is soft grayish brown, its tail is black and square, its forehead and underparts range from delicate pink to purplish brown. The female is similar, but with pale brownish gray forehead and underparts. When disturbed the birds rise on whistling wings, displaying a flash of red under the wings.

Voice. Common Ground-Doves repeat a soft *woo-oo*, which they deliver with a rising inflection.

Habitat. Within their range, Common Ground-Doves can be found in farmlands, orchards, backyards, open woods, small villages, ranches, cultivated fields, river bottoms, and roadsides.

Habits. A male sometimes settles on a perch—anything from a fence or tree branch to a roof—and coos its mournful call for hours with only an occasional break. In backyards, these birds sometimes become so tame that they do not fly until someone nearly steps on them.

Nest and eggs. On the ground or up to 20 feet above the ground in a tree, the Common Ground-Dove builds a nest of well-matted and twisted plant fibers. They frequently use the abandoned nests of other birds as foundations. After one brood has moved on, the pair often renovates the nest and uses it for subsequent broods. The male and female share the 12- to 14-day incubation of the 2 white eggs.

Food. Common Ground-Doves glean weed seeds and waste grain as they forage on the ground. They also eat insects and some berries.

Greater Roadrunner

Greater Roadrunner
(Geococcyx californianus)

The Greater Roadrunner is a popular, plucky bird, famous for its diet of lizards and snakes and for its speedy running. The roadrunner got its name from its habit of running down the road ahead of horse-drawn vehicles. Observers have clocked its running speed at 15 miles per hour, but there is some speculation that the bird may exceed that speed over short distances.

Description. This is a slender bird about 2 feet long. It has a shaggy crest, a heavy black bill, strong legs, and a tail as long as its body. It is heavily streaked brown with pale blue and red-orange patches behind its eyes.

Voice. The Greater Roadrunner's cooing is dovelike. It starts at a high pitch that becomes lower with each succeeding *coo*. The bird usually utters 6 to 8 *coos*. It also makes a clattering sound with its mandibles.

Habitat. The Greater Roadrunner favors semiarid or dry open country with scattered thickets of mesquite, juniper, pinyons, and other low trees and thick shrubs.

Habits. The Greater Roadrunner's nesting season depends upon the availability of food. Nesting usually occurs in April and May but may be as early as March or as late as September. As part of its mating ritual, the male sings from a perch at dawn, beginning with its bill pointed so far down that it almost touches the bird's toes. With each hoarse, throaty coo, it raises its head a little more until the bill points upward.

Nest and eggs. In a low tree or bush the Greater Roadrunner arranges a foundation of sticks and lines it with leaves, feathers, grass, roots, and an occasional snakeskin or dried bit of cattle or horse manure. Observers believe that the female alone incubates the 3 to 6 white eggs, beginning before the clutch is complete. The eggs hatch in about 18 days.

Food. The Greater Roadrunner's diet of lizards and snakes includes rattlesnakes. It also eats rodents, crickets, grasshoppers, and other insects, seeds and fruit, and some birds' eggs and young.

Eastern Screech-Owl

H. Cruickshank/VIREO

Great Horned Owl

G.C. Kelley/Tom Stack & Associates

Eastern Screech-Owl
(Otus asio)

The call of an Eastern Screech-Owl is not a screech but rather a kind of wail. Though it is strictly nocturnal and rarely observed, the owl's eerie wailing confirms its presence.

Description. The Eastern Screech-Owl is the smallest owl with "horns," or tufts, on its head. Though they look like ears, these feather tufts are simply ornamental. Their ears are at the borders of the feathered eye disks. In the East, this 8- to 10-inch owl may be either reddish or gray. In the West, nearly all are gray. Pairs mate without regard to color.

Voice. This owl's "song" is a tremulous cry, an eerie, ghostly sound that carries well on a still night, often rising at first then descending in a pronounced waver. The superstitious sometimes believe that hearing it is a bad omen.

Habitat. Eastern Screech-Owls live in open woods, woodland edges, and fields with scattered trees. In the Southwest they live in desert areas. It is not unusual to find a Screech-Owl in a suburban yard or garden.

Habits. The Eastern Screech-Owl spends the day hidden in a cavity or in the seclusion of a heavily foliaged tree, often against the trunk. In its search for prey, selection of nest site, and habitat preference, this bird is the nighttime counterpart of the diurnal American Kestrel.

Nest and eggs. The pair does not build a nest. In addition to using natural cavities in many kinds of trees, these owls often take over the abandoned nesting holes of Northern Flickers and Pileated Woodpeckers. Sometimes Eastern Screech-Owls lay their eggs in the crevices of buildings, and they occa-

sionally occupy birdhouses erected for flickers and Wood Ducks. The female lays 4 or 5 eggs in the rotting wood chips and rubble at the bottom of the cavity, then undertakes most of the incubation duties until the eggs hatch. The eggs require about 26 days of incubation.

Food. Eastern Screech-Owls eat almost any available animal food. They prey on insects, crayfish, small mammals and birds, fish, spiders, and reptiles. They swallow their food whole or in large pieces. Later, they regurgitate indigestible parts as pellets.

Great Horned Owl
(Bubo virginianus)

Of all native North American birds, the Great Horned Owl is one of the earliest to nest. The female lays eggs in February, and because the eggs must be protected against freezing, it is not unusual to find the female covered with snow while sitting on the nest. One of the largest and most powerful owls on the continent, the Great Horned Owl is among the very few

Burrowing Owl

H. Cruickshank/VIREO

creatures that includes skunk on its menu. The strong odor lingers after an adult bird brings a skunk back to feed its youngsters; bird-watchers often track the odor when searching for an owl's nest.

Description. The Great Horned Owl is a very large brown owl; an adult is about 2 feet tall with a wingspan of 4 to 5 feet. The only large owl with ear tufts, it has a heavily barred belly and a conspicuous white collar or bib.

Voice. *Hoo, hooo-oo, hoo, hoo* is the familiar resonant sound made by the Great Horned Owl.

Habitat. Great Horned Owls feel at home from wilderness to suburban backyard. Look for them on farms or ranches, in heavy forests, open country, swamps, deserts, city parks, canyons, or by streamsides.

Habits. The Great Horned Owl sometimes hunts during the day, but, typically, it is nocturnal. On silent wings it swoops to snatch its live prey, which can be nearly anything that the big, strong owl is capable of attacking. During the day it roosts near the top of a tree. If a flock of crows or jays discovers it, the flock noisily mobs the owl, forcing it to. fly from its roost.

Nest and eggs. Great Horned Owls generally renovate the nest of some other large bird, such as a Red-Tailed Hawk, Osprey, Great Blue Heron, eagle, or crow. Some use the leaf nests of squirrels; others nest in tree cavities. Except for a few feathers or breast down, Great Horned Owls add little nesting material. The incubation of the 1 to 4 white eggs takes 28 to 35 days. The average clutch contains 2 eggs, and the female usually does most of the incubation—a process that begins after the first egg is laid.

Food. The Great Horned Owl preys on small mammals, especially cottontail rabbits, as well as some waterfowl, songbirds, frogs, and fish.

Burrowing Owl
(Athene cunicularia)

Sharp-eyed bird-watchers often spot the Burrowing Owl while motoring through the wide open areas of the West or in Florida. Standing atop the earthen lookout mound at the entrance to its burrow, this small brown owl bobs up and down when it is alarmed. The owl uses the burrow both as a nest site and as a year-round shelter.

Description. The Burrowing Owl is small (about 9 to 11 inches long) with a round, tuftless head, a stub of a tail, and legs that seem too long. Its wingspread is 20 to 24 inches.

Voice. The Burrowing Owl's song is a series of mournful coos similar to the call of a dove but higher pitched, *coo-coo-roo*, or *co-hoo*. The alarm note, often heard as the owl takes flight or makes a quick dash for the safety of its burrow, is a chattering *cack, cack, cack.*

Habitat. Burrowing Owls are birds of the open country; they prefer deserts, prairies, grassy plains, canal dikes, farms, airports, large vacant lots, or highway edges.

Habits. The Burrowing Owl spends most of the day on the ground. It uses a fence post or the mound at its nesting burrow as a vantage point. The little owl stands erect, but at the sight of anything threatening, it begins bowing and bobbing on its long legs.

Nest and eggs. Using their feet, Burrowing Owls dig a tunnel that ends in a nest chamber. Excavated earth accumulates at the entrance to form the large observation mound. Some Burrowing Owls use the abandoned burrows of prairie dogs or other animals. They usually line their nests with dry cattle or horse manure. The eggs, pure white when laid, soon become stained from contact with the surroundings. The parents share incubation duties until their 5 to 9 eggs hatch after about 3 weeks.

Food. Insects and rodents are the mainstay of the Burrowing Owl's diet. Particularly important are grasshoppers, caterpillars, beetles, and moths. Hunting from twilight until dawn, the Burrowing Owl also preys on mice, gophers, chipmunks, prairie dog young, ground squirrels, and other small mammals. Sometimes it captures and eats small birds and reptiles, including lizards, frogs, toads, snakes, salamanders, fish, scorpions, centipedes, and crayfish.

Whip-poor-will
(Caprimulgus vociferus)

The clear call of a Whip-poor-will is one of the delights of spring nights. The Whip-poor-will is more often heard than seen because it is nocturnal. During the day its protective coloration allows it to blend well with its woodland surroundings. Early American settlers were oblivious to the existence of the Whip-poor-will; they believed the three-syllable call was the voice of the nighthawk. The Whip-poor-will is particularly talkative during the breeding season. Listeners never hear just one *whip-poor-WILL*; the phrase bursts persistently from the bird, sometimes for hours at a time. These oratorios leave no question as to how this member of the Nightjar family got its name.

Description. About 9 or 10 inches long, the Whip-poor-will is a barred brown bird with a small bill and "whiskers." These bristles around the bill increase the functional size of the mouth, making it easier to catch insects while on the wing. The male is identified by a white throat patch and white outer tail feathers. These areas are buff on the female.

Voice. Some people find the *whip-poor-WILL*, repeated over and over again, tiresome. Naturalist John Burroughs once counted 1,088 consecutive calls from a single bird. The calls are often given in rapid succession, about one per second.

Whip-poor-will

Bill Dyer/Lab of Ornithology

Common Nighthawk

O.S. Pettingill, Jr./VIREO

Habitat. This is a country bird that favors woodlands, especially those composed predominantly of hardwoods.

Habits. The Whip-poor-will feeds at night, darting about with mouth agape to catch insects on the wing. If flushed from its hiding place during the day, it flies off looking very much—according to Roger Tory Peterson—like a large brown moth.

Rather than perching crosswise on a branch or a fence rail, Whip-poor-wills sit parallel to their perch.

Nest and eggs. With its natural camouflage, this species can get by without building a nest. The female lays 2 white eggs with brownish gray spots on the ground on top of dead leaves. When it sits on the eggs during the incubation period of about 19 days, it blends with its surroundings to such a degree that it is almost indistinguishable.

Food. Whip-poor-wills are insectivores that dine on moths, beetles, grasshoppers, mosquitoes, crickets, and other flying insects.

Common Nighthawk
(Chordeiles minor)

The Common Nighthawk, often a city dweller, is not actually a hawk; it is a member of the Nightjar family like its country cousin, the Whip-poor-will. Over towns and cities on summer evenings, the Common Nighthawk captures

Chimney Swift

Michael Hopiak/Lab of Ornithology

insects by flying high overhead on long, pointed wings and scooping them into its wide mouth. The Common Nighthawk is often in the company of other evening flyers like swifts and bats. In late August, flocks of nighthawks begin their leisurely migration south; some travel as far as Argentina.

Description. The gray-brown 9- to 10-inch body is accented by a conspicuous white patch on the underside of each wing, which serves as a field mark for observers who see the bird pass overhead. The Common Nighthawk flies gracefully on slender wings and can execute quick and effortless changes of direction in midair.

Voice. While darting about, the Common Nighthawk produces a nasal *peent.* During courtship, the male makes a nonvocal noise as a result of spectacular diving. Flying

high into the air, it executes a power dive, rocketing to earth with partly closed wings. Just as a crash seems inevitable, it spreads its wings and, with a booming noise like a hollow *woof,* zooms upward again.

Habitat. The Common Nighthawk is found in urban and suburban communities throughout most of North America and also lives in open woodlands, farmlands, and plains.

Habits. Observers sometimes spot a Common Nighthawk in full daylight, but the bird is generally nocturnal. From dusk into the night, it flies through the air seeking its insect prey.

Nest and eggs. Flat gravel roofs and railroad rights-of-way provide nesting sites for the nighthawk throughout its range, but the bird's natural nesting site is on the ground in pastures, plains, and burned-over areas. Common Nighthawks do not construct nests. The female incubates the 2 creamy eggs, which are heavily dotted with gray and brown. The eggs hatch after about 19 days.

Food. The insectivorous nighthawk consumes large quantities of beetles, grasshoppers, moths, and other nocturnal insects.

Chimney Swift
(Chaetura pelagica)

The civilization of North America decimated the populations of many birds, but some species have adapted and actually thrived because of the human advance. Chimney Swifts have put the chimneys of human settlements to such good use, for example, that the species has prospered. The birds seldom nest in hollow trees anymore. Chimneys serve not only as nesting sites for single pairs, but migrating hordes of these fast-flying birds find shelter in huge chimneys. Flocks of several thousand birds visit particularly suitable chimneys year after year.

Unfortunately, a nest occasionally meets a disastrous end if a late cold spell necessitates a warm fire below.

Description. Chimney Swifts in flight display their distinctive long, very slender, curved wings and stiff, stubby tails. Their whole bodies are sooty gray, and the sexes look alike. A common description is "a cigar with wings."

Voice. These birds produce a rapid, loud chippering, chattering, or twittering series of notes.

Habitat. Swifts are birds of the air; they rarely perch except in chimneys. They may be found in any type of environment within their range, for their habitat is the open sky.

Habits. Chimney Swifts often fly in threes; two males chase a female during courtship and nesting. The Chimney Swift's wings do not appear to move in unison during flight, but slow-motion photography has proved that the lack of synchrony is an illusion. Inside a chimney the birds cling with sharp claws to the vertical, sooty walls. The short barb-tipped tail helps prop the bird as it perches. Every fall season brings flocks of swifts descending at sunset in a swirling funnel-shaped mass into an enormous chimney to spend the night.

Nest and eggs. The bird uses its glutinous saliva to attach a bracketlike nest cup of twigs to a vertical surface. The surface is usually the inside of a chimney but may be the inside of a hollow tree, open well, cistern, barn, or shed. While in flight, the swift breaks off twigs for the nest with its feet. Working together, a pair takes 3 to 6 days to complete a nest. The female lays one moderately glossy white egg every other day until there are 4 or 5. Both sexes share the job of incubation over the 18- to 21-day period. Occasionally, both occupy the nest at the same time. The quill-covered young instinctively cling to the chimney wall with their sharp claws until their feathers are fully developed.

Food. A Chimney Swift's diet consists entirely of flying insects caught on the wing.

Ruby-throated Hummingbird

Robert A. Tyrrell

Ruby-throated Hummingbird
(Archilochus colubris)

Of the 325 species of hummingbirds in the world, 23 occur in North America. Only one of these, the Ruby-throated Hummingbird, nests in the eastern United States. This mite of a bird is attracted to gardens by brightly colored flowers (red is a favorite color) and by red vials of sugar water. Despite its small size, the Ruby-throated Hummingbird is a strong and fast flier. It has been timed at up to 60 miles per hour. In forward flight the wings beat about 75 times per second and appear as blurs to the human eye. These hummingbirds are often pugnacious, and have been known to attack and drive off birds as large as hawks.

Description. The male is iridescent; the color you see depends on your angle of vision. Reflected light may reveal the fiery red throat and brilliant green back. At certain angles in the shade, how-

ever, the bird may appear black. The female is similarly colored, but its throat is white and its outer tail feathers are tipped with white. Like most hummingbirds, the Ruby-throated Hummingbird is sometimes mistaken for a day-flying sphinx moth.

Voice. With a voice to match its size, the Ruby-throated Hummingbird's song is a series of high-pitched squeaks uttered in rapid succession. In flight, the beating wings create a dull buzzing sound.

Habitat. Ruby-throated Hummingbirds are attracted to mixed woodlands, orchards, and shade trees, and are commonly seen in gardens where nectar and insects are available.

Habits. Hummingbirds can fly forward and backward as they hover near a source of nectar. The male performs a spectacular "pendulum flight" during courtship. While chattering like a mouse, it sweeps before a preening female in deep arcs, displaying its flaming throat to best advantage. The male's devotion is short-lived; it leaves the female the entire responsibility of building the nest, incubating the eggs, and feeding the young.

Nest and eggs. The female creates a tiny cup of plant down, fibers, and bud scales and attaches it to a twig or small branch with spider silk.

It lines it with soft plant down and covers the exterior with greenish gray lichens. The female lays 2 pea-sized, pure-white eggs and incubates them for 14 to 16 days.

Food. Ruby-throated Hummingbirds lap flower nectar with a brush-coated tongue. They also consume tiny insects and spiders. Hummingbird feeders containing sugar water often attract these tiny beauties to backyards.

Anna's Hummingbird

Robert A. Tyrrell

Anna's Hummingbird
(Calypte anna)

Anna's Hummingbird, the common backyard hummingbird of California, is the largest hummingbird in most of its range, and is the only one commonly present in winter. It is also the only hummingbird that nests generally within a single state—California. Like others of its family, this bird can fly backward, forward, upward, and down.

Description. The crown and throat patch of the male Anna's Hummingbird are a brilliant rose-red in good light; otherwise, these parts appear dull black. No other North American hummingbird shows rose-red on the crown. The back of both sexes is a bright green, and a green wash covers the sides. Females are grayish below. They lack red on the crown but their throats usually have flecks of rose-red and are heavily spotted. Young males resemble females.

Voice. A series of squeaky phrases, probably the most definitive of all hummingbird songs, is sung either in flight or from a perch. Both sexes utter *chick*, especially when feeding.

Habitat. Predominately a bird of gardens and backyards, it is also found in canyons, foothills, river bottoms, and occasionally in dense chaparral. After the breeding season the sight of the Anna's Hummingbird in the high coniferous forests is not uncommon.

Broad-tailed Hummingbird

Robert A. Tyrrell

Rufous Hummingbird

Robert A. Tyrrell

Habits. In courtship the male soars high into the air until almost lost from sight, then it dives vertically at great speed toward a female perched in a tree or bush. At the end of the flight the male typically spreads its tail feathers and utters a sharp *peek*.

Nest and eggs. The Anna's Hummingbird is one of the first California birds to nest. They sometimes build their nests as early as December, although nesting usually begins in January or February and continues into late spring. The birds employ a variety of sites—from power lines, to trees, to shrubs in remote wooded canyons—for their nest, which is made of plant down secured with spider silk and lined with fine down and feathers. The nest is large for a hummingbird, and holds 2 white eggs, which are incubated only by the female. A pair usually raises two broods per year.

Food. The favored food of the Anna's Hummingbird includes nectar from blossoms and sap from the bleeding bark of injured trees. Like other hummers, it enjoys sugar water from feeders. The Anna's Hummingbird eats more insects than other North American hummingbirds.

Broad-tailed Hummingbird
(Selasphorus platycercus)

The Broad-tailed Hummingbird is one of the most abundant birds of the Rocky Mountains. The male is easily distinguishable from other species because of the insect-like buzzing of its wings in flight, a sound similar to the shrill notes of a cicada. When hovering near a food source, however, the male's wings hum in true hummingbird fashion.

Description. In general appearance, the 4-inch-long Broad-tailed Hummingbird resembles the Ruby-throated Hummingbird of the East. Its rose-pink throat patch and green crown distinguish the male from other western hummers. The female, green above and buff below, has

bronze specks on its throat and a bit of red on its outer tail feathers.

Voice. The Broad-tailed Hummingbird may utter a high-pitched *chip*, but the sound commonly associated with this species is made by the male's wings.

Habitat. This hummingbird lives in forests, wooded canyons, mountain glades, willow thickets, and in the backyards of Rocky Mountain homes.

Habits. After wintering anywhere from central Mexico to Guatemala, the vividly colored male usually returns to summer breeding grounds in the Rocky Mountains in the middle of May, before the female. When the female arrives, the male courts a mate by performing an aerial display involving a high-speed dive from far above.

Nest and eggs. The Broad-tailed Hummingbird builds a dainty cup of plant down adorned with shreds of bark, bits of leaves, and other plant fibers on a low horizontal branch—usually a willow, cottonwood, alder, juniper, or oak. The 2 tiny white eggs hatch after 14 to 16 days of incubation by the female.

Food. While feeding on the nectar of flowers, the Broad-tailed Hummingbird also eats many of the small insects and spiders that may be on or in the blossoms. Within its

range, it is a common visitor to backyard hummingbird feeders that offer sugar water.

Rufous Hummingbird
(Selasphorus rufus)

The Rufous Hummingbird is probably the most abundant of all western hummingbirds, and it is certainly one of the most spectacularly colored. Like the Allen's Hummingbird, a close relative, the Rufous Hummingbird migrates early; it may already be moving north from its winter home in Mexico by February. Males precede females to breeding grounds as far north as Alaska—farther north than any other hummingbird. By August, the birds begin their return south. The Rufous and Allen's hummingbirds are similar in both size and appearance. The males of both species have flaming scarlet throat patches, though Allen's Hummingbirds have a green back. The females of the two species are indistinguishable from each other.

Description. Rufous Hummingbirds are about 3½ inches long. The male has a reddish back and flaming scarlet throat patch. The female has a greenish back. The female Rufous lacks the scarlet patch, but may have scarlet spots on its throat. In flight, the wings make a quiet humming sound.

Voice. The call note of the Rufous Hummingbird is a soft *chup.* In flight, the male's wingbeats produce a trilling buzz or whistle.

Habitat. During the nesting season, the Rufous Hummingbird inhabits parks, gardens, and woodland edges and openings. During migration, it often frequents mountain meadows. Gardens that include trees and shrubs for cover and flowers and blossoms for nectar provide an ideal environment in both spring and summer.

Habits. The male Rufous Hummingbird performs a towering courtship display by flying in an oval pattern with a rapid sweep downward, then a slower flight upward. The female sometimes joins him, with copulation in the air. Both sexes aggressively defend their nesting and feeding territories.

Nest and eggs. For a nesting site the Rufous Hummingbird chooses the low-drooping branches of conifers, vines, or the roots of upturned trees. The nest consists of a tiny cup of plant fibers, mosses, lichens, and spider silk. The birds cover the cup with lichens and bind it to a limb with spider silk. Rufous Hummingbirds sometimes nest in a loose colony. A clutch usually contains 2 white eggs, which the female incubates for about 2 weeks.

Food. Red flowers are especially attractive to the Rufous Hummingbird for nectar and insects—columbines, penstemons, tiger lilies, paintbrushes of alpine meadows. The Rufous Hummingbird is also attracted to tree sap and favors hummingbird feeders with sugar water.

Belted Kingfisher

H. Cruickshank/VIREO

Belted Kingfisher
(Ceryle alcyon)

Well known to anglers, the Belted Kingfisher livens a streamside with its fishing habits. It dives from a perch to seize a small fish in its powerful bill, or hovers in the air, anywhere from 20 to 40 feet above water, then dives, disappearing under the surface for a few seconds. With a fish in its bill, the bird then rises and returns to perch. There it beats the fish, tosses it in the air, and swallows it headfirst. Of the world's approximately 90 species of kingfishers, only 3 are found in North America: the Green, the Ringed, and the Belted.

Description. A rather large bird, the 11- to 14-inch Belted Kingfisher is bluish gray with a broad white collar, an unkempt-looking crest, a large head, and a heavy, pointed bill. This is one of the few species in which the female boasts brighter colors than its mate. The male has one wide blue band across its white breast; the female Belted has two breast bands, or belts. The second belt is chestnut brown.

Voice. The kingfisher's loud, rattling call is unmistakable: *richety-crick-crick-crick.*

Habitat. Belted Kingfishers always live near water: streams, rivers, lakes, ponds, quarries, and seashores.

Habits. Kingfishers are most often seen perched on a limb or snag overhanging water. From this vantage point, the bird can spot prey in the water below. When it does, it dives, makes its catch, returns to its perch, beats the food against the limb, tosses it into the air, catches it in its bill, and gulps it down headfirst.

Nest and eggs. A pair of Belted Kingfishers spends 2 to 3 weeks excavating their nesting burrow in a bank near water. Taking turns, they burrow inward to create a tunnel about 4 inches in diameter and 3 to 6 feet long. (In rare instances the tunnel may extend up to 15 feet.) At the end the passage widens to a diameter of 10 to 12 inches—this is the domed nesting chamber. If the nest is undisturbed, the pair may use the same burrow year after year. The clutch usually contains 6 or 7 pure white eggs. The male and female share the duties during the 23- to 24-day incubation period.

Food. Small fish are the staple diet of the Belted Kingfisher. It also catches insects, tadpoles, crabs, frogs, toads, and other small aquatic creatures. After eating, it regurgitates the indigestible portions, such as bones and scales, in the form of pellets.

Northern Flicker

J.R. Woodward/VIREO

Northern Flicker
(Colaptes auratus)

One of the best known North American woodpeckers is a rebel in the family ranks. Unlike other woodpeckers, the Northern Flicker does most of its feeding on the ground. Its favorite food? Ants. Birdwatchers in the East used to refer to their flicker as the yellow-shafted flicker; those in the West called it the red-shafted flicker; and the desert species was known as the gilded flicker. Ornithologists have decided that the three birds are one and the same; therefore, all are now called the Northern Flicker. The birds show a marked difference in breeding range and color (though not in pattern), but they prove their relationship by interbreeding where ranges overlap.

Description. The Northern Flicker, at 13 to 14 inches in length, is bigger than a robin. It is adorned with black bars on a brown back, a black crescent on the breast, and a white rump. Males sport a black mustache in the East and a red mustache in the West. In the East, these flickers flash golden yellow under the wings and tail; in the West, the underwing feathers are salmon-red. Adult females have no mustache, but in juvenile plumage, both sexes display mustaches.

Voice. Of their many loud, distinctive calls, the most common call of the Northern Flicker is a series of identical notes: *wicker, wicker, wicker.* The young call *klee-yer.*

Habitat. Northern Flickers prefer open country—particularly farms, orchards, and woodlots—but are also common in city streets and parks.

Habits. Flicker flight is usually undulating—several wingbeats take them upward before they swoop downward with closed wings, and they repeat the cycle over and over again. The bird is built for tree climbing. Although it does most of its foraging on the ground, its awkward hopping indicates that it is not at home there.

Red-bellied Woodpecker

J.R. Woodward/VIREO

Nest and eggs. Both sexes dig the nest hole in a live tree, dead tree, stub, utility pole, fence post, or at the side of a building. A Northern Flicker will sometimes use a birdhouse built to suitable specifications. The female usually lays 6 to 8 glossy white eggs, one per day. Both sexes incubate the eggs during the day; the male takes over at night.

Food. Ants make up about half the flicker's diet. Instead of being barbed, as it is in other woodpeckers, the flicker's tongue is smooth, long, and sticky so that ants adhere to it. In fall the Northern Flicker eats berries, nuts, and seeds. Suet and peanut butter often attract flickers to feeding stations.

Red-bellied Woodpecker
(Melanerpes carolinus)

Ornithologists used to think that the Red-bellied Woodpecker was common only in the southeastern United States. Recently, however, the species has expanded its breeding range as far north as Wisconsin, Michigan, and southern Ontario. The Red-bellied Woodpecker is still an abundant year-round resident in the South, but northern breeders tend to withdraw to a warmer climate in winter. Few other woodpeckers are as easily attracted to backyard feeding stations and, like the Northern Flicker, the Red-bellied Woodpecker is often attracted to birdhouses near suburban homes.

Description. The zebra-striped back and scarlet patch on the head distinguish this bird. The reddish tinge on the belly that gives the Red-bellied Woodpecker its name is usually difficult to see, but its white rump and wing patches are conspicuous in flight. The sexes look alike, except that the female has red only on the nape; on the male, both the crown and nape are red. Juveniles have streaked breasts and gray crowns.

Voice. The Red-bellied Woodpecker's most common call is *churr-churr-churr*, but the species has a variety of other noisy calls. Both sexes drum and tap with their sturdy bills.

Habitat. Bottomland woods, swamps, coniferous and deciduous forests, and shade trees in towns and suburban gardens are ideal habitats.

Habits. This woodpecker makes its presence known throughout the day with noisy calls and persistent drumming. Of the Woodpecker family the Red-bellied is one of the tamest around humans.

Nest and eggs. Both sexes—but mostly the female—dig out a nesting cavity in a live tree (the cabbage palm is a favorite nest site in Florida), a dead tree, a utility pole, or even a wooden building. They might choose the deserted nesting hole of another woodpecker or, frequently, a birdhouse. The female lays one pure white egg each day until the clutch of 4 or 5 is complete. Both sexes incubate the eggs for about 2 weeks. In the North a pair usually produces one brood per year; in the South parents rear two broods each year.

Food. The diet of the Red-bellied Woodpecker consists primarily of vegetable matter, but the bird occasionally gleans beetles and insect larvae from tree bark. The Red-bellied Woodpecker sometimes forages for food on the ground and avails itself of suet, peanut butter, sunflower seed, and cracked corn at feeding stations.

Red-headed Woodpecker
(Melanerpes erythrocephalus)

Loss of habitat and competition from European Starlings for nesting cavities have reduced the number of Red-headed Woodpeckers. This is especially true in the Northeast, but these birds are not abundant in any part of their range. This woodpecker is somewhat migratory, particularly in regions where the winter food supply is not dependable.

Description. The entire head and throat of this woodpecker is red. The 8½- to 9½-inch body has clearly contrasting areas of black and white. Characteristic patches of white on the dark wings and tail show up in flight. Adult males and females are indistinguishable, but young birds have brown heads, which they retain until the fall molt.

Voice. A common call note is a loud *queer, queer.*

Habitat. Farmlands, open woods, bottomlands, gardens, parks, and highway shoulders provide a habitat for the Red-headed Woodpecker. In towns and cities dead or dying trees in orchards or gardens seem to attract the species. With natural habitat constantly diminishing, individual pairs have adopted telephone poles for perching spots and even for nesting cavities.

Habits. The Red-headed Woodpecker forages on the ground and in shrubs. Unlike many other woodpeckers, it seldom bores into live trees for insects, although it occasionally does so in dead wood. Like its close relative

Red-headed Woodpecker

the Red-bellied Woodpecker, it stores food—especially acorns—in handy cavities: the cracks of telephone poles, fence posts, tree cavities, and crevices in tree bark. Much of this stored food is never used.

Nest and eggs. The nesting pair excavates a hole 8 to 80 feet above ground in a live tree, dead stub, utility pole, or fence post. They do not add nesting material. The female lays from 4 to 7 white eggs; the average clutch contains 5. Parents share the 2-week-long task of incubation. This species shuns birdhouses.

Food. Insects constitute about 50 percent of this bird's diet. It also eats corn, acorns, berries, wild and cultivated fruit, and the sap from wells drilled by sapsuckers in tree trunks. These birds come to bird feeders for suet, bread, sunflower seeds, nuts, and cracked corn.

Yellow-bellied Sapsucker
(Sphyrapicus varius)

Other woodpeckers occasionally drill holes for tree sap, but the Yellow-bellied Sapsucker is the only one that uses sap as a major source of food. With its bill the sapsucker drills holes just through the bark in a characteristic pattern of horizontal rows. Many other species of birds, small mammals, and insects feed on the sap in these "sapsucker wells." Homeowners are often ambivalent about sapsuckers. The birds are entertaining, but their drilling may make yard and garden trees vulnerable to fungal organisms and harmful insects. They may also disfigure prized ornamentals.

Yellow-bellied Sapsucker

John Gerlach/DRK Photo

Hairy Woodpecker

J.R. Woodward/VIREO

Description. The Yellow-bellied Sapsucker is a medium-sized bird with a red crown and throat. The sexes look alike, except that females in the North and East have white chins and throats. In both sexes, the underside is dull yellow, the body is mottled black and white, the wings have white patches, and the face has two horizontal white stripes.

Voice. The sapsucker makes a mewing cry that resembles the mew of a cat. It also uses a downward slurring *cheerrr.* Drumming by both sexes starts with a rapid thumping and ends with a number of disconnected taps.

Habitat. Yellow-bellied Sapsuckers prefer openings in mixed coniferous-deciduous forests and wooded river bottoms. They are especially attracted to aspen groves.

Habits. This noisy bird is conspicuous though shy on its northern breeding grounds, but is quiet and secretive during migration and in winter. Males precede females to their nesting grounds by about a week. The first migrants to arrive in March or April occasionally find snow on the ground.

Nest and eggs. Both sexes excavate a gourd-shaped hole 8 to 40 feet above ground in a live tree or stub. They add no material to the cavity before the female lays the clutch that contains 4 to 7 white eggs. Both sexes incubate the eggs for 12 to 13 days.

Food. Tree sap is the major source of food for Yellow-bellied Sapsuckers, but they also eat insects, larvae, fruit, and berries. Insects attracted to sap wells are eaten along with the sap. Suet, peanut butter, and occasionally sugar water from hummingbird feeders attract this species to feeding stations.

Hairy Woodpecker
(Picoides villosus)

A familiar and welcome visitor to backyard bird feeders across North America, the Hairy Woodpecker is especially fond of beef suet. Using its two feet and sturdy tail as a tripod, the Hairy Woodpecker rests comfortably against the tree bark to tap off a bit of suet, or to move effortlessly up and down the trunk. Wherever it is found, the spunky Hairy Woodpecker is a year-round resident, active even on the most frigid winter days.

Description. Like a larger version of its cousin the Downy Woodpecker, the Hairy Woodpecker has black wings accented with white spots, a white back, black tail, and white underparts. Like the Downy, only the male has a red spot on the back of its head. Close observation, however, reveals that the red spot on the Hairy Woodpecker's head is divided; the Downy Woodpecker's is in one piece. Also, in proportion to its body, the Hairy Woodpecker's bill is larger and heavier than that of the Downy Woodpecker.

Voice. The Hairy Woodpecker often utters a sharp *peek* and a rattling call reminiscent of the kingfisher's voice. Its "song," however, is not a vocalization, but a long, rolling drumming made with its bill on a tree trunk. Both sexes drum.

Habitat. Found in deciduous and coniferous woodlands, wooded swamps, river bottoms, and mountain forests, the Hairy Woodpecker is also a visitor to backyards with mature trees—especially if they offer feeding stations with suet. The Hairy is not as common in most backyards as the Downy Woodpecker.

Downy Woodpecker

J.R. Woodward/VIREO

Habits. The Hairy Woodpecker's habits are similar to those of the Downy Woodpecker, but it is generally much shyer. Its typical woodpecker flight is graceful and deeply undulating—several wingbeats take it upward before it swoops downward with closed wings, a cycle that repeats over and over again. The Hairy Woodpecker roosts in cavities that it excavates. Hammering into tree bark with its strong bill, it finds wood-boring insects, which comprise up to 40 percent of its diet.

Nest and eggs. Both parents spend from 1 to 3 weeks digging a cavity in a tree or stub, usually 5 to 30 feet above ground. They add no nesting material to the wood chips that fall into the nesting hole. The female Hairy Woodpecker lays 4 pure-white eggs on the chips. The male and female share nest duties in the 11- to 12-day incubation period.

Food. The Hairy Woodpecker consumes great numbers of insects, especially wood borers. It also eats tree-dwelling beetles, ants, and spiders. Occasionally, it eats berries and nuts such as acorns and hazelnuts. At backyard feeding stations, the bird eats beef suet, peanut butter, and sunflower seeds.

Downy Woodpecker
(Picoides pubescens)

When summer nesters go south in the fall, a handful of hardier birds remains in the North to forage for winter food. One of these is the smallest of North American woodpeckers, the Downy Woodpecker. It is our best-known woodpecker, probably because it is not as shy as other members of its tribe. The Downy Woodpecker is a regular visitor to the beef suet at winter backyard feeding stations. On cold nights the Downy insists on a warm bed in the form of a cavity, much like a nesting hole, which it drills and chisels for a roosting place.

Description. The Downy Woodpecker looks like a 6½- to 7-inch version of the Hairy Woodpecker. Though smaller, it has the same white back,

white spots on black wings, and barred outer tail feathers. The male has a red patch on the back of its head; the female does not.

Voice. A common call is a flat *pick*, which is not as loud and sharp as the *peek* of the Hairy Woodpecker. In courtship, males often emit a loudly repeated *wick, wick, wick, wick*. In late winter and early spring, both sexes drum in courtship and territorial declarations.

Habitat. Most areas with many trees, including suburban gardens, city parks, orchards, bottomlands, and small woodlots, appeal to Downy Woodpeckers, but they prefer deciduous trees.

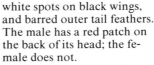

Eastern Kingbird

J.D. Young/VIREO

Habits. The Downy Woodpecker is well equipped for seeking its livelihood. Aided by a sharp, strong tail, which it uses like a campstool, it searches for food while clinging to tree trunks. Its skull is thick and adds great force to its hammering. Its bill is pointed like a carpenter's chisel. The bird can extend its tongue about 2 inches beyond the end of the bill. Sharp barbs lie on the tongue, so even deeply hidden wood borers do not escape.

Nest and eggs. Both sexes—but mostly the female—excavate a nesting cavity in a tree, stump, stub, fence post, or in rotting wood, from 3 to 50 feet above ground. By day both sexes incubate the clutch of 3 to 6 white eggs; the male assumes the responsibility at night. The incubation period lasts 12 days. This species does not favor birdhouses.

Food. A Downy Woodpecker's diet is primarily grubs, insects, and insect eggs from the bark of trees. It also eats nuts and berries. Feeding stations with suet, peanut butter, and sunflower seeds attract these birds.

Eastern Kingbird
(Tyrannus tyrannus)

The Eastern Kingbird, like its western counterpart, the Western Kingbird, is a member of the Tyrant Flycatcher family. Bird-watchers often see it perched upright on a utility line or a fence post, keeping a constant watch for passing insects. When an insect flies by, the kingbird darts out and snares it in typical flycatcher fashion—a quick dart into the air that often involves complicated maneuvers, and a loud snap of the bill as it seizes its prey. Then the bird returns to its perch on fluttering wings and fans its tail as it alights.

Description. Like most flycatchers, the color of the Eastern Kingbird is somewhat dull. A white throat, breast, and belly are topped with blackish gray upperparts. The fanlike tail is banded with white at the tip. The Western Kingbird is similar, but has a yellow abdomen. In addition, the western species lacks a white band on the tail tip, but it does have white outer tail feathers.

Voice. The Eastern Kingbird's song is a rollicking stutter of *pe-cheer-ry* or *dzee-dzee-dzeet.* The call note is a nasal *tzeeb.*

Habitat. The Eastern Kingbird can adapt to various habitats. Throughout much of its range, it is a bird of orchards and open farm country. The species also inhabits woodland edges, fencerows, river bottoms, and parks, but it avoids heavy forests.

Habits. The Eastern Kingbird seems to be fearless. Without hesitation it harasses a hawk or crow that has invaded its territory, even though the interloper is many times larger. According to reports, one bird repeatedly attacked a low-flying airplane. For the winter season, it migrates to South America as far as Bolivia and Peru.

Nest and eggs. The male and the female construct the nest, which is a bulky cup of weeds, grasses, and moss lined with soft plant down and fine grass. They often place the nest well out on a tree limb, frequently over water. Their 3 to 5 eggs are creamy white and heavily spotted with brown and lavender. The female incubates the clutch alone during the 12- to 13-day incubation period.

Food. The Eastern Kingbird usually feeds upon flying insects that it catches on the wing. Occasionally it finds beetles and grasshoppers on the ground.

Great Crested Flycatcher
(Myiarchus crinitus)

Naturalist John Burroughs dubbed the Great Crested Flycatcher the "wild Irishman" of the flycatchers because of the fierce and aggressive manner in which it rules its woodland domain. From its lofty perch—often a dead stub—the bird may startle a human intruder and often momentarily silence other creatures with its shrill *wheerp!*

Great Crested Flycatcher

C.H. Greenewalt/VIREO

Description. The Great Crested Flycatcher has a gray throat and breast and a sulfur-yellow belly. Its cinnamon wings and tail are topped by a tousled gray crest.

Voice. The Great Crested Flycatcher calls a loud *wheerp! wheerp! wheerp!* or *wheep! wheep! wheep!*

Habitat. A woodland dweller, the Great Crested Flycatcher especially favors those woods that offer large shade trees, wooded borders, abandoned orchards, swamps, and parks.

Habits. Like its fellow flycatchers, the Great Crested Flycatcher darts out to catch flying insects that pass its perch. An aggressive defender of its territory, the male fights off other males, sometimes engaging in aerial combat. This species spends the winters anywhere from Mexico to Colombia.

Nest and eggs. The Great Crested Flycatcher raises its family in a natural tree cavity or an abandoned woodpecker hole. A breeding pair will occasionally use a birdhouse. The nest is a bulky mass of twigs, feathers, leaves, and other debris. Both the male and the female share in its construction and line it with soft materials. Nearly every nest includes a shed snakeskin, although sometimes the birds settle on a piece of cellophane instead. Nest construction may take up to 2 weeks. Then the female lays from 4 to 8 whitish eggs with brown and purple streaks. She keeps the eggs warm during the 13- to 15-day incubation period.

Food. The bird darts out from its perch to seize flying insects on the wing. The Great Crested Flycatcher also eats insects and bugs that it finds in the crevices of tree bark or on the ground. Sometimes it eats wild berries.

Eastern Phoebe

C.H. Greenewalt/VIREO

Black Phoebe

Peter M. La Tourrette

Eastern Phoebe
(Sayornis phoebe)

The Eastern Phoebe is not likely to visit a feeding station, but it does frequent suburban yards and farms. One of the hardiest of the North American flycatchers, it returns to the North from its wintering grounds in the southeastern United States and Mexico in March or April and remains long after many other birds have gone.

Description. Its gray-brown upperparts and white underparts, its black bill, and the absence of eye-rings or distinct wing bars distinguish the Eastern Phoebe from other flycatchers. Its habit of wagging its tail is this bird's most obvious field mark.

Voice. Eastern Phoebes repeat their name again and again: *FEE-bee* or *fee-BEE.*

Habitat. These birds prefer a waterside habitat that might include wooded country roads with bridges over small streams. In the nesting season they seek barns, sheds, and rocky ravines.

Habits. The Eastern Phoebe has favorite perches at vantage points throughout its territory. Perched upright on a dead limb or twig, constantly and conspicuously bobbing or wagging its tail, it searches for flying insects. The Eastern Phoebe darts out swiftly, snaps up a bug, twists gracefully in midair, and sails back to its perch.

Nest and eggs. The Eastern Phoebe's nest is large and well constructed of mud, weeds, grasses, and plant fibers and lined with finer grasses and hair. It is built on a shelflike projection—a windowsill, the rafter of a shed, or a girder under a bridge—or is plastered to the side of a rocky ledge or a concrete or wooden wall. The female usually builds the nest by itself, then lays 5 eggs in it. Most of the eggs are white, though a couple may be sparsely spotted. The eggs hatch after 15 to 16 days of incubation by the female. Parents usually raise two broods per year. Youngsters leave the nest about 3 weeks after hatching.

Food. In spring, summer, and early fall, the Eastern Phoebe's diet consists almost entirely of insects. In winter its diet is vegetarian—sumac fruits, poison-ivy berries, and various other fruits and berries.

Black Phoebe
(Sayornis nigricans)

The Black Phoebe, a flycatcher, is a year-round resident in valleys and coastal plains of the Southwest. In harsher climates, especially at high altitudes, it sometimes migrates south for the winter. This phoebe rarely roams far from water; garden pools, water-filled roadside ditches, and small ponds attract it. Although the Black Phoebe and Say's Phoebe occupy much the same range, each shows a preference for its own particular type of habitat. The Say's Phoebe lives in dry, barren country, in sagebrush plains, and around bluffs and cliffs.

Eastern Wood-Pewee

Description. The Black Phoebe is the only flycatcher with a sooty black breast, head, and upperparts and a sharply contrasting white belly. The color pattern is similar to that of a junco, but the Black Phoebe's thin, flattened bill and its behavior distinguish it.

Voice. The Black Phoebe sings a thin, high-pitched repetition of two pairs of notes: *ti wee, ti wee* or *pi-tsee, pi-tsee*. The call note is a sharp *tsip* or *tsee*.

Habitat. Civilization has contributed immeasurably to the Black Phoebe population by providing many more water areas than existed naturally. Lowland marshes, mountain streams, lakes, and other natural habitats still attract this bird, but ranch stock tanks, irrigation ditches, garden pools, canals, and reservoirs have expanded the amount of suitable territory.

Habits. Like most flycatchers, the Black Phoebe is a solitary bird except when nesting. It perches in an erect posture, slowly raising and lowering its tail when hunting insects. The bird darts from fences, stubs, and the shaded lower branches of trees and other low perches to snap up bugs close to the ground or on water surfaces. A careful listener will hear the click of the bird's bill as it captures wild bees, wasps, beetles, flies, and other airborne insects.

Nest and eggs. Black Phoebes plaster their mud nests to rocky cliff faces, concrete walls, wooden buildings, bridges, old wells, and other structures. They often choose a site that offers overhead protection. When building, the birds mix mud with hair, grasses, and forbs to construct the nest shell, then line the shell with wool, hair, fine roots, strips of bark, and, occasionally, feathers. Except for the last egg laid, which has tiny dustlike spots, the 3 to 5 eggs are white. The female incubates the eggs for 15 to 17 days. Black Phoebes typically produce two broods per year, and sometimes three.

Food. The Black Phoebe's diet is typical of phoebes; it consists almost entirely of insects.

Eastern Wood-Pewee
(Contopus virens)

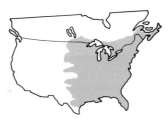

An insistent yet plaintive *pee-o-wee* whistled from high in a shade tree announces the presence of this nondescript little member of the Tyrant Flycatcher family. After its return to northern breeding grounds in spring until late summer, the Eastern Wood-Pewee's sweet, slow, gliding song fills the air. "The sweetest, most soul-searching voice in nature," is the way one naturalist described it. Ornithologist Frank Chapman wrote, "The notes are as musical and restful, as much a part of Nature's hymn as the soft humming of a brook."

Description. The Eastern Wood-Pewee is 6 to 6½ inches long—about the size of a sparrow. Olive brown above and whitish below, its two white wing bars distinguish it from the Eastern Phoebe. Unlike other small flycatchers, the Eastern Wood-Pewee lacks a conspicuous eye-ring. It is impossible to distinguish the Eastern Wood-Pewee from the Western Wood-Pewee by sight in the field. Their songs, however, are quite different. The Eastern Wood-Pewee's nasal *peeer* is similar to the Common Nighthawk's *peent*.

Voice. The song that gives the Eastern Wood-Pewee its name is a plaintively whistled *pee-o-wee*.

Habitat. A wooded area with mature trees is a promising habitat for the Eastern Wood-Pewee. Orchards, groves, parks, backyards, mature forests, and woodlots are also attractive to the species.

Habits. By April or May the Eastern Wood-Pewee has returned from its winter home in Central and South America to its breeding grounds in the eastern United States and southern Canada. Like other flycatchers, it darts out from its perch to catch passing insects.

Nest and eggs. The shallow, dainty nest of the Eastern Wood-Pewee is a masterpiece of bird architecture. Constructed to resemble a natural growth on the horizontal limb to which it is attached, it is built of mosses, rootlets, plant fibers, and fine grasses; covered with lichens; and reinforced with spider silk. Three white eggs, wreathed at the large end with brown spots, make up the usual clutch. The 12- to 13-day incubation of the eggs is entirely the responsibility of the female.

Food. Like other flycatchers, the Wood-Pewee feeds on insects—especially flying bugs—and occasionally eats wild berries.

Violet-green Swallow

Herbert Clarke

Tree Swallow

Herbert Clarke

Violet-green Swallow
(Tachycineta thalassina)

Sleek and slender, with long, pointed wings, the Violet-green Swallow darts gracefully through the air, catching insects as it goes. Where its range overlaps that of the Tree Swallow, bird-watchers might easily confuse the two species. To tell the difference, look for the two conspicuous white rump patches that nearly meet over the base of the tail of the Violet-green Swallow.

Description. About sparrow-sized (5 to 5½ inches long), this streamlined bird is glossy dark green and purple above and bright white below. Its short bill is quite wide and is well adapted to catching insects in flight. The pointed wings are so long that the wing tips extend to the tail tip when the bird sits. Juvenile birds are brown in the areas that are green and purple on the adults.

Voice. Twittering best describes the sound made by the Violet-green Swallow. The song is a rapid, thin *tseet, tseet, tseet* or *chit-chit-chit.*

Habitat. Look for the Violet-green Swallow in open forests, parks, towns and villages, farms, cliffs, canyons, and suburbs.

Habits. Like other swallows, the Violet-green spends much of its time in the air. A skillful flier capable of split-second maneuvers, it catches insects on the wing. During courtship, the male flies about before daylight singing *tseet, tseet, tseet.* When the nesting season ends, Violet-green Swallows gather into large flocks before their fall migration southward. During this time, Violet-green Swallows often perch in great numbers on utility wires.

Nest and eggs. Though they sometimes nest in colonies, Violet-green Swallows are just as likely to nest singly. They choose natural tree cavities, abandoned woodpecker holes, birdhouses, and holes in buildings or cliffs. The female incubates the white eggs—usually 4 or 5—for 13 to 14 days.

Food. Insects form a complete diet for the Violet-green Swallow. The bird snaps them up in midair while flying over land or water.

Tree Swallow
(Tachycineta bicolor)

Like many other species that nested in natural cavities before backyard bird-watching became such a popular pastime, the Tree Swallow has adapted readily to birdhouses—especially ones located near water. Tree Swallows breed from April into the summer months. They are quite tolerant of close neighbors of their own species and are, in fact, so colonial that two pairs sometimes occupy boxes in the same tree. This is the only swallow that habitually winters in the southern United States. Tree Swallows are among the first birds to arrive back in the North from the southern United States and Central America. Great flocks sometimes starve to death when caught in an unexpected freeze.

Barn Swallow

Herbert Clarke

Description. Adults are blue-green-black above and white below. Youngsters have dusky brown backs and incomplete breast bands.

Voice. A sweet, liquid twitter—a variation of *weet, trit, weet*—is the song of the Tree Swallow. The call note is *cheet* or *silip*.

Habitat. Large and small bodies of water, marshes, or wet meadows are essential to Tree Swallows.

Habits. The rapid wingbeats and slightly flickering flight of this swallow are distinctive. It sails with shoulders forward and wing tips pointed upward. Late summer and fall flocks may contain thousands of birds.

Nest and eggs. A Tree Swallow pair may choose an old woodpecker hole, a fence post, a rural mailbox, a hole in a building, or a birdhouse (even a large Wood Duck box) for a nest site. The nest itself is an accumulation of dry grasses hollowed in the center or a corner. The female lays 4 to 6 pure-white eggs. Tree Swallows line the nest cup with feathers (usually white chicken feathers), which the female often places so the curved tips curl over the eggs.

Food. Most of their diet consists of insects caught on the wing. In winter, 30 percent of their food is fruits and berries. Tree Swallows seem to especially enjoy bayberries.

Barn Swallow
(Hirundo rustica)

When early settlers discovered this bird's affinity for nesting in barns, they added the word *barn* to the simple European name *swallow*. The westward spread of farming helped the bird extend its range in America. A farmer who discourages Barn Swallows from using a barn as a nest site is ill advised, for no feathered neighbor is a more useful friend. To satisfy their exclusive diet of insects, Barn Swallows sweep the countryside from morning to night, gleaning a livelihood from a farm's unwelcome guests. Year after year, Barn Swallows return to the same nest sites. In spring, they leave their winter home in South America and fly north. Some travel as far as Alaska.

Description. The Barn Swallow's dark blue back contrasts with cinnamon-buff below. The throat is dark, and the tail is deeply forked with white spots. Females and immature birds look like males but with duller color.

Voice. Barn Swallows usually utter a series of twittering notes—*kittick, kittick*—in flight. The male twitters constantly in its courtship flight with the female.

Habitat. Barn Swallows are attracted to open country that lies near water. Look for them around meadows, parks, golf courses, pastures, large lawns, and agricultural fields. During migration they sometimes forage on ocean beaches.

Habits. Barn Swallows are tireless fliers and may range far on their daily hunts. They drink and bathe on the wing, and dart at high speed in and out of the small openings of their nest sites. Its large mouth and short, flat, triangular bill are adapted to its habit of feeding on the wing.

Nest and eggs. Barn Swallows often nest in colonies within or under barns, sheds, bridges, wharves, boathouses, and culverts. Constructed of mud and straw, the nest is plastered to beams, upright walls, or eaves, and is profusely lined with feathers. The birds seem to prefer white feathers as a lining material. They will often repair old nests for a new brood. A typical clutch contains 4 or 5 white eggs with brown spots. Both sexes incubate the eggs and change places on the nest often during the day.

Food. The Barn Swallow is exclusively insectivorous.

Cliff Swallow

D. & M. Zimmerman/VIREO

Cliff Swallow
(Hirundo pyrrhonota)

Before Europeans settled in America and built barns and sheds, Cliff Swallow was an appropriate name for this bird, for it built its mud nest on the perpendicular sides of rocky cliffs. Today a more suitable name for the Cliff Swallow might be "Eaves Swallow," for this colorful bird has largely forsaken its traditional haunts for the eaves of buildings, barns, sheds, and even houses.

Description. A pale reddish rump and almost square tail distinguish this species from other swallows. Most have blackish throats and pale foreheads. A southwestern race has a cinnamon forehead like the Cave Swallow, but the throat is dark.

Voice. The Cliff Swallow often produces a rapid twittering chatter in flight. The call is a low *chrrr.*

Habitat. The Cliff Swallow prefers farmlands, villages, and cliffs, especially cliffs near fresh- or saltwater areas. Like the Barn Swallow, the Cliff Swallow requires much open country over which to hunt for its insect food.

Habits. Cliff Swallows are extremely social. They nest close, feed together in wheeling and crisscrossing flocks, and preen together. After nesting and during migration, they perch by the hundreds on telephone wires.

Nest and eggs. Nests are gourd-shaped structures built of mud and clay pellets which the birds plaster to the sides of buildings or under bridges. The side of a cliff is the traditional nest site, but modern birds seem to prefer human architecture. Hundreds of nests form dense colonies on the side of a single barn. One Wisconsin farmer counted 2,015 Cliff Swallow nests on his barn. The nest chamber is globular and extends forward into a tubular entrance tunnel. Built by both parents, the nest is sparsely lined with grasses, hair, and feathers. The 4 or 5 white eggs are spotted with brown. Both parents incubate the eggs until they hatch after about 15 days. Parents sometimes raise two broods per year.

Food. The Cliff Swallow feeds almost entirely on insects caught on the wing.

Purple Martin
(Progne subis)

Every spring the Cliff Swallows that return from South America to San Juan Capistrano Mission have received widespread publicity. Other birds, like the Purple Martin, maintain just as rigid an itinerary. Year after year, the Purple Martins return on schedule from South America to locations where they have found birdhouses in the past. Males usually arrive in April, ahead of the females. But the early arrival sometimes proves fatal; entire flocks may starve if cold, prolonged rains or unexpected snowstorms eliminate the insects these birds depend on for food. The Purple Martin has been a well-liked bird for many generations. In the past Indians attracted them by hanging hollow gourds for nesting from the ends of crossed sticks on a pole, a practice that is still common in the South. Today bird fanciers set up special martin houses in gardens and backyards throughout its breeding range.

Description. The Purple Martin is the largest North American swallow. Adult males are purple-black above and below and darker on the wings and tail. No other swallow has a black belly. The females and immature Purple Martins have gray or white underparts.

Purple Martin

Herbert Clarke

Blue Jay

J.R. Woodward/VIREO

of the best-known birds in the eastern United States.

Description. Blue above with paler underparts, the Blue Jay carries a saucy blue crest and a black necklace. The Blue Jay's wings and tail are barred with white.

Voice. A noisy *jay, jay* or *jeer, jeer* is the Blue Jay's familiar call, but a bell-like double note, *tull-ull,* is also characteristic. The Blue Jay can also imitate the calls and cries of other birds. Its imitation of a Red-shouldered or Red-tailed Hawk has fooled bird-watchers as well as birds at feeding stations.

Habitat. Open woods, parks, farmlands with trees, yards, and gardens appeal to Blue Jays.

Habits. After nesting, Blue Jays form noisy flocks that roam woods or residential areas and call to one another. Nothing arouses a flock of Blue Jays more than the sight of a roosting owl during the day. With a great uproar the shrieking blue attackers descend upon and harass the luckless owl. The noisy Blue Jay is surprisingly quiet and secretive around its nest.

Nest and eggs. The Blue Jay's nest is bulky but well hidden 5 to 50 feet above ground in a crotch or the outer branches of a tree. Both sexes contribute to the structure of thorny twigs, bark, mosses, string, and leaves and line it with rootlets. Incubated by both parents, but mostly by the female, the 4 or 5 eggs hatch in 17 to 18 days. Blue Jay eggs occur in two distinct colors; most eggs are olive, but some are buff marked with dark brown and grayish spots. They often look like miniature American Crow eggs.

Food. About 75 percent of the Blue Jay's diet is fruit, grain, and nuts. The remainder consists of insects and small animals. The Blue Jay's fondness for the eggs of other birds has gained it a reputation as a nest robber. Sunflower seeds and suet attract Blue Jays to feeding stations.

Voice. In flight Purple Martins utter a pleasant twittering sound. A more complex song is a long gurgling that begins with descending notes and ends with a prolonged twitter.

Habitat. The ideal habitat for a Purple Martin is a grassy, open streamside, a river bottom, a marsh, or a forest opening near a lake or pond. The best garden habitats include lawns and meadows that are near large bodies of water.

Habits. Purple Martins dart about, turning quickly on rapidly beating wings. Short glides alternate with rapid flapping. They usually nest in colonies. The natural cavities in trees and cliffs were the birds' original dwellings. Today, Purple Martins accept birdhouses that range from single dwellings to elaborate "apartment houses" with 200 or more compartments.

Nest and eggs. Purple Martins frequently build their nests in birdhouses set 15 to 20 feet above ground on poles. A pair gathers grasses, twigs, bark, paper, leaves, and string for the outer nest, and lines the egg cup with fine grasses and fresh green leaves. A clutch usually contains 4 or 5 slightly glossy white eggs. The female incubates the eggs by itself. When the young fly, some 4 weeks after hatching, the colony leaves the nesting house for the year.

Food. Purple Martins are entirely insectivorous.

Blue Jay
(Cyanocitta cristata)

The Blue Jay certainly makes more than its share of noise wherever it goes, and humans do not appreciate some of its habits. Nevertheless, this big, bold, dashing bird is a most colorful addition to any feeding station. The Blue Jay has adapted well to civilization and is abundant in backyards, especially where sunflower seeds are available. It is one

Steller's Jay
(Cyanocitta stelleri)

The only crested jay in the western United States is the Steller's Jay, the western counterpart of the Blue Jay. It is named for George Wilhelm Steller, a German zoologist who collected the first specimens along the coast of Alaska in 1741. The Steller's Jay can imitate the calls of many birds, including the Red-tailed Hawk, American Crow, and even the Common Loon. This jay is not often seen in suburban gardens but may be abundant in parks, picnic grounds, and campsites. It seems less gregarious than other jays and usually travels alone or in pairs.

Description. The crest and front parts of the Steller's Jay are black, and the rest of the body is dark blue. Juveniles are duller than adults and have grayish underparts.

Voice. In addition to their amazing ability to imitate the calls and cries of other birds, the calls of the Steller's Jays shatter the forest silences: *shaack!* This jay also produces a soft whisper song, however, which is somewhat like the song of a robin.

Habitat. Steller's Jays are found mostly in deep coniferous forests, including those at high elevations. In fall and winter Steller's Jays seek more open woods at lower elevations.

Habits. Around camps and picnic areas, the bird is bold and well known, but in its forest habitat it is shy and difficult to approach. It searches for food from high in the treetops to the ground. It raids the nests of smaller birds and eats eggs and even nestlings.

Steller's Jay

Gary W. Hanlon

Nest and eggs. The Steller's Jay generally nests in coniferous trees but sometimes selects shrubbery or bushes. The nest is usually 8 to 40 feet above ground. Both sexes build the large rough-looking mud structure of plant fibers, dry leaves, moss, sticks, trash, and paper. The 3 to 5 eggs are pale greenish blue or bluish green and marked with fine brown dots. The female is often the only parent to incubate the eggs.

Food. The bird's diet is mostly vegetation, and acorns make up a good portion of it. It also eats insects. Sunflower seeds will attract Steller's Jays to feeding stations.

Scrub Jay
(Aphelocoma coerulescens)

The distribution of this jay is unusual. Ornithologists believe that centuries ago the species ranged from coast to coast. For some reason, it has disappeared from all of the eastern United States except Florida, where it now inhabits only the central portion of the peninsula. In the West, however, the Scrub Jay is common and is found as far east as Texas and Oklahoma.

Description. About the size of a Blue Jay but more slender and with a longer tail, the Scrub Jay has no crest. Its wings and tail are blue, and it is distinguished by its gray back, light throat, and dark breast band.

Voice. The Scrub Jay has a variety of calls, including a raspy *quick, quick, quick.* In addition to loud, boisterous calls, the bird also has a soft, sweet, high-pitched call.

Habitat. Scrub Jays live in thickets of sand pine, scrub oak, and, in Florida, saw palmetto. In the West they prefer chaparral-covered mountain slopes, dense shrubbery and pinyon, scrub oak thickets, and juniper. They also may live in backyards where dense shrubs predominate.

Scrub Jay

Frans Lanting

Black-billed Magpie

A. Cruickshank/VIREO

Habits. In Florida the Scrub Jay is bold and often tame, willing to feed from the hand. In California, it is much wilder and is often disliked because of its shrieks and its habit of following those who intrude into its territory. Like other members of the Crow family, this jay often collects bright and shiny objects which it buries, as it does some of its food.

Nest and eggs. Scrub Jays nest from 3 to 30 feet above ground in trees, bushes, and shrubs. The nest is a compact, well-constructed platform of twigs, moss, and dry grass that the birds line with hair and fine roots. In Florida these jays sometimes live in colonies of up to 6 pairs. The 3 or

4 eggs are either pale green with spots and blotches of deep olive or grayish white to green with spots of reddish brown. The female sits on the clutch during the 16-day incubation period.

Food. The Scrub Jay favors acorns, pinyon seeds, fruits, and berries as well as a wide variety of insects, small reptiles, and rodents. It gathers food by hopping around on the ground or in thick shrubbery where its food grows. The bird sometimes eats the eggs and young of songbirds. Feeding stations that offer seeds and suet often attract these jays.

Black-billed Magpie
(Pica pica)

The Black-billed Magpie is a striking resident of the open country of the West. Graceful in flight with its long, iridescent greenish black tail leveled off behind, it is a handsome bird. It is, however, a member of the family Corvidae, which includes crows and jays, and the Black-billed Magpie has family character-

istics that humans find unattractive. For example, it occasionally eats the eggs and young of smaller birds.

Description. The Black-billed Magpie is a large bird—17½ to 22 inches in total length. About half of its length consists of the long, wedge-shaped tail. Its plumage is iridescent black, with white on the shoulders and abdomen. In flight, white wing patches flash with every wingbeat.

Voice. Its call is a harsh *quag quag quag.*

Habitat. The Black-billed Magpie occupies rangeland, sagebrush, river thickets, prairies, open woodlands, and foothills in much of the West.

Habits. Observers usually see Black-billed Magpies on the ground foraging for grasshoppers and other insects. Like most of the Corvidae family, they are gregarious and, except in nesting season, prefer to travel in small flocks. In winter, the flocks are larger, sometimes containing as many as 50 birds.

Nest and eggs. The large nests of Black-billed Magpies are scattered in small colonies, often in thorny bushes. A pair sometimes spends 6 weeks constructing the structure, which is usually about 3 feet in diameter. They build it with mud or manure and fine plant materials, then cover the nest bowl with a dome of sticks. Openings on opposite sides serve as the entrance and escape exits. When it has laid its clutch, usually 7 green-gray eggs blotched with browns, the female undertakes the 18-day incubation period.

Food. Magpies enjoy a varied diet. They feed on the ground, gleaning grasshoppers and other insects; they pick ticks off the backs of large game animals such as elk and deer; they scavenge carrion from road kills; and occasionally they raid a songbird nest or catch a small rodent or reptile.

American Crow
(Corvus brachyrhynchos)

Conservationists concerned about endangered species have no reason to worry about the American Crow. This raucous bird is extremely adaptable and intelligent. With a reputation for eating corn and other farm crops, as well as for occasionally eating the eggs of game birds and songbirds, the crow has survived the bombing of its roosts, organized shooting, and poisoning.

Description. At a length of 17 to 21 inches, the American Crow is a large bird. It is entirely black, from its big bill to its legs.

Voice. A distinctive *caw* or *cah* uttered once or in a series is the Amercian Crow's typical call. It sometimes mimics the calls of other birds.

Habitat. Human alteration of the landscape has favored the crow. The bird inhabits farmlands, roadsides, orchards, forests, and parks.

Habits. Crows fly with deep, steady wingbeats—some describe the motion as rowing through the air. Following the nesting season they gather in enormous flocks of up to 200,000 birds. They roost and feed together until late winter or spring.

Nest and eggs. Crows are solitary nesters. They choose deciduous or coniferous trees and build the nest 10 to 70 feet above ground in a crotch or near the trunk on heavy supporting limbs. The male and female construct a large, substantial basket of twigs, sticks, bark, and vines. They line it with shredded bark fibers, moss, grass, feathers, fur, hair, and roots. The fe-

American Crow

H. Cruickshank/VIREO

male lays from 3 to 8 eggs; a typical clutch contains 4 to 6. The eggs are bluish or grayish green and are irregularly blotched with browns and grays. Both parents incubate the eggs until they hatch after 18 days.

Food. Crows consume grain and feast on waste grain after harvest. They also eat insects that could damage fields and orchards. Crows scavenge garbage, dead fish, carrion, and road kills. They eat the eggs and young of many songbirds. Around backyard feeding stations crows are wary and easily frightened.

Clark's Nutcracker
(Nucifraga columbiana)

The Clark's Nutcracker bears the name of its discoverer, Captain William Clark of the Lewis and Clark expedition. The Clark's Nutcracker is familiar at campsites and picnic grounds throughout the high western mountains.

Clark's Nutcracker

H. Cruickshank/VIREO

Black-capped Chickadee

J.D. Young/VIREO

Anyone who has driven along Trail Ridge in Rocky Mountain National Park has probably been entertained by the Clark's Nutcrackers that congregate at the scenic lookouts. But it is not the spectacular view that attracts these gray scamps; it is the handouts that they beg so successfully from the tourists.

Description. The Clark's Nutcracker is an average-sized jay about 12 inches long. It is distinguished by a light gray body, black wings with conspicuous white patches, and a black tail.

Voice. Hardly musical, this bird's call is a harsh, grating, squawk: *krasak!*

Habitat. A bird of the high country, the Clark's Nutcracker is usually found in the coniferous forests near timberline.

Habits. The noisy, boisterous ways of the Clark's Nutcracker are like those of a jay. Like its cousin the Gray Jay, it is sometimes called a camp robber because it boldly approaches humans for handouts. It eats seeds offered at bird feeders and will occasionally even go so far as to enter a human home in its search for food.

Nest and eggs. The breeding pair works together to build its nest and often begins early in spring when snow still lies on the ground. After choosing a site in a conifer, they construct a platform of twigs and bark strips, then create a deep nest cup of grasses, pine needles, and bark shreds. The parents take turns incubating the 2 to 4 pale green eggs, which are spotted with brown and gray. The incubation period is 16 to 18 days.

Food. The bird gleans much of its food from the seeds, kernels, and nuts of the conifers among which it lives. It is adept at prying seeds from cones with its bill. The Clark's Nutcracker often stores food for later use. It eats insects, carrion, and sometimes the eggs or young of small birds, as well as bread and other treats that humans offer.

Black-capped Chickadee

(Parus atricapillus)

It is safe to say that where you find one chickadee, you will find others. When not nesting, chickadees travel in little bands much of the year. Searching for food, these roving flocks often include the chickadee's close relative, the Tufted Titmouse. They also travel with White-breasted or Red-breasted Nuthatches, Downy Woodpeckers, kinglets, and occasionally Brown Creepers. The Black-capped Chickadee is nonmigratory throughout its range. Some travel south of the breeding range for the winter, however, sometimes invading the home territory of the Carolina Chickadee. The two chickadees are difficult to distinguish by appearance, but their songs are somewhat different: The Carolina's song has four notes; the Black-capped's has two or three.

Description. This little acrobat is a ball of gray and buff feathers with a bright black bib and skullcap and white cheeks.

Voice. During nesting the Black-capped Chickadee whistles a plaintive *phee-bee,* the first note higher than the second. Although listeners may hear the whistle the year around, the call that gives the bird its name, *chicka-dee-dee-dee,* is more characteristic.

Habitat. Woodlands are the typical habitat of Black-capped Chickadees, but they regularly visit orchards and backyards.

Habits. No birds are friendlier than Black-capped Chickadees. At home in the woods, they are curious about strange noises and visitors. At feeding stations some become tame; they may allow close approach, and some may fly to outstretched hands that offer food. When feeding in trees, Black-capped Chickadees often hang upside down.

Nest and eggs. The nesting cavity of a Black-capped Chickadee is a 5- to 8-inch hole that both sexes construct in the soft, rotting wood of a stub. The typical cavity is 4 to 10 feet above ground. They also use natural cavities, abandoned woodpecker holes, and birdhouses. The birds line the bottom with wool, hair, fur, moss, feathers, and cotton fibers. The 6 to 8 eggs are white and evenly spotted with reddish brown. The female incubates the clutch for 12 to 13 days.

Food. A Black-capped Chickadee's primary food is insects, but during the winter, when insects are scarce, vegetables may constitute up to 50 percent of its diet. Pine seeds are an important food. Sunflower seeds, suet, cracked corn, and shelled peanuts are attractive to Black-capped Chickadees at feeding stations.

Karl & Steve Maslowski

Carolina Chickadee

Carolina Chickadee
(Parus carolinensis)

The perky Carolina Chickadee is almost a carbon copy of its close relative, the Black-capped Chickadee. Fortunately for most bird-watchers, the ranges of these two overlap only in the mountains of North Carolina. There, they can be distinguished most easily by their voices. The Carolina Chickadee sings a four-syllable song; the Black-capped Chickadee sings two or three syllables.

Description. One of the smallest chickadees, the Carolina is a tiny, 4½-inch-long sprite. A jet-black cap and bib and white cheek patches accent gray upperparts over buff underparts.

Voice. The Carolina Chickadee's four-syllable whistled song is *phee-bee, phee-bay.* Its *chicka-dee-dee-dee* call is faster and higher pitched than that of the Black-capped Chickadee.

Habitat. The Carolina Chickadee is more of a woodland bird than the Black-capped Chickadee; it prefers coniferous and deciduous forests and swamps. It also resides in backyards that offer sufficient trees and shrubbery.

Habits. The Carolina Chickadee may visit backyard bird feeders and seems especially fond of suet. It is a year-round resident within its range. Mated pairs often stay together for several years. In fall and winter, they form small flocks with others of their species, as well as Tufted Titmice, Brown-headed Nuthatches, Downy Woodpeckers, and some warblers.

Nest and eggs. Beginning as early as February, Carolina Chickadee pairs begin to excavate their nesting cavity. The birds' small bills are not strong enough to hammer out a hole in hard wood, so they dig in soft, rotting tree stubs or stumps. The digging often takes 2 weeks. The pair lines the bottom of the cavity with soft materials: feathers, fur, down, moss, and hair. The 5 to 8 eggs are white dotted with reddish brown. The female incubates the eggs for the approximately 13-day incubation period.

Food. Insects, many of them harmful to trees and other plants, make up nearly half of the Carolina Chickadee's diet. They supplement this with seeds from shrubs, pines, and weeds, and often visit bird feeders.

Chestnut-backed Chickadee
(Parus rufescens)

Compared with the Black-capped Chickadee, the Chestnut-backed Chickadee of the forests of the Pacific Northwest is not well known. It is not shy, but because of its coloring it is inconspicuous in the shade of towering redwoods, pines, and firs. These birds are somewhat gregarious after the nesting season and often travel in flocks with other small birds.

Description. The Chestnut-backed Chickadee looks like other chickadees, but its back and sides are bright reddish brown, and its cap is sooty rather than black.

Chestnut-backed Chickadee

P. La Tourrette/VIREO

Voice. This chickadee has no whistled song, but its call, *tsick-a-see-see*, is somewhat like that of the Black-capped Chickadee. A harsh *zee* is its common call note.

Habitat. The Chestnut-backed Chickadee prefers dense coniferous forests, woods at the edges of streams, or a similar habitat in a backyard. In California it often chooses eucalyptus groves.

Habits. The behavior of this species is much like that of other chickadees.

Nest and eggs. The birds tend to nest in loose colonies. For example, in one small area, seven nests were found, some not more than 50 yards apart. The birds dig a nesting cavity in a rotted stump or use natural cavities and abandoned woodpecker holes. Nests are usually less than 10 feet above ground. The birds line the cavity with mosses, hair, fur, small feathers, and trash. The 6 or 7 eggs are white and sprinkled sparingly with reddish brown dots.

Food. Insects constitute the bulk of this chickadee's diet, but in winter up to 40 percent of its diet is vegetation. Pine seeds are an important natural food. At feeding stations, sunflower seeds and suet often prove attractive.

Tufted Titmouse
(Parus bicolor)

The Tufted Titmouse is one of the most delightful birds to visit a feeding station. If the station provides sunflower seeds—its favorite food—this little gray bird is likely to be a constant visitor throughout the winter. Ornithologists used to consider the Tufted Titmouse a southern bird, but like the Northern Cardinal, the Northern Mockingbird, and the Carolina Wren, it has been extending its range northward for many years. Today it nests as far north as southern New England, Wisconsin, and Michigan.

Tufted Titmouse

J.R. Woodward/VIREO

Description. The Tufted Titmouse is a small gray bird with a crest, a blackish forehead, brown flanks, and bright black eyes.

Voice. This bird produces a loud, clear whistle of *peto, peto, peto*, throughout spring and summer. The winter notes are harsh and scolding. Its occasional *day-day-day-day* is reminiscent of the chickadee's call but has a wheezy, coarse tone.

Habitat. The Tufted Titmouse inhabits deciduous and coniferous forests, moist bottomlands and swamps, orchards, suburban shade trees, parks, and mesquite areas.

Habits. Titmice are very active, vivacious birds. They flit through shade trees and often hang upside down when searching for food. In winter, they wander through the woods in flocks with other birds. They are bold around humans and will sometimes accept food from the hand.

Nest and eggs. A Tufted Titmouse rarely, if ever, excavates its own nest cavity; it finds a natural tree cavity or abandoned woodpecker hole or occasionally nests in a birdhouse. The nest is usually 2 to 80 feet above ground. The birds line the bottom of the cavity with shed snakeskins, bark strips, dead leaves, moss, and grass. They pad the nest cup with hair, fur, bits of string, and cloth. The 5 or 6 white eggs are speckled with small spots, which are often concentrated at the larger end. When unattended, the eggs are covered with nest material. The female incubates the eggs for the 13 to 14 days required for them to hatch. Pair-bonds may be lifelong.

Food. In spring, summer, and fall, insects are the Tufted Titmouse's primary food. In winter, however, more than 70 percent of its diet is made up of plant food, such as berries, acorns, seeds, nuts, and the sunflower seeds it finds at feeding stations.

Plain Titmouse

Herbert Clarke

Bushtit

P. La Tourrette/VIREO

Plain Titmouse
(Parus inornatus)

Its scientific name, *inornatus*, means "unadorned," and the name certainly is appropriate for this little gray bird. The Plain Titmouse is the western counterpart of the Tufted Titmouse. It too has a crest, but it is plain and gray and not always noticeable.

Description. This is the only small, plain, gray bird with a crest throughout its range. The shade of its gray plumage varies from one area to another. Coastal birds are gray-brown; interior birds are commonly a drab gray.

Voice. In the spring the Plain Titmouse whistles *witt-y, witt-y, witt-y* or *ti-wee-ti-wee-ti-wee.* Its call follows the pattern of the call of other members of the Titmouse family and closely resembles the *dee-dee* notes of the chickadee.

Habitat. The bird's habits are in many ways similar to the chickadee's. The Plain Titmouse prefers oak woods but also lives in pinyon and juniper woodlands and a variety of deciduous woods, thickets, and shrublands with scattered trees. Streamsides and forest edges seem especially attractive. The Plain Titmouse is an adaptable bird and is a frequent garden resident.

Habits. The Plain Titmouse is likely to retain the same mate from year to year. Unlike its close relatives, it is rarely seen in large flocks. The Plain Titmouse is an inquisitive little bird that often feeds by hanging by its feet in an upside-down position.

Nest and eggs. The birds build their nest from 3 to 35 feet above ground in the natural cavities of trees, in old woodpecker holes, fence posts, birdhouses, and crevices in buildings. They fill the nest hole with moss, grass, forb stems, and fibers and line it with feathers and fur. The clutch contains 6 to 8 eggs, which require 2 weeks of incubation by the female. The eggs are white and usually unmarked but occasionally they have minute dots of pale reddish brown.

Food. Insects are the spring and summer diet of the Plain Titmouse; in winter it is primarily vegetarian. These birds often visit feeding stations for sunflower seeds, peanut butter, and suet.

Bushtit
(Psaltriparus minimus)

This western bird is among the smallest of all North American bird species—smaller than its close relatives, the chickadees and titmice. It is a permanent resident throughout its range, and during much of the year, it travels in loose, noisy flocks of a few to as many as 50 birds.

White-breasted Nuthatch

J.R. Woodward/VIREO

Description. Bushtits are tiny, long-tailed birds with dull gray backs and wings and light brown caps and tails. The sexes look similar, except that females have pale yellow eyes; the male's eyes and those of newly hatched young are dark brown. There are no pronounced markings on the adult's plumage. Bushtits with black ears live near the Mexican border.

Voice. Bushtits have no recognizable voice. Their call note is a high-pitched twittering or a note they produce while foraging: *tseet* or *tsip.*

Habitat. Bushtits prefer deciduous and coniferous forests, forest edges, streamsides, alder thickets, oak woodlands, and chaparral. They are frequently found in oak, juniper, and pinyon groves of the mountainous Far West.

Habits. Bushtits are gregarious in winter and spend the season with their own species or in mixed flocks. The flocks break up into pairs for nesting in spring. The Bushtits' gray coloring is so nondescript that the birds would be hard to see if they were not constantly on the move.

Nest and eggs. The Bushtit nest is most unusual—a marvelous piece of avian architecture. It is a long, gourd-shaped hanging pocket, usually 7 to 10 inches deep; one nest has been found that was 21 inches long. Six to thirty-five feet above the ground, the carefully camouflaged nest is woven into and supported by twigs and branches. The nest materials include mosses, lichens, leaves, cocoons, and grasses, which are woven with spider silk and lined with plant down, wool, hair, and feath-

ers. The birds fashion an entrance hole on the side near the top. Building this elaborate nest requires the efforts of both birds, who work on it for between 13 and 51 days, a time period that may also include egg laying and incubation. The typical clutch contains 5 to 7 unmarked white eggs, and both parents take turns incubating them over 12 to 13 days. The parents usually spend the night in the nest together.

Food. Foraging flocks of Bushtits glean enormous quantities of aphids, beetles, and many other insects. Bushtits do not generally visit feeding stations. The birds also eat poison oak and some berries and fruits.

White-breasted Nuthatch
(Sitta carolinensis)

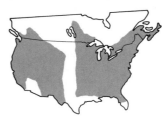

When Europeans watched this nervous little bird wedging nuts into crevices in trees and hacking them open with its long bill, they called it a *nuthack.* Colonists on American shores saw the same bird doing the same thing, and as language evolved the word changed to *nuthatch.* The White-breasted Nuthatch is by far the best known of all nuthatches. It is the largest member of the family, but its size does not limit its characteristic acrobatic qualities. It frequents feeding stations and is sometimes so tame that it will accept food from the hand.

Description. White-breasted Nuthatches are distinguished by a black cap and beady black eyes on an all-white face. The sexes are much alike—blue-gray above and white below, with a short, square tail.

Voice. The call of the White-breasted Nuthatch is a low *yank-yank.* The spring song is a series of high, shrill notes variously interpreted as *ha, ha, ha, ha, ha* or *wee-wee-wee-wee-wee-wee* or *to-what, what, what, what, what.*

Habitat. In the West White-breasted Nuthatches inhabit coniferous as well as oak or juniper woodlands. In the East they show a preference for deciduous woods, especially beech and oak, and for orchards and groves of large trees in towns.

Habits. The nuthatch's most characteristic habit is traveling down tree trunks head first. These birds seem to remain paired throughout the year, and they maintain a feeding territory as well as one for nesting. Permanent residents wherever they are found, in winter they join small roving flocks of other birds to search for food.

Nest and eggs. The nest site is usually a natural tree cavity 15 to 50 feet above ground, but the birds occasionally use an old woodpecker hole or a birdhouse. Experts doubt that this species ever excavates its own cavity. The female lines the nest with bark shreds, twigs, grasses, rootlets, fur, and hair. A normal clutch contains 7 or 8 eggs, but there may be as many as 10. The eggs are white and usually are heavily marked with light brown and lavender spots. The female undertakes the 12-day chore of incubation.

Food. The primary food sources are insects gleaned from tree bark and the nuts of deciduous trees—especially acorns and beechnuts. Pine seeds, waste grains, and the seeds and berries of various plants are important supplements. At feeding stations, nuthatches are attracted by sunflower seeds, suet, and peanut butter.

Red-breasted Nuthatch

J.R. Woodward/VIREO

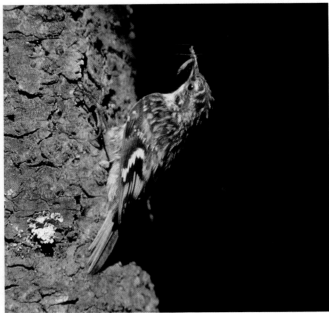

Brown Creeper

O.S. Pettingill, Jr./VIREO

Red-breasted Nuthatch

(Sitta canadensis)

Like the White-breasted Nuthatch, the Red-breasted Nuthatch is found in many parts of the country at various times of the year. Some individuals in the far north are migratory; others are permanent residents.

Description. A small bird, the Red-breasted Nuthatch is blue-gray above, buff or reddish brown below. It has a black stripe through the eye, a white stripe above the eye, and a black cap. Females and juveniles have duller heads and underparts.

Voice. The common call is a high-pitched, nasal *ank, ank, ank.* Another call is an explosive *kick* which sounds like a high-pitched trumpet or tin horn.

Habitat. These nuthatches are residents of the spruce and fir forests of the North. The cultivation of ornamental conifers has contributed to a gradual southward extension of their range.

Habits. The Red-breasted Nuthatch works over the trunks and limbs of conifers in typical nuthatch fashion; it moves up and down, almost always head first. Searching for food, it moves quickly to the ends of twigs and beneath hanging cones. When traveling in small family bands at the end of summer, individuals constantly chatter.

Nest and eggs. The nest is usually in an excavated cavity in a rotting stub or branch 5 to 40 feet above ground. The birds sometimes use an old woodpecker hole or natural cavity but rarely use a birdhouse. They line the cavity with bark shreds, grass, moss, and feathers. The tarlike resin of an evergreen tree is often smeared around the entrance hole. A typical clutch contains 5 or 6 white eggs

dotted with reddish brown, which the female alone incubates for 12 days.

Food. This bird's diet is comprised of seeds of conifers and insects gleaned from tree bark. It often stores food in bark crevices.

Brown Creeper

(Certhia americana)

Tree bark provides the Brown Creeper's food, shelter, and unique nesting site. Its long claws and stiff tail are excellent tools for clinging to a trunk when hunting for insects and eggs with its needle-sharp bill. This bird seldom moves straight up or down or sideways; it spirals its way up tree trunks. When it flattens itself against a trunk, the Brown Creeper's plumage serves as ideal camouflage.

Description. The Brown Creeper is brown above and speckled and streaked with white. It has a reddish rump and tail, white underparts, and a slender downward-curved bill.

Voice. The song of this bird is a thin, high-pitched, but musical series of notes. The call note, *seep,* is similar to a kinglet's faint, short, lisp.

Habitat. Any type of forest habitat is suitable for the Brown Creeper. It commonly summers in mature coniferous and deciduous forests, and seems to prefer densely wooded swamps.

Habits. This species has the distinctive habit of spiraling up a tree trunk, then dropping to the base of another tree to repeat the performance. Throughout the winter, the Brown Creeper is active from morning to night, searching incessantly on trees for insects and insect eggs.

Nest and eggs. The Brown Creeper uses tree bark even in nesting. It builds its nest behind a slab of bark that is loosely attached to a tree. The nest is built of twigs, leaves, and bark shreddings and is lined with finer bark shreds, grasses, mosses, and occasionally with feathers. The male sometimes carries material, but the female does the

Wrentit

Herbert Clarke

actual building. The shape of the finished nest conforms to the narrow space behind the bark. The 5 or 6 eggs are peppered with reddish brown spots, which sometimes appear in a wreath. Both sexes sit on the eggs during the 2-week incubation period.

Food. The Brown Creeper eats insects almost exclusively, although its diet does include some nuts and seeds. It does not appear to be interested in feeding stations.

Wrentit
(Chamaea fasciata)

The Wrentit family contains only one species and is the only family of birds whose range is restricted to North America. The Wrentit's nearest relatives belong to the Babbler family of Europe, Asia, Africa, and Australia.

This secretive little brown bird is classified between a titmouse and a wren and shows no close relationship to any other American songbird.

Description. About 6½ inches long, the Wrentit is usually brown with a dusky back and faintly streaked, buff-cinnamon underparts. The iris of its eye is conspicuously white, and its tail is long, rounded, and tilted up from the body.

Voice. The male sings a series of whistles on the same pitch, which run together and end in a trill: *yip-yip-yip-yi-ytr-tr-tr-r-r-r.* The female sings a similar song without the trill. Their call is a low churring noise.

Habitat. Wrentits live in dense, brushy chaparral, in brushy areas near forests and streams, and in gardens and parks. They are seldom seen, however, because they rarely venture out from their brushy habitat.

Habits. The Wrentit chooses one mate and one homesite for life. The pair does almost everything together: They feed together, preen each other, and roost together, leaning against each other with feathers interlaced and legs drawn up.

House Wren

H. Cruickshank/VIREO

Nest and eggs. The nest site is usually in chaparral and is about 18 to 24 inches above ground. Horizontal or vertical twigs built into or lashed to the nest provide support. Leafy twigs screen it from view. Both parents build the compact cup of bark fibers bound with spider silk. They line it with fine fibers and sometimes add hair and fine grasses. The 3 to 5 eggs are pale greenish blue with no markings. Both birds take part in incubation during the day, but only the female incubates the eggs at night. Parents usually raise one brood per year, but if the nest is continually destroyed, Wrentits may lay up to five clutches per year.

Food. Wrentits glean insects from the bark of shrubs and small trees and eat fleshy fruits and berries. It is almost impossible to attract them to a feeding station unless it is very close to shrubby cover.

House Wren
(Troglodytes aedon)

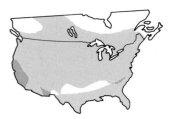

The House Wren is one of the best known and best loved of our summer birds. It is also one of the most valuable because of the tremendous amount of insects it consumes. No other wild bird has taken as completely to birdhouses as this little wren has.

Description. This is the plainest wren in the East. Its upperparts are unstreaked grayish brown with darker bars on the wings and tail; its underparts are dull white. It lacks a pronounced eye line.

Voice. Many know the male's rapid, bubbling, repetitive musical chatter. When aroused, House Wrens are great scolders; they fuss and fume in a harsh, grating chatter.

Winter Wren

C.H. Greenewalt/VIREO

Habitat. Wrens prefer low deciduous woods and shrubby woodland edges and openings. They often live in backyards—particularly where there are trees and shrubs around a lawn or a patio.

Habits. When establishing a territory a male fills all available cavities or nesting boxes in its domain with sticks, which seems to protect the nest sites from encroachment by other wrens. When it arrives, the female selects a nest site, throws out much of the material deposited by the male, and builds another nest. A male often attracts two mates. Males sometimes puncture other birds' eggs, possibly in defense of their nesting territory.

Nest and eggs. The House Wren's nest site is usually a natural cavity in a tree, stub, or fence post, an old woodpecker hole, or a birdhouse. On a base of twigs, the female builds a cup of grasses, plant fibers, rootlets, feathers, hair, and rubbish. The 5 to 8 eggs are white and heavily speckled with minute reddish brown dots. The female House Wren incubates the eggs for about 2 weeks. A pair of House Wrens produces up to two broods a year.

Food. House Wrens are almost entirely insectivorous. They rarely visit feeding stations but might come for suet or bread.

Winter Wren
(Troglodytes troglodytes)

The Winter Wren is as shy and retiring as the House Wren is sociable and trusting. It is a rare backyard that entices this diminutive bird near human habitation. Most birdwatchers happen upon the Winter Wren as a winter visitor or a migrant.

Description. This wren is one of North America's smallest songbirds; it is only about 4 inches long. It is dark reddish brown above and pale brown below, with barred feathers and a stubby, upturned tail. It has a narrow buff line over its eye.

Voice. The Winter Wren's series of loud tinkling trills and tumbling warbles lasts for about 6 seconds. This summer song is one of the most delightful in the northern woods. The call note is a sharp *tick.*

Habitat. The Winter Wren lives mostly among rotting logs and fallen tree trunks. It prefers areas with little sunshine near cool swamps and in coniferous forests, rocky ravines, and mountainous areas of the North.

Habits. The Winter Wren creeps like a mouse about woodpiles and brush heaps and bobs through woodland tangles with its stubby tail tilted far back over its back.

Nest and eggs. The nest is usually in a well-hidden cavity in the upturned root of a fallen tree, but it may also be under a tree stump, in the root of a live tree, or in an abandoned woodpecker hole, mossy hummock, or rocky crevice. Occasionally, the nest consists of a round mass of twigs and mosses attached to the open branch of a coniferous tree. The nest cavity is filled with moss, grasses, weed stems, fine twigs, and rootlets and has a lining of hair and feathers. The size of the nest varies with the space available, but it is unusually large for so small a bird. The male builds dummy nests to fill up a nesting site so that other birds will not use it. The average clutch contains 5 or 6 eggs. The eggs resemble those of the Black-capped Chickadee but are less round. The shell is white, with reddish brown spots, which often wreathe the large end.

Food. Ornithologists believe that the Winter Wren is almost exclusively insectivorous. It does, however, occasionally eat the berries of red cedar.

Carolina Wren
(Thryothorus ludovicianus)

The Carolina Wren, the state bird of South Carolina and the largest eastern member of its family, is nonmigratory. The species has gradually extended its breeding range northward. Today it lives as far north as Wisconsin, Minnesota, and southern New England. Bird-watchers detect it more often by ear than by sight because of its clear, easily recognizable song.

Description. Rusty brown above and buff below, this wren has a conspicuous white line over the eye.

Voice. There are many interpretations of the song of this versatile singer. The most common is *tea-kettle, tea-kettle, tea-kettle. Chirrrrrrr* is a common call note. The Carolina Wren is known to occasionally imitate the voices of other birds.

Habitat. This wren lives the year around in brushy forests; on rocky slopes thick with brush; in shrubby thickets, farmlands, and parks; and in woody suburban gardens that have a dense undergrowth of shrubs.

Carolina Wren

Habits. The energetic Carolina Wren is seldom still; it darts in and out of brush piles, fallen trees, and dense shrubbery. The best way to see the bird is to make a loud and unusual sound to attract its attention. Produce a loud squeak by blowing hard with your lips pressed against the back of your hand. The inquisitive Carolina Wren will usually come to investigate the strange noise, bobbing up and down and scolding at the intrusion.

Nest and eggs. The Carolina Wren builds in anything: a natural tree cavity, a woodpecker hole, a birdhouse, an upturned root, or a nook or cranny in a stone wall, under a bridge, or around a human dwelling. Sometimes the nest site is unique, such as a roll of wire, an open tin can, a garbage bag, the pocket of an old piece of clothing, or a mailbox. The nest is a bulky mass of leaves, twigs, mosses, grasses, strips of bark, and debris. It is generally domed, has a side entrance and a lining of feathers, hair, moss, and fine grasses. The 5 or 6 eggs are white or pale pink and marked with heavy brown spots. The female incubates the clutch, and the male carries food to its mate during the 2 weeks it takes

for the eggs to hatch. In the South pairs may raise three broods per year, but two broods is typical.

Food. Insects make up the bulk of this wren's diet. Only about 10 percent of its intake is plant matter, which it tends to eat only in winter. Suet, peanut butter, sunflower seeds, and nuts attract Carolina Wrens to backyard feeding stations.

Cactus Wren
(Campylorhynchus brunneicapillus)

Humans probably find the thought of life among needle-sharp cactus spines unpleasant. The Cactus Wren, however, seeks out the cholla cactus because predators—including humans—shun it. The nearly impenetrable thicket offers a safe refuge. The largest of its family, this wren is the state bird of Arizona.

Cactus Wren

Description. The Cactus Wren is similar in size and shape to a small thrasher. Its back is a rich brown marked with broken white stripes and blackish spots. Its underparts are whitish or buff and heavily spotted with black. A white eyebrow borders the rust-colored crown, and the long tail has barring on the outer feathers.

Voice. The song of the Cactus Wren is one of the most familiar year-round sounds of the desert. The unmusical sound has been likened to that of a car that refuses to start: *chur-cha-ra, chur-cha-ra, chur-cha-ra.*

Habitat. The chief requirement for this desert wren is an abundance of prickly, thorny shrubs and cacti. It lives along brushy streamsides and in residential areas adjacent to deserts.

Habits. The wren flies jerkily from one perch to another and sings in a conspicuous location. As unlike a wren as it is in many respects, the male nevertheless displays a trait shared with other

wrens—it builds dummy nests to keep other birds away from area nesting sites.

Nest and eggs. Cholla, prickly pear, and other cacti are favorite nesting sites. The nests are bulky cylindrical or spherical masses of straw-colored plant stems and grasses and are lined with fine grass, feathers, fur, and cotton. The nest rests horizontally, with the entrance in one end. A long passageway about 3 inches above the level of the chamber floor extends down to the chamber. The 2 to 5 eggs are salmon-buff or pinkish white and covered evenly with brown spots that nearly conceal the background color. The female incubates the eggs for 16 days.

Food. The Cactus Wren eats primarily insects and occasionally lizards and tree frogs. It also eats cactus fruits, including prickly pears, some berries, and some seeds.

Northern Mockingbird
(Mimus polyglottos)

"Listen to the Mockingbird"—the words of the famous old song provide unnecessary advice for southerners who live the year around with this songster at their doorsteps. Indeed, some have threatened violence to the melodious bird that serenades outside the bedroom window at 4:00 a.m. The name *mockingbird* is well chosen. No bird is more adept at imitating the songs of other birds. Its habit of repeating phrases several times is often the best clue to identifying the sound as that of a Northern Mockingbird and not of the bird it imitates.

Description. The Northern Mockingbird is gray above, white to light gray below, and has white wing bars. In flight it displays white outer tail feathers and large white patches on the upper wings.

Voice. The Northern Mockingbird's repertoire of songs and calls, not to mention the number of songs of other birds it can imitate, is so large and varied that it defies description. Experts have recorded 50 mockingbird call notes and imitations of 39 different species.

Habitat. Farmlands, open woods, parks, gardens, cities, and villages are the traditional habitats of the Northern Mockingbird. Today mockingbirds are common in towns and gardens.

Northern Mockingbird

C. Allan Morgan

Gray Catbird

J.R. Woodward/VIREO

Habits. Intensely territorial, the Northern Mockingbird attacks any creature—including a human—that invades its domain. When perched, it often flicks its tail sideways. It flashes its wings and fans its tail as it runs across the ground.

Nest and eggs. The male mockingbird often places material in more than one nest site as a part of courtship. On the occasions that a male attracts more than one female, it is polygynous. The female chooses a location, then both sexes construct the nest in a tree, shrub, or vine 3 to 10 feet above ground. The nest is bulky, with a loosely laid outer layer of thorny twigs and an inner layer of dry leaves, plant stems, moss, hair, and rootlets. A clutch usually contains 4 eggs, which are blue or green and heavily marked with brown spots and blotches. The female alone incubates the eggs for 12 to 13 days.

Food. The Northern Mockingbird's diet is about 60 percent insects; the remainder consists of a wide variety of fruits and berries. Mockingbirds often visit feeding stations in search of suet cakes, bread crumbs, and dried fruit. They particularly seem to enjoy raisins.

Gray Catbird
(Dumetella carolinensis)

The Gray Catbird is famous for its excellent voice. It is also closely related to wrens, and there is something wrenlike about the Gray Catbird; it displays the same sort of nervousness, flicking its tail and quivering its wings. The Gray Catbird also carries its tail in the same saucy, erect manner.

Brown Thrasher

J.D. Young/VIREO

Description. The Gray Catbird's slate-gray plumage is broken by a black cap and chestnut feathers on the underside of its tail. No other American bird has the same combination of colors. It is about an inch shorter than a robin.

Voice. The Gray Catbird's catlike *meow* is familiar to anyone who has disturbed the bird. The Gray Catbird can produce a variety of songs and can imitate other birds, but unlike the Northern Mockingbird, it does not repeat imitated phrases in succession. It often sings on moonlit nights.

Habitat. The Gray Catbird prefers woodland undergrowth, shrubby marsh borders, and hedgerows. It frequently nests in gardens quite close to houses. Human settlements have greatly expanded the bird's range by providing more forest edges.

Habits. A sprightly running gait with a sudden lunge into the air for a passing insect is characteristic of the Gray Catbird. No other bird responds more quickly to the sound a bird-watcher can make by blowing air through lips pressed tightly to the back of the hand. With *meows* and saucy flicks of its tail, the Gray Catbird peers inquisitively at the noise.

Nest and eggs. The female builds the nest among briars, in a dense thicket, vine tangle, shrub, or low tree. The bulky, substantial nest is deeply cupped and lined with rootlets. The female usually lays 4 deep greenish blue unmarked eggs, then incubates them for 12 to 13 days.

Food. The Gray Catbird's diet is about 50 percent fruits and berries and 50 percent insects. Catbirds visit feeding stations in search of dried berries, fruits, peanut kernels, crumbs, and suet.

Brown Thrasher
(Toxostoma rufum)

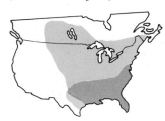

Like its close relatives the mockingbird and catbird, the Brown Thrasher mimics the songs of other birds but not as often as its cousins. The Brown Thrasher is migratory and arrives on its northern territory in mid- or late April. It is much shyer than its relatives, but it will nest in backyards that offer sufficient cover. Observers sometimes mistake it for the Wood Thrush, but a quick reference to its description will dispel confusion.

Description. The back is reddish brown, and the heavily streaked (not spotted) whitish underparts are washed with buff on the sides and breast. The eyes are usually yellow but sometimes orange. The long, curved bill, long tail, and streaked underparts distinguish it from thrushes.

Voice. The Brown Thrasher usually repeats each phrase twice in succession. Its voice sounds something like *plant-a-seed, plant-a-seed; drop-it, drop-it; cover-it-up, cover-it-up; eat-it-all, eat-it-all; chew-it, chew-it.* The bird's utterances include a loud smack, hisses, and bill clicks.

Habitat. Dry thickets, brushy fields and pastures, hedgerows, woodland borders, and occasionally garden shrubbery are the Brown Thrasher's haunts.

Habits. The Brown Thrasher feeds mostly on insects on or near the ground, digging among and tossing aside dead leaves and debris with its bill. Occasionally it leaps into the air to catch flying insects. Around its nest the Brown Thrasher occasionally attacks intruders, including humans. For such a large bird, this bird conceals itself remarkably well. Brown Thrashers are easily attracted to backyard birdbaths and pools, where they seem to enjoy drinking and bathing.

Nest and eggs. The Brown Thrasher nests up to 14 feet above ground in a tree or shrub or on the ground under a small bush. A loose foundation of thorny twigs is a base for a large cup made of layers of leaves, twigs, grasses, grapevine, and thin bark. The female usually produces 4 pale bluish white eggs, which are evenly and thickly covered with reddish brown marks. The sexes share the nest building and the incubation duties, which last from 12 to 13 days.

Food. Brown Thrashers eat many kinds of insects as well as salamanders, lizards, snakes, and tree frogs. These birds also eat some berries, figs, acorns, and waste grain. In many areas they visit feeding stations for scratch feed, millet, suet, and raisins.

Western Bluebird

Herbert Clarke

Mountain Bluebird

Peter M. La Tourrette

Description. The bright iridescent blue of the male's upperparts extends to its wings and tail. Its throat and breast are reddish brown. The females are similar but duller and grayer. Like true thrushes, the young have spotted breasts.

Voice. In addition to its whispered song, *tru-al-ly*, the Eastern Bluebird has a musical call: *chur-lee.*

Habitat. The Eastern Bluebird favors farmlands, roadside fence lines, open woods, swamps, and gardens. Loss of nesting sites and the indiscriminate use of pesticides have decimated the population, and competition with other cavity-nesting species (especially European Starlings) has contributed greatly to its decline.

Habits. When perched on a fence post or in a small tree, the Eastern Bluebird appears to be hunched in a vertical position. From its perch, the bird makes short, quick forays to the ground to catch insects, twitching or lifting one wing when it alights.

Nest and eggs. Bluebirds are the only cavity nesters of the Thrush family. They use natural cavities in trees, old woodpecker holes, or the birdhouses erected for their use on farms and along roadsides. In a cup of grasses, the female lays 4 or 5 pale blue (occasionally white) unmarked eggs. A pair produces two broods, sometimes three, annually.

Food. Insects make up about 80 percent of the Eastern Bluebird's diet in spring and summer. It eats fewer insects in winter when fruits and berries are available.

Western Bluebird
(Sialia mexicana)

The simple song of the Western Bluebird in no way rivals the lovely warble of its eastern relative. Easterners familiar with the sweet, warbling song of their own bluebird may find the Western Bluebird's song disappointing.

Description. The 6½- to 7-inch Western Bluebird differs from the Eastern Bluebird in that the Western male has a blue throat and a rusty upper back. The female and immature birds have upperparts that are browner than those of the Eastern variety. The grayish fledglings have speckled breasts and no rusty red.

Voice. The spring song of the male is a double or triple whistle of *pa-wee.* The male also sings *f-few, f-few* in the rhythm of a robin's song. It often calls a short *mew* in flight.

Habitat. This bird prefers open woodlands, farmyards, roadsides, and orchards.

Habits. The bird appears to have its shoulders hunched as it sits on one of its conspicuous perches. It often darts into the air from its perch to catch an insect on the wing or drops to snatch one from the ground. Except during the nesting season, Western Bluebirds are usually found in small flocks.

Nest and eggs. The typical Western Bluebird nest is in a natural tree cavity or an abandoned woodpecker hole. Western Bluebirds also compete for birdhouses with Violet-green Swallows and House Wrens. Accompanied by its mate, the female fills the cavity with grasses and stems then with a lining of finer grasses. The 4 to 6 pale blue eggs, which are incubated by the female for 2 weeks, are indistinguishable from those of the Eastern Bluebird. A typical pair raises two broods per year.

Food. Like its eastern relative, the Western Bluebird consumes large quantities of insects—especially beetles, caterpillars, and grasshoppers—as well as spiders and ants. It also eats some berries, earthworms, and snails.

Blue-gray Gnatcatcher

J.R. Woodward/VIREO

Mountain Bluebird
(Sialia currucoides)

A brilliant turquoise Mountain Bluebird hovering low over a western alpine meadow, then dropping to the ground to snatch an insect, is a breathtaking sight. Beloved throughout its high-country range, the Mountain Bluebird was chosen as the state bird by both Idaho and Nevada.

Description. Measuring 6½ to 7½ inches, the Mountain Bluebird is a little larger than a House Sparrow. The male in breeding plumage is blue overall with lighter blue underparts and a white belly. It is distinguished from the Western Bluebird by its blue underparts. The female is dull brown with a blue wash on the rump, tail, and wings. Immature birds resemble the female. The Mountain Bluebird is easily distinguished from other bluebirds because it does not have a red breast.

Voice. At dawn the male gives a clear, soft, warbling whistle that is reminiscent of the American Robin's song.

Habitat. Living in the foothills up to 10,000 or 12,000 feet (just below timberline), Mountain Bluebirds prefer mountain meadows and clearings, pine ridges, and open forests. They also live around mountain ranch structures, towns, and parks.

Habits. The perching posture of the Mountain Bluebird is not as round-shouldered as that of other bluebirds. When hunting for its insect prey, it often hovers low to the ground. Other times it darts out from a low perch to catch a passing insect.

Nest and eggs. Natural cavities, woodpecker holes, fence posts, bird houses, cavities around buildings, and even old Cliff Swallow nests suit the Mountain Bluebird's nesting requirements. Experts believe that both the male and the female build the nest of grasses, rootlets, and weed stems, which they sometimes line with a few feathers. The female incubates the 5 or 6 pale blue eggs for 14 days.

Food. The Mountain Bluebird's diet consists mostly of insects, including beetles, weevils, ants, bees, wasps, cicadas, caterpillars, grasshoppers, and crickets. It also eats some berries, currants, grapes, and mistletoe.

Blue-gray Gnatcatcher
(Polioptila caerulea)

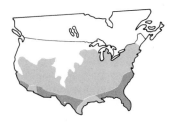

Blue-gray Gnatcatchers are nervous mites that are always on the move—jerking their tails, drooping or fluttering their wings, peering here and there, and uttering wheezy, rasping high-pitched notes. Gnatcatchers belong to the family of Old World Warblers, which include kinglets.

More like flycatchers, the Old World Warblers are in no way related to American Wood Warblers. The Blue-gray is the only gnatcatcher in the eastern United States.

Description. This tiny 4- to 5-inch bird resembles a pint-sized mockingbird. Grayish blue above and white below, it has a narrow white eye-ring. The comparatively long tail is black in the middle, white on the sides, and it is often cocked like a wren's tail.

Voice. A thin, squeaky wheeze is the characteristic song of the Blue-gray Gnatcatcher. Its call note is a distinctive *zpee*, a sound like the twang of a banjo string.

Habitat. Blue-gray Gnatcatchers favor the treetops of moist forests and open woods of oaks, pinyon, juniper, and chapparal.

Habits. In flycatcher style, the Blue-gray Gnatcatcher often darts into the air to snare a passing insect in a complicated maneuver. A fidgety, active little bird, it frequently twitches its long tail or holds it upright in the manner of a wren.

Nest and eggs. Placed in a crotch or saddled on a horizontal limb in the manner of a hummingbird's nest, the Blue-gray Gnatcatcher's home is a masterful piece of bird architecture. Constructed of plant fibers and down and covered with lichens, the compact cup is held together with spider silk. It takes the male and female 1 to 2 weeks to build the nest; egg laying begins 10 to 14 days later. Both birds share the 13-day incubation of the 4 or 5 pale blue, red-dotted eggs.

Food. The Blue-gray Gnatcatcher busily inspects leaves, flowers, and twigs for beetles, ants, gnats, flies, spiders, insect eggs, and larvae.

Golden-crowned Kinglet

Herbert Clarke

Ruby-crowned Kinglet

D. & M. Zimmerman/VIREO

Golden-crowned Kinglet
(Regulus satrapa)

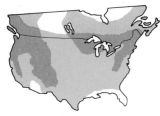

The two kinglets, the Ruby-crowned and the Golden-crowned, belong to a large and diverse family called Old World Warblers, whose members are much more numerous in Europe.

Description. The Golden-crowned Kinglet is a chunky little bird, only 3½ to 4 inches long. Its drab plumage—olive green above and paler below—is accented by a conspicuous bright orange crown patch bordered by black. It also sports a white stripe over the eye and two whitish wing bars. The sexes look similar, but the female's crown patch is yellow.

Voice. Although the Golden-crowned Kinglet's song is not as remarkable as that of the Ruby-crowned Kinglet, it is distinct. A series of ascending thin notes ends in a descending chattering of harsher notes. It seldom sings its true song except on the breeding grounds. Its call note is a three-phrased *tsee, tsee, tsee.*

Habitat. The Golden-crowned Kinglet is a bird of the conifers, but during migration it may feed in deciduous woods.

Habits. Golden-crowned Kinglets nervously flick their wings as they feed and flit from one twig to another, a characteristic that distinguishes them from warblers. They are surprisingly tame around humans.

Nest and eggs. Working on a branch in a conifer, the female takes about 9 days to construct the hanging open-topped nest of mosses and lichens lined with fine rootlets, tiny strips of inner bark and feathers. The 8 or 9 whitish eggs are spotted and blotched with browns and grays. The female begins incubating the eggs before the entire clutch is laid.

Food. Insects and their eggs and larvae form the primary diet of the Golden-crowned Kinglet. It also drinks some tree sap.

Ruby-crowned Kinglet
(Regulus calendula)

In winter and while migrating, kinglets sometimes travel with other birds—warblers, titmice, creepers, and nuthatches. Most sightings occur in winter, for in summer they breed in the far North. Naturalist John Burroughs marveled that "so small a body can brave the giant cold of our winters."

Description. The Ruby-crowned Kinglet is smaller than our smallest Wood Warbler. It is olive gray above with white wing bars and is dusky beneath. The male has a scarlet crown patch that is usually concealed unless the bird is excited. A large white eye-ring creates the impression of staring. Its tail is stubby.

Voice. Its bubbling, melodious warbling song seems impossibly loud for such a tiny bird. One description transcribes its song as a high-pitched *tee, tee, tee* that drops to a lower *tew, tew, tew* and ends with a repeated rolling chant of *ti-da-dee* or *li-ber-ty.*

Habitat. Coniferous forests, woodlands, thickets, and brush are typical habitats of the Ruby-crowned Kinglet.

Habits. Kinglets forage for aphids and other tiny insects and their eggs on the delicate tips of conifer branches. One way of distinguishing this bird from the Golden-crowned Kinglet is that the Ruby-crowned Kinglet flicks its wings almost constantly.

Cedar Waxwing

O.S. Pettingill, Jr./VIREO

Nest and eggs. The Ruby-crowned Kinglet attaches its nest to twigs dangling beneath a horizontal branch of a conifer. The typical site is a spruce, in which the nest hangs from 2 to 100 feet above ground. It is well concealed at the end of the branch where the foliage is thickest. The birds line the soft cup of mosses, lichens, and small twigs with fur and feathers. The deep cup narrows at the rim to form a circular opening. The nesting female is completely concealed inside. Kinglets lay 5 to 11 eggs in a clutch, but 7 or 8 are average. The eggs are pale buff white, dirty white, or clear white and are covered evenly with fine reddish brown dots.

Food. Kinglets feed almost entirely on insects.

Cedar Waxwing
(Bombycilla cedrorum)

Except during the nesting season, which is relatively late in the summer, Cedar Waxwings roam the countryside in flocks ranging in size from about a dozen to a hundred or more birds. During most of the year, if you see one Cedar Waxwing, you will see several. These nomadic flocks can show up almost anywhere at any time in fall, winter, or spring. The Cedar Waxwings' preference for fruit and berries explains their restless travels over much of the United States and also their late nesting. Since they do not migrate in a typical north-south pattern, they are described as wanderers.

Description. This sleek, beautiful, crested bird is distinguished by its gray-brown color; its dramatically contrasting black mask, yellow belly and tail band; and the red, waxy wingtips from which the bird gets its name.

Voice. The Cedar Waxwing's call is just a few high, thin, lisping notes strung together. The call has a faint ringing quality.

Habitat. In the breeding season, pairs seek nesting territories in open woodlands and orchards. In the non-breeding season, Cedar Waxwings live in orchards, parks, and woodlands along streams.

Habits. Cedar Waxwings perform an unusual ritual. They pass cherries back and forth as flock members perch side by side on a tree limb. During courtship a pair may pass a flower petal or an insect back and forth. Cedar Waxwings feed regurgitated cherries or berries to their nestlings.

Nest and eggs. The nest sits 4 to 50 feet above ground on the horizontal limb of a tree or in a crotch. It is loosely woven of grasses, twigs, string, and yarn and has a lining of rootlets and fine grasses. The female lays 4 or 5 pale gray or bluish gray eggs that are lightly spotted with dark brown and blotched with pale brownish gray. The male feeds the female during incubation. A pair usually produces two broods per year.

Food. About 90 percent of the Cedar Waxwing's food is wild and cultivated fruit and berries. They eat an unusually wide variety of plants. A birdbath often attracts Cedar Waxwings more successfully than a bird feeder.

European Starling

J.R. Woodward/VIREO

White-eyed Vireo

C.H. Greenewalt/VIREO

European Starling
(Sturnus vulgaris)

Most bird-watchers are more interested in learning how to repel the Starling than how to attract it. It was introduced into the United States in 1890 when 60 birds were released in New York City's Central Park. Since then, it has spread prolifically to all parts of the country. Although its consumption of harmful insects is of great benefit, the bird is generally considered a nuisance. Its constant struggle with native birds for cavity nest sites, its habit of roosting by the thousands in noisy flocks, and its pillaging of fruit and grain crops make the European Starling an unpopular visitor.

Description. The European Starling is chunky, short-tailed, and has a long pointed bill and pointed wings. In winter, its glossy black plumage with a metallic sheen is speckled with light spots. In spring, its bill is yellow; at other seasons, dusky brown.

Voice. A series of squeaks, rattles, and chirps are interspersed with a rising "wolf whistle," *sweeeuu*. Starlings mimic the songs of other birds and even imitate barking dogs and mewing cats.

Habitat. This adaptable bird is found in cities, suburbs, wooded farmlands, orchards, parks, gardens, and cliffs.

Habits. Gregarious except when nesting, Starlings gather in enormous flocks with blackbirds, cowbirds, and grackles to roost and feed together. Flying in flocks, Starlings achieve perfect timing and coordination in their flawless maneuvering.

Nest and eggs. Nests are solitary or in colonies in cavities or holes such as old or new woodpecker holes, natural tree cavities, birdhouses, holes in abandoned buildings, or crevices in rock cuts. The cavity is filled with a mass of grasses, weed stems, twigs, corn husks, leaves, cloth, feathers, and debris. A cup is then formed where 4 to 6 pale bluish or greenish white eggs are laid. Both sexes incubate for 11 to 13 days. They typically have two broods a year.

Food. Starlings feed on the ground, eating primarily insects. Large flocks invade bird feeders, driving away other birds and eating large quantities of food.

White-eyed Vireo
(Vireo griseus)

This pert little bird is loquacious and not at all like a vireo in its many kinds of utterances. It changes both the tune and tempo of its song completely and rapidly and often imitates the songs of other birds. Although it is shy and seldom seen, its song is so loud and distinctive that its presence is easy to detect.

Description. Two white wing bars accent a grayish green upper body. The underpart of the body is either white or grayish. The lores, which resemble spectacles, are yellow. Only the adult has a white iris; the iris of the immature bird is dark.

Voice. The White-eyed Vireo's common song is *chick-a-per-weeoo-chick* or *chick-per-weo-chick*. The bird has several calls, including a harsh mewing note.

Habitat. White-eyed Vireos favor streamsides that include thickets and dense shrubbery, deciduous forest undergrowth, briars, and old fields.

Habits. The White-eyed Vireo is extremely active and inquisitive. It comes readily to a series of squeaks from the bird-watcher. It is seldom far from the ground.

Red-eyed Vireo

R. Cardillo/VIREO

Warbling Vireo

Herbert Clarke

Nest and eggs. The nest is suspended from the forked twigs of a shrub or low tree, 1 to 8 feet above ground. Its conelike pointed bottom distinguishes it from the round, cup-shaped nest of the Red-eyed Vireo. The nest is woven of small pieces of soft wood and bark shreds held together by cobwebs and lined with fine plant stems and grass. The typical clutch contains 4 white eggs marked with only a few scattered fine brown or black dots. The sexes share the 14- to 15-day incubation period.

Food. Insects captured on or near the ground are the White-eyed Vireo's primary food, but in fall plant material forms as much as 30 percent of its diet. The White-eyed Vireo consumes more fruit and berries than do other members of its family. It seldom, if ever, visits feeding stations.

Red-eyed Vireo
(Vireo olivaceus)

The Red-eyed Vireo is one of the most common North American songbirds. The Vireo family is closely related to the American Wood Warblers and like them, they are small, tree-inhabiting birds whose diet is largely insectivorous. Observers often mistake vireos for warblers, but vireos are less active, less fluttery in their movements, generally duller in color, with larger heads and thicker bills.

The Red-eyed Vireo is one of the most common hosts to parasitic Brown-headed Cowbirds. No other species is victimized more in number of nests parasitized.

Description. Olive green above and white below, the Red-eyed Vireo's best field mark is the black-bordered white stripe over its ruby-red eye and black stripe through the eye. The gray cap is difficult to see and the red eye is of little help at a distance.

Voice. The Red-eyed Vireo sings *Here I am! Here I am! See me? See me? Here I am! See me? See me?* in ceaseless repetition. This bird sings more persistently than any other during the hottest summer days. During one 10-hour period, a Red-eyed Vireo sang the phrase 22,197 times.

Habitat. In its range the Red-eyed Vireo may be found almost anywhere that has deciduous trees: open woods, forest clearings, and the edges or thick undergrowth of saplings. The bird occasionally lives among conifers.

Habits. Despite its incessant singing (which inspired the nickname "preacher bird") the Red-eyed Vireo is hard to spot as it moves about the high, slender branches of leafy trees. Though they do not migrate in flocks, vast numbers of Red-eyed Vireos leave the United States for South America in the fall and return in the spring to breed throughout the United States and southern Canada.

Nest and eggs. A deep-cupped hanging structure, the nest is suspended from a horizontal fork of a slender tree branch. The Red-eyed Vireo binds its nest of grasses, paper, bark strips, and rootlets with spider silk to supporting twigs. The 4 white, sparingly spotted eggs are incubated, mostly by the female, for almost 2 weeks.

Food. In spring the Red-eyed Vireo eats insects almost exclusively. Later in the season its diet is about 25 percent plant material.

Warbling Vireo
(Vireo gilvus)

In order to find the Warbling Vireo, it is a good idea to learn its song well. Although it breeds over a vast area throughout the United States, it is hard to see, for it is a plain bird with no conspicuous field marks, and it spends much of its time in the tops of tall elms, oaks, maples, and other shade trees along village streets. Its song does not resemble the typical voice of the vireo.

Description. The Warbling Vireo is the grayest and palest of North American vireos. Its upper body is grayish or olive, its underparts are whitish, and a faint white line runs above the eye.

Voice. As the name implies, this bird's song is a warble. It is similar to that of the Purple Finch but more languid. The scolding note is a harsh *quee*.

Habitat. Warbling Vireos are attracted to leafy treetops in open, mixed, or deciduous woods; orchards; and roadside and village shade trees. In the West they often inhabit mountain canyons.

Habits. Like most vireos, this bird looks for food with slow, leisurely movements. The male sings persistently throughout the day, often while on the nest.

Nest and eggs. The nest is often in a poplar tree and tends to be higher above ground than most vireo nests—a site 20 to 90 feet up in a horizontal fork of a slender branch is typical. The birds tend to build at a distance from the trunk. They construct a closely woven cup of bark strips, leaves, grasses, feathers, and plant down, fastened to the twigs and held together with spider silk. They line the nest with plant stems and hair and narrow the rim over the deep cup. Both sexes incubate the eggs. The 3 to 5 eggs are white and sparsely dotted with browns and blacks.

Food. With the exception of some berries, Warbling Vireos subsist almost entirely on insects. Caterpillars picked from foliage and twigs are their primary food. Warbling Vireos do not visit feeding stations.

Yellow Warbler
(Dendroica petechia)

The migration records of this dainty little warbler emphasize how little time some summer birds actually spend in the North. The Yellow Warbler arrives in apple-blossom time in late April. By May it is nesting, and the young are on the wing in June. If a second nesting follows an unsuccessful first attempt, the young are out of the nest in July. By the end of that month, many Yellow Warblers are already heading southward. By the end of August, the warblers have disappeared from their breeding ground and are already settled in winter homes in Mexico and South America.

Description. The Yellow Warbler is the only small bird (it measures 5 inches) that appears to be all yellow. Close up, however, reddish brown streaks are visible on the male's breast. These streaks are faint or absent on the female, which is duller and greener than the male.

Voice. Ornithologists recognize several transcriptions of the song: *sweet, sweet, sweet, sweeter, sweetest,* and *wee-chee, we-chee, we-chee.* The Yellow Warbler's song is often used as a basis for comparing a number of other warbler songs that contain similar *sweet-sweet* notes.

Habitat. Yellow Warblers live close to waterways, swamps, marshes, orchards, brushy bottomlands, hedgerows, and roadside thickets. They prefer small trees.

Yellow Warbler

B. Schorre/VIREO

Nest and eggs. Nests are often in colonies along waterways, marshes, orchards, swamps, hedgerows, and thickets. The birds choose an upright fork or crotch of a shrub, tree, or briar as a building site. Then they construct a strong, compact cup made of firmly interwoven milkweed fibers, hemp, grasses, and plant down. Matted plant down, hair, and fine grasses form the inner lining. The typical clutch consists of 4 or 5 eggs that are grayish, bluish, or greenish white and splashed with brown and gray markings. The Yellow Warbler has devised an ingenious way to negate the parasitism of the Brown-headed Cowbird, which lays eggs in other birds' nests: The warbler builds a second story on top of the cowbird eggs in its nest and buries them.

Food. The Yellow Warbler's diet consists of insects—caterpillars and other larvae in particular. Yellow Warblers do not visit feeding stations.

Yellow-rumped Warbler
(Dendroica coronata)

The classification of bird species frequently changes as new facts come to light. In this case bird-watchers discovered that the western Audubon's warbler and the eastern myrtle warbler interbreed freely where their ranges overlap. As a result ornithologists now group the two types as a single species, the Yellow-rumped Warbler. Next to the Yellow Warbler, the Yellow-rumped Warbler is probably the best known of North American wood warblers. Both the eastern and western Yellow-rumped Warblers migrate to some extent but not nearly as far as most in the Wood Warbler family. Their fall sojourn often takes them no farther than the southern United States.

Yellow-rumped Warbler

J.D. Young/VIREO

House Sparrow

H. Cruickshank/VIREO

Description. Both types are distinguished by a yellow rump, a yellow patch on the crown, and one yellow patch on each side. The eastern form has a white throat; the western race has a yellow throat.

Voice. Yellow-rumped Warblers sing a musical trill that often changes to a higher or lower pitch. Some listeners believe that, of the two races, the western bird has a richer tone. The call is a sharp *check*.

Habitat. Yellow-rumped Warblers inhabit mixed and coniferous forests in both the East and West. These warblers are likely to visit gardens in winter when the stresses of the season force them to enlarge their habitat.

Habits. This is a hardy, active, and abundant warbler, and it is the only member of the Wood Warbler family that seems able to survive winters as far north as New England. In the West the Yellow-rumped Warbler moves from the mountains to the lowlands in winter.

Nest and eggs. The nest is a deep, neat cup of small twigs, bark strips, plant down, and fibers lined with hair and fine grasses. It is typically 4 to 50 feet above ground on a horizontal branch of a conifer, often near the trunk. Many feathers are woven into the nest rim with tips bent inward over the cup. The 4 eggs are greenish or creamy white spotted with brown. The female incubates the eggs for 12 to 13 days.

Food. In spring and summer the Yellow-rumped Warbler's diet consists almost entirely of insects; in winter the bird switches to plant food. The availability of bayberries and juniper berries in the East explains the bird's ability to survive in the North. The Yellow-rumped Warbler may be enticed to feeding stations with fruit, berries, suet, and peanut butter.

House Sparrow
(Passer domesticus)

Formerly known as the English sparrow, the House Sparrow was introduced in America in 1850, when eight pairs were released in Brooklyn. Within 50 years the House Sparrow spread to all corners of the United States and Canada.

The success of the House Sparrow is due to the fact that it is a nonmigratory, hardy, adaptable, and almost omnivorous bird. The House Sparrow's greatest enemies have been the automobile and the European Starling. When the automobile replaced the horse, the bird lost a great food supply of spilled grain, stable refuse, and manure; the European Starling competes with the House Sparrow for nesting sites.

Description. In breeding plumage, the male has a gray crown, chestnut nape, black bib, and black bill. The female has a streaked back, buff eye stripe, and unstreaked breast. Juveniles resemble adult females.

Voice. Although technically a songbird, this species has no true song. Both sexes repeat notes of *cheep, cheep*.

Habitat. The House Sparrow is a year-round resident of cities, towns, farms, and parks—anywhere near human habitation.

Habits. These birds are always gregarious. Except when paired for nesting, they assemble at night in large flocks in protected places. They roost in or on buildings, in dense trees, shrubs, or in vines that cover walls.

Bobolink

O.S. Pettingill, Jr./VIREO

Nest and eggs. The nest site is usually a cavity; it could be in a building, behind a billboard, over a sign, in a traffic light, or between house rafters. House Sparrows frequently use birdhouses, but competition for these sites from starlings and bluebirds is fierce. The House Sparrows stuff the cavity with grass, feathers, paper, and trash. They occasionally build tree nests from a large ball of the same kinds of nesting material and form an opening in the side. The 5 or 6 grayish white eggs are speckled with brown. The parents raise several broods annually.

Food. For the most part these birds are vegetarian, but during the summer they feed on a variety of insects. In winter, small seeds and grain picked off the ground are staple foods. At feeding stations they prefer to eat on the ground or on tray feeders.

Bobolink
(Dolichonyx oryzivorus)

"This flashing, tinkling meteor bursts through the expectant meadow air, leaving a train of tinkling notes behind," Thoreau once said of the Bobolink. Its cheerful song—bubbling and tumbling in a series of rollicking notes—fills the summer days over fields and meadows until farmers arrive with mowing equipment. Bobolink populations have been decreasing, especially in the East, because early hay cutting disrupts its nesting cycle and destroys many nests and eggs.

Description. In spring breeding plumage, the Bobolink male is black beneath and mostly white above, with a large buff patch on the back of the head. When fall arrives, the male has molted to match the buff, heavily streaked female. The Bobolink, 6½ to 8 inches long, is the only member of the Troupial (blackbird) family with pointed tail feathers.

Voice. Hard to put into words, the joyous sound of the Bobolink's song is best described as an exuberant tumble of *spink-spank-spink-spank-spink-spank*. Its call is a clear, metallic *pink*.

Habitat. Bobolinks are attracted to green meadows, especially hayfields. During migration, they sometimes stop in marshes.

Habits. In late summer, Bobolinks start their migration, which takes them to wintering grounds as far as Brazil and Argentina—nearly 5,000 miles south of their northern breeding grounds. In spring a male courts a female with chasing flights and ground displays in which it lowers its head, partly opens its wings, fluffs its nape feathers, and drags its spread tail on the ground.

Nest and eggs. Extremely well concealed, the Bobolink's nest is usually built on the ground in dense hay, clover, alfalfa, or weeds. The female scrapes out a slight hollow in the ground, fills it with coarse grasses and weed stalks, then lines it with finer grasses. It lays 5 or 6 buff eggs, which are heavily splotched with browns. During the 13 days of incubation, it is almost impossible to follow the female to the nest or to flush the bird from it; it is very secretive. Instead of flying off the nest, the female runs some distance through the grass first. On nestbound flights it alights at a distance and walks the rest of the way.

Food. The Bobolink's summer diet is composed largely of insects such as beetles, caterpillars, alfalfa weevils, and grasshoppers. It also eats some weed seeds and grain. On southward migrations, Bobolinks sometimes descend in large numbers on unharvested grain fields.

Eastern Meadowlark
(Sturnella magna)

The Eastern Meadowlark is not actually a lark; it is a member of the Troupial family, which includes blackbirds, orioles, bobolinks, and cowbirds.

Description. The fairly chunky Eastern Meadowlark has a bright yellow breast emblazoned with a broad black V. The 9- to 11-inch-long bird has a brown streaky back and white outer tail feathers. Its western counterpart, the Western Meadowlark, is nearly identical in appearance. Differentiating the two species where their ranges overlap would be almost impossible if it were not for the difference in their songs.

Voice. *Spring o' the year!* is what the voice of the Eastern Meadowlark seems to proclaim. More often, the four syllables sound like *tee-you, tee-year*. The Western Meadowlark pours out a loud, warbling, flutelike song of six or more notes.

Habitat. Pastures, meadows, prairies, and open fields are home to the Eastern Meadowlark.

Eastern Meadowlark

Habits. The Eastern Meadowlark frequently sits on top of a fence post, pole, or wire at the edge of an open field. Its flutter-sail-flutter flight is reminiscent of a quail's. Males often have more than one mate at a time.

Nest and eggs. Carefully hidden in dense cover and attached to surrounding vegetation, the grass nest of this species has a domed roof and a side entrance. It takes the female Eastern Meadowlark 3 to 8 days to scrape out a depression and construct the nest. The bird incubates the 3 to 5 white eggs, which are heavily blotched with brown and lavender, for about 14 days. The nests and eggs of the Eastern and Western meadowlarks are virtually indistinguishable.

Food. The Eastern Meadowlark eats beetles, grasshoppers, crickets, caterpillars, weevils, ants, wasps, spiders, and bugs. Grain and weed seeds round out the Eastern Meadowlark's diet.

Red-winged Blackbird
(Agelaius phoeniceus)

In spring, a small band of hardy Red-winged Blackbirds, arriving from the South, sings at twilight in the marshes. From the top of the highest cattail a pretty redwing (as the species is sometimes called) spreads its shiny black feathers and pours out its song: *conk-kar-ree!* To intruders in its recently acquired sanctuary, the redwing extends a disgruntled *check.* Another week passes before the drab females join the jet-black males.

Description. The shiny black adult male displays red shoulder patches with yellow borders along the bottom.

Red-winged Blackbird

(The red patches may not be visible when the bird is at rest.) First-year males look more like the streaked brown females, except that some red shows in the epaulets. Female Red-winged Blackbirds are brown above and heavily streaked with brown below.

Voice. The male's song is a gurgling *conk-kar-ree* or *oka-leeee,* and ends in a trill. The call note is *check* or *cack.*

Habitat. In winter Red-winged Blackbirds wander in flocks that may include grackles and cowbirds. They feed in open agricultural fields and roost together in trees in immense flocks. In the nesting season, Red-winged Blackbirds breed in freshwater marshes throughout the country.

Habits. Red-winged Blackbirds are unusually aggressive. They attack crows, hawks, ravens, magpies, grackles, and most any other bird that invades their territories. Courtship consists of much bowing and flashing of the male's gaudy red epaulets as well as a good deal of chasing. Nesting colonies often have an overabundance of females, so males are often polygynous.

Nest and eggs. Although cattail marshes are favored, this species also nests in meadow grass, low bushes, and trees. Their nests are deep cups of sedge leaves, rushes, rootlets, and mosses, which they bind to surrounding vegetation. The 3 or 4 pale bluish green eggs, blotched and scrawled with black, are incubated by the female for 10 to 12 days.

Food. About 75 percent of a Red-winged Blackbird's diet is plant food, although the proportion ranges from about 60 percent in summer to 100 percent in winter. At backyard feeders it devours all kinds of seeds and grains.

Orchard Oriole
(Icterus spurius)

Most male songbirds acquire adult plumage in the spring following their hatching, but, except for having the male's black chin and throat, Orchard Oriole males resemble females through their second summer. Although young males with this second-year plumage sometimes breed, older, brighter-colored rivals lessen their chances of attracting a willing female.

Description. No other North American oriole is colored like the Orchard Oriole. The adult males have black heads, backs, wings, throats, and tails; their underparts and rump patches are burnt orange. The female is greenish above and yellow below and has two white wing bars.

Voice. The song of the Orchard Oriole has a robinlike quality but is high-pitched and hurried: *look here, what cheer, what cheer, whip yo, what cheer, wee-yo.* The male sometimes sings in flight.

Habitat. As its name implies, this species inhabits orchards and shade trees, especially in the southern and central states, where it is most abundant. It shuns heavy forests in favor of farms, suburbs, country roadsides, and open woodlands.

Habits. Many observers have remarked on the Orchard Oriole's propensity to nest in the same tree with a pair of Eastern Kingbirds. Although not especially shy, the Orchard Oriole is usually well hidden in foliage as it sings while hopping among twigs, searching for food.

Orchard Oriole

B. Schorre/VIREO

Northern Oriole

C.H. Greenewalt/VIREO

Nest and eggs. The typical Orchard Oriole nest hangs between the horizontally forked twigs of a tree or shrub. The basketlike, thin-walled structure is deeply hollowed, securely woven of grasses, and well concealed by leaves. The 4 or 5 pale bluish white eggs, which are blotched with browns, purples, and grays, are incubated by the female for 12 to 14 days.

Food. More than 90 percent of the Orchard Oriole's diet is insects, although it occasionally eats fruit and berries.

Northern Oriole
(Icterus galbula)

Ornithologists now consider the Bullock's oriole and its eastern counterpart, the Baltimore oriole, as one species, the Northern Oriole. The name *Baltimore oriole* has its roots in early American history. English colonists in Maryland named this member of the Troupial family after Lord Baltimore because it wears the same color as the lord's family crest. Why the colonists applied the word *oriole* to the American bird is less apparent; the Baltimore oriole is quite different from the European oriole.

Description. The male Northern Oriole of the eastern, or Baltimore, race is bright orange and black with one narrow white wing bar. Its head, neck, upper breast, wings, and tail are black, and its underparts are orange-yellow. Its all-black head distinguishes it from the similar male of the western race. The female and young are olive above and yellow below.

Common Grackle

O.S. Pettingill, Jr./VIREO

Voice. The songs of the two races are quite similar. The typical song is a flutelike series of notes. The typical call of the Baltimore oriole is *hewli*; the Bullock's race utters an emphatic *skip*.

Habitat. The Northern Oriole prefers tall shade trees with shrubby undergrowth, open woods, oak savannahs, and stream borders with tall willows. In the Southwest its habitat includes mesquite groves in dry streambeds. It is a regular inhabitant of tree-lined streets in towns and villages.

Habits. The male Northern Oriole does not lose its bright plumage in the fall molt. It goes south to its wintering grounds in Central America and northern South America clad just as brilliantly as when it arrives north in the spring. The female retains its drab olive plumage the year around. The male arrives at the breeding grounds in the northern United States and Canada a few days before the female. Many backyard bird-watchers consider the spring season complete when they see the first Northern Oriole dart across their lawn.

Nest and eggs. Among songbirds the female Northern Oriole is an accomplished nest builder. The deep hanging basket is woven skillfully of strings, fibers, weed stalks, hair, and similar materials. It hangs high in a tree at the end of a swaying limb. A typical clutch contains 4 pale grayish or bluish white eggs scrawled with browns and blacks. The female incubates the eggs for the approximately 2-week incubation period.

Food. Insects form the basic diet of the Northern Oriole, but fleshy fruits and berries provide variety in the summer and fall. Chopped fruit and orange halves may attract them to backyard stations, and they sometimes visit hummingbird feeders.

Common Grackle
(Quiscalus quiscula)

The Common Grackle is a beautiful bird with a bad reputation. A pompous-looking black creature, it struts about lawns in search of food. In sunlight its sleek black feathers gleam with beautiful iridescent hues. Its bad reputation derives from its habit of stealing large quantities of domestic grain and fruit, and its propensity for feeding on the eggs and young of other birds.

Description. From beak to tail tip, the Common Grackle is 11 to 13 inches long. It creases its long tail in the middle by depressing the central feathers. This keeled tail is conspicuous in flight. Males are black with yellow eyes; females are smaller and duller than their mates.

Voice. Common Grackles are persistent singers, but their song is about as musical as a rusty hinge on a barn door—and that is just what it sounds like. The call note is a harsh *chuck* or *cack*.

Habitat. This bird inhabits a wide variety of urban and suburban environments, including parks and suburban lawns and gardens. The fields and woodlots of farming areas seem particularly attractive. Common Grackles also live in marshes, swampy thickets, and coniferous groves.

Habits. Common Grackles not only flock together by the thousands in fall and winter to feed and roost, but in spring and summer they nest together in small colonies of 20 to 30 pairs. The birds are often considered a nuisance in city parks because they litter walks with their droppings and nesting materials and raise a great commotion. Wildlife managers have made exhaustive studies on how to control the huge flocks of Common Grackles and other blackbirds, without much success.

Nest and eggs. The colonies tend to be in deciduous or coniferous trees, but the birds sometimes choose shrubs or roadside plantings. Common Grackles also nest in natural cavities, on ledges, in cattail marshes, and in birdhouses. Nests are loose, bulky structures of weed stalks, grasses, and debris. The clutch consists of 5 pale greenish white eggs, which are blotched and scrawled with dark browns and purples. The female incubates the eggs for 11 to 12 days.

Food. Omnivorous and adaptable, Common Grackles usually forage on the ground but also feed while wading in water or searching in trees and shrubs. Their diet includes earthworms, seeds, insects, and the eggs and young of other birds. They visit feeding stations readily.

Brown-headed Cowbird

J.R. Woodward/VIREO

Western Tanager

D. & M. Zimmerman/VIREO

Brown-headed Cowbird
(Molothrus ater)

The female Brown-headed Cowbird practices an unusual scheme to propagate its species. With apparently no instinct for building a nest of its own, it resorts to parasitism. It lays its eggs in the nests of other birds—usually birds smaller than itself—and leaves the hatching and raising of its offspring to foster parents.

Description. The female Brown-headed Cowbird is uniformly gray. The male is more conspicuous, with a black body and a coffee-brown head. It is the only bird marked in this way.

Voice. A few gurgling notes, *glug-glug-glee,* serve as the Brown-headed Cowbird's song. Its call note is *chuck.*

Habitat. Almost any habitat is suitable for Brown-headed Cowbirds: farmland, open woodlands, forest edges, ranches, suburban backyards, roadsides, river groves, and city parks.

Habits. Brown-headed Cowbirds often travel in flocks with other blackbirds, especially grackles and Red-Winged Blackbirds. In spring a female may be accompanied by an entourage of males. As a courtship gesture, the male spreads its wings, bows low before the female, and sings a gurgling song.

Nest and eggs. Most birds tolerate the encroachment of cowbird eggs, but some, like the Gray Catbird and American Robin, throw the foreign eggs out of the nest. The female Brown-headed Cowbird often chooses the nests of Yellow Warblers and Song Sparrows as targets. It lays its egg at dawn (often around 4:30 a.m.) before its hostess returns to the nest to lay its own egg for that day. The cowbird usually removes an egg from the target nest the day before or the day after its own egg is laid. The interloping female lays one egg per day—usually in different nests—until it has produced 6 or more. After several days, it

begins a second clutch. The Brown-headed Cowbird produces 3 or 4 clutches of eggs during the nesting season—a total of 11 to 20 eggs. The surrogate mother incubates the cowbird egg with its own until the cowbird hatches, then raises the youngster as part of its brood.

Food. The Brown-headed Cowbird's diet includes many weed seeds, some berries, and many insects. Grasshoppers are a staple.

Western Tanager
(Piranga ludoviciana)

The Western Tanager male is one of the most colorful birds of the Rocky Mountains. Against the dark green of an evergreen forest, the male is a conspicuous and beautiful creature. His song reminds many easterners of the Scarlet Tanager.

Description. With a bright yellow body, black wings and tail, and a crimson head, the male Western Tanager cannot be confused with any other bird. The female Western Tanager (like its relative, the female Scarlet Tanager) is dull in comparison—greenish above and yellowish below. The Western Tanager is the only North American tanager with strong white wing bars. In fall and winter, the red disappears from the male's face and head and changes to yellow-green.

Voice. The Western Tanager's song is robinlike, but hoarser, a repetition of short *pit-ic* or *pit-i-tic* phrases with rising and falling inflections. The call note is *chee-tik.*

Habitat. A bird of coniferous forests, the Western Tanager especially favors mature firs and pines in elevations to 10,000 feet.

Habits. After wintering in Mexico and Central America, Western Tanagers make their way northward at a leisurely pace, occasionally loitering. They arrive on their breeding grounds in April and May. Western Tanagers often visit backyard birdbaths for a quick dip.

Scarlet Tanager

H. Cruickshank/VIREO

Northern Cardinal

B. Schorre/VIREO

Nest and eggs. The Western Tanager saddles its shallow nest 15 to 65 feet above the ground in a fork well out on a horizontal limb of a pine or fir tree. The compact saucer is constructed of twigs and rootlets and lined with hair and rootlets. The 3 to 5 spotted bluish green eggs are incubated by the female for about 13 days. A pair raises only one brood per year.

Food. Western Tanagers enjoy a diverse menu. They eat wasps, ants, caterpillars, cicadas, grasshoppers, and many other insects. They also enjoy cherries, elderberries, crabapples, and other fruits. Western Tanagers may be attracted to backyard feeding stations that offer fresh orange halves and other fruit or baked goods such as doughnuts, bread, and cake.

Scarlet Tanager
(Piranga olivacea)

If a poll were taken to determine the ten most beautiful birds in North America, the Scarlet Tanager would probably be among them. Birdwatchers are continually surprised at how difficult it is to see this bird, despite its brilliant plumage, in the leafy canopy of deciduous trees. Of the four members of the Tanager family that nest in the United States, the Scarlet Tanager has the longest migration and the northernmost breeding range. It also has the dubious distinction of being parasitized more than other tanagers by the Brownheaded Cowbird, which lays eggs in other birds' nests.

Description. The female Scarlet Tanager is olive green and is as conservatively colored as its scarlet-and-black mate is conspicuous. The male sports its fiery plumage only in spring and summer, however; except for black wings and tail it emerges from a late summer molt looking as drab as the female.

Voice. The Scarlet Tanager's song is a hurried, hoarse caroling. Some say it sounds like a robin with a sore throat. The alarm note is a distinctive *chip-churr.*

Habitat. Scarlet Tanagers prefer dense, mature, deciduous or coniferous forests. They may inhabit suburban areas with many large shade trees.

Habits. The male is difficult to locate in treetops because it perches motionlessly for long periods of time, and its red feathers look black in the shade. In courtship it sings and spreads its wings to display its scarlet back.

Nest and eggs. The nest sits 8 to 75 feet above ground, well out on a horizontal limb. An oak is a typical site. Built by the female, the nest is a small, shallow saucer of twigs and rootlets lined with weed stems and grasses. It is sometimes so flimsy that the eggs may be seen through the bottom. The 3 to 5 pale blue or pale green eggs are irregularly spotted with browns. The female incubates the eggs for almost 2 weeks.

Food. Insects are the mainstay of the Scarlet Tanager's diet, but it also eats fleshy fruits and berries. Although usually a treetop feeder, a Scarlet Tanager may occasionally be lured to a summer feeding station, especially one well above ground.

Northern Cardinal
(Cardinalis cardinalis)

John James Audubon wrote that the Northern Cardinal, "in richness of plumage, elegance of motion, and strength of song, surpasses all its kindred in the United States." Illinois, Indiana, Kentucky, North Carolina, Ohio, Virginia, and West Virginia seem to agree, for they have made the Northern Cardinal their state bird.

Once a southern bird, this species has gradually extended its range northward until it now reaches the Canadian border, southern New England, and South Dakota. Cardinals are not truly migratory, but some wander after nesting—especially birds that are less than a year old.

Description. The male is unmistakable with its brilliant red color and crested head. The female's plumage is much more subdued—olive gray back, dull reddish wings and crest, soft pink-brown underparts, and a red bill.

Voice. The male Northern Cardinal is a master songster with a broad repertoire. Its typical song is *what cheer! what cheer!*, *whit-whit-whit-whit*. Another is *purty, purty, purty, purty*, and still another is *cue, cue, cue*. Unlike most female birds, the female Northern Cardinal sings, but normally in a softer voice than that of its mate.

Habitat. Preferred habitat includes dense thickets, woodland margins, and briar tangles; areas along washes and streams; and parks and gardens with thick shrubbery. The Northern Cardinal usually shuns deep forests.

Habits. Cardinals often fly in mixed flocks during the winter, but pairs isolate themselves in spring and summer. The birds may remain mated throughout the year.

Nest and eggs. Northern Cardinals place their nests in dense shrubbery, small trees, thickets, and vines and briar tangles. The nests are loosely built of twigs, vines, leaves, bark strips, and rootlets and have a lining of fine grasses. Three or four grayish blue or greenish white eggs dotted with browns, grays, and purples form the typical clutch. Pairs raise two or three broods annually.

Food. For seed eaters, Northern Cardinals eat a great many insects, especially during the breeding season. They also eat many kinds of fruits and berries and are attracted to feeding stations that offer sunflower seeds.

Rose-breasted Grosbeak
(Pheucticus ludovicianus)

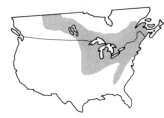

It is unusual to find a brightly colored male bird incubating eggs, but the male Rose-breasted Grosbeak does just that. As if its bright plumage were not enough to jeopardize the hidden nest, it sings while sitting on the eggs. The female is one of the few female songbirds that sings; its song is similar to that of the robin.

Description. These birds are 6½ to 7½ inches long. The male is easily distinguished by its plumage. A black and white finch about the size of a Northern Cardinal, it has a shield-shaped rose breast tapering to a rose streak down the middle. The bird's large beak looks like a great white nose. Its delicate pink wing linings are noticeable in overhead flight. The drab female has been aptly described as resembling an overgrown sparrow. Heavily striped above and brown streaked below, the female has white spots on its wings and a white line over each eye.

Voice. The Rose-breasted Grosbeak's long, broken warble is similar to the song of a robin but sweeter and more varied. The song also resembles the Scarlet Tanager's but lacks its hoarseness. The call note is an unmistakable metallic *kink*.

Habitat. Rose-breasted Grosbeaks prefer moist, deciduous woods, swamp borders, thickets, old orchards, suburban trees, and shrubs. They frequently nest in backyards in towns and suburbs where dense plantings of small trees, shrubs, and hedges afford thick cover.

Rose-breasted Grosbeak

B. Schorre/VIREO

Habits. Several male Rose-breasted Grosbeaks sometimes fight fiercely over one female during courtship. They hover over the female and pour out their finest vocal renditions. Mated pairs appear quite affectionate; they often touch bills in courtship.

Nest and eggs. The nest is a thin, curved structure of many twigs and dried weed stalks, which the birds line with finer materials. It is generally 6 to 26 feet above ground in the fork of a deciduous tree or shrub, though the birds occasionally choose a conifer. A nest is sometimes so flimsy that eggs may be seen through the lining from the ground. The 4 eggs are greenish blue and speckled with shades of brown. The pair shares the incubation duties over the 12- to 14-day incubation period.

Food. The Rose-breasted Grosbeak consumes large numbers of harmful insects, especially potato beetles. In spring and summer about 40 percent of their diet is plant food, mostly seeds and flower buds. Sunflower seeds may attract them to feeding stations.

Black-headed Grosbeak
(Pheucticus melanocephalus)

The Black-headed Grosbeak is to the West what the Rose-breasted Grosbeak is to the East. Like its eastern cousin, the male Black-headed Grosbeak shares incubation of the eggs and attends the young. The songs of the two species are similar and their feeding habits are alike. Besides range, the only important difference between the two birds is the plumage.

Description. The Black-headed Grosbeak is the same shape and size as the Rose-breasted Grosbeak, about 6½ to 7½ inches long. The jet-black head of the male contrasts with an orange-brown breast, a chestnut-colored nape, and black wings boldly

Black-headed Grosbeak

D. & M. Zimmerman/VIREO

Indigo Bunting

Herbert Clarke

marked with white. The female resembles the female Rose-breasted Grosbeak but has an unstreaked brown breast and extremely fine streaking on its sides.

Voice. Much like the song of its close relative, the Rose-breasted Grosbeak, the Black-headed Grosbeak's song resembles that of the American Robin but is richer and mellower with clear whistled trills that rise and fall. The call note is a sharp *eek.*

Habitat. The Black-headed Grosbeak favors open woodlands but may also be found along streams, near ponds and swamps, and in thickets, orchards, and parks.

Habits. Black-headed Grosbeaks seem to have little fear of people and readily come into camps, parks, and picnic grounds for handouts. The male arrives back from the Mexican wintering grounds about a week before the female. When the female arrives, the male sings to its mate from a nearby perch. The male sometimes rises suddenly into the air to per-

form its courtship song in flight. Where their ranges overlap (mostly in Nebraska and North Dakota), Black-headed Grosbeaks are known to sometimes interbreed with Rose-breasted Grosbeaks.

Nest and eggs. A bulky cup of twigs, stems, and other plant material is placed in the fork of a small tree or a shrub. Built by the female in 3 to 4 days, the nest is so loosely woven that it is not unusual to see the eggs through the bottom when looking up from the ground. Both parents share in the incubation of the 3 or 4 brown-spotted bluish green eggs. Grosbeaks sometimes sing while sitting on the eggs—the male seems especially prone to song.

Food. With their strong, conical bills, Black-headed Grosbeaks easily crack sunflower seeds, pine seeds, and other wild seeds. They also eat berries and a number of insects.

Indigo Bunting
(Passerina cyanea)

The male Indigo Bunting that you see singing *sweet-sweet* from the top branch of a roadside tree, bathed in bright morning sun, is as blue as any bird. On a rainy day you might not recognize it as the same bird, for now it appears brown. When the Indigo Bunting's feathers are wet, they cannot reflect the light that ordinarily makes them appear blue. Blue, green, and purple birds all actually have brown feathers that are covered with a thin, transparent coating that refracts light rays to produce bright colors.

Description. The male Indigo Bunting is the only North American finch that appears blue all over. Female Indigo Buntings are brown above with buff and faintly streaked underparts.

Voice. The male sings a series of high-pitched notes from a conspicuous perch: *sweet-sweet, where-where, here-*

here, see it, see it. Each syllable pair is a different pitch.

Habitat. Open brushy fields, clearings, hedgerows, roadside thickets, edges of woods, and overgrown fencerows are typical habitats.

Habits. Indigo Buntings usually migrate in the fall to Mexico, the West Indies, and Central and South America, but some individuals winter in Florida and occasionally stop even farther north.

Nest and eggs. The female Indigo Bunting builds the nest 2 to 12 feet above ground in dense cover. It is likely to be in the crotch of a bush, shrub, or low tree; in a tangle of blackberries; or in a cane thicket. On a base of leaves, the nest is a woven cup of dried grass, bark strips, twigs, forbs, and sometimes snakeskin lined with fine grasses, cotton, rootlets, and hair. The 3 or 4 eggs are white or pale bluish white and unmarked. Incubation is 12 to 13 days and there are usually two broods a year. The nests are frequently parasitized by Brown-headed Cowbirds.

Food. Thistle seeds are a primary food source for Indigo Buntings. They also eat the seeds of goldenrod, asters, and grasses, as well as grains and insects. Indigo Buntings may be lured to feeding stations where they prefer to eat on the ground.

Evening Grosbeak

O.S. Pettingill, Jr./VIREO

Purple Finch

Herbert Clarke

Evening Grosbeak
(Coccothraustes vespertinus)

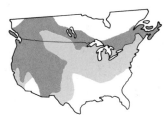

Within the last hundred years or so, these colorful birds have extended their range east of the Great Lakes. During the winter, plantings of box elders and maples provide the seeds and buds that lured them eastward, but little is more inviting to them than a backyard feeding station with a quantity of sunflower seeds.

Description. Evening Grosbeaks are chunky birds with short tails. Their plumage and their undulating flight make them look like large American Goldfinches. The male has a yellow forehead, black crown and tail, olive brown back, yellow underparts, and black wings with white secondary feathers. The female Evening Grosbeak is grayish and yellow, with black on its wings. Both sexes have large whitish beaks.

Voice. This bird sings a short, uneven warble reminiscent of the notes of a Purple Finch. Its chirping notes are much like those of the common House Sparrow but shriller and more harsh.

Habitat. Fir and spruce forests are the year-round home of the Evening Grosbeak. It winters in the southern part of its range and visits inhabited areas only to obtain sunflower seeds.

Habits. Evening Grosbeaks are gregarious throughout the year; they roost and feed together even while nesting. In courtship, the male seeks a mate within the flock and feeds it as part of the courting ritual.

Nest and eggs. Evening Grosbeaks situate their nests 20 to 60 feet above ground in conifers. The female builds a frail, loosely constructed cup of twigs interwoven with mosses and lichens, which it lines with rootlets. The 3 or 4 eggs the female lays are blue or blue-green blotched with browns, grays, and purples. In captivity the eggs are incubated for 12 to 14 days by the female; the length of the incubation period in the wild is not reported.

Food. In summer, especially while nesting, Evening Grosbeaks consume large quantities of insects. Besides eating sunflower seeds at winter bird feeders, they also forage for buds and seeds in the wild.

Purple Finch
(Carpodacus purpureus)

Bird-watchers who attract Purple Finches to their backyard feeders have the privilege of seeing one of the most strikingly colored North American birds. For many years, eastern bird-watchers were able to identify the raspberry-colored birds easily, but in recent years the invasion of the House Finch has made identification more difficult.

Description. The Purple Finch is actually a dull rose-red. Roger Tory Peterson describes it as looking "like a sparrow dipped in raspberry juice." Female and immature Purple Finches are brown, heavily striped, and sparrowlike.

Voice. This finch sings a rich, musical, rising and falling warble, sometimes while in flight. Its call is a sharp metallic *tick* or *tuck*, which it also gives in flight.

Habitat. Coniferous (and sometimes deciduous) forests, roadside conifers, Christmas tree farms, and ornamental evergreens provide breeding grounds for Purple Finches.

Habits. The flight of this species is conspicuously undulating. The Purple Finch is an erratic migrant; a dwindling supply of seeds in the North accounts for the large flocks that move southward during severe winters.

Nest and eggs. The nest is almost always placed on the horizontal branch of a conifer or in a crotch at the trunk of a small tree. The female builds the well-concealed, shallow cup of grasses, twigs, forb stems, bark strips, and rootlets, then lines the cup with fine grasses and hair. A typical clutch contains 4 or 5 greenish blue eggs spotted with dark brown, which the female incubates for almost 2 weeks.

Food. The adult's staple foods are buds, fruits, berries and seeds; nestlings sometimes eat insects and caterpillars. Purple Finches are fond of sunflower seeds and prefer elevated feeders to ground feeding.

House Finch

D. & M. Zimmerman/VIREO

Common Redpoll

J.R. Woodward/VIREO

House Finch
(Carpodacus mexicanus)

Abundant in the western United States, the common House Finch was almost unknown to eastern bird-watchers until it was introduced illegally in the 1940s by caged-bird dealers. Like the House Sparrow, the House Finch thrived, adapting quickly to human settlements. This bird is less aggressive than the House Sparrow, has a much prettier song, and a pleasing bright color.

Description. Although it is often confused with the Purple Finch, the red on the crown, breast, and rump of the male House Finch is brighter than the wine color of the Purple Finch. The male House Finch can also be distinguished by its brown-streaked flanks. The female House Finch lacks the red of the male. It is similar to the female Purple Finch but is smaller, more finely streaked, and bears no contrasting stripes on the face.

Voice. Both the male and the female sing a lively, warbling song that they repeat many times. Their call note is *kweet* or *pit.*

Habitat. In the West the House Finch is found in brushy deserts, chaparral, old fields, and areas around abandoned buildings. In the East this species inhabits towns, gardens, and open woodlands. It adapts easily to a civilized environment.

Habits. Flocks that visit feeding stations during the cold months divide into mated pairs in spring. In courtship the male follows the female, fluttering its wings and repeating a warbling refrain.

Nest and eggs. For a nest site the House Finch may choose a branch of an ever-green, a tree cavity, a birdhouse, a ledge, or the eaves of a building. The site may be in a town or along a roadway. In the West the House Finch frequently nests in a cactus or desert shrub. The 4 or 5 eggs are pale bluish green spotted with black. The female incubates the eggs for 12 to 14 days. A pair usually produces two broods annually.

Food. Seeds, fruits, and berries are mainstays of the House Finch's diet. They capture a few insects, but usually feed them to the young. House Finches are regular patrons at feeding stations in both the East and West.

Common Redpoll
(Carduelis flammea)

A lone Common Redpoll in the United States is an unusual sight. Large flocks of these little arctic finches occasionally visit the northern states in winter. They are sociable with other species as well as with their own; they fly and feed regularly with goldfinches, crossbills, siskins, and Evening Grosbeaks. They do not fight over territories even on their nesting ground. Pairs occasionally nest close together.

Description. The jaunty red cap on the forehead and the black chin patch are the field marks of these small, 5- to 5½-inch-long birds. Their upperparts are streaked grayish brown; the abdomen is white. The male's breast and rump have a pinkish wash. Hoary Redpolls occasionally join in flocks with Common Redpolls. The two birds look alike, but the Hoary Redpoll has a frostier coloration and a white rump.

Voice. The Common Redpoll's song is a trill followed by a rattling *chet, chet, chet, chet.* Their call, *swee-e-et,* is similar to the American Goldfinch's but a bit coarser.

Habitat. Tundra scrub, coniferous forests, swamps, and birch woods make up the Common Redpoll's usual habitat. In some winters, they wander south into the northern United States.

Pine Siskin

Wayne Lankinen/DRK Photo

American Goldfinch

J.R. Woodward/VIREO

Habits. This tiny bird can survive in colder temperatures than any other songbird. Americans see Common Redpolls only in winter—and not every winter—in flocks that wander about snowy landscapes. Common Redpolls are generally quite tame, and eagerly use backyard bird feeders.

Nest and eggs. The female builds the nest close to the ground on a branch or in the crotch of a willow, alder, or spruce. A loose base of twigs supports a cup of smaller twigs, grasses, and mosses, which it lines with a thick blanket of ptarmigan feathers. The 4 to 7 pale green or blue eggs are spotted with dark purple. The female incubates them for 10 to 11 days.

Food. Common Redpolls eat some insects in the summer and feed them to their young, but for the most part they are seed eaters. At backyard feeders they prefer niger and sunflower seeds.

Pine Siskin
(Carduelis pinus)

Pine Siskins are the gypsies of the bird world. Pine Siskins wander most of the year in noisy flocks, sometimes with their own kind, sometimes—especially in winter—with large flocks of goldfinches, redpolls, and crossbills.

Description. Pine Siskins are the smallest of the winter finches. They are heavily streaked on a gray-brown back and buff-gray underparts. Some yellow shows in their wings and tail. The sexes look similar.

Voice. The Pine Siskin's song is similar to that of the American Goldfinch and the canary but coarser and wheezier. Their call notes are *tit-a-tit*, which the birds sing while flying in compact flocks.

Habitat. Pine Siskins roam over coniferous forests from the Atlantic to the Pacific.

Habits. Pine Siskins fly relatively high in swift, compact flocks and give their call notes during characteristic undulating sweeps. When courting, the males feed the females while they are still in flocks, and there is much singing and chasing until pairs are formed. Siskins have no fixed home for nesting. In spring, after roaming the evergreen forests in flocks of 50 to 200, they form pairs that nest in the area where courtship took place, though they do not always return to the same nesting area. After the young leave the nest, the birds resume their roving.

Nest and eggs. Pine Siskins nest in singles and in pairs, but loose colonies are not uncommon. The nest is well concealed on a horizontal conifer branch, usually at a distance from the trunk, in a natural stand or planting of evergreens. The nest is a large, shallow cup of twigs, grasses, mosses, lichens, and rootlets. It has a lining of finer rootlets, hair, fur, and feathers. The 3 or 4 greenish blue eggs are spotted with brown. The female incubates the eggs, and the male feeds its mate throughout the 13-day period.

Food. Pine Siskins eat weed seeds and the seeds of trees most of the year. During the nesting season adults and nestlings also eat many insects. The birds enjoy seeds at winter feeding stations. They will eat from hanging feeders or collect seeds from the ground.

American Goldfinch
(Carduelis tristis)

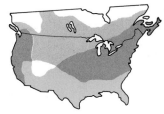

The common name, wild canary, is certainly appropriate for the American Goldfinch, for it looks like a canary and sings like one. When a flock of these bright yellow birds swoops down on a bed of ripening cosmos, dandelions, bachelor's buttons, or coreopsis, you could easily believe that someone left the cage door open on a canary farm.

Description. The American Goldfinch is the only small yellow bird with black wings, cap, and tail. The female is olive yellow with dusky wings and two white wing bars. In winter both sexes look much like the summer female but grayer.

Voice. The male has a canarylike song that is marked with a series of trills and twitters. His undulating flight is marked by a *per-chick-o-ree* song with each downward swing. Bands of goldfinches utter low *swee-swee* notes as they flit from one flower stalk to another during the summer or vie for perches on feeders during the winter.

Habitat. American Goldfinches spend most of the year in little roving bands that forage over the countryside. Many move South in the fall, but others winter in the North. Backyard feeders that feature sunflower and niger seeds are often on their daily itinerary as they roam over the landscape in their deeply undulating flight.

Habits. When the thistles ripen in July and August, long after most birds have nested, cheery bands of these finches divide into mated pairs and establish nesting territories. The American Goldfinch tolerates an ill-kept and unclean nest. A bird-watcher can identify an American Goldfinch's nest long after the young have left by the thick layer of excrement piled around the rim.

Nest and eggs. An American Goldfinch places its nest deep among several upright branches or on the fork of a horizontal limb. The nest is a durable, neat cup of fine interwoven vegetable fibers and is lined with thistle and cattail down. Some nest cups tend to be deeper than they are wide. Five bluish white unmarked eggs form the typical clutch, and the female incubates them for 12 to 14 days. The male feeds its mate during incubation.

Food. In the spring, as much as half of their diet is insects, which they also feed to their young. At other times of the year weed seeds are the primary food source. Feeding stations with niger and sunflower seeds attract American Goldfinches.

Lesser Goldfinch
(Carduelis psaltria)

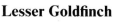

Once known as the Arkansas goldfinch because it was first seen along the Arkansas River in Colorado, the Lesser Goldfinch is the smallest North American goldfinch. This sweet songster bears the species name *psaltria*, which means one who plays the lute. There are two races of the Lesser Goldfinch: The more western form, sometimes called the green-backed goldfinch, has a dark green back; the so-called dark-backed goldfinch, more common in the eastern part of the range, has a solid black back.

Lesser Goldfinch

Description. This tiny finch is a mere 3¾ to 4¼ inches long. The male has dark green or black upperparts and is bright canary yellow below. Bold white patches on the wings become visible when the bird is in flight. The female Lesser Goldfinch looks like a somewhat smaller version of the American Goldfinch female but is more greenish and has a dark rump.

Voice. A sweet, canarylike, rising *tee-yee* and a falling *tee-yer* is the plaintive song of the Lesser Goldfinch. The bird often sings these notes in flight.

Habitat. The Lesser Goldfinch is as likely to live in suburban backyards as open woodlands, brushy fields, farmland, roadsides, and streamsides.

Habits. Lesser Goldfinch pairs stay together throughout the winter, joining flocks of their own kind to rove the countryside in search of seeds. In spring courtship the male sings to and feeds the female. It continues to feed its mate during incubation.

Nest and eggs. With some help from the male, the female constructs a dainty cup of plant fibers, fine grasses, and moss. Well concealed in a tree or bush, the nest is lined with plant down, a few feathers, and other soft materials. The 4 or 5 pale blue eggs, indistinguishable from those of the American Goldfinch, hatch after 12 days of incubation by the female.

Food. Like other goldfinches, the Lesser Goldfinch is an avid seed eater; weed seeds make up about 95 percent of its diet. It has a particular fondness for wild thistle seeds and often visits backyard water areas to drink.

Rufous-sided Towhee

C.H. Greenewalt/VIREO

Brown Towhee

D. & M. Zimmerman/VIREO

Rufous-sided Towhee
(Pipilo erythrophthalmus)

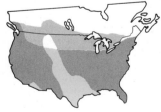

The towhee belongs to a small group of birds named for their songs or calls. In its call, the towhee slurs the first part of its name so that it sounds like *t'whee*. Its other common call, *che-wink*, is the source of its often-used English name, chewink. Because it looks somewhat like a robin and spends much of its time on the ground, it has also been called a ground robin.

Description. The male Rufous-sided Towhee has a black head, bill, throat, upper breast, back, wings, and tail. Its sides are rich brown. The white in the wings and in the corners of the long, rounded tail are good field marks. Females have the same pattern but are brown where the male is black.

Voice. *Towhee* and *chewink* are the call notes of the Rufous-sided Towhee. Its real song consists of three musical syllables that may be interpreted as *drink your teeeeeeee.* The third syllable is delivered in a quavering voice.

Habitat. The Rufous-sided Towhee is attracted to open brushy fields, barrens, hedgerows, thickets, slashings, woodland, roadside edges, suburbs, and parks.

Habits. Rattling and scuffling among dry leaves is a common habit of the Rufous-sided Towhee. Foraging on the ground in thick cover, the bird scratches with both feet, creating a surprising amount of commotion with its flurry of activity.

Nest and eggs. Rufous-sided Towhees typically place their nests on or near the ground, under or in a small bush. Second or late nests may be in small trees or bushes. The nest is bulky and firmly built of leaves, bark strips, weed stalks, twigs, and grasses. It has a lining of fine grasses and hair, bark shreds, and pine needles. The 4 or 5 white eggs are finely dotted with reddish brown. The female builds the nest and incubates the eggs for 12 to 13 days until they hatch. Northern pairs usually raise two broods per year; southern birds sometimes raise three.

Food. The diet of the Rufous-sided Towhee is half insects and half plant food. They visit feeding stations but prefer to be on the ground under the feeder. When they do alight on elevated feeders, their furious scratching sends seeds flying in all directions.

Brown Towhee
(Pipilo fuscus)

The only facet that seems to distinguish this drab, gray-brown bird is its commonness. Next to the House Finch and Brewer's Blackbird, the Brown Towhee is the most common and most obvious bird about gardens, ranch buildings, and roadside brush within its Southwest range.

Dark-eyed Junco

J.D. Young/VIREO

Description. This towhee is uniformly dusky with a reddish patch under its rather long tail and a light buff throat bordered faintly by dark streaks. Its short, small sparrowlike bill distinguishes it from similar thrashers.

Voice. The Brown Towhee's calls and songs produce the sounds *ssip* or *chip.* Its song is a monotonous succession of *chips* with a frequent trill at the end of the series.

Habitat. Though still common in its natural habitat of open oak woods, wooded valleys, canyons, chaparral, and sage, the Brown Towhee is far more numerous about towns and backyards where trees are plentiful.

Habits. Like its relative, the Rufous-sided Towhee, this species scratches the ground with vigorous backward kicks, using both feet at once. Wary in wild country, the Brown Towhee is quite tame around gardens and backyards. The pair is mated for life.

Nest and eggs. The nest is a bulky, well-made, deep cup of small twigs, forb stems, and grasses and is lined with fine grasses, rootlets, and hair. The birds place nests in low bushes, vines, or small trees. Usually 3 or 4 eggs constitute a clutch, which the female incubates for 11 days. Eggs vary greatly with the races of this species that occur in different regions, but they are usually white with brown spots or scrawls.

Food. A ground feeder, the Brown Towhee scratches for seeds of forbs and grasses under shrubs and in dense grassy patches. It comes to bird feeders for small seeds and is well known for scratching the seed out of the feeder and onto the ground.

Dark-eyed Junco
(Junco hyemalis)

Until recently, ornithologists believed that the birds known as the white-winged junco, the slate-colored junco, and the Oregon junco were separate species, but they interbreed freely where their ranges overlap and are now considered one species, the Dark-eyed Junco.

Description. Dark-eyed Junco males are mantled with black or sooty gray "ponchos," and their white underparts are sharply defined. White outer tail feathers usually show in flight. Their bills are pink and their eyes are brown. Females are similar, but they are brown where the males are sooty and their ponchos are not defined. Some western races show more of brown. The race known as the Pink-sided Junco has brown upperparts and a gray hood; the Oregon race has brown upperparts and a black hood.

Voice. The musical trill of the Dark-eyed Junco is on one pitch. It is similar to that of the Chipping Sparrow but shorter, faster, and more musical. The call is a series of clinking notes.

Habitat. Coniferous and mixed forests, forest edges, and roadside embankments are favored nesting areas.

Habits. During the winter, flocks roam the countryside throughout most of the United States. In April they become restless and head north to their breeding range.

Nest and eggs. Dark-eyed Junco nests are usually on the ground under concealing forbs and grasses; on slopes, rock ledges, or roadside banks; in fallen tree roots; under fallen trees and logs; and—occasionally—low in a tree. The female builds a compact nest of grasses, rootlets, bark shreds, mosses, and twigs and lines it with finer grasses, rootlets, and hair. The 4 or 5 pale bluish white eggs are spotted with brown, purple, and gray. Egg markings may vary considerably. The female incubates the eggs for 12 to 13 days.

Food. Dark-eyed Juncos generally eat weed seeds, but in spring and summer they consume many kinds of insects. Juncos prefer to feed on the ground, though they sometimes come to low platform feeding stations. Millet and finely cracked corn attracts them.

American Tree Sparrow

J.R. Woodward/VIREO

American Tree Sparrow
(Spizella arborea)

The American Tree Sparrow spends little time in trees. This sparrow is rarely seen in the summer; its breeding grounds are just south of the tundra, from Alaska across northern Canada. But in winter, hardly a feeding station in the northern United States fails to attract this seed eater. It is most common at feeders during the harshest and snowiest weather. Unlike other winter invaders from the North (like crossbills and siskins), American Tree Sparrows are influenced in their southward migration more by weather than by food supply. The number of American Tree Sparrows in the United States is noticeably smaller during mild winters.

Description. A dark brown spot in the center of a whitish gray breast distinguishes the American Tree Sparrow. The gray head with a reddish crown and ear stripe and the streaked brown back are also distinctive.

Voice. In spring sweet canarylike notes and trills are sometimes heard as these winter chippies prepare to move northward. The winter call heard most often, a *teelwit* note, is likened to the merry tinkling of tiny sleigh bells.

Habitat. In winter, flocks wander over weedy fields, marshes, hedgerows, and backyards that offer food. In the North during the nesting season, American Tree Sparrows live in tundra edges in open areas with scattered trees and bushes.

Habits. American Tree Sparrows come to the United States only in a wandering flock in search of food in winter. The flocks arrive in October and November and leave during warm April days.

Nest and eggs. Few have seen the nest of the American Tree Sparrow because the birds nest in such a remote area. The nest is usually on the ground, but may be in a low bush. It is built of grasses and forb stems and lined neatly with feathers. The female lays 5 or 6 eggs, then incubates them for 12 to 13 days. The eggs resemble those of the Song Sparrow. Nesting does not begin until June, and pairs attempt only one brood per year.

Food. Weed seeds compose most of this bird's diet; therefore, winter feeding stations are attractive. American Tree Sparrows prefer to eat on the ground or on a tabletop rather than at hanging feeders.

Chipping Sparrow

J.R. Woodward/VIREO

Chipping Sparrow
(Spizella passerina)

Over much of its range in the East, the Chipping Sparrow has forsaken its home in the wild and has become one of the most domesticated North American sparrows. A birdwatcher with a medium-size garden is almost certain to see the chippy each summer. Two other sparrows with chestnut caps are easily confused with this bird. The American Tree Sparrow, which is in the continental United States only in winter, wears a distinct central breast spot. The Field Sparrow, which rarely visits backyards, has a pink bill and no eye line.

Description. The Chipping Sparrow's upperparts are brown streaked with black; the underparts, sides of the face, and the rump are gray. The chestnut crown and white eyebrow with a black line through the eye are good identifiers.

Voice. Some say that the Chipping Sparrow sounds like a sewing machine. The bird repeats the monotonous series of short notes so rapidly that it is almost a trill. The alarm note is a single *chip*.

Habitat. Look for Chipping Sparrows in towns, farms, orchards, gardens, lawns, shrubbery, open woodlands, and conifer plantings.

Habits. The Chipping Sparrow is an inconspicuous little bird. It makes no bid for attention except when it sings its trilling song. In fall small flocks often forage for seeds in lawns and gardens.

Nest and eggs. For nesting, Chipping Sparrows choose trees (often conifers), shrubs, or vines. The female builds a nest of fine dead grasses, forb stalks, and rootlets and lines it with hair and fine grasses. The nest is placed up to 25 feet above ground. A clutch of 4 pale bluish green eggs spotted, blotched, and scrawled with dark brown, black, and purple is typical. The female incubates the eggs for 11 to 14 days. These sparrows usually produce two broods in one nesting season.

Food. In spring and summer most of the Chipping Sparrow's diet consists of insects, such as weevils, leaf beetles, leafhoppers, caterpillars, grasshoppers, ants, spiders, and wasps. In fall and winter it consumes grass and weeds in great quantities. In winter Chipping Sparrows visit southern feeding stations where they forage on the ground under bird feeders.

Field Sparrow

J.R. Woodward/VIREO

Field Sparrow
(Spizella pusilla)

In pastures, meadows, and abandoned fields, this little sparrow sings its melancholy trill from morning to night during the nesting season. On hot afternoons when other songbirds are silent, the Field Sparrow persists. It may even be heard singing on occasional moonlit nights.

Description. A pink bill is one of the best identification marks of this 5¼- to 6-inch sparrow. It sports a rusty red cap, somewhat rusty upperparts, and a clear, unstreaked buff breast.

Voice. Beginning with several notes delivered slowly and on the same pitch, the Field Sparrow's song accelerates and ends in a rapidly repeated trill: *see-u, see-u, see-u, seeu, seeu, seeu, seeu, wee, wee.*

Habitat. Abandoned fields, brushy pastures, fencerows, meadows, woodland edges, and briar thickets suit the Field Sparrow's requirements.

Habits. Unlike its close relative the Chipping Sparrow, the Field Sparrow is shy and avoids human habitation. Though it rarely nests near houses, it sometimes visits backyard water areas in summer to drink and bathe and feeding stations during migration to gather seeds.

Nest and eggs. Accompanied by its mate, the female weaves a nest cup of grass and leaves on or near the ground. They then add a lining of rootlets, fine grasses, and hair. The 3 or 4 creamy, bluish or greenish eggs spotted with reddish brown hatch after about 11 days of incubation by the female. A pair usually produces two broods a year; sometimes they produce three. Young can leave the nest one week after hatching and can fly at two weeks; at one month, they can survive on their own.

Food. Basically insectivorous, the Field Sparrow mostly forages on the ground for beetles, weevils, caterpillars, leafhoppers, grasshoppers, ants, flies, wasps, and spiders. The birds also consume some weed seeds.

White-crowned Sparrow

D. & M. Zimmerman/VIREO

White-throated Sparrow

J.R. Woodward/VIREO

White-crowned Sparrow
(Zonotrichia leucophrys)

Most sparrows enjoy the company of mixed flocks in migration, but the White-crowned Sparrow remains aloof, moving over ancestral routes alone or in small bands of its own kind. It migrates about two weeks later than its close relative, the White-throated Sparrow, with which it is often confused.

Description. The White-crowned Sparrow has a pearl gray breast, a black-and-white striped crown, and a pinkish or yellowish bill.

Voice. The White-crowned Sparrow's song is composed of soft, rich, plaintive whistles, similar to the song of the White-throated Sparrow's *peabody* song. The song varies with the races of this species.

Habitat. White-crowned Sparrows prefer clearings, forest edges, alpine meadows, parks, and gardens with shrub cover. They also inhabit stream borders, marshes, and other watery places.

Habits. This species has the distinctive habit of partially extending its crown to form a low crest, a maneuver that shows off the white feathers to advantage. While feeding on the ground, the birds vigorously scratch for seeds and some insects with both feet at the same time. During the breeding season, males sing from a stalk of grass or a twig near the pair's nest.

Nest and eggs. The nests of White-crowned Sparrows are on or a few feet above the ground under or within dense vegetation. Ground nests may be in tussocks of grass or densely matted vegetation. The female builds the nest of fine twigs, rootlets, grasses, feathers, and hair. The structure usually holds 4 or 5 pale greenish or creamy white eggs, which are heavily marked with reddish brown blotches. The female incubates the eggs for 12 days.

Food. Small seeds of forbs and grasses are the mainstays of this bird's diet. In spring and summer the White-crowned Sparrow also eats insects. At winter feeding stations it prefers to forage for seed at tray feeders or on the ground.

White-throated Sparrow
(Zonotrichia albicollis)

The lyrics of the song of the lovely White-throated Sparrow are open to interpretation. In Canada, where many of these birds nest, it is often interpreted as *sweeeet canada, canada, canada.* New Englanders often report its song as *old sam peabody, peabody, peabody.* But William L. Dawson, the famous Ohio ornithologist, said that "the bird does not utter anything remotely resembling *peabody* when it is in Ohio."

Description. A distinct white throat patch, a yellow mark between the eye and bill, a darker bill, and flatter head distinguish the White-throated Sparrow from the White-crowned Sparrow. Adults of both species have black-and-white head stripes.

Song Sparrow

J.R. Woodward/VIREO

Voice. The White-throated Sparrow's song is beautiful in its sweet simplicity and rich tone quality. The call is a lisping *tseet*. The female sometimes sings.

Habitat. These birds live in undergrowth, at the edges of coniferous and northern deciduous forests, in clearings, brushy thickets, brush piles, cut-over woods, and park and garden shrubbery.

Habits. On their nesting territories, White-throated Sparrows work their way somewhat noisily over the ground in search of food. They sometimes come close to a quiet observer and often visit feeders.

Nest and eggs. The female builds the nest on or close to the ground under a grassy hummock, a brush pile, prostrate tree branch, or mat of dead fern or dead grass. The structure of coarse grasses, rootlets, pine needles, twigs, bark fibers, and mosses has a lining of fine grasses, rootlets, and hair. The 4 creamy or bluish white eggs are heavily spotted and blotched with browns that sometimes obscure the background color. The female broods for 12 to 14 days.

Food. White-throated Sparrows feed primarily on weed seeds. At feeders, where they eat cracked corn, millet, and hulled sunflower seeds, they prefer to feed on the ground close to cover.

Song Sparrow
(Melospiza melodia)

The spring melody of the Song Sparrow is one of the best-known North American bird songs. The Song Sparrow, whose beautiful song belies its drab appearance, is a permanent resident in much of its vast range, but individuals in the extreme northern United States and southern Canada move farther south for the winter.

Description. The Song Sparrow's upperparts are usually a streaked brown. The underparts are whitish with streaks on the sides and breast that join to form a dark spot. The crown is brown with a narrow gray stripe, and a broad grayish stripe runs over the eye. The Song Sparrow's appearance varies by region. In desert areas it is pale; in humid regions it is dark.

Voice. The male's song begins with three clear notes of *sweet, sweet, sweet* followed by short notes and a trill. The Song Sparrow's distinctive call note is *chimp*. To describe its song, Thoreau wrote the following in his journal in 1853: "*Maids, maids, maids . . . hang on your tea kettle . . . ettle, ettle, ettle, ettle.*"

Habitat. Song Sparrows inhabit farms, cities, suburbs, gardens, backyards, roadsides, brushy fields, thickets, swamps, hedgerows, and woodland edges.

Habits. In flight, the Song Sparrow pumps its long, round tail. Where many Song Sparrows are nesting, the song of one male arouses all the others in the vicinity to answer. Silence follows, only to be broken again when a male announces its presence to all of its neighbors.

Nest and eggs. The Song Sparrow's nest is well hidden on the ground under a tuft of grass, bush, or brush pile, or in a low bush or tree. The cup of grasses, weed stems, leaves, and bark fibers is lined with fine grasses, rootlets, and hair. The 3 to 5 eggs are greenish white and heavily spotted and splotched with reddish brown and purple. The female incubates them for 12 or 13 days. Song Sparrows usually produce two clutches per year.

Food. In fall and winter Song Sparrows eat small seeds of grasses and weeds. In summer, insects constitute as much as half of their diet. Winter residents are frequent visitors to feeding stations.

Index

Note: Page numbers in **bold** refer to the Gallery of Birds. Page numbers in *italics* refer to photographs.

A

ABA. *See* American Birding Association
Accidental injury, 227–28
Accidentals (strays), 14
Aerodynamics, 126, 129
Airfoils, 126, 132
Akepa, 106
Akialoa, Kauai, 106
Akiapolaau, 106
Albatross, 28, 31, 46, 127, 129, 132, 133, 143
Albatross, Laysan, *129, 133, 238, 256*
Albatross, Royal, *31*
Albatross, Short-tailed, 106
Albatross, Wandering, *78*
  nesting behavior, 79
  wing span, 133
Alerting behavior, 60
Altricial birds, 80, 81
Amakihi, *90*
Ambiortus, 26
American Birding Association (ABA), 13, 14
American Ornithologists' Union (AOU), 11, 25, 113
Anhinga, *14,* 28, 31
Anis, 37
Antbird, 41
AOU. *See* American Ornithologists' Union
Aquatic ecosystems, 90
Archaeopteryx, 26, 37, 117
Arctic-breeding songbirds, 50
Attracting birds
  See also Backyard habitat
  bird feeders, 195–204, 220
  bird-food garden for, 172
  birdhouses, 214–23
  in city, 173
  with food. *See* Feeding birds
  garden pools, 179–80
  gardens, *166,* 166–72, *212*
  for nesting, 205–9, 213, 214–22
  roosting boxes, 219
  safety, 224–28
  water sources, 172, 174–83
  in winter, 183, 184–85, 219
Audubon Society, 17, 113, 189, 233
Auk, 2, 30, 35
Auklet, 76
Aves, 21, 22
Aviaries, 254–55
Avocet, 29, 36, 55
Avocet, American, *35*

B

Backyard habitat
  See also Attracting birds; *specific habitat elements.*
  buildings, 165
  for cavity nesters, 214–23
  creating, 92, 166–72
  for hummingbirds, 212–13
  in cities, 173
  nesting materials, 207–9
  nesting sites, 206, 220
  parallels to natural habitat, 164, 165

range expansion, 85
  specialization, 94
Banded birds, 152–53, 228
Barbets, 29, 39, 40
Barn-Owl, 29, 46
Barriers, 45
Bathing, 174. *See also* Birdbaths
Bee-eater, 29, 39
Behavior, 44–49
Aggressive behavior, 47, 59
  antipredator, 56–60
  bathing, 174
  mating, 65–75
    establishing and defending territories, 61–64
  evolution of, 44
  feeding, 50–55
  grooming, 174
  individual characteristics, 44–47
  movement, 43, 47
  nest defense, 76–77
  nesting, 75–81, 213
  one-on-one interactions, 47–48
  preening, 174
  sensory, 44–47
  societal interactions, 48–49, 68
  sounds, 43
  territorial, 61–64
Bills, 51, 96–97, 187–88
Biochemical classification of birds, 21
Birdathons, 16–17
Bird banding, 152–53, 228
Birdbaths, *171,* 175–78
  for city birds, 173
  equipment suppliers, 233
  placement of, 171
Bird boxes. *See* Birdhouses
Birdcalls. *See* Songs; Sounds; *specific birds, Gallery pages*
Bird feeders, 195–201
  for city birds, 173
  filling with homemade seed, 190–91
  for hummingbirds, 212–13
  placing in backyard, 169, 171, 201–2
  problems, 202–4
  sources of, 233
Birdhouses, 94, 214–23
  cleaning of, *221*
  dimensions for, 215, 216
  equipment suppliers, 233
  hardware for, 218
  location for, 220, 225
  maintenance, 220–21
  materials for, 216, 218
  predator danger, 224, 225
  waterproofing, 218
  winter shelter, 219, 221
Bird netting, 186
Bird of Paradise, 68
Birdseed, 188–91, 233
Birds of prey
  as backyard bird danger, 201, 224
  classification, 28, 33
  DDT poisoning, 111
  feeding behavior, 54
  mating behavior, 67
  nest-building behavior, 77
  nest locations, 76
  territorial behavior, 63
  wing shape, 127
Bird-watching, 11–17, *229*
  in cities, 173
  organizations, 233
  equipment for, 229–33
  feeding as part of, 16, 53

nest locating, 77
  observing migration, 152–55
  periodicals, 233
  territorial behavior, 61, 63
Bittern, 45
Bittern, American, *245*
  camouflage ability, 57
  mating system, 75
Bittern, Least, 32, *84*
Blackbird, 41, 61, *61,* 84, 153
Blackbird, Red-winged, *48, 146,* **331,** *331*
  food preferences, 193
  mating system, 70, 71, 72, 75
  migration timing, 147
  nest, *77*
Blinds, 250, 265, 266, 267
Bluebird, 75, 94, 100, 193, 214, *214,* 215, 216, 220
Bluebird, Eastern, *95, 321,* **321–22**
  endangered, 111
  habitat destruction, 214, *214*
  nesting box, *215*
Bluebird, Mountain, **323,** *322*
Blue Bird of Paradise, 68
Bluebird, Western, **322,** *322*
Blue Warbler, Black-throated, 75
Bobolink, *75, 144,* **330,** *330*
Bobwhite, Northern, *11,* 106, 193, **280,** *280. See* Quail
Booby, 28, 54
Brant, *53*
Breeding range, 85
Breeding sites, 260
Brood parasitism, 37, 40
Buildings, as habitat, 165
  nesting sites, 95
  planting near, 168–69
Bulbul, 91
Bunting, 29, 41
Bunting, Indigo, 24, *24, 42,* **337,** *337*
  food preferences, 193
  mating system, 75
  in orientation cages, *157*
Bunting, Lark
  ecosystem, 89
  food preferences, 193
Bunting, Lazuli, 24, *24*
Bunting, Snow, *184*
  ecosystem, 88
  food preferences, 193
  nesting territory, 206
Bushtit, *312,* **312–13**
Bustard, 28, 35
Button-Quail, 28
Buzzard. *See* Vulture, Turkey

C

Calamus (quill), 123
Camouflage
  feathers for, 123
  for nest defense, 77
  with precocial chicks, 80
  as predation defense, 57–58
Canary, Wild. *See* Goldfinch, American
Canvasback, *33*
Caracara, 33
Cardinal, 16, 41, 51, *164,* 165, 185, *185,* 187
Cardinal, Northern, *12,* 52, 67, *185,* 236, *335,* **335–36**
  birdseed preferences, 190
  range expansion, 85
  mating behavior, 65, 67, 68
  mating system, 75

singing by, 68
Carrion eaters, 33
  Bald Eagle, **277,** *277*
  storks, 32
  Turkey Vulture, *274,* **275**
Cassowary, 27, 28
Catbird, Gray, *318,* **318–19**
  food preferences, 193
  territorial behavior, 61
Cavity-nesting birds
  attracting, 214–23
  primary vs. secondary, 94
  winter shelter for, 219
Chachalaca, 34
Charting migratory paths, 157–58
Chat, Yellow-breasted, 193
Chickadee, 58, 62, 63, 94, 190, 191, 193, *199, 201,* 205, 206, 214, 215, 216, 219, 220, 257
Chickadee, Black-capped, *199, 201,* **309,** *309*
  birdhouse, 215
  birdseed preferences, 190
  ecosystem, 87
  nesting territory, 206
  territorial behavior, 63
Chickadee, Boreal, 87
Chickadee, Carolina, **310,** *310*
  ecosystem, 88
  mating system, 75
  territorial behavior, 63
Chickadee, Chestnut-backed, 63, **310–11,** *311*
Chickens, 78
Chicks, 79–81
Circulatory system, 123
Classification of birds, 20–25
  fossils, 26–27
  modern birds, 28–29
Climate, 98–104
  adaptations to, 100, 101–2
  habitat generalists and, 97
  photoperiod, 98–99
  precipitation, 102
  temperature, 100–2
Cock of the Rock, Guianian, *254*
Cockatoo, 29
Cockatoo, Lesser Sulphur-crested, *237*
Communal breeding, 74–75
Communal roosting, 219
Communication, 47–49
Condor, 127, 130
Condor, California, 106, *107*
  lead-poisoning danger, 111
Conservation groups, 113
Coot, 28, 34
Coot, American, *34,* 106
Cormorant, 28, 31, 64
Cormorant, Double-crested, *31*
Courser, 29
Courtship, 65–69
  photoperiod and, 99
Cowbird, Brown-headed, *62,* **334,** *334*
  as ecosystem generalist, 86
  food preferences, 193
  habitat, 84
  as nonterritorial, 48, 62
Crab-Plover, 29
Crane, 28, 34, 128, 147, 153
Crane, Sandhill, 106, *145*
Crane, Whooping, *105,* 106
Creeper, 40, 147, 187
Creeper, Brown, *314,* **314–15**
  feeding behavior, 53
  roosting behavior, 100
Creeper, Hawaii, 106
Creeper, Molokai, 106

Creeper, Oahu, 106
Crested-Swift, 29
Crops, protecting, 186
Crossbill, 139, 168, 187
Crossbill, Red, *96*
  food preferences, 193
  as food specialist, 97
Crossbill, White-winged, feeding behavior, 53
Crow, 61, 98, 165, 193
Crow, American, **308,** *308*
  flight style, 133
Crow, Hawaiian, 106
Cuckoo, 29, 37, 147
Cuckoo, Coral-billed, *37*
Cuckoo-Roller, 29, 39
Curassow, 133
  mating system, 75
Curlew, 140
Curlew, Eskimo, 106

D

Darters, 31
DDT. *See* Pesticide contamination
Defense
  See also Territorial behavior
  aggressive, 59
  of nest locations, 58, 76–77, 80
  in nesting colonies, 64
  one-on-one interactions for, 47–48
  against predation, 56–60
  vision and, 45
Desert ecosystems, 89–90
  nest-site specialization, 95
  water as bird lure in, 172
Dickcissel, 75
Diet, 187–94
  generalists vs. specialists, 50, 51, 96–97
  migration and, 144, 148
  photoperiod and, 98, 99
  summer, 187
  winter, 184–85
Dipper, 41, 45, 53
Dipper, American, *52*
Display
  broken wing, 58, 80
  communal grounds, 68
  communicating by, 48
  feathers for, 123, 124–25
  by lekking species, 72
  mating behavior, 65–68
  for nest defense, 58, 77, 80
  rodent run, 58, 80
  singing, 68
Diving-Petrel, 28, 31, 35
DNA studies, 21
Dove, 29, 36, 202
  See also Ground-Dove
Dove, Brown-backed Emerald, *36*
Dove, Mourning, *251,* **286,** *286*
  food preferences, 190, 193
Dove, Rock, 173, **285,** *285*
Dove, Turtle. *See* Dove, Mourning
Dove, White-Winged, *285,* **285–86**
Duck, 28, 33, 55, 56, 77, 80, 81, 90, 101, 111, 140, 160, *160,* 260
Duck, Hawaiian, 106
Duck, Laysan, 106
Duck, Ruddy, 65
Duck, Wood, **274,** *274,* 288
Dunlin, 73, *73*